Personality and Stress:
Individual Differences in the
Stress Process

WILEY SERIES ON STUDIES IN OCCUPATIONAL STRESS

Series Editors

Professor Cary L. Cooper
Manchester School of Management
University of Manchester
Institute of Science and Technology

Professor S. V. Kasl
Department of Epidemiology
School of Medicine
Yale University

Personality and Stress: Individual Differences in the Stress Process

Edited by

Cary L. Cooper

University of Manchester Institute of Science and Technology, UK

and

Roy Payne

Manchester Business School, University of Manchester, UK

JOHN WILEY & SONS

Chichester · New York · Brisbane · Toronto · Singapore

Other Wiley Editorial Offices

John Wiley & Sons, Inc., 605 Third Avenue,
New York, NY 10158-0012, USA

Jacaranda Wiley Ltd. G.P.O. Box 859, Brisbane,
Queensland 4001, Australia

John Wiley & Sons (Canada) Ltd, 5353 Dundas Road West,
Fourth Floor, Etobicoke, Ontario M9B 6H8, Canada

John Wiley & Sons (SEA) Pte Ltd, 37 Jalan Pemimpin #05-04,
Block B, Union Industrial Building, Singapore 2057

Library of Congress Cataloging-in-Publication Data:

Personality and stress : individual differences in the stress process
/ edited by Cary L. Cooper and Roy Payne.
    p. cm. — (Wiley series on studies in occupational stress)
    Includes bibliographical references and index.
    ISBN 0-471-93063-6 (ppc.)
    1. Stress (Psychology) 2. Individual differences. I. Cooper.
Cary L. II. Payne, Roy. III. Series.
BF575.S75P46 1991   91–3269
155.9′42—dc20   CIP

British Library Cataloguing in Publication Data:

A catalogue record for this book is available from the British Library.

ISBN 0-471-93063-6

Typeset in 10/12pt Times by Inforum Typesetting, Portsmouth
Printed and bound in Great Britain by Biddles Ltd, Guildford and King's Lynn

Contents

List of Contributors

CARY L. COOPER
Editor
Manchester School of Management, University of Manchester Institute of Science and Technology, UK

ROY PAYNE
Editor
Manchester Business School, University of Manchester, UK

AARON ANTONOVSKY
Department of the Sociology of Health, Ben-Gurion University of the Negev, Israel

TOM COX
Department of Psychology, University of Nottingham, UK

JEFFREY R. EDWARDS
Darden Graduate School of Business Administration, University of Virginia, USA

EAMONN FERGUSON
Department of Psychology, University of Nottingham, UK

DANIEL C. GANSTER
Department of Management, University of Nebraska, USA

JOSEPH J. HURRELL, JR.
Applied Psychology and Ergonomics Branch, National Institute for Occupational Safety and Health, Ohio, USA

RACHEL JENKINS
Institute of Psychiatry, London, UK

STANISLAV V. KASL
Department of Epidemiology, School of Medicine, Yale University, USA

LAWRENCE R. MURPHY
Applied Psychology and Ergonomics Branch, National Institute for Occupational Safety and Health, Ohio, USA

STEPHEN R. RAPP
Department of Psychiatry, Wake Forest University, Winston-Salem, North Carolina, USA

ETHEL ROSKIES   *Department of Psychology, University of Montreal, Quebec, Canada*

JOHN SCHAUBROECK   *Department of Management, University of Arkansas, USA*

ANDREW STEPTOE   *Department of Psychology, St George's Hospital Medical School, University of London, London, UK*

Editorial Foreword to the Series

This book, *Personality and Stress: Individual Differences in the Stress Process*, is the nineteenth* book in the series of *Studies in Occupational Stress*. The main objective of this series of books is to bring together the leading international psychologists and occupational health researchers to report on their work on various aspects of occupational stress and health. The series will include a number of books on original research and theory in each of the areas described in the initial volume, such as Blue Collar Stressors, The Interface Between the Work Environment and the Family, Individual Differences in Stress Reactions, The Person–Environment Fit Model, Behavioural Modification and Stress Reduction, Stress and the Socio-technical Environment, The Stressful Effects of Retirement and Unemployment and many other topics of interest in understanding stress in the workplace.

We hope these books will appeal to a broad spectrum of readers—to academic researchers and postgraduate students in applied and occupational psychology and sociology, occupational medicine, management, personnel, and law—and to practitioners working in industry, the occupational medical field, mental health specialists, social workers, personnel officers, lawyers and others interested in the health of the individual worker.

CARY L. COOPER,
University of Manchester Institute of
Science and Technology
STANISLAV V. KASL,
Yale University

*Five earlier titles are now out of print.

Abbreviations

BDHI	Buss–Durkee Hostility Inventory
CAD	coronary artery disease
CFA	confirmatory factor analysis
CHD	coronary heart disease
EPT	Eysenck Personality Inventory
I–E	Internal–External
JAS	Jenkins Activity Scale
LOC	locus of control
MBTI	Myers–Briggs Type Indicator
MRFIT	Multiple Risk Factor Intervention Trials
NA	negative affectivity
SE	self-efficacy
SI	structured interview
SOC	sense of coherence
TABP	Type A behaviour pattern
WCGS	Western Collaborative Group Studies

Chapter 1
Introduction

Cary L. Cooper, University of Manchester Institute of Science
and Technology, UK and
Roy Payne, University of Manchester, UK

The recognition of the need for a book on personality, individual differences
and stress was stimulated by the chapter on "Individual differences and
occupational stress" in our book, *Causes, Coping and Consequences of Stress
at Work* (Cooper and Payne, 1988). Writing that chapter revealed a range of
issues about individual differences and stress.

Perhaps the most obvious was the variation in the amount of research on
different individual-difference variables. There has been a huge amount of
research on Type A behaviour. Not only have there been many studies, but
they have included some of the largest epidemiological studies in the
medical literature. An interesting aside about this huge body of work
seems worth making. The Type A Behaviour Pattern (TABP) has been
investigated because it has been hypothesised that it is associated with
(causes?) coronary heart disease (CHD). Since the Type A pattern
includes elements of hostility, and since stress has been assumed to
stimulate, if not cause, the onset of CHD, it has been implicitly argued that
Type A is associated with stress. Hostile, workaholic types must be
stressed people. While the evidence that Type A is associated with CHD is
now considered to be equivocal (see Edwards's Chapter 7 in this volume)
the evidence that it is associated with stress measures is equally equivocal.
Furthermore, that particular relationship has rarely been the central stand
in studies of Type A.

The reason for raising this point is to propose that, even in a large body of
literature such as exists about Type A, these fundamental issues have not
been adequately articulated. We wish to argue that this is because there has
been little effort put in to conceptualising the role of individual differences in
the study of stress generally, and that this is even true of the one variable that
has been extensively included in stress studies. Thus, another reason for

Personality and Stress: Individual Differences in the Stress Process. Edited by C.L. Cooper and R. Payne
© 1991 John Wiley & Sons Ltd

producing this book was a concern for conceptualising the role of individual differences in the stress process.

If Type A has been extensively studied, it is perhaps surprising that the same individual-difference variables that one might expect to relate to stress (trait anxiety, introversion, pessimism) have been largely ignored. Introver- sion and anxiety were included in the seminal study of role conflict and ambiguity carried out by Kahn et al. (1964), but subsequently anxiety had hardly been studied at all within the stress literature until it re-emerged in the late 1980s as "negative affectivity" (Watson and Clark, 1984). This is some- what surprising since even a layperson might quickly conclude that being anxious might make you more inclined to see the world as more threatening (i.e. anxiety affects perceptions of stress), as well as affecting how one copes with that stress whether it is "real" or not.

Without a study by an expert in the sociology of knowledge, we might be on weak ground in claiming that these omissions may be due to the fact it was in the early 1960s that personality theory itself came under heavy criticism. Even then doubts were raised about the wisdom of this. This waning of interest in personality appeared to be due to worries about the validity of personality measures, and to the fact that they account for very small proportions of variance in variables such as educational achievement, job performance, psycho-social adjustment and so on. Another reason for believing that this volume is a timely one is the recent trend towards greater awareness of individual differences and their role in the stress process, and to acknowledge that in complex human behaviour a plethora of small, interrelated relation- ships is all we can reasonably expect.

Two other issues appeared important to us. The first was the interrelation- ships among individual-difference variables themselves. In most studies of stress people study one or two such variables but we felt it was important to consider how the major individual-difference variables relate to each other. Does anxiety relate to Type A, and if it does, is the relationship between Type A and CHD due to Type A or to anxiety? Or, a related question, is locus of control linked to social class, and if so does that explain why it relates to psychological distress (since social class is related to mental and physical ill- health)?

A more general issue of course is, "What are the origins of the individual differences themselves?" Understanding the genesis of variations in these individual-difference variables provides another justification for the more comprehensive examination of this topic which we have tried to accomplish in this book.

All these concerns raise methodological issues about how best to investi- gate the role of individual differences as they interact with changes in environ- mental stress, and efforts to cope with the consequences of that stress. This latter issue pervades many of the chapters in the book, but as is obvious from the contents page and the description of the structure of the book which appears below, methodological issues are dealt with specifically in some chapters rather than others.

In attempting to design a book which at least met the requirements of dealing with the above issues we decided to start by inviting Tom Cox and Eamon Ferguson to provide a framework chapter indicating how individual-difference variables are relevant to different parts of the stress process.

Part II of the book provides a different kind of background in that it deals with the question as to how the different individual-difference variables that are common in the stress literature relate to each other. This chapter is written by John Schaubroeck and Daniel Ganster and provides a useful map of these interrelationships. Hopefully this will alert researchers to these patterns, and to the syndromes to which particular variables belong.

The second chapter in Part II is by Aaron Antonovsky who considers several of the major personality syndromes (for example, hardiness and efficacy) as well as his own syndrome of salutogenesis. He offers some fascinating suggestions about how people come to acquire these patterns of beliefs and behaviours. Suggestions are given as to how to create these conditions and to help people to acquire such psychologically positive attributes.

The third part of the book is designed to probe our knowledge about major individual-difference variables. Rachel Jenkins reviews the effects of background variables such as gender, social class and marital status showing how they influence psychological health. Joseph Hurrell and Lawrence Murphy concentrate on locus of control and have confined their review to the occupational stress literature, though their concluding model can be applied to any kind of environment.

Jeff Edwards also confines himself to a single aspect of Type A in concentrating on the validity of measures. There have been several, major reviews of Type A recently and Jeff refers to these to reveal the major relationships between Type A, CHD and stress, but as he convincingly shows, further progress depends very much on refining and improving the measures of variables that make up the Type A syndrome.

Roy Payne's chapter looks at the role of cognitive factors and discovers that they have been little studied in the literature on real-life stress. He ends with a call for further work, arguing that they account for as much of the variance in psychological strain and coping as any other type of variable.

Part IV of the book specifically considers *coping*, and Andrew Steptoe cogently and comprehensively examines the relationship between physiological functioning and psychological coping. Ethel Roskies considers two contrasting health-related behaviours (smoking and exercise), and examines how individual differences influence the practice or cessation of these two activities. Their role in the two activities appears quite different, which suggests that a knowledge of the role of individual differences can have considerable practical value in selecting people for treatment and designing treatment for individuals of different types.

The final section of the book falls to Stan Kasl and Stephen Rapp, who bring wisdom and insight to evaluating and criticising the broad area of individual differences and health. Their suggestions for further work are, as ever, a challenge to the research community and ones we hope will be taken up and progressed through the ideas and the scholarship that we believe this book contains.

REFERENCES

Cooper, C. L. and Payne, R. (1988). *Causes, Coping and Consequences of Stress at Work*, John Wiley, Chichester.

Kahn, R. L., Wolfe, D. M., Quinn, R. P., Snoeck, J. D. and Rosenthal, R. A. (1964). *Organizational Stress: Studies in Role Conflict and Ambiguity*, John Wiley, New York.

Watson, D. and Clark, L. A. (1984). Negative affectivity: The disposition to experience negative affective states, *Psychological Bulletin*, **96**, 465–90.

PART I

Theory and Methodological Framework

Chapter 2

Individual Differences, Stress and Coping

Tom Cox and Eamonn Ferguson, University of Nottingham, UK

INTRODUCTION

Essentially there have been three different approaches to the study of stress (see Cox, 1978, 1990; or Cox and Mackay, 1981): the stimulus-based or engineering approach; the response-based or medico-physiological approach; and a more psychological approach exemplified by "interactional" and "appraisal" theories of stress.

The engineering approach treats stress as a stimulus characteristic of the person's environment, usually cast in terms of the load or level of demand placed on the person or some adverse or noxious element of that environment. Stress, so defined, produces a strain reaction. In contrast, the medico-physiological approach considers stress as a "generalized and non-specific" response to aversive or noxious environmental stimuli. This approach owes much to the pioneering work of Hans Selye (1950) Stressors give rise, among other things, to a stress response. Despite a certain popularity, these approaches have been judged to be inadequate both in terms of their ability to account for the available data and in terms of their theoretical sophistication. Essentially, they fail to take account of the individual differences which are so obvious in relation to stress, and the perceptual cognitive processes which underpin such differences.

The question of individual differences in relation to the experience and effects of stress and in relation to coping is virtually a defining characteristic of the more psychological approaches. As a result, much research effort has been expended in exploring their nature and role, and in trying to establish the natural "laws" which govern their behaviour. Developing an understanding of such differences must begin with some consideration of the relevant conceptual and methodological issues, and the resolution of these, in turn, hinges on the model of stress that is adopted as the framework for study.

Personality and Stress: Individual Differences in the Stress Process. Edited by C.L. Cooper and R. Payne
© 1991 John Wiley & Sons Ltd

A PSYCHOLOGICAL FRAMEWORK

It has been argued above that stimulus- and response-based models of stress have been found to be inadequate in two respects: first, they fail to account convincingly for much of the available data, and second, they do not reflect current thinking in psychology (or many of the other contributing disciplines). The more psychological models have attempted to overcome the obvious weakness in these approaches. Various have been offered: most may be categorised as either "interactional" or "transactional" in nature. Transactional models, which are the more process orientated of the two, have tended to focus on the concept of "appraisal", and owe much to the work of Lazarus (for example, 1966, 1976). Such models are used here as a framework for discussing the role of individual differences in stress and coping.

APPRAISAL MODELS OF STRESS

Appraisal models of stress make explicit its psychological nature. They treat stress as a psychological state which is the internal representation of a particular and problematic transaction between the person and their environment. This state, however, is effectively a "snap shot" of a wider and *dynamic* "stress process" which involves an ongoing sequence of person–environment transactions (Cox, 1978, 1985, 1990; Lazarus and Folkman, 1984). Appraisal is the evaluative process that imbues these transactions with meaning (Holroyd and Lazarus, 1982). According to Lazarus and his colleagues (see, for example, Lazarus, 1966; Folkman and Lazarus, 1986), the outcome of a stressful transaction is mediated by appraisal and coping. Individual differences are obvious in relation to both.

Appraisal is said to be comprised of primary and secondary processes. When involved in primary appraisal, the person asks themselves: "Is this particular encounter relevant to well-being, and in what way?". If the encounter is relevant to well-being then the person might judge it to involve, in terms of Lazarus and Folkman's (1984) model: challenge, threat or harm/loss. These authors have more recently suggested a fourth appraisal, that of "benefit".

In a recent study (Ferguson and Cox, 1991), the present authors have argued that the architecture of primary appraisal should be explored using "situational" rather than "psychological" reasoning. Subjects in studies of primary appraisal should be confronted with questions or scales asking them about their relationship with particular situations in terms of the characteristics of those situations rather than their own feelings (items such as "the situation was frightening" rather than "I was frightened"). Their studies, based on the use of factor-analytic and LISREL techniques, confirmed the existence of three dimensions of primary appraisal but suggested that these are more appropriately conceputalised, in terms of situations, as: challenging, anxiety-producing and depressing. Initial validity data suggest that only the latter two are associated with the self-reported experience of stress.

Primary appraisal is associated with the stressful characteristics of situations: secondary appraisal is concerned with the question: "What, if anything, can be done to resolve them?". As such, it is a decision-making process (Cox, 1987) which must take into account the coping resources and options available to the person, their preferred style(s) of coping and the nature of the stressful situation.

TRANSACTIONAL MODEL OF OCCUPATIONAL STRESS

Influenced by the work of Lazarus and his colleagues, and also by that of McGrath (1970), the theoretical contribution of Cox, and of Cox and Mackay, has attempted to set appraisal mechanisms in the wider context of the stress process and with particular reference to occupational health.

Originally their transactional model of occupational stress was set within "general systems theory", and was described in terms of five stages (Cox, 1978). The first stage, it was argued, represents the sources of demand faced by the person and reflects the characteristics of their environment. The person's perception of these demands in relation to their ability to cope represents the second stage: effectively primary appraisal. Stress was described as the psychological state which arose when there was a personally significant imbalance or mismatch between the person's perceptions of the demands on them and their ability to cope with those demands. The psychological and physiological changes which are associated with the self-recognition of such a stress state, and which include secondary appraisal and coping, represent the third stage of the model, which leads into the fourth stage, which is concerned with the consequences of coping. The fifth stage is the general feedback (and feed forward) which occurs in relation to all other stages of the model.

Development of Transactional Model

This model has been further developed in three respects. First, the authors have attempted to describe the process of primary appraisal in more detail (Cox, 1985; Cox and Mackay, 1981; Ferguson and Cox, 1991). They have argued that primary appraisal takes into account a number of different person and situational factors, and results in the person judging a particular situation as challenging, anxiety-producing or depressing. It is only the latter two appraisals which are experienced as stressful. The four factors which contribute to the appraisal process are:

- the external and internal demands that the person experiences, matched against

- their personal coping ability and resources,
- the control they have over coping, and
- the support that they receive from others in coping.

The concept of control, or conversely constraint, has been given increasing importance in the transactional model and its contribution to secondary, as well as primary, appraisal is now being considered.

Second, the stress process (including coping) has been set in the context of "problem solving" and a clear distinction has been made between primary appraisal (is there a problem?) and secondary appraisal (how and how well can I cope with it?) (Cox, 1987). Primary appraisal is seen as a continual process of monitoring while secondary appraisal is seen as a more discrete activity involving decision making and somewhat contingent on the outcome of primary appraisal. However, anecdotal evidence suggests that the interface between the two is "fuzzy".

Third, there has been some discussion of the problem of measuring stress based on this approach (Cox, 1985, 1990) with the development of possible subjective measures of its attributional and experiential (mood) correlates (see Mackay et al., 1978; Cox and Mackay, 1985; Cox, 1990; Ferguson and Cox, 1991).

Response to Stress: Stage 3

A stress state is usually accompanied by a characteristic mood change, and possibly by a more intense and focused emotional experience: the person feels anxious or tense, worn out or depressed. Such moods and emotions are unpleasant, and on many occasions serve to define the stress state for the individual (Cox, 1985, 1990).

Together, an awareness that a stressful problem exists and is anxiety producing or depressing normally initiates a cycle of changes in the person's perceptions and cognitions, and in their behavioural and physiological function. Some of these changes are attempts at attenuating the experience of stress and mastering the problem and have been termed "coping" by Lazarus (1966). Coping usually represents either an adjustment *to* the situation or an adjustment *of* the situation. There are marked individual differences in how people attempt to cope with stress.

In addition to these psychological responses to stress, there may be significant changes in physiological function, some of which might facilitate coping, at least in the short term, but in the longer term may threaten physical health.

ROLE OF INDIVIDUAL DIFFERENCES

In 1988, Payne suggested that individual differences might be involved in the stress process in at least five different ways. He presented these in the form of a series of questions which he argued could be asked for every individual-difference variable separately. His questions were:

(1) Do individual differences play a role in selecting individuals into jobs which differ in stressfulness?
(2) How do individual differences relate to the development of symptoms of psychological strain?
(3) How do individual differences relate to perceptions of stress in the environment?
(4) Do they act as moderators of the stress–strain relationship?
(5) Do they affect the way people cope with stress?

Setting aside the first question, there would appear to be two different approaches to research on individual differences based on Payne's (1988) questions. Effectively individual-difference variables have been investigated as *either*; (1) components or mediators of stress appraisal *or* (2) moderators of the stress–outcome relationship. Hence, researchers have asked, for example, to what extent does the experience of stress depend on the match between the *person's attitudes, knowledge and skills* and the demands made on them by their job; or, for example, to what extent does, say *"hardiness"* moderate the relationship between job characteristics and employee well-being?

Individual Differences and the Transactional Model

This distinction between individual differences as mediators of stress appraisal and moderators of the stress–outcome relationship can be mapped on to the transactional model.

Primary appraisal, as described by the present authors, is by its very nature, subject to mediation by individual differences. First, individual differences may exist in relation to the person's perception of job demands and pressures. Kahn (1974), for example, found a modest relationship between objective and subject measures of role conflict. The objective measure was based on the sum of pressures to change behaviour as reported by the role senders who had formal influence on the person in the focal role. Further analyses revealed that this relationship largely resulted from those in the sample who were high on anxiety proneness. In the same vein, Payne and Hartley (1987) found a positive correlation between perceptions of the severity of problems facing unemployed men and an abbreviated measure of locus of control (see below). Second, people will vary in their ability to cope with demands, and in their perceptions of those abilities. Such variation may be a function of their intelligence, their experience and education, or their beliefs in their ability to cope (self-efficacy: Bandura, 1977). Third, people may vary in the amount of control that they can exercise over any situation but not only as a function of that situation but also as a function of their beliefs about control (Finally) people may vary in their need for social support and the skills that they have for exploiting such support, and in their perceptions of support.

The stress–outcome relationship is obviously moderated by individual differences not only in secondary appraisal and related decision making and in coping, but also in emotional and physiological response tendencies, latencies and patterns. The latter are well documented in the psychophysiological literature. The former are discussed later in this chapter.

MEDIATORS AND MODERATORS

The conceptual distinction between individual differences as *mediators* of stress appraisal and as *moderators* of the stress–outcome relationship has important implications for research methodology. However, many studies do not make their conceptual position clear. Some appear not to appreciate the difference between the two positions. As a result, the terms mediator and moderator are often confused and used interchangeably, both with each other and with a variety of other words—for example, buffer or vulnerability factor and modifier (Kessler, 1983). Some clarification is required.

A *mediator* variable is one that is responsible for the transmission of an effect, but does not alter the nature of that effect (Baron and Kenny, 1986; Kessler, 1983). On the other hand a *moderator* variable is one whose presence or level alters the direction or strength of the relationship between two other variables (Arnold, 1982; Saunders, 1956). Here mediator variables, for example, offer some explanation of *how* external physical events take on psychological meaning (primary appraisal), while moderator variables specify *when* certain responses to stress will occur. Mediator-focused research tends to be interested in *mechanisms* while moderator-driven research is much more interested in *predictors* (Baron and Kenny, 1986). These conceptual differences between moderators and mediators require that different statistical procedures be adopted in their study.

Mediators

The role of mediators in the stress process is often tested for using regression procedures. For example, and following Baron and Kenny (1986), the following sequence of regressions could be used to test for a hypothesised mediator effect:

eq1 Regress the mediator variable on to the independent variable: the latter must affect the mediator.

eq2 Regress the dependent variable on to the independent variable: the latter must affect the dependent variable.

eq3 Regress the dependent variable on to the mediator and independent variables: the mediator (but not the independent variable—see below) must affect the dependent variable.

Mediation is indicated if all these conditions are met and the effect of the independent variable on the dependent variable is *greater* in eq2 than in eq3. Full mediation is demonstrated when the strength of the association between the independent and dependent variables is reduced to zero once the effect of the mediator has been controlled for. However, as with most psychological effects those under discussion here are undoubtedly mediated by several variables. Hence, in reality a reduction in the regression coefficient between the independent and dependent variables would be all that is required to indicate (partial) mediation.

   This method requires that there is no measurement error. However, as mediators are likely to be assessed by latent variables, such error is likely to occur. This error will tend to cause an underestimation of the effects of the mediator and exaggerate the direct link between the independent and dependent variables (Judd and Kenny, 1981).

Moderators

Several different analytical strategies can be suggested for the study of individual differences as moderator variables dependent on the nature of the data under investigation. The following discussion draws heavily on Baron and Kenny (1986).

Scenario 1

In experimental designs, where both the independent and moderator variables are dichotomous, then the moderation effect can be made apparent by the interaction term in ANOVA (Bobko, 1986).

Scenario 2

Where the moderator variable is dichotomous and the independent variable is continuous, the usual approach has been the compare the correlation coefficients (independent–dependent variables) between the two groups which defined the independent variable. However: (1) it assumes that the independent variable has equal variance at each level of the moderator; (2) it assumes that the amount of measurement error in the dependent variable does not vary as a function of the moderator variable causing spurious correlations between the independent and dependent variables (Dunlap and Kemery, 1987); and (3) it recognises that this strategy tests the difference between the amounts of variance explained by the correlations rather than their regression slopes (Cohen and Edwards, 1989).

Scenario 3

When the independent variable is dichotomous and the moderator variable is continuous, regression analyses may be used or the data may be reduced to fit scenario 1. A prior knowledge of the moderation function is needed. This may suggest: (1) a linear function, in which case a cross-product term can be used in a hierarchical regression analysis; (2) a quadratic function, which may be tested by adding the quadratic term into the analysis; or (3) a step function. The latter can be tested by dichotomising the moderator at the point where the step is believed to occur and reverting to scenario 1.

Scenario 4

Both the independent and moderator variables are viewed as continuous. Here the most appropriate analysis strategy is hierarchical linear regression (Cohen and Cohen, 1975); where the interaction term is assessed by the cross-product function (Saunders, 1956) of deviation scores (see Finley et al., 1984). If there is evidence that the moderation is, however, a polynomial function then one should include this in the cross-product term. Cohen and Cohen (1975) argue for the use of hierarchical multiple linear regression (HMLR) instead of step-wise techniques. This approach allows for theories about the relationships between variables to be tested and reduces the problem posed by correlated variables (see also Martin, 1981).

Subsequent chapters in this book will explore these and other methodological issues in greater depth. Other chapters review the literature on particular mediator and moderator variables in more detail. Suffice that in this chapter, attention is now drawn to some of the more pouplar individual differences in stress research, and, arguably, more important to our understanding of the stress process.

POPULAR MEDIATOR AND MODERATOR VARIABLES

Many individual differences have been explored as possible mediator or moderator variables in relation to the stress process. Interestingly, a number of those studied appear to be related, either implictly or explicitly, to the concept of *perceived control*. This concept has achieved almost universal recognition within the psychological literature, and has generated much research in many different areas of the subject.

Such research appears to be concerned either with *belief* states (for example, locus of control) or with *attributions*. Although often combined in psychological research (Calhoun, Cheney and Dawes, 1974; Hiroto, 1974; Nelson and Cohen, 1983; Sandler and Lakey, 1982), these two domains are viewed here as psychologically different yet related. Beliefs are treated as antecedents of attributions and as more stable and trait like in nature. Attributions are viewed as state dependent and likely to fluctuate over time (see Gregory, 1981 and Palenzuela, 1984 for a discussion of this position). Both belief states and attributions can produce future expectancy judgements with the difference that the latter tend to be situation specific and the former more general in nature.

These two broad categories of research can be further broken down by research method into that conducted either in the field (sometimes quasi-experimental in nature) or that conducted in laboratory settings. The laboratory studies may then be further broken down into that involving human subjects or conducted on other animals. Only research which relates to individual differences in perceived control and stress in humans is discussed here, and both laboratory and field data are considered.

Three particular individual-difference variables are reviewed: hardiness, locus of control and the nature of coping. The first includes the notion of control as one component of essentially a personality construct, while the second focuses on generalised beliefs about control loosely based on reinforcement theory. Albeit at a different conceptual level, coping is itself an individual-difference variable, one possibly influenced, in turn, by other such variables. Differences in coping style or the functional architecture of coping (see below) are obvious between individuals when attempting to deal with stressful transactions. These differences may well *moderate* the stress–outcome relationship.

HARDINESS

Hardiness has been defined as a personality construct composed of three characteristics: *control*, which refers to a belief in one's ability to influence events; *commitment*, which refers to an approach to life marked by curiosity and a sense of meaningfulness; and *challenge*, which refers to an expectation that change is normal and stimulates development (Kobasa, Maddi and Courington, 1981). Kobasa and her colleagues variously argue that individual differences in "hardiness" *moderate* the stress–outcome relationship (Kobasi et al., 1981; Kobasa, Maddi and Kahn, 1982; Kobasa and Puccetti, 1983; Gallen and Blaney, 1984).

In a prospective study, Kobasa et al. (1981) collected three sets of data separated by one year intervals from a sample of over 250 US executives. Hardiness was measured using a weighted total score from five different scales chosen to tap the different components of the construct. Stress and recent illness were also measured by questionnaire. The data collected suggested a main effect of hardiness (and constitutional predisposition: parents' illness) on recent illness, summed over the second and third data sets, after controlling for illness at time 1. Although no interactions were significant in these data, the pattern of group means was taken to be consistent with a moderating effect for hardiness. The possibility of such moderation has been explored in a variety of other occupational groups, including lawyers, accountants, nurses and secretarial staff (Kobasa et al., 1982; Kobasa and Puccetti, 1983; Topf, 1989; Schmied and Lawler, 1986).

However, according to Cohen and Edwards (1989), the evidence for individual differences in hardiness moderating the stress–outcome relationship is weak and there have been many failures to demonstrate such an effect (Funk and Houston, 1987; Hull, Van Treuren and Virnelli, 1987; Manning, Williams and Wolfe, 1988; Roth et al., 1989; Schmied and Lawler, 1986; Topf, 1989; Wiebe and McCallum, 1986).

Kobasa et al. (1982) have also suggested that "hardiness" has a *mediating* effect in relation to primary appraisal. Using the Baron and Kenny (1986) assessment technique, Rhodewalt and Zone (1989) appear to provide evidence to support this contention, as do Rhodewalt and Agustsdottir (1984). The latter authors, using the same hardiness scales as Kobasa and her colleagues (1982), examined the relationship between this measure and the report of recent life events, psychological distress and Type A behaviour. For each life event, subjects indicated the degree to which the event was desirable, controllable and expected. Only data from subjects scoring in the upper or lower third of *both* the hardiness and Types A scales were used for analysis. The final sample used by Rhodewalt and Agustsdottir (1984) comprised 339 undergraduate students. The data indicated that for low-hardiness students, life events which were perceived as either undesirable or not totally controllable were related to the experience of psychological distress. For high-hardiness students, only life events which were moderately controllable were related to psychological distress. Cohen and Edwards (1989) criticise this study on a number of grounds, including the inappropriateness of the design for testing buffering (mediating) effects.

The difficulty in demonstrating moderating or mediating effects with hardiness may be partly due to probelms with the construct and its measurement. Several have been cited in the literature: three are mentioned here.

First, hardiness may not be unidimensional. Kobasa et al., (1982) report relatively low correlations between pairs of scales used to measure each of the three components of hardiness, ranging from 0.15 to 0.53. Their factor analysis of the five scales in question revealed a single factor but one which only accounted for 46.5% of the total variance. When the separate components of hardiness have been tested, only control and commitment appear related to well-being (Hull et al., 1987; Roth et al., 1989; Schmied and Lawler, 1986; Topf, 1989). Second, there is a suggestion that the construct may only be relevant to a male population, at least in terms of physical illness, (Schmied and Lawler, 1986; but see Rhodewalt and Zone, 1989). Finally, hardiness may be confounded with neuroticism (Hull et al., 1987): those low on hardiness may only report more illness because the measure might be correlated with neuroticism, and neurotics tend to report more illness.

LOCUS OF CONTROL

The notion of locus of control (Rotter, 1966) is based on the belief that outcomes (reinforcements) are either due to personal factors (internality) or caused by factors external to the individual (that is, fate, chance or significant others). Rotter's (1966) scale was designed to measure a unidimensional, generalised expectancy of control over a wide variety of life domains. Measures of locus of control have been widely used in stress research as possible *moderators* of the stress–outcome relationship. Studies have been conducted using a variety of groups including teachers, managers, soldiers and the elderly (Anderson, 1977; McIntyre, 1974; Solomon, Mikulincer and Benbenishty, 1989; Solomon, Mikulincer and Avitzer, 1988; Brownell, 1982; Heaven, 1990). Spector (1982) and Jackson (1987) have provided reviews of locus of control in relation to behaviour in organisations.

Many subsequent factor-analytical studies suggest a multidimensional interpretation of locus of control. For example, Mirels (1970) reported two dimensions, one concerning control over personal goals, achievements and outcomes, and the other concerning control over socio-political systems. Reid and Ware (1973) described the former as "fatalism" and the latter as "social systems control". These authors later elaborated these dimensions with the development of a three-factor model (Reid and Ware, 1974). This model, in addition to fatalism and social systems control, contained a factor relating to the ability to regulate one's own responses. This, the authors termed "self-control".

More recent studies on the locus-of-control construct appear to agree on a two-dimensional structure (for example, Harter and Connell, 1984; Palenzuela, 1984, 1987; Skinner, Chapman and Baltes, 1988; Wiesz, 1983, 1986; Wiesz and Stipek, 1981; Wallston et al., 1987). Such models appear to separate situation-specific control attributions and ability judgements from generalised control beliefs. Control has been variously described in these studies in terms of: competence and contingency, self-efficacy and response outcome contingency, agency beliefs and means–end beliefs, and self-efficacy and locus of control.

Folkman (1984) has proposed a theoretical framework which is relevant to this type of model. She distinguishes between situational control judgements (including self-efficacy) and locus of control, arguing that the former affects secondary appraisal and the latter primary appraisal. The present authors are in agreement with her general thesis but would state it slightly differently in terms of event-dependent attributions and event-independent beliefs. Thus event-independent control beliefs should affect primary appraisal while event-dependent control attributions should affect secondary appraisal.

Despite these developments, there are still many "locus of control" scales which do not distinguish between its different dimensions (see Palenzuela, 1987). However, the significance of this is arguable (see below).

Several studies have examined the *moderating* effects of locus of control on the stress–outcome relationship (for example, Johnson and Sarason, 1978; Krause and Stryker, 1984; Lefcourt et al., 1981; Sandler and Lakey, 1982; Turner and Noh, 1983; Wheaton, 1982). Lefcourt et al. (1981) have reported three cross-sectional studies of the impact of various measures of locus of control on the relationship between life events and psychological strain. In their first study, they used the Rotter (1966) scale. Fifty-nine undergraduate students completed a life-events scale, the Rotter scale, another locus of control scale and a measure of affect. Separate hierarchical regression analyses, each using the affect measure as the dependent variable, were performed for both measures of locus of control (plus the measure of life events). Main effects were found for negative life events and the Rotter scale. The interaction between these two variables was significant, and a moderating effect was thus indicated. However, the interaction term only accounted for 7% of the variance in the affect measure. No effects were found with the other measure.

Overall, the demonstration of a moderating effect of locus of control on the stress–outcome relationship seems to depend on the instrument used to measure the construct and the outcome variable under consideration (Cohen and Edwards, 1989). Most studies that report moderation appear to have used the unidimensional Rotter (1966) scale and some measure of psychological distress (Johnson and Sarason, 1978; Krause, 1986; Krause and Stryker, 1984; Lefcourt et al., 1981; Turner and Noh, 1983; Wheaton, 1982, 1983). However, several of these apparently successful studies suffer methodological problems, such as inappropriate statistical analyses (Johnson and Sarason, 1978) or failure to provide enough data to determine the form of the reported interaction (Johnson and Sarason, 1978; Krause and Stryker, 1984). Notwithstanding this, the success of the Rotter (1966) scale may reflect its generality, and attempts to produce multidimensional models of locus of control may sacrifice its power.

COPING

The appraisal of a particular person–environment transaction as anxiety producing or depressing, with a subsequent experience of stress, is usually associated with changes in psychological and physiological function some of which are attempts at coping. That appraisal is mediated by individual differences, and the coping which may follow varies between individuals, and this variation may *moderate* the stress–outcome relationship. Coping is, in a sense, an individual-difference variable.

In everyday discourse, the idea of coping tends to imply success, as when people say "they are coping" (Stone and Neale, 1984). However, for the purposes of research, definitions of coping need to be independent of outcome (Folkman and Lazarus, 1986; Lazarus and Folkman, 1984). Methodologically, this would suggest not using the terms "cope" or "coping" in interviews or questionnaires because they are value laden (Stone and Neale, 1984).

Cox (1987) has offered a simple definition in terms of

> the cognitions and behaviours adopted by the individual, following the recognition of a stressful transaction, that are in some way designed to deal with that transaction.

This is taken as a starting point for the present discussion.

Cox (1987) has also suggested that research into coping tends to fall into one of two broad categories—that which is (1) typological and (2) concerned with the *process* of coping (and problem solving). Typological research is largely to do with the functionality of coping: that is, the coping typologies presented so far have been attempts to describe the functions that coping behaviours are believed (or designed) to perform. The rest of this discussion will address itself to this issue. A discussion of coping as "process", and in particular relation to problem solving, is offered elsewhere by Cox (1987).

COPING TYPOLOGIES

There have been two main approaches to the study of coping typologies: that based on the notion of *coping styles*, and that more concerned with the functional *dimensions* which underpin the coping process—the architecture of coping. Individual differences play an important role in both.

Coping styles appear to be trait-like combinations of cognitions and behaviours brought into play as a result of the experience of stress and expressed somewhat independently of the nature of the situation. There have been many attempts to describe such styles: for example, monitor–blunter (Miller, 1979; Miller, 1987; Miller and Mangan, 1983; Miller, Brody and Summerton, 1988) or repressor–sensitiser (Houston and Hodges, 1970). Roth and Cohen (1986) list twelve such differences. In contrast to trait-like models of coping, there has been an interest in the functional dimensions which underpin coping strategies (for example, Lazarus and Folkman,

1984). This approach assumes that individuals have a repertoire of coping options available to them from which they can build what they believe to be the most effective strategy, depending on the nature of the situation. It further assumes that such coping will alter the nature of the person–situation transaction and this in turn will force the development of new coping strategies. This approach differs from the first in that it does not assume that individuals have one particular style of coping but seeks the functional dimensions which best describe the virtually infinite number of options and strategies that can be employed in response to stressful situations. Despite the apparently unlimited number of coping strategies that can be built up, there is an implicit assumption here that there are a small number of at least general functional dimensions. The present authors are currently involved with this approach.

There are two overlapping methods which have been employed in the study of the functional dimensions or architecture of coping. First, scales have been developed to describe coping with stress *in general* (for example, Aldwin and Revenson, 1987; Carver, Scheier and Weintraub, 1989; Folkman and Lazarus, 1986; Folkman et al., 1986a, 1986b; Holahan and Moos, 1990; Patterson, Smith, Grant, 1990; Wood et al., 1990). Second, other scales have been developed to describe coping in response to *specific types of stressful situation,* such as marriage, parenting, finance and occupation (Fleishman, 1984; Pearlin and Schooler, 1978), chronic pain (Brown and Nicassio, 1987; Brown, Nicassio and Wallson, 1989; Turner and Clancy, 1986), hazardous emergency work (McGammon et al., 1988; Pijawka, Cuthbertson and Olson, 1988), insulin-dependent diabetes mellitus (Hanson et al., 1989), family life (Ventura and Boss, 1983), sports injuries (Smith, Smoll and Ptacek, 1990) and hypertension (Jalowiec, Murphy and Powers, 1984).

Both methods have tended to rely on factor analysis. The typical study has involved factor analyses of respondents' endorsements of a list of possible coping cognitions and behaviours, then the naming and treatment of the emergent factors as the functional dimensions underpinning coping. Such studies effectively describe how people behave and then decide what those behaviours achieve.

THE FUNCTIONAL ARCHITECTURE OF COPING

The most popular and widely used description of the functional architecture of coping is that offered by Lazarus and Folkman (1984). They distinguish between problem- and emotion-focused options and strategies. The former are concerned with directly addressing the problem while the latter attack the emotional response to it. Those authors attempt an assessment of such strategies using the "Ways of Coping" questionnaire. When factor analysed, data from this questionnaire tend to an eight-factor solution. Lazarus and Folkman

(1984) describe this solution in terms of a single problem-focused factor, six emotion-focused factors and one that combines both (social support). The rotation technique used in their studies was oblique and the eight factors are correlated. A subsequent higher order factor analysis may have suggested a simpler model, and, in general, three-factor models are popular in the recent literature (Endler and Parker, 1990; Moos and Billings, 1982; Parkes, 1984; Pearlin and Schooler, 1978; Rhode et al., 1990).

Parkes (1984), for example, using the VSS technique (Rocklin and Revelle, 1980), produced a three-factor solution for data obtained with the "Ways of Coping" questionnaire. The first factor, termed "direct action", involved behaviours designed to change the situation; the second factor, "suppression", involved avoidance behaviours; and the third factor described general coping behaviours. Endler and Parker (1990) have also described a three-factor model based on coping which is: (a) task orientated (problem focused), (b) emotion orientated (emotion focused) and (e) avoidance (spending time with a special friend, seeing a movie and so on).

Pearlin and Schooler (1978), working in an occupational context, described coping in terms of: problem-focused behaviours, emotion-focused behaviours and reappraisal. A somewhat similar three-factor model has been suggested by Moos and Billings (1982). Their first factor is *problem focused* and includes:

(1) information seeking involving social support;
(2) problem solving (making plans); and
(3) developing alternative rewards, say through religion.

Their second factor is *emotion focused* and includes:

(1) affect regulation or wishful thinking;
(2) resigned acceptance or submission; and
(3) emotional disengagement (crying).

The third factor is *appraisal focused* coping and includes:

(1) logical analysis (causal search and relying on past experience);
(2) cognitive redefinition (acceptance, social comparison); and
(3) cognitive avoidance (denial).

While the models offered by Pearlin and Schooler (1978) and Moos and Billings (1990) are consistent with the original two-factor formulation of Lazarus and Folkman (1984), they usefully extend it by adding a third factor in a way which fits the appraisal framework.

Jalowiec et al. (1984), noting the debate over the architecture of coping, reported that raters had immense difficulty categorising descriptions of coping behaviour using just two categories (problem and emotion focused). Using factor analysis, they then went on to produce a *four*-factor solution: the initial factor described problem-oriented coping; the second factor appeared to relate to appraisal (acceptance, optimism, resignation, humour and so on); the third factor, which they said was the hardest to classify, included behaviours such as swearing, crying, eating and smoking; and the fourth factor related to social support.

When coping with a specific problem, pain, is considered two general factors of *passive* and *active* coping appear to emerge (Brown and Nicassio,1987; Brown et al., 1989). When Sickle Cell Disease was the problem to cope with, Gil et al. (1989) also produced a two-factor model: (1) active problem and appraisal-focused coping, and (2) passive acceptance. Similarly, Hanson et al. (1989), working with the diabetes, described a two-factor model: they termed the first factor "personal and interpersonal resources" and the second factor "ventilation and avoidance".

However, Turner and Clancy (1986), reproducing the findings of Rosentiel and Keefe (1983), have suggested a slightly more complex three-factor model for coping with pain. Their first factor was concerned with ignoring or reinterpreting the pain, their second factor related to diverting attention and praying, while the third factor was to do with helplessness. A three-factor model also emerged in a study of depressives (Beckman and Adams, 1984): emotional expression, emotional containment and general activity.

The data reviewed here, and that provided elsewhere, suggest that descriptions of coping need to include, but also go beyond, a simple problem—emotion–focused dichotomy. Perhaps there are, at least, two additional dimensions which might be considered: one concerned with reappraisal and the other with avoidance. At the same time, it must be remembered that these are offered here as functional dimensions underpinning coping options and strategies and not as coping strategies in themselves. Any particular strategy will have elements of the different dimensions shot through it: thus it is sometimes difficult for raters to place strategies into a single (dimensional) category. This problem may also extend to research activity and the naming of factors and dimensions. Callan and Hennessey (1989) examined coping with infertility. They categorised a factor called "keep busy, avoid and deny" as appraisal-focused coping. Such a factor could easily be said to suggest avoidance. Any one coping option or strategy may perform more than one function and may perform different functions for different individuals in the same situation, or different functions for the same individual over time. In a sense the functional nature of coping can only be defined by the individual involved. For the purpose of research, there must be a shift in emphasis from what the individual *does* to what the behaviours *do* (psychologically) for the individual.

A Working Model of Coping

On the basis of the preceding discussion, the following model of coping is proposed by the authors. Initially all coping serves one overall function, that of dealing with the emotional correlates of a stressful transaction and creating a sense of control. Beyond this, coping strategies have three functions: (1) problem solving (directly confronting or dealing with the source of stress); (2) reappraisal (rethinking the meaning of the transaction); and (3) avoidance (avoiding or being distracted from the problem or doing something "off line"). Any one strategy may perform all or some of these three functions and to some extent. All serve to reduce the emotional correlates of the problem, no but "off line" activities (avoidance) may be most directly targeted on managing emotion.

Coping may now be defined as:

cognitions and behaviours which, following a stressful transaction and defined independently of outcome, have the primary function, consciously decided, of dealing with the emotion caused by the transaction and developing a sense of personal control. This is achieved by those cognitions and behaviours combining into strategies which perform a mixture of functions: problem solving, reappraisal and avoidance. Any particular option or strategy may perform any one or a number of these functions in the space of dealing with one stressful transaction.

From the existing literature it seems that if a time-based analysis is made then avoidance strategies should be more beneficial in the initial stages of coping and problem-focused strategies at latter stages (Roth and Cohen, 1986; Suls and Fletcher, 1985). However, no one coping function is seen as more adaptive than any other. Rather, a successful outcome is engineered by the individual fitting the right strategy to the situation (Rothbaum, Wiesz and Snyder, 1982).

Individual differences are implicit in the repertoire of coping options available to the person, in the person's decisions on combining options into strategies, in the functions that these strategies are designed to fulfil and in the way they are "fitted" to particular person–environment transactions. Such individual differences may be partly expressed in terms of differences in the functional architecture of coping and as such moderate the stress–outcome relationship.

Assessment of Coping

This emphasis on coping *strategies* and their functional architecture may force a need for a new assessment technique. The following procedure is suggested. The respondent is asked to describe a stressful situation that they have recently experienced. They are then requested to describe the "behaviour(s) they adopted in attempting to deal with the stressful situation that they have described". These instructions (1) do not mention the word cope or coping; (2) use the phrase "in attempting to deal with" and thus avoid any connotation of success; and (3) allow the subject to mention more than one behaviour. Following this, each respondent, using six-point scales (where 0 = not at all to 5 = completely), then rates those cognitions and behaviours according to a number of items designed to assess the management of emotion and feelings of control, and the problem-focused, reappraisal and avoidance (and "off-line") functions.

This method has a number of advantages for the researcher. First, new scales do not have to be developed for each new situation. The respondent describes the strategies adopted and then makes judgements concerning their function. Second, it avoids the problems of imposed sampling from the universe of possible cognitions and behaviours as there is no limit built into the device. Finally, the richness of description offered allows some analysis of the sequence of cognitions and behaviours. This last point raises the rather interesting possibility of applying cognitive causal mapping and sequence analysis to these data.

CONCLUSIONS

This chapter has been concerned with the nature and role of individual differences in relation to stress and coping. It has examined a number of sources of difference and in doing so has attempted to distinguish between those that mediate the various stages of the overall process and those that moderate it. It was argued that although these concepts of mediation and moderation are distinct, they have often been confused in the literature. A clearer distinction was attempted here and analytical procedures were offered that might both assess the two processes and offer some formal separation between them.

In considering particular differences, attention was paid to three notions, those of hardiness and locus of control, and that of coping. The studies reviewed questioned the role played by hardiness, both as a mediator and a moderator, but there was evidence that locus of control, when assessed using Rotter's (1966) uni-dimensional scale, acted in a way consistent with the moderation hypothesis. Coping was treated both as a source of individual difference and as an outcome of other such differences. Its architecture and measurement were discussed within the general framework offered by the transactional model of stress, which was used to provide the overall structure to this chapter.

REFERENCES

Aldwin, C. and Revenson, T. (1987). Does coping help? A re-examination of the relation between coping and mental health. *Journal of Personality and Social Psychology,* **53**, 337–48.

Anderson, C. (1977). Locus of control, coping behaviour, and performance in a stress setting: A longitudinal study, *Journal of Applied Psychology,* **62**, 446–51.

Arnold, H. (1982). Moderator variables: A clarification of conceptual, analytic, and psychometric issues, *Organizational Behavior and Human Performance,* **29**, 143–74.

Bandura, A. (1977). Self-efficacy: Towards a unifying theory of behavioural change, *Psychological Review,* **84**, 191–215.

Baron, R. and Kenny, D. (1986). The moderator–mediator variable distinction in social psychological research: Conceptual, strategic, and statistical considerations, *Journal of Personality and Social Psychology,* **51**, 1173–82.

Beckman, E. and Adams, R. (1984). Coping behavior in depression: Report on a new scale, *Behavioral Research and Therapy,* **22**, 71–5.

Billings, A. and Moos, R. (1984). Coping, stress, and social support among adults with unipolar depression, *Journal of Personality and Social Psychology,* **46**, 877–91.

Bobko, P. (1986). A solution to some dilemmas when testing hypotheses about ordinal interactions, *Journal of Applied Psychology,* **71**, 323–6.

Brown, G. and Nicassio, P. (1987). Development of a questionnaire for the assessment of active and passive coping strategies in chronic pain patients, *Pain,* **31**, 53–64.

Brown, G., Nicassio, P. and Wallston, K. (1989). Pain coping strategies and depression in rheumatoid arthritis, *Journal of Consulting and Clinical Psychology,* **57**, 652–7.

Brownell, P. (1982). The effects of personality–situation congruence in a managerial context: Locus of control and budgetary participation, *Journal of Personality and Social Psychology,* **42**, 753–63.

Calhoun, L., Cheney, T. and Dawes, S. (1974). Locus of control, self reported depression, and perceived cause of depression, *Journal of Clinical and Consulting Psychology,* **42**, 736.

Callan, V. and Hennessey, J. (1989). Strategies for coping with infertility, *British Journal of Medical Psychology,* **62**, 343–354.

Carver, C., Scheier, M. and Weintraub, J. (1989). Assessing coping strategies: A theoretically based approach, *Journal of Personality and Social Psychology,* **56**, 267–83.

Cohen, J. and Cohen, P. (1975). *Applied Multiple Regression/Correlation Analysis for the Behavioral Sciences,* Lawrence Erlbaum Associates, New York.

Cohen, S. and Edwards, J. (1989). Pesonality characteristics as moderators of the relationship between stress and health. In R. W. Neufeld (ed.) *Advances in Investigations of Psychological Stress,* Wiley & Sons, New York.

Cox, T. (1978). *Stress,* MacMillan Press, London.

Cox, T. (1985). The nature and measurement of stress, *Ergonomics,* **28**, 1155–63.

Cox, T. (1987). Stress, coping and problem solving, *Work and Stress,* **1**, 5–14.

Cox, T. (1990). The nature and recognition of stress: Conceptual and methodological issues. In E. N. Corlett and J. Wilson (eds) *Evaluation of Human Work,* Taylor & Francis, London.

Cox, T. and Mackay, C. (1981). A transactional approach to occupational stress. In E. N. Corlett and J. Richardson (eds) *Stress, Work Design and Productivity,* Wiley & Sons, Chichester.

Cox, T. and Mackay, C. J. (1985). The measurement of self-reported stress arousal, *British Journal of Psychology,* **76**, 183–6.

Dunlap, W. and Kemery, E. (1987). Failure to detect moderating effects: Is multicolinearity the problem?, *Psychological Bulletin*, **102**, 418–20.

Endler, N. and Parker, J. (1990). Multi dimensional assessment of coping: A critical review, *Journal of Personality and Social Psychology*, **58**, 844–54.

Ferguson, E. and Cox, T. (1991). The nature of primary appraisal, *British Journal of Psychology*, (submitted).

Finney, J., Mitchell, R., Cronkite, R. and Moos, R. (1984). Methodological issues in estimating main and interactive effects: Examples from coping/social support and stress field, *Journal of Health and Social Behavior*, **25**, 85–98.

Fleishman, J. (1984). Personality characteristics and coping patterns, *Journal of Health and Social Behaviour*, **25**, 229–44.

Folkman, S. (1984). Personal control and stress and coping processes: A theoretical analysis, *Journal of Personality and Social Psychology*, **46**, 839–52.

Folkman, S. and Lazarus, R. (1985). If it changes, it must be a process: Study of emotion and coping during three stages of a college examination, *Journal of Personality and Social Psychology*, **48**, 150–70.

Folkman, S. and Lazarus, R. (1986). Stress process and depressive symptomology, *Journal of Abnormal Psychology*, **95**, 107–13.

Folkman, S., Lazarus, R., Greun, R. and DeLongis, A. (1986a). Appraisal, coping, health status, and psychological symptoms, *Journal of Personality and Social Psychology*, **50**, 571–9.

Folkman, S., Lazarus, R., Dunkel-Schetter, C., DeLongis, A. and Gruen, R. (1986b). Dynamics of a stressful encounter: Cognitive appraisal, coping, and encounter outcomes, *Journal of Personality and Social Psychology*, **50**, 992–1003.

Funk, S. and Houston, B. (1987). A critical analysis of the Hardiness Scale's validity and utility, *Journal of Personality and Social Psychology*, **53**, 572–8.

Gallen, R. and Blaney, P. (1984). Hardiness and social support as moderators of the effects of life stress, *Journal of Personality and Social Psychology*, **47**, 156–63.

Gil, K., Abrams, M., Philpips, G. and Keefe, F. (1989). Sickle cell disease pain: Relation of coping strategies to adjustment, *Journal of Clinical and Consulting Psychology*, **57**, 725–31.

Gregory, W. (1981). Expectancies for controllability, performance attributions and behaviour. In H. Lefcourt (ed.) *Research with the Locus of Control Construct*. Academic Press, New York.

Hanson, C., Cigrang, J., Harris, M., Carle, D., Relyea, G. and Burghen, G. (1989). Coping styles in youths with insulin-dependent diabetes mellitus, *Journal of Consulting and Clinical Psychology*, **57**, 644–51.

Harter, S. and Connell, J. (1984). A model of children's achievement and related self-perceptions of competence, control and motivation orientation, *Advances in Motivation and Achievement*, **3**, 214–250.

Heaven, P. (1990). Suggestions for reducing unemployment: A study of protestant work ethic and economic locus of control beliefs, *British Journal of Social Psychology*, **29**, 55–65.

Hiroto, D. (1974). Locus of control and learned helplessness, *Journal of Experimental Psychology*, **102**, 187–93.

Holahan, C. and Moos, R. (1990). Life stressors, resistance factors and improved psychological functioning: An extension of the stress resistance paradigm, *Journal of Personality and Social Psychology*, **58**, 909–17.

Holroyd, K. A. and Lazarus, R. S. (1982). Stress, coping and somatic adaptation. In L. Goldberger and S. Breznitz (eds) *Handbook of Stress*, Free Press, New York.

Houston, B. and Hodges, W. (1970). Situational denial and performance under stress, *Journal of Personality and Social Psychology*, **16**, 726–30.

Hull, J., Van Treuren, R. and Virnelli, S. (1987). Hardiness and health: A critique and alternative approach, *Journal of Personality and Social Psychology*, **53**, 518–30.

Jackson, S. (1987). Does job control control job stress?, paper presented at NIOSH Conference on Stress and Control, Cincinnati, Ohio.

Jalowiec, A., Murphy, S. and Powers, M. (1984). Psychometric assessment of the Jalowiec Coping Scale, *Nursing Research*, **33**, 157–61.

Johnson, J. and Sarason, I. (1978). Life stress, depression and anxiety: Internal–external control as a moderator variable, *Journal of Psychosomatic Research*, **22**, 205–8.

Judd, C. and Kenny, D. (1981). *Estimating the Effects of Social Interventions*, Cambridge University Press, Cambridge.

Kahn, R. L. (1974). Conflict, ambiguity and over work: Three elements in job stress, In A. McLean (ed.) *Occupational Stress*, Charles C. Thomas, Springfield, Illinois.

Kessler, R. (1983). Methodological issues in the study of psychosocial stress. In H. Kaplan (ed.) *Psychosocial Stress*, Academic Press, New York.

Kobasa, S. (1979). Stressful life events, personality, and health: An inquiry into hardiness, *Journal of Personality and Social Psychology*, **37**,1–13.

Kobasa, S. and Puccetti, M. (1983). Personality and social resources in stress resistance, *Journal of Personality and Social Psychology*, **45**, 839–50.

Kobasa, S., Maddi, S. and Courington, S. (1981). Personality and constitution as mediators in the stress–illness relationship, *Journal of Health and Social Behaviour*, **22**, 368–78.

Kobasa, S., Maddi, S. and Kahn, S. (1982). Hardiness and health: a prospective study. *Journal of Personality and Social Psychology*, **42**, 168–77.

Krause, N. (1986). Stress and coping: Reconceptualizing the role of locus of control beliefs, *Journal of Gerontology*, **41**, 617–22.

Krause, N. and Stryker, S. (1984). Stress and well being: The buffering role of locus of control beliefs, *Social Science and Medicine*, **18**, 783–90.

Lazarus, R. S. (1966). *Psychological Stress and the Coping Process*, McGraw-Hill, New York.

Lazarus, R. S. (1976). *Patterns of Adjustment*, McGraw-Hill, New York.

Lazarus, R. and Folkman, S. (1984). *Stress, Appraisal and Coping* Springer Publishing, New York.

Lefcourt, H. M., Miller, R. S., Ware, E. E. and Sherk, D. (1981). Locus of control as a modifier of the relationship between stressors and moods. *Journal of Personality and Social Psychology*, **41**, 357–69.

McCammon, S., Durham, T., Allison, J. and Williamson, J. (1988). Emergency workers' cognitive appraisal and coping with traumatic events, *Journal of Traumatic Stress*, **1**, 353–72.

McGrath, J. E. (1970). *Social and Psychological Factors in Stress*, Holt, New York.

McIntyre, T. (1984). The relationship between locus of control and teacher burnout, *British Journal of Educational Psychology*, **54**, 235–8.

Mackay, C., Cox, T., Burrows, G. and Lazzerini, T. (1978). An inventory for the measurement of self-reported stress and arousal, *British Journal of Social and Clinical Psychology*, **17**, 283–4.

Manning, M., Williams, R. and Wolfe, D. (1988). Hardiness and the relationship between stressors and outcomes, *Work and Stress*, **2**, 205–16.

Martin, R. (1981). Techniques for data acquisition and analysis in field investigation of stress. In R. W. Neufeld (ed.) *Advances in Investigations of Psychological Stress,* Wiley & Sons, New York.

Miller, S. (1979). Controllability and human stress: Method, evidence and theory, *Behavioural Research and Therapy,* **17**, 287–304.

Miller, S. (1987). When to whistle while you work: Toward a cognitive social learning analysis of the coping process, paper presented at the Stress and Control Conference, NIOSH, Cincinatti, Ohio.

Miller, S. and Mangan, C. (1983). Interacting effects of information and coping style in adapting to gynecologic stress: Should the doctor tell all?, *Journal of Personality and Social Psychology,* **5**, 223–36.

Miller, S., Brody, D. and Summerton, J. (1988). Styles of coping with threat: Implications for health, *Journal of Personality and Social Psychology,* **54**, 142–8.

Mirels, H. L. (1970). Dimensions of internal versus external control, *Journal of Consulting and Clinical Psychology,* **34**, 226–8.

Moos, R. and Billings, A. (1982). Conceptualizing and measuring coping resources and processes. In L. Goldberger and S. Breznitz (eds) *Handbook of Stress: Theoretical and Clinical Aspects,* Free Press, New York.

Nelson, D. W. and Cohen, H. (1983). Locus of control and control perceptions and the relationship between life stress and psychological disorders, *American Journal of Community Psychology,* **11**, 705–22.

Palenzuela, R. (1984). Critical evaluation of locus of control: Towards of reconceptualisation of the construct and its measurement, *Psychological Reports,* **54**, 683–709.

Palenzuela, R. (1987). Sphere-specific measures of perceived control: Perceived contingency, perceived competence, or what? A critical evaluation of Paulus and Christi's approach, *Journal of Research in Personality,* **21**, 264–86.

Parkes, K. (1984). Locus of control, cognitive appraisal and coping in stressful episodes, *Journal of Personality and Social Psychology,* **6**, 655–68.

Patterson, T., Smith, L. and Grant, I. (1990). Internal vs external determinants of coping responses to stressful life-events in the elderly, *British Journal of Medical Psychology,* **63**, 149–60.

Payne, R. (1988). Individual differences in the study of occupational stress. In C. L. Cooper and R. Payne (eds) *Causes, Coping and Consequences of Stress at Work,* Wiley & Sons, Chichester.

Payne, R. and Hartley, J. (1987). A test of a model for explaining the affective experience of unemployed men, *Journal of Occupational Psychology,* **60**, 31–47.

Pearlin, L. and Schooler, C. (1978). The structure of coping, *Journal of Health and Social Behavior,* **19**, 2–21.

Pijawka, D., Cuthbertson, B. and Olson, R. (1988). Coping with extreme hazard events: Emerging themes in natural and technological disaster research, *Journal of Death and Dying,* **18**, 281–97.

Rhode, P., Lewinshon, P., Tilson, M. and Seeley, J. (1990). Dimensionality of coping and its relation to depression, *Journal of Personality and Social Psychology,* **58**, 499–511.

Rhodewalt, F. and Agustsdottir, S. (1984). On the relationship of hardiness to the type A behaviour pattern: Perceptions of life events versus coping with life events, *Journal of Research in Personality,* **18**, 212–23.

Rhodewalt, F. and Zone, J. (1989). Appraisal of life change, depression, and illness in hardy and non hardy women, *Journal of Personality and Social Psychology,* **56**, 81–8.

Reid, D. and Ware, E. E. (1973). Multi dimensionality of internal–external control: Implications for past and future research, *Canadian Journal of Behavioural Science,* **5**, 264–71.

Reid, D. and Ware, E. (1974). Multidimensionality of internal versus external control: Addition of a third dimension and the non-distinction of self versus others, *Canadian Journal of Behavioural Sciences,* **6**, 131–42.

Rocklin, T. and Revelle, W. (1980). VSIMPL: A program to estimate the number of interpretable factors, *Behavior Research Methods and Instrumentation,* **12**, 69–70.

Rosentiel, A. and Keefe, F. (1983). The use of coping strategies in chronic low back pain patients: Relationship to patient characteristics and current adjustment, *Pain,* **17**, 33–44.

Roth, D., Wiebe, D., Fillingim, R. and Shay, K. (1989). Life events, fitness, hardiness, and health: A simultaneous analysis of proposed stress-resistance effects. *Journal of Personality and Social Psychology,* **57**, 136–42.

Roth, S. and Cohen, L. (1986). Approach, avoidance, and coping with stress, *American Psychologist,* **41**, 813–19.

Rothbaum, F., Wiesz, J. and Snyder, S. (1982). Changing the world and changing the self: A two process model of perceived control, *Journal of Personality and Social Psychology,* **42**, 5–37.

Rotter, J. (1966). Generalised expectancies for internal versus external control of reinforcement, *Psychological Monographs: General and Applied,* **80** whole issue.

Sandler, I.N. and Lakey, B. (1982). Locus of control as stress moderator: The role of control perceptions and social support, *American Journal of Community Psychology,* **10**, 65–79.

Saunders, D. (1956). Moderator variables in prediction, *Educational and Psychological Measurement,* **16**, 209–22.

Schmied, L. and Lawler, K. (1986). Hardiness, type A behaviour, and the stress–illness relation in working women, *Journal of Personality and Social Psychology,* **51**, 1218–23.

Selye, H. (1950). *Stress,* Acta Incorporated, Montreal.

Skinner, E., Chapman, M. and Baltes, P. (1988). Control, means–ends, and agency beliefs: A new conceptualization and its measurement during childhood, *Journal of Personality and Social Psychology,* **54**, 117–33.

Smith, R., Smoll, F. and Ptacek, J. (1990). Conjunctive moderator variables in vulnerability and resiliency research: Life stress, social support and coping skills, and adolescent sports injuries, *Journal of Personality and Social Psychology,* **58**, 360–70.

Solomon, Z., Mikulincer, M. and Avitzer, E. (1988). Coping, locus of control, social support, and combat related post traumatic stress disorder: A prospective study, *Journal of Personality and Social Psychology,* **55**, 279–85.

Solomon, Z., Mikulincer, M. and Benebenishty, R. (1989). Locus of control and combat-related post tramatic stress disorder: The intervening role of battle intensity threat appraisal and coping, *British Journal of Clinical Psychology,* **28**, 131–44.

Spector, P. (1982). Behavior in organizations as a function of employee's locus of control, *Psychological Bulletin,* **91**, 482–97.

Stone, A. and Neale, J. (1984). New measure of daily coping: Development and preliminary results, *Journal of Personality and Social Psychology,* **46**, 892–906.

Suls, J. and Fletcher, B. (1985). The relative efficacy of avoidant and non avoidant coping strategies: A meta-analysis, *Health Psychology,* **4**, 249–88.

Topf, M. (1989). Personality hardiness, occupational stress, and burnout in critical care nurses, *Research in Nursing and Health,* **2**, 179–86.

Turner, J. and Clancy, S. (1986). Strategies for coping with chronic low back pains: Relationship to pain and disability, *Pain*, **24**, 355–64.

Turner, R. J. and Noh, S. (1983). Class and psychological vulnerability among women: The significance of social support and personal control, *Journal of Health and Social Behaviour*, **24**, 2–15.

Ventura, J. and Boss, P. (1983). The family coping inventory applied to parents with new babies, *Journal of Marriage and the Family*, **12**, 867–75.

Wallston, K., Wallston, B., Smith, S. and Dobbins, C. (1987). Perceived control and health, *Current Psychological Research and Reviews*, **6**, 5–25.

Wheaton, B. (1982). A comparison of the moderating effects of personal coping resources in the impact of exposure to stress in two groups, *Journal of Community Psychology*, **10**, 293–311.

Wheaton, B. (1983). Stress, personal coping resources and psychiatric symptoms: An investigation of interactive model, *Journal of Health and Social Behaviour*, **24**, 208–29.

Wiebe, D. and McCallum, D. (1986). Health practices and hardiness as mediators in the stress–illness relationship, *Health Psychology*, **5**, 425–38.

Wiesz, J. (1983). Can I control it? The pursuit of veridical answers across the life span. In P. Baltes and O. Brim (eds) *Life Span Development and Behaviour* (vol. 5), Academic Press, New York.

Wiesz, J. (1986). Contingency and control beliefs as predictors of psychotherapy outcomes among children and adolescents, *Journal of Consulting and Clinical Psychology*, **54**, 789–95.

Wiesz, J. and Stipek, D. (1981). Competence, contingency and the development of perceived control, *Human Development*, **25**, 250–81.

Wood, J., Saltzberg, J., Neale, J., Stone, A. and Rachmiel, T. (1990). Self-focused attention, coping responses, and distressed mood in everyday life, *Journal of Personality and Social Psychology*, **58**, 1027–36.

PART II

Stress, Personality and Individual Differences: Their Relationships and Origins

Chapter 3

Associations among Stress-related Individual Differences

John Schaubroeck, University of Nebraska, USA and
Daniel C. Ganster, University of Arkansas, USA

The purpose of the present chapter is to review the nomological evidence concerning personality variables that are frequently studied in the stress literature. The reviewed personality traits include Type A behavior pattern (TABP), anger and hostility, hardiness, sense of coherence, locus of control (LOC), self-esteem, power motivation, and trait positive and negative affectivity (including extraversion, neuroticism, and trait anxiety). We also review major conclusions regarding these constructs' relationships to demographic variables such as income, age, gender, and marital status as well as other factors such as heretability. It is hoped that this broader perspective on individual differences will facilitate theory building and data analysis in applied stress research. Epidemiological researchers developing hypotheses that include personality as an independent variable frequently focus exclusively on the evidence pertaining to the stress effects of the focal trait. However, much nomological evidence relating to personality traits has accumulated in the literatures of personality and social psychology, and it has been shown that this knowledge can be applied effectively to enhance theory building. For example, as is described in a subsequent chapter of this volume, Kobasa and other researchers have utilized a broad range of findings concerning associations among personality traits in their development of the hardiness construct and its specification in theoretical models.

The chapter begins by defining the personality constructs and briefly summarizing evidence for their role in the etiology of stress symptoms. The personality constructs in the present review were chosen because each has a large body of accumulated evidence regarding its stress effects. Therefore some personality factors previously idenfitied as having a role in the stress process are excluded. Our omission of such constructs as sex role orientation, field

Personality and Stress: Individual Differences in the Stress Process. Edited by C.L. Cooper and R. Payne
© 1991 John Wiley & Sons Ltd

dependence, and authoritarianism does not imply that their role in the stress process is unimportant, but rather that it is less revealed. The remainder of the chapter reviews linkages among the personality variables and the other important indiviudal differences. Much of the review makes operational distinctions within the construct domains because these distinctions often have substantive ramifications. For example, in reviewing TABP associations we focus chiefly on the Strucured Interview (SI) and Jenkins Activity Survey (JAS) because of their wider use in the literature. Further, the JAS is weighted less heavily in the review than the SI because the evidence for the toxic effects of the latter is broader and more convincing (Friedman and Booth-Kewley, 1988).

Conversely, certain distinctions among personality construct conceptualizations that are judged to be important by personality theorists are in some cases collapsed together in our review in the interest of parsimony. For example, more specific facets of locus of control (e.g. health LOC) are not accorded separate treatment.

Demographic differences and other non-personality variables are also discussed. Reliable associations between demographic variables and personality or subpopulation differences in the effects of the personality variable may suggest the need to include the demographic variable in analyses. We do not review the effects of the demographic variables on health or their relationships with one another. Some of these relationships are interesting and important for epidemiological research. For example, social mobility and status incongruity variables have been related to cardiovascular disease and there are interesting associations between variables within these domains (Kasl, 1978). Space limitations encouraged us to limit the focus of our review to the personality constructs.

STRESS-RELATED PERSONALITY VARIABLES

In this section we identify the epidemiological outcomes of the personality constructs that are frequently observed in the literature. The reviewed constructs include the Type A behavior pattern (TABP), anger, hostility and aggression, hardiness, locus of control and sense of coherence, trait negative and positive affectivity (including neuroticism, anxiety, and extraversion), power motivation, and self-esteem.

Type A Behavior Pattern

Since the original work of M. Friedman and Rosenman in the 1950s, researchers in the fields of behavioral medicine and psychology have found evidence of psycho-behavioral risk factors that partially explain coronary heart disease (CHD) and coronary artery disease (CAD). Friedman and

Rosenman conceptualized the Type A Behavior Pattern as "an action–emotion complex that can be observed in any person who is aggressively involved in a chronic, incessant struggle to achieve more and more in less and less time, and if required to do so, against the opposing efforts of other things or other persons" (Friedman and Rosenman, 1974, p. 67). Behavioral elements of the pattern are said to include: (a) an exaggerated sense of time urgency, (b) excessive competitiveness and achievement striving, and (c) hostility and aggressiveness (Friedman, 1969). Due to the success of some exemplars of TABP in predicting coronary morbidity, TABP and "coronary prone behavior" are generally equated in both the scientific and popular lexicons, despite the vagueness and multiplicity with which TABP is conceptualized and measured in the literature (H. S. Friedman and Booth-Kewley, 1988).

The Structured Interview (SI) developed out of Friedman and Rosenman's work and is the most successful among the TABP indices at predicting cardiovascular morbidity in prospective studies. The SI is an instrument assessing "the outcome of a set of [individual] predispositions interacting with specific types of eliciting situations, including those that might be considered stressful" (Matthews, 1985, p. 154). While current forms of the SI vary in format, all contain variables relating to speech characteristics (SC's; e.g. explosive speech; response latency), physically expressed attitudes (e.g. hostility and competitiveness with the interviewer), and answer content in which individuals describe their Type A tendencies. The effects of these variables on morbidity have been independently examined, and the hostility components, measured by stylistics and answer content, and observed SCs often correlate with CAD and CHD severity (cf. Dembroski et al., 1985; Siegman et al., 1987b). Type A categorization is done using a global A versus B classification and also a four- or five-category assignment that essentially represents a continuous A–B scale. Because SI Hostility is conceptually and empirically distinct from other TABP constructs and a literature has developed around them, SI Hostility and other measures related to anger, hostility, and aggression will be discussed separately from TABP in this chapter.

Although the SI is the only Type A measure that has consistently demonstrated validity in predicting coronary morbidity (Matthews and Haynes, 1986), the Jenkins Activity Scale (JAS) has been used in a great many studies and is frequently associated with CHD and related complaints (see the review by Friedman and Booth-Kewley, 1987b). Quantitatively cumulating the results of many independent studies in a meta-analysis, Harbin (1989) found that both global JAS and global SI were reliably associated with blood pressure reactivity and other forms of autonomic nervous system arousal in response to stressors. These forms of arousal have been implicated as possible mediators of the CHD and CAD effects of the traits. Because of their prominence in the epidemiological literature, our review focuses chiefly on the SI and JAS. There are, however, other self-report TABP measures that are infrequently associated with coronory morbidity. These are examined as well.

Anger, Hostility, and Aggression

Although dimensions of anger, hostility, aggression and cynicism were included in Friedman and Rosenman's original Type A conceptualization, there is enough evidence concerning their unique effects on coronary morbidity and autonomic nervous system reactivity to warrant their classification as separate constructs. The relative lack of hostility-related variables in self-report Type A measures reinforces such a distinction. Indeed, hostility, broadly defined, is emerging as the central personality factor in the etiology of CHD and CAD (Siegman, 1989). SI-measured hostility, based on behavioral stylistics and answer content, is particularly predictive of CHD.

The original self-report hostility instrument is the Buss–Durkee Hostility Inventory (BDHI). The BDHI has been significantly correlated with CAD severity in post-infarct samples (Siegman, 1989). The Minnesota Multiphasic Personality Inventory (MMPI) derived Cook–Medley Ho scale primarily measures cynicism and feelings of persecution. Although labelled as a hostility instrument, it does not measure anger, aggression, or even irritability. This instrument has demonstrated considerable success in predicting severity of CAD, physiological arousal that provides a marker of coronary risk (Williams, 1989), and CHD mortality in prospective studies (Barefoot, Dahlstrom and Williams, 1983; Shekelle et al., 1983).

Hardiness, Locus of Control, and Sense of Coherence

Hardiness is defined by the additive effects of high commitment, personal control, and challenge seeking in daily life. Hardy persons believe in what they are doing, believe they can influence important events in their lives, and welcome change and personal challenge (Kobasa, Maddi and Zola, 1983). Based on the work of Kobasa and her colleagues, hardiness has emerged as an individual difference that appears to buffer the debilitating effects of stressful events and is sometimes linearly related to physical symptoms. Whereas Type A and Hostility variables reliably predict coronary morbidity and peripheral arousal under stress but are not related to noncardiovascular physical illness and psychological strain (Suls and Sanders, 1988), hardiness is related only to the latter stress outcomes.

An internal locus of control (LOC) is an integral aspect of the hardy personality and hence its constituent measures are frequently employed in hardiness research. Because there are independent epidemiological and psychological literatures associated with internal-external LOC relevant studies from that literature are reviewed separately in this chapter. Internals have been associated with a higher resistance to illness caused by stress, and studies have found an internal LOC to be positively associated with systolic blood pressure (SBP) reactivity (cf. Manuck, Craft and Gold, 1978), diastolic blood pressure (DBP) reactivity (cf. DeGood, 1975), and heart rate (HR) reactivity (cf. Houston, 1972). In fact, in his review of psychological predictors of reactivity, Houston (1986) stated that LOC is among the most important correlates of cardiovascular reactivity (p. 222).

A construct that fits closely with the LOC and hardiness constructs is Sense of Coherence (SOC). Antonovsky (1987) developed the SOC constellation after observing the health status of women concentration camp survivors. He was struck by the surprisingly good health of these women despite their prior experiences. Antonovsky developed a perspective he labelled the "salutogenic" model to explain the conditions that predict well-being, as opposed to sickness, under conditions of adversity. Antonovsky's (1987) definition of SOC is as follows:

> The sense of coherence is a global orientation that expresses the extent to which one has a pervasive, enduring though dynamic feeling of confidence that (1) the stimuli deriving from one's internal and external environments are structured, predictable, and explicable; (2) the resources are available to one to meet the demands posed by these stimuli; and (3) these demands are challenges, worthy of investment and engagement.
>
> (p. 19)

Like hardiness, there is some evidence that SOC serves a buffering role in stressful situations. Antonovsky and Sagy (1986) tested the anxiety responses of subjects in an ego threatening stress setting and reported that high-SOC subjects were less anxious than low-SOC subjects. In a study of 60 married couples having a disabled male, Antonovsky and Sourani (1988) found that SOC correlated positively with family and community life satisfaction.

Negative and Positive Affectivity

Negative affectivity (NA) "subsumes a broad range of aversive mood states, including anger, disgust, scorn, guilt, fearfulness, and depression . . ." (Watson and Pennebaker, 1989, pp. 234–5). Although various indexes of NA, including trait anxiety and neuroticism, have been found to be correlated significantly with cortisol (Anisman and LaPierre, 1982), salivary immunoglobulins (S-IgA; Ursin et al., 1984), and somatic complaints (see the review by Costa and McCrae, 1987), the only cardiovascular outcome with

NA has been found to affect is angina pectoris (cf. a prospective study conducted by Costa et al., 1982).

Positive affectivity is the disposition to experience positive emotional states. It represents the degree to which one is characteristically enthusiastic and full of energy (Watson and Tellegen, 1985). It is frequently measured using extraversion self-reports such as the Eysenck Personality Inventory (EPI; Eysenck and Eysenck, 1968). Extraversion appears to be consistently associated with emotional well-being (see the review by Costa and McCrae, 1980). It has also been correlated negatively with CHD and related complaints, although these effects are not robust, as evidenced by the meta-analysis results of Friedman and Booth-Kewley (1987a). H. Eysenck and his colleagues have also found links between neuroticism and extraversion and various cancers (see Eysenck, 1983). These characteristics were particularly predictive when used interactively with stressors. Combinations of these traits interacting with stressors have also been shown to predict subjective well-being (Hotard et al., 1989).

Power Motivation

High N-Powers are posited to be competitive and aggressive, interested in the accumulation of *things* and memberships, and to prefer action over reflection (McClelland and Burnham, 1976). Several empirical studies conducted in university student populations indicate a positive linear relationship between N-Power and stress symptoms and reactivity (cf. Fodor, 1984). Inhibited power motivation, the combination of high N-Power, low need for affiliation, and high activity inhibition, has been associated with significantly higher norepinephrine (NE) saliva concentration and a significantly greater subsequent drop in salivary immunoglobulin (S-IgA; McClelland, Ross and Patel, 1985b; McClelland *et al.*, 1985a). Both of these effects indicate depressed immune system functioning. Inhibited power motivation has also been associated with elevated diastolic blood pressure (McClelland, 1979), and physical illness (McClelland and Jemmott, 1980).

Self-esteem

Although there is little evidence that self-esteem is directly related to CHD (Friedman and Booth-Kewley, 1987a), it may be reliably correlated (negatively) with blood pressure reactivity to stressors in the laboratory (Scherwitz, Berton and Leventhal, 1978). Self-esteem has been regarded as a critical element in mental health. For example, Rosenberg's (1965) study of over 5000 high-school students found moderate to strong correlations between self-esteem and depressive affect and a list of physiological indicators of anxiety that included trembling hands, pounding heart, pressures or pains in the head, sweating hands, and dizziness. Beck's (1967) research on depression also indicated the important role of low self-esteem in that disorder.

INTERRELATIONSHIPS AMONG THE INDIVIDUAL DIFFERENCES

Type A Personality

Recent research has attempted to refine the TABP conceptualization and to distinguish the characteristics associated with coronary morbidity. Relationships between TABP measures and other personality variables have been frequently studied. This has provided a more thorough understanding of the psychological dimensions underlying TABP. A second area of research has correlated factors that may help to explain the onset and maintenance of TABP traits as well as TABP's toxic effects. Each of these streams has implications for the nomological validity of the TABP. Our review focuses on the more toxic TABP factors, examining first their interrelationships with one another and then their associations with different individual differences.

The SI and JAS do not appear to share much common variance. Matthews et al. (1982) found very little convergence between global SI and the JAS in two male samples. Content ratings of pressured drive were highly correlated with the JAS global rating, but other components were not. Across the JAS dimensions and global rating, Chesney et al. (1981) observed correlations with global SI ranging from .12 (Job Involvement) to .26 (global JAS) among 384 male workers. Using a Dutch adaptation of the JAS in a sample of 2712 males in the Netherlands, SI categorization was predicted with success at a rate only 23% better than chance (Appels, Jenkins and Rosenman, 1982). As observed by Matthews (1982), these findings are fairly typical. She concluded from her review that the JAS corresponds with SI categorization at an average rate of only 10% to 20% among males.

Similarly disappointing convergence has been found within female samples. Studying a sample of 88 white women, Anderson and Waldron (1983) found a correlation of .27 between the SI and JAS global ratings. Mayes, Sime and Ganster (1984) found even less correlation between global SI and global JAS and its constituent subscales among 63 working women. The average correlation was zero across the "Job Involvement", "Speed and Impatience", and "Hard-Driving Competitive" JAS subscales and the global rating. At the component level of the SI, correlations were statistically significant but of modest size. The highest correlation was .36, between JAS-Speed and Impatience and answer content from the SI.

In sum, across male and female populations, the global ratings from the two most pouplar TABP instruments tend to share less than 10% common variance. Higher correlations are observed between certain common components, but even these seldom reflect more than 25% shared variance and common use of the self-report method of measurement probably inflates these estimates. In light of this evidence and the frequent support for the null hypothesis in studies assessing JAS effects on coronary morbidity, we are led to agree with Siegman (1989), who stated:

> To the extent, then, that the SI has been successful in predicting CHD, it is probably not by virtue of it measuring the same components of the TABP construct that are being measured by the JAS, but rather by virtue of it tapping a dimension that is not being measured by JAS.

(pp. 68–9)

Other self-report TABP instruments commonly used in research include the Bortner Type A Scale (Bortner, 1969), which, like the JAS, was developed from the Western Collaborative Group Studies (WCGS) data, the Thurstone Temperament Schedule, the Framingham Type A Scale, and the Bortner Type A Scale. The Thurstone instrument, which primarily measures speed and hurriedness, has been positively associated with blood pressure and pulse rate reactivity (Pittner, Houston and Spiridigliozzi, 1983) and indicated some potential as a predictor of CHD (Brozek, Keys and Blackburn, 1966). It has demonstrated convergence with the SI global rating at a level superior to all other TABP questionnaires in six studies (Chesney et al., 1981; Dodd, Conti and Sime, 1983; MacDougall, Dembroski and Musante, 1979; Mayes et al., 1984; Rahe, Hervig and Rosenman, 1978; Rosenman and Chesney, 1980). The correlations are nonetheless unimpressive, typically ranging below 10% common variance. The higher correlations have been observed between Thurstone and SI answer content, with correlations of .39 and .38 observed by Mayes et al. (1984) and Ganster et al. (1991), respectively. Musante et al. (1983) observed a correlation of .42 between SI global and Thurstone in their female subsample (the correlation was only .17 in the male subsample). It was not surprising that the highest SI component correlations with Thurstone occurred with the SI speed, impatience, and competitiveness variables inasmuch as items tapping these domains largely comprise the Thurstone measure.

Very few studies have examined the Framingham or Bortner Type A scales in conjunction with the SI since the WCGS. The Bortner instrument was more highly correlated with SI global Type A and SI components than Thurstone and the JAS variables in the Mayes et al. (1984) study. The SI and Framingham were significantly, but again modestly, correlated in a sample of undergraduate women (MacDougall et al., 1979), but the same variables' correlation was nonsignificant in an adult sample (Haynes, Feinleib and Kannel, 1980). Content reports of pressured drive, competitiveness, and impatience from the SI were associated with Framingham Type A in the Musante et al. (1983) study, but the SI global A/B rating was correlated with Framingham only within the female subsample. Again, however, most of the significant findings involve small correlations in large samples.

The SI has been called the "gold standard" of TABP because of its superior predictive validity in epidemiological studies (Dembroski and Czajkowski, 1989). In fact, studies frequently interpret convergent validity with the SI as evidence that a self-report TABP measure indeed measured (Type A (cf. Appels et al., 1982). If the SI is to be used as the criterion of coronary prone behavior, these studies provide evidence that self-reported historical data are not informative about coronary proneness. Indeed, answer content from the SI, a self-report albeit not paper and pencil, is the only SI component demonstrating reasonable convergence with self-report exemplars, and it has been shown to be quite benign in epidemiological studies (Ganster et al., 1991). The lack of association is probably a function of the self-report measures' deficiency in capturing the Type A conceptualization. In terms of their ability to measure an action–emotion complex elicited in response to stressful stimuli, reminiscences of prior behavior fall far short of a stimulus-intense interview that includes observations of physical responses *in situ*. On the other hand, if indeed researchers wish to continue refinement of self-report TABP measures and use these in health-related studies, the Thurstone instrument would appear to deserve at least as much attention as does the JAS.

A great many studies have identified separate personality variables that are associated with Type A. We will briefly review a sample of these studies in which stress-related personality variables appear to be informative about the development and maintenance and/or the nature of TABP.

Much of the social psychology literature on the TABP has investigated Type A's unique reactions to performance-related stimuli. Type A's are known to react with more arousal than Type B's to settings that contain incentives for accomplishment and a moderate probability of failure. Type A's also respond to a greater extent than B's when they are harassed or annoyed (Houston, 1983), and their attributions for personal failure are more self-focused (Strube, 1985). Each of these mechanisms offers a potential explanation for the stressfulness of TABP. Interpretations of these effects vary, but most tend to cite the Type A's greater need for control as the causal agent. We will not review the abundant laboratory evidence in which control-related variables have been manipulated and frequently found to interact with TABP variables in predicting physiological as well as interpersonal outcomes (see Matthews (1982) and Janisse and Dyck (1988) for reviews). Rather, we will focus on the control-related variables that are often themselves cited as being related to stress outcomes.

Achievement and power orientations have been studied in relation to stress and the TABP because of their clear conceptual link to driving, ambitious, control-oriented behaviors. The avoidance of easy and extremely difficult goals would seem to be consistent with the Type A's drive to accomplish many things. Individuals high in the need for achievement (N-Ach) are similarly characterized. The competitive, control-seeking aspect of TABP is descriptive of high N-power. Type A variables can therefore be expected to correlate positively with N-Ach and N-Power. As noted in Matthews's (1982) review, N-Ach is fairly consistently associated with Type A categorization using the SI and the JAS. However, she notes that the SI studies primarily involved middle-aged, middle-class Caucasian men. Given the influence of socialization variables on N-Ach (Stewart and Chester, 1982), research using population-based studies is needed to determine whether the SI–N-Ach correlation is generalizable across sexes, age groups, and social backgrounds.

Studies directly focused on the TABP and its relation to power motivation, however, are surprisingly scarce. Blumenthal, Lane and Williams (1985) observed that SI-measured TABP was related to the Personality Research Form (PRF) measure of need for dominance, but it was not associated with the Thematic Apperception Test (TAT) operationalization of N-Power. As measured by the Manifest Needs Questionnaire (MNQ), N-Power was significantly and positively correlated with both the SI global rating and the Thurstone Type A instrument in the Ganster *et al.* (1991) study. In the latter study, a multivariate regression including demographics and several other personality variables resulted in N-Power being one of only a few of the traits that maintained its significant association with SI content ratings. A positive SI correlation with N-Power was also reported by Matthews and Saal (1978).

A number of studies have observed positive associations between Type A and constructs that are similar to N-Power. Musante et al. (1983) found the SI global score and the JAS composite to correlate significantly with the Desirability of Control scale (Burger and Cooper, 1979) in a male subsample, but not relations were observed within their female subsample. Fontana et al. (1984) did not observe a relationship between power motivation and the SI or the JAS, but using subjects from the same all-male sample Fontana et al. (1987) found that inhibited power motivation had a sizable relationship with both Type A measures.

Two studies have observed sex differences in the correlation between TABP and manifest needs. Bergman and Magnusson (1986) conducted an interesting longitudinal study of Swedish males and females. Measures of various personality variables including "overambition" and "overachievement" were measured at age 13 (in 1968) and an adapted short version of the JAS was administered at age 27. The time-lagged correlation was significant for overambition ($r = .22$, $p < .05$) but not for overachievement ($r = .01$) among men, whereas the opposite pattern (correlation of .07 for overambition and .18 for overachievement) was observed among women. Using a gender-mixed sample of undergraduates, Yarnold and Grimm (1986) found that an instrument measuring dominance was positively correlated with composite JAS, and Chesney et al. (1981) reported a significant positive relationship between dominance from an adjective check-list and the SI global rating.

Self-esteem has been positively correlated with SI categorization (for example, Chesney et al., 1981). In recognition of suggestions made by Matthews (1982) and Strube (1985), among others, that ". . . Type A's are particularly concerned with self-esteem enhancement and protection" (p. 785), Friedman and Booth-Kewley (1987b) included the Rosenberg (1965) measure of self-esteem in their predictive study of SI and JAS categorization and health status. They observed negligible correlations with each of these outcomes. Ganster et al. (1991) found the same self-esteem instrument to correlate significantly with SI global Type A, SC's, and content ratings, but the effect sizes were quite small. In multiple regression analyses, self-esteem appeared to buffer the effects of Hostility on palmar sweat responses to the stress of the interview. Only individuals scoring low on self-esteem exhibited a positive relationship between Hostility and reactivity or recovery time. Hubbs-Tait and Blodgett (1989) similarly found that low SE Type A's became more tense and hostile than their high SE counterparts during a frustrating task.

The two major prospective studies of the TABP, the WCGS and Multiple Risk Factor Intervention Trials (MRFIT), sampled a narrow demographic substrate of men and are therefore uniformative about demographic variation in TABP. Several studies have reported higher Type A scores among males than females (cf. the Framingham Heart Study—(Haynes et al., 1978). Haynes et al. (1978) noted, however, that women who are employed during at least half of their adult life exhibit Type A scores comparable to males. Several other studies have failed to find sex differences, especially those using undergraduate samples. Controlling for occupational status and education-based socio-economic status (SES) scores eliminated the relationship between gender and TABP in the large-scale Chicago area study reported by Shekelle, Schoenberger and Stamler (1976). As suggested by Baker et al. (1984), ". . . observed sex differences in the prevalence of the Type A behavior pattern diminish to insignificance when occupation, education, or socioeconomic status are controlled" (p. 481).

Significant gender differences in the relationship between TABP and coronary morbidity have not been the norm, although male white-collar workers evidenced a significantly stronger relationship between Framingham Type A and diastolic blood pressure than did other groups (Haynes et al., 1978). In the laboratory, female Type A's and Type B's exhibit less autonomic nervous system reactivity than their male counterparts. Houston (1986) suggests that this may be explained by females' sex-role orientations concerning performance in the laboratory:

> . . . Type A–Type B differences in cardiovascular responses are less likely to be found for women when the situation with which they are confronted is not congruent with traditional sex-role expectations for good performance . . .
>
> (p. 212)

As noted by Baker et al. (1984), studies of the relationship between age and TABP have been inconclusive, although large sample population-based studies have reported age differences in female samples using the JAS (cf. Shekelle et al., 1976). In the large-scale, population-based Minnesota Heart Survey reported by Sprafka et al. (1990), black and white, male and female groups showed a negative relationship between age and each of the JAS components except competitiveness. In a probability sample of 903 Michigan (US) residents, Moss et al. (1986) observed an inverted U-shaped relationship between age and the SI global rating.

Although Blacks have repeatedly been shown to exhibit a higher propensity to hypertension than demographically comparable Whites and, in certain stressful situations, greater physiological reactivity (especially comparing Black and White hypertensives; Anderson, 1989), few studies have sought to compare these groups on TABP indices. It is noteworthy, however, that in the large-scale population studies conducted by Sprafka et al. (1990) and Moss et al. (1986), Blacks had *lower* age- and education-adjusted scores on the JAS and SI, respectively. Due to these opposing effects, researchers studying the relationship between TABP and reactivity should beware of a possible racial suppressor effect.

Social and economic status variables are other important demographic correlates of the TABP. Although there was no relation between the SES composite and SI-categorization in the all-male WCGS, as observed in the first population-based study of TABP, the Framingham study, as well as large samples in countries outside the US (cf. Belgium; Kittel et al., 1983), Type A behavior as measured by most standard instruments tends to be positively correlated with SES composites, income, white-collar occupation, and years of education. SES–TABP correlations often appear to be predominantly a function of income (Moss et al., 1986).

Marital status was associated with all JAS dimension in the Belgian Physical Fitness Study (Kittel et al., 1983). Married men provided the higher JAS scores. Finally, family histories and personality characteristics of parents appear to increase proclivity toward development of the TABP (Woodall and Matthews, 1989). Some studies have found significant relationships between parental and offspring Type A. For example, using a random sample of 12-, 15-, and 18-year-old subjects in Sweden, Keltikangas-Jarvinen (1988) observed significant correlations within parent–child dyads; interestingly, relationships were substantially stronger for opposite-sex dyads. Studies comparing twins reared apart, however, do not support a hypothesis of heritability (Rahe, Hervig and Rosenman, 1978).

Summary

The SI "gold standard" of TABP converges poorly with other TABP measures. A few studies have identified sex differences in the relationship between SI categorization and self-report TABP. Within narrow demographic ranges, the SI has been correlated positively with N-Ach, and there is considerable evidence to suggest a positive relationship between TABP and power and control needs. Type A's also appear to score high on self-esteem and multiplicative combinations of self-esteem and TABP show promise for improving stress outcome prediction.

Frequently observed sex differences on TABP scores are probably an artifact of the socioeconomic status/gender correlation. Gender appears to moderate the relationship between TABP and physiological reactivity to laboratory-induced stressors.

Age is negatively associated with SI categorization. Black–White racial differences and marital status have also been correlated with TABP, but there is not a great deal of evidence to be confident about population differences.

Anger, Hostility, and Aggression

Despite a recently proliferating literature on the role of anger, hostility, and aggression as coronary risk factors, several issues concerning the nomological validity of these constructs remain. In particular, the psychological dimension underlying anger, hostility, aggression, and cynicism are not fully understood. The more we understand about these factors, the more able we will be to identify the unique components that explain the toxic effects and possibly develop a taxonomy of coronary prone behavior. The findings discussed below indicate that there is considerable movement in this direction.

The Buss–Durkee Hostility Inventory (BDHI) is positively correlated with expert ratings of physical aggressiveness (Matthew, Jamison and Cottington, 1985). Musante et al. (1989) found SI Hostility from the SI, which measures both arousal and demonstration of anger and hostility, to be correlated with BDHI subscales of verbal expression of hostility, and self-reported physical assault and irritability, but not negativism, indirect expression of hostility, resentment, suspicion, or guilt. On the other hand, the Cooke–Medley Ho scale's correlations with the BDHI are quite high, ranging from .60 to .70 in two samples of male and female undergraduate students across the Resentment, Suspicion, and Irritability BDHI subscales in a study conducted by Smith and Frohm (1985).

The Ho instrument also correlated significantly with the remaining BDHI subscales, but controlling for social desirability substantially attenuated these correlations. Indeed, composite scale Ho correlations with the Marlowe–Crowne Social Desirability scale averaged – .53 across the two samples. This points up the difficulty of obtaining valid measures of such emotionally charged variables. Costa et al. (1986a) found that the Ho instrument's subscales of Cynicism and Paranoid alienation had the same pattern of association with various personality markers of psychopathology taken from the MMPI, including neuroticism, psychoticism/infrequency, and inadequacy. The positive infrequency correlation is striking in view of the strong negative relationship with social desirability observed by Smith and Frohm (1985). It is not clear whether hostiles are deceiving in their reports or are actually quite forthcoming and merely inattentive during questionnaire administration.

Buss and Durkee (1957) extracted two factors from the BDHI instrument in a principal components analysis. The first was defined by the Resentment and Suspicion subscales, and the second included the Physical Assault and Verbal Expression subscales. These two factors were interpreted to represent experience (or awareness) of hostility and expression of hostility, respectively. This two-factor structure of covert and overt hostility has been widely replicated across various other instruments (Musante et al., 1989). In the Musane et al. study, Hostility scores from the SI were correlated most strongly with the factor represented by variables measuring anger expression. SI Hostility was uncorrelated with variables measuring suspicion (r = − .04), mistrust (r = .03), guilt (r = − .09), and anger expressed inward (r = .14). Between these two dimensions, expression (or overt hostility) has been found to be more toxic in its effects on coronary morbidity. Siegman (1989) views these dimensions as "neurotic" and "expressive" hostility. In an angiographic study conducted by Siegman, Dembroski and Ringel (1987a), the experience of hostility and neuroticism each correlated *negatively* with CAD; expressive hostility, on the other hand, correlated positively with CAD. As will be made clear in our review of hostility variables' correlations with independent personality constructs, this distinction is important to the normological validity of hostility.

If anger and hostility instruments are to purport to measure some unique construct, they should demonstrate substantially higher correlations with measures of both expressive and experienced anger and hostility than with measures of other affective traits. In the Siegman et al. (1987a) study, the Taylor Manifest Anxiety Scale (MAS), known variously to index trait anxiety and neuroticism or, in a more general conceptual context, trait negative affectivity (Watson and Tellegen, 1985), was highly correlated with experienced hostility from the BDHI. The Spielberger, Gorsuch and Lushene (1970) trait anxiety measure and a depression inventory were each significantly correlated with the Cooke–Medley Ho instrument in the Smith and Frohm (1985) study. Ho scores also correlated significantly with state anxiety among the 50 men studied by Friedman and Booth-Kewley (1987a). The Spielberger et al. trait anxiety instrument was uncorrelated with Hostility from the SI in the Ganster et al. (1991) study. This latter null result may be indicative of SI Hostility's capturing expressive hostility variance as opposed to the experiential (or neurotic) hostility that may be captured by Ho.

On the basis of Siegman et al.'s (1987a) study and the null results of cross-sectional and prospective studies of CHD, Siegman (1989) concluded that it is not likely that personality tests that also measure neuroticism and trait anxiety will correlate positively with severity of CHD . . . Depending on the level of confounding, the correlation can even be significantly negative.

(p. 70)

However, as observed by Costa et al. (1986a), Ho is highly correlated with neuroticism. Neurotic hostiles may be more prone to experience symptoms and seek treatment for CHD symptoms. In light of this nomological evidence indicating its unusually strong relationships to both NA and CHD, examination of the unique components underlying the toxicity of the Ho instrument is in order.

Inasmuch as the SI Type A/B designation and various indexes of hostility appear to be reliably associated with CHD, the relative paucity of studies examining their relationships is surprising. Ganster et al. (1991) found that SI Hostility from the SI correlated .61 (p < .0001) with the two-point SI global rating, and .70 with the five-point SI rating. This was in contrast to the nonsignificant correlation (r = .13) between SI Hostility and the Thurstone Type A instrument. Aggression from an adjective check-list was also significantly related to SI global Type A in the Chesney et al. (1981) study.

The Cooke–Medley Ho instrument, however, is in general weakly associated with the SI and JAS Friedman and Booth-Kewley (1987a) observed a nonsignificant correlation of .13 between the Ho instrument and the SI global rating. The even smaller effect size for the Ho–JAS Type A relationship suggested that it was not simply a lack of behavioral exemplars explaining the weak results. Matthews et al. (1982) and Musante et al. (1983) found similarly weak associations between SI Hostility and both the JAS global rating and the JAS subscales. This may reflect the relative lack of negativity content in the JAS as compared to the SI, Thurstone, and Framingham Type A instruments. Irritation and hostility from the SI were weakly correlated with the JAS in the Anderson and Waldron (1983) study.

In the Smith and Frohm (1985) study, the Ho scale was not significantly correlated with the JAS after controlling for social desirability, but it was significantly correlated (r = .34) with the Framingham Type A scale even after partialling social desirability. However, the Framingham instrument is unusual for self-report Type A measures because it includes some hostility items. It was positively correlated with anger-out (r=.19) but not anger-in in the Framingham study (Haynes et al., 1978). Herman et al. (1981) suggests that social desirability is an important factor in accounting for the generally weak relationship between Type A and hostility. They suggested that Type A's will endorse hostile self-descriptors only when the descriptors are socially acceptable. For instance, aggressive behavior in an achievement context may be acknowledged by the Type A, but random physical abuse will not.

One study has examined interactions between hostility and Type A in the prediction of health outcomes. Testing SI Hostility's interactions with content and speech characteristics (SC's) from the SI, only individuals scoring high on Type A answer content exhibited a positive relationship between Hostility and somatic complaints in the Ganster et al. (1991) study. This Hostility–Content interaction was not observed across a range of dependent reactivity measures, however.

Inasmuch as they involve use of strong, forceful actions to control others, power motivation constructs may bear a positive relation to expressive hostility as measured by SI Hostility. Literature from the field of social psychology on aggression also suggests that there should be some relation between overt power motivation and hostility. According to McClelland (1975), provided that it is matched by low needs for affiliation and low activity inhibition, men with high N-Power will exhibit more physical aggression. There is a paucity of studies examining such a relationship, however. Musante et al. (1983) reported a significant correlation between SI Hostility and Burger and Cooper's (1979) Desirability of Control Scale (r = .31), and this was stronger than the latter's correlations with other SI dimensions. Fontana et al. (1984) also found a significant positive relation between SI Hostility and N-Power, and in a subsequent paper (Fontana et al., 1987) they reported that there was also a significant positive relationship between *inhibited* power motivation and SI Hostility. Ganster et al. (1991), however, found no relation between manifest needs questionnaire (MNQ) measured N-Power and SI Hostility. Mason and Blankenship (1987) reported that high N-Power was positively associated with physical abuse by men of their intimate female partners, but high N-Power female partners did not exhibit the same tendency.

Aggression and anger expressed inward are plausible psychological strategies used to protect low self-esteem (Novaco, 1975). However, we find no evidence that self-esteem is correlated with either "neurotic" or "expressive" hostility. Ganster et al. (1991) and Musante et al. (1983) each found no relationship between SI Hostility and measures of self-esteem from Rosenberg (1965) and the California Psychological Inventory (CPI), respectively. The Rosenberg measure was also not correlated with the Cooke–Medley Ho measure in the Friedman and Booth-Kewley (1987a) study. Kernis, Granneman and Barclay (1989) offer a possible explanation for these weak associations. Persons whose self-esteem was shown to be high and unstable across multiple measurements expressed significantly more neurotic hostility than persons with stable high self-esteem. Stable and unstable low self-esteem fell between these extremes. Ganster et al. (1991) observed an interaction between hostility and self-esteem in predicting palmar sweat reactivity that is more consistent with the plasticity hypothesis of buffering role for self esteem (SE). Hostility was positively related to reactivity among low SE's and negatively related among high SE's. It is likely that the degree of threat perceived upon presentation of a noxious stimulus (in this case the harassment of the SI) may be moderated by self-image.

It is also plausible that individuals perceiving less control over events and outcomes in their lives would resort to aggression in lieu of effective problem-solving strategies (Doherty, 1983). Hence, expressive hostility should correlate positively with an external LOC. Various laboratory studies of social relationships (cf. Bhatia and Golin, 1978) and field studies of marital relationships (cf. Doherty and Ryder, 1979) support this hypothesis. Contrary results are found in studies utilizing instruments to assess hostility, however. Ganster et al. (1991) and Musante et al. (1983) observed negligible relationships between SI Hostility and LOC. A significant *positive* relationship between the Cooke–Medley Ho scale and internal LOC was reported by Friedman and Booth-Kewley (1987a). It should be noted, however, that each of these results is based on analyse of predominantly male samples. Furthermore, they tell us nothing about how externals respond to provocation, short of the harassment contained in the SI interview in the Ganster et al. and Musante et al. studies. Because the subject has submitted freely to the SI and can presumably terminate the interview at will without consequence, the type of threat (harassment) confronting an external in the SI may not be conducive to control-relevant attributions as are marital disputes.

Due to a lack of population-based studies and the emphasis on post-infarct and other clinical samples for investigating anger and hostility, very little is known about their demographic correlates. Gender is an exception, however. One probabilistic sample of traig anger data was recently collected by Zeidner (1990). Among 923 Israeli adults, women scored significantly higher than men on the Spielberger et al. (1983) anger index. In the Framingham study, women scored significantly higher on the anger-in index, but not on the anger-out index (Haynes et al., 1978). In the broader social psychology literature on aggression, a meta-analysis conducted on a large sample of independent field and laboratory studies by Eagly and Steffen (1986) found that males were significantly more aggressive than females. This gender difference was particularly pronounced when the aggressive behavior was directed toward physical rather than psychological injury. Extrapolating from these findings, it is very possible that male gender is associated with higher scores on measures of expressive hostility. Indeed, in the Jorgensen and Houston (1986) study males scored significantly higher than females on the Physical Assault subscale of the Buss–Durkee Hostility Inventory.

One recent study suggests that males and females may differ on the relationships among SI Type A and SI Hostility variables. The male and female undergraduates studied by Musante et al. (1983) provided SI scores that differed substantially on factor structure. One key difference was that hostility variables did not load congenerically among females but rather combined with the impatience variables. These results and differences between males and females in the pattern of correlations between hostility and other variables suggest that certain gender-specific motivational bases may underly hostility (Woodall and Matthews, 1989). Gender may moderate the relationship between anger and hostility and some measures of the TABP. Significant anger–Type A correlations were observed among females in the Framingham Heart Study (Haynes et al., 1978), but not among males. Waldron et al. (1980) reported that interviewer and self-ratings of anger were correlated with Type A among females but not males. In the prospective investigation conducted by Bergman and Magnusson (1986), aggression reports at age 13 correlated significantly and positively with JAS scores at age 27 among males, but the same indices at equivalent points in the lifespan did not correlate among women. These results are consistent with the Mason and Blankenship (1987) findings discussed above, wherein N-Power, a TABP correlate, was associated with the infliction of phsyical abuse only among men.

Smith and Frohm (1985) reported that Cooke–Medley Ho scores correlated positively with positive life event scores among undergraduate females, but there was no correlation among their male counterparts. In addition, Ho was correlated more strongly with depression among the females but not the males. While only white-collar males exhibited a link between Type A and diastolic blood pressure in the Framingham study, only females exhibited a positive association between anger-in and DBP. On the basis of these few studies and the emotion-charged nature of anger and hostility indices, potential gender-specific socialization on these variables requires that the assumption of homogeneous regression coefficients be tested in mixed-gender samples.

Summary

The "neurotic" and "expressive" dimensions of hostility are differentially related to other personality variables. Neurotic hostility measures such as Ho correlate positively with neuroticism and trait anxiety. Neither form of hostility correlates well with self-report TABP. SI Hostility (a measure of expressive hostility) correlates positively with N-Power but not negative affectivity. In research that has been limited to predominantly male samples, SI and Ho hostiles appear to have a more external LOC.

If there is a gender difference in anger/hostility, males appear to exhibit more of such tendencies than females. Gender may also moderate TABP–hostility associations.

Locus of Control, Hardiness, and Sense of Coherence

As stated by Friedman and Booth-Kewley (1987b), an internal LOC appears to be the major aspect of hardiness that relates consistently to other personality characteristics. They found that a less internal LOC was positively related to anxiety reports but the other hardiness indices were not. However, neither LOC nor hardiness was significantly correlated with JAS or SI Type A or hostility as measured using the Cook–Medley Ho instrument. The relationship between LOC and hardiness and trait anxiety has been observed in other studies (cf. Powell and Vega, 1972; Richert, 1981). In contrast with the Friedman and Booth-Kewley (1987b) findings, however, trait anxiety and other measures of negative affectivity are frequently shown to be so highly correlated with hardiness composities that they explain the latters' personality and health correlations. Rhodewalt and Zone (1989) controlled for trait NA and found that a significant positive zero-order correlation between hardiness and illness reports disappeared. Among a sample of male undergraduates, Allred and Smith (1989) observed that neuroticism accounted for a significant positive correlation between hardiness and self-esteem.

As stated by Strickland (1978), "Type A individuals . . . sound strikingly like internals" (p. 1195). However, hardiness and LOC do not appear to share a significant amount of common variance with TABP. Using participants from the MRFIT study, Friedman, Hall and Harris (1985) found that Type A's, defined by triangulating the JAS and the Affective Communication Test, a behavior observation system very similar to the stylistic components of the SI, scored significantly higher on internal locus of control than persons scoring low on either the JAS or ACT. Among males in the Musante et al. (1983) study, there were significant correlations between drive and competitiveness components of the SI, JAS, and an internal LOC as measured by Rotter's (1966) instrument, but the SI stylistics and the global rating were not correlated with LOC. Levenson's (1973) Internal LOC subscale was not significantly correlated with any SI Type A measure (including content) or the Thurstone instrument in the Ganster et al. (1991) study. Friedman and Booth-Kewley (1987b) also did not find a relationship between Rotter's instrument and the SI global rating, and the JAS was *negatively* associated with internal LOC. Keenan and McBain (1979) and Nowack and Sassenroth (1980) found JAS-defined Type A's to be more *external* in their LOC. Type A externals also exhibited higher trait anxiety. Besides Musante et al. (1983), only Glass (1977) has reported a positive significant relationship between the JAS and internal LOC as assessed by the Rotter instrument. Along similar lines, Perloff, Yarnold and Feltzer (1988) found that JAS-defined Type A designation was positively correlated with health LOC, but this was not replicated in non-college adult study conducted by Leikin (1990). On the whole, then, the findings suggest that there is little, if any, relationship between toxic Type A and internal LOC, and there may in fact be a negative relationship between the JAS and internal LOC.

One possible explanation for these equivocal findings has been supported in several laboratory studies. While Type A's attribute success to internal causes, they attribute failure and other negative outcomes to external causes in order to maintain control and self-esteem (Strube, 1985). The Matthews (1982) review indicates that Type A's are more easily threatened by a loss of control than are Type B's. As further evidence that Type A's may perceive more or less self-control over stressors and other environmental influences, Brunson and Matthews (1981) observed that Type A's attributed their failures on a difficult laboratory task to be caused by a lack of ability (an internal cause) whereas B's attributed failure to external factors such as luck and task difficulty. Contrada, Wright and Glass (1985) similarly observed that Type A's made more use of control mechanisms to avoid noxious stimulation than did B's, suggesting that B's experienced helpless cognitions more readily than A's.

Similarly weak TABP associations are found in the literature studying the broader construct of hardiness. Schmeid and Lawler (1986) found no correlation between hardiness and SI. Hardiness also does not correlate very well with the JAS (Kobasa et al., 1983; Schmeid and Lawler, 1986). This general lack of association between TABP and hardiness is consistent with their differences in epidemiological prediction. Hardiness appears to correlate well with illness and psychological strains, whereas TABP does not correlate well with general strain but the SI operationalization of it is reliably associated with cardiovascular disorders and physiological reactivity.

When combined, however, hardiness and TABP appear to increase the amount of strain variance explained. Rhodewalt and Augustsdottir (1984) found that individuals scoring high on JAS Type A and low on hardiness were most prone to physical symptoms. Kobasa et al. (1983) obtained similar results in their sample of male executives. Using the Framingham measure of TABP, Nowack (1986) observed that hardy Type A's were least prone to burnout and other psychological strains. Howard, Cunningham and Rechnitzer (1986) observed a three-way interaction in which extreme SI Type A subjects who scored low on hardiness and role clarity experienced more pronounced physical symptoms. Schmeid and Lawler (1986), however, found no such interactions between hardiness and the SI or JAS in their female sample.

Internal LOC's relationships with achievement needs deserve mention because the latter are closely related to the Type A conceptualization; in fact, achievement striving items form a subscale of the JAS. An internal LOC also tends to be positively correlated with achievement needs (cf. Powell and Vega, 1972, Zuckerman and Gerbasi, 1977). There is reason to believe that this correlation should be stronger among males. As revealed in Findley and Cooper's (1983) meta-analysis of several independent field studies, internal LOC tends to be much more strongly related to actual achievement among males than among females. Because this finding was based primarily on studies conducted in the 1960s and 1970s, however, these sex differences may be expected to be less pronounced in current and future studies given the changes in gender-related mores and socialization patterns throughout the world.

Based on her program of research begun in the 1970s, Kobasa et al. (1983) stated that hardiness bears little relationship to demographic variables (p. 45). They found no correlation with age or education in a diverse sample. Nowack (1986) found no correlation between hardiness and education, but hardiness had a negative correlation with age. Contradictory results were observed by Schmeid and Lawler (1986). Hardiness was positively correlated with age as well as education and marital status.

The research evidence for demographic correlates of LOC in particular is not remarkably different from the broader domain of hardiness. In a national probability survey conducted by Ryckman and Malikiosi (1975), age was unrelated to internal LOC. Occupational differences were observed, however. Specifically, professionals were more internal than blue-collar workers and college students (Ryckman and Malikiosi, 1974). Further, Blacks have been found to be more external than Whites (Hall, Joesting and Woods, 1977; Powell and Vega, 1972). These latter findings could possibly be explained by the consistently positive correlation between internal LOC and SES (Powell and Vega, 1972).

Sex differences in LOC are observed infrequently. When they are found, however, females have tended to report a more internal LOC (cf. Nowicki and Segal, 1974; Zika and Chamberlain, 1987).

Empirical and conceptual relationships between Antonovsky's Sense of Coherence and Kobasa's Hardiness are discussed in a subsequent chapter in this volume. Along separate lines, Antonovsky's 29-item SOC scale does appear to correlate positively with internal LOC (Antonovsky, 1987). In addition, Antonovsky (1987) reported a correlation of – .79 between an SOC scale adapted for adolescents and Trait Anxiety. Antonovsky and Sagy (1986) found moderately high negative correlations between SOC and trait anxiety (– .56 and – .62) in two adolescent samples. Based on the SOC conceptualization we would speculate that it should also be correlated positively with self-esteem and demonstrate associations with occupational status variables that are similar with self-esteem (these are discussed below). However, we know of no research examining the SOC–SE linkage, and there is too little data to provide definitive conclusions about demographic correlates of SOC.

Summary

An internal LOC in particular and hardiness and sense of coherence in general appear to be negatively associated with trait anxiety. Although it is not reliably correlated with TABP, LOC's multiplicative relationship with TABP may improve prediction of general illness. An internal LOC is also positively linked to N-Ach. There is little consistent evidence for demographic subgroup differences on hardiness or LOC, however.

Positive and Negative Affectivity

Much of our review of the personality correlates of trait anxiety and neuroticism, constructs that are both posited to represent the broader domain of trait negative affectivity, has appeared in the foregoing sections. In this section we will briefly review findings concerning relationships between NA and positive affectivity measures and other personality variables. We will also return to a most important issue discussed above, the association between NA and hostility, and review demographic findings that shed more light on that relationship.

As the Matthews (1982) review noted, with the possible exception of the Framingham scale, TABP in all its operationalizations is generally unassociated with psychological stress or anxiety. This evaluation appears to be quite accurate, especially as it pertains to the SI. However, the exceptions in SI and self-report Type A studies deserve notice. To our knowledge, Bass (1984) is the only published study to report a significant correlation (positive) between trait anxiety and the SI global rating. On the other hand, through the Murray (1971) review, three of six studies he cited had reported a significant negative correlation between trait anxiety and response latency, a major component of SI SC's (low response latency is seen as a Type A characteristic). In addition, only SC's were positively correlated with trait anxiety in the Ganster et al. (1991) study. Even though it was very highly correlated with trait anxiety, neuroticism bore no correlation with SC's, other SI dimensions, or the Thurstone scale. This provides fairly strong evidence for the discriminant validity of these constructs with respect to their association with expressive hostility.

Trait anxiety was related to the Framingham self-report measure but not to any other self-report TABP exemplar in the Chesney et al. (1981) study. This correlation is to be expected given its item domain emphasis on antagonism and neuroticism. We find little evidence of other correlations between anxiety and self-report TABP, however. One interesting exception reported by Lundberg (1980) points up a possible sex difference. Among Swedish undergraduates, the JAS composite was positively correlated with anxiety proneness and neuroticism among females, but not among males.

Extraversion is frequently found to correlate positively with the SI and other TABP exemplars (cf. Chesney et al., 1981; Ganster et al., 1991). One major sex difference finding was reported by Musante et al. (1983). Although significant positive correlations have been observed between extraversion and SI Hostility in field studies (cf. Ganster et al., 1991), Musante et al. (1989) observed negative correlations with indirect (or neurotic) hostility and null relationships with expressive hostility in undergraduate samples. In addition, there was no correlation between extraversion and Ho in the large, mixed-gender Costa et al. (1986a) study. This suggests the possibility that demographic differences, such as a disproportionate number of males in the sample, may contribute to extraversion–hostility correlations.

Among the undergraduates studied by Musante et al. (1983), males and females provided substantially different patterns of correlations between California Psychological Inventory (CPI) scores and JAS and SI global ratings. Interestingly, extraversion from the Eysenck Personality Inventory (EPI) correlated significantly with the SI global rating only among females, and extraversion correlated significantly with the JAS composite only among males.

Relationships between extraversion and the other personality constructs discussed in this chapter are similarly variable and probably subject to artifactual inflation. It appears quite clear, however, that negative affectivity and positive affectivity are only very weakly, if at all, correlated with each other (Watson and Tellegen,1985).

There is probably a negative relationship between age and both NA and PA. In a population-based study of Israeli adults, Zeidner (1990) found the Spielberger et al. (1970) trait anxiety instrument to correlate negatively with age, but it was uncorrelated with gender and ethnicity. Analyzing a probability sample of 10063 US survey participants, Costa et al. (1986b) found age to be negatively correlated with neuroticism and extraversion.

In a nonlinear multiple regression analysis of the Costa et al. data, women showed a higher tendency towards neuroticism than men and there was a greater decline in extraversion with age among Blacks. Spielberger et al. (1970) concluded from their review that their trait anxiety measure exhibits no main sex differences and, as with neuroticism, there appeared to be a slight decrease with age. Among a sample of 1000 undergraduates sampled by Jorgensen and Houston (1986), female students were found to score higher than their male counterparts on a composite of neuroticism, trait anxiety, irritability, and resentment. In the manual for the EPI, Eysenck and Eysenck (1968) reviewed previous studies and concluded that women, members of lower economic strata, and urban subjects tend to score higher on neuroticism. Males and urban subjects also were seen to score higher on the composite extraversion scale.

Both extraversion and neuroticism demonstrated evidence of heritability in a study of monozygotic and dizygotic twins conducted by Pederson et al. (1988). Matching twins reared apart with similar twins reared together, 23% to 45% of the total variation in these constructs appeared attributable to genetic sources, whereas a shared environment accounted for only 10% of the variance.

Summary

There may be a positive relationship between trait anxiety and SI Speech Characteristics. Generally, however, negative affectivity is unassociated with TABP. Positive affectivity, in the form of extraversion, is positively related to TABP as well as hostility. There may be sex differences in the latter relationships, however.

Age appears to be negatively correlated with neuroticism and extraversion. Studies have also found evidence for possible gender, socioeconomic status, and urban–rural effects on neuroticism.

Power Motivation

Our discussion of power motivation constructs (e.g. N-Power, dominance) and their relationships with other personality constructs is subsumed within the prior sections. With regards to demographic correlates, there is very little evidence linking power motivation to SES or occupational status. As stated in a very thorough review by Stewart and Chester (1982), however, the sexes diverge considerably on some of the behavioral correlates of N-Power. These authors and others have reasoned that such differences are probably caused by the sexes' differential socialization regarding appropriate behavior. On the other hand, the conditions that elicit the power motive appear the same for men and women.

Self-esteem

As we noted above, self-esteem tends to be higher among those classified as Type A by the Structured Interview, and it is at least weakly related to the SI components with the exception of Hostility. Though it bears some positive relation with Type A classification, there is no evidence that self-esteem contributes to what might be considered the toxic outcomes of the behavior pattern. Moreover, its most important role seems to be as a potential buffer of the effect of Type A and Hostility on physiological reactivity and tension during stressful episodes (Ganster et al., 1991; Hubbs-Tait and Blodgett, 1989). This potential buffering role of self-esteem was also illustrated in a study of reactions to work stressors. Mossholder, Bedeian and Armenakis (1981) studied the attitudinal and behavioral repsonses of nurses in a hospital setting to role conflict and role ambiguity stresses. They found that there were significant negative relationships between these stressors and both job satisfaction and performance among low-SE nurses but not among high-SE nurses. Ganster and Schaubroeck (1990) observed the same SE buffering effect on the relationship between role stress and physical symptoms in a sample of police force workers.

There is a large literature that investigates the associations of SE with a variety of demographic variables. For socioeconomic status, Rosenberg (1979) reported small significant relationships between SE and education, occupation, and income. These relationships were found after controlling for race, which acted as a suppressor variable. Although consistent relationships between social class and SE are not evident for children and adolescents, SE and social standing tend to be positively related among adults (Weidman, Phelan and Sullivan, 1972; Yancey, Rigsby and McCarthy, 1972). Kohn (1969) and Kohn and Schooler (1969) proposed that the relationship between social class and SE is primarily a function of the types of occupational activities engaged in at different levels of occupational status. Specifically, those holding higher status jobs have more opportunity to exercise independent judgment and they enounter more substantive complexity in their work demands. Kohn (1969) reported that the significant relationships between SE measures and social class disappeared when occupational self-selection was controlled.

The finding that SE is positively associated with occupational self-direction converges with results suggesting that high SE's generally have stronger perceptions that they can exercise control over their environment than do low SE's. In this regard Dweck (1975) and Fitch (1970) report positive correlations between SE and internal LOC.

Self-ratings of the extent to which individuals are characterized as having sex-related attributes are also correlated with SE. Spence, Helmreich and Stapp (1975) found that male and female students who perceived themselves as having stereotypically male-valued attributes (e.g. independence, competitiveness, self-confidence, ambition, outspokenness) scored significantly higher on a measure of self-esteem ($r = .77$ for males and $r = .83$ for females). However, self-ratings of stereotypically female-valued attributes (e.g. emotionality, consideration, tactfulness, gentleness) were also positively related to SE for both males and females. It is not clear what role social desirability plays in these relationships, but it is conceivably a source of artifactual inflation of these correlations given the ostensibly socially desirable nature of both male and female stereotypes.

Summary

Self-esteem is such an integral component of mental health that it probably makes more sense to view it as an indicator of well-being than as a predictor. Its role as a moderator of relationships between stress and health and between other individual differences (e.g. Type A) and health is probably the best reason to incorporate it in studies of stress. There do not appear to be strong demographic correlates of SE (including age, race, and sex) with the exception of social class, particularly occupational status.

CONCLUDING REMARKS

In researching this review we were struck by the wealth of information pertaining to the nomological validity of various stress-related personality variables. Figure 3.1 attempts to summarize graphically the more consistently supported relationships among the personality and demographic characteristics examined in this chapter. Given the large number of established connections, it would appear that much has been learned and researchers can rely confidently on this literature in developing testable hypotheses. As we have casually reviewed throughout this chapter, however, there are several more possible connections that remain to be established conclusively or may have a nonlinear connection. Moreover, the figure does not include the many interactive relationships between the variables in predicting stress outcomes we reviewed, or the likely set of relationships that escaped our attention or that await discovery.

Much of the more reliable nomological information could be applied to enhance the precision and generalizability of substantive stress studies. In stress studies that include personality as an independent variable, measurement of established personality and demographic correlates could eliminate spuriousness or suppression caused by the variable's omisison from the analysis. Furthermore, identification of subpopulation differences in the effects of

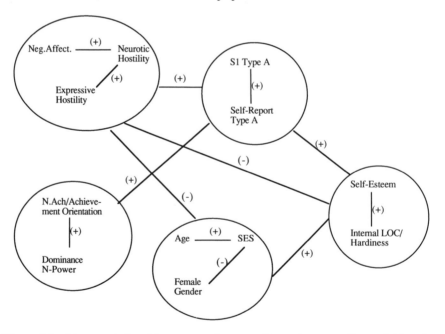

Figure 3.1   Linear relationships among demographic and personality variables that are observed consistently

the personality variable can be facilitated. For example, progress can be made in identifying differences among occupations in terms of the health risk posed by TABP or the extent to which TABP varies across occupations. Little headway has been provided in this direction since Kasl's (1978) call for such research.

It would also be advantageous if researchers paid more attention to the literature or stress-related individual differences in studies in which occupations or environmental variables are the focus. Such information adds complexity to the data analysis and interpretation of such studies, but we believe the increased understanding of the etiology of stress disorder provided by such a perspective outweighs the inconvenience.

REFERENCES

Allred, K. D. and Smith, T. W. (1989). The hardy personality: Cognitive and physiological responses to evaluative threat, *Journal of Personality and Social Psychology*, **56**, 257–66.

Anderson, J.R. and Waldron, I. (1983). Behavioral and content components of the structured interview assessment of the Type A behavior pattern in women, *Journal of Behavioral Medicine*, **6**, 123–34.

Anderson, N.B. (1989). Racial differences in stress-induced cardiovascular reactivity and hypertension: Current status and substantive issues, *Psychological Bulletin*, **105**, 89–105.

Anisman, H. and LaPierre, Y. (1982). Neurochemical aspects of stress and depression: formulations and caveats. In R. W. Neufeld (ed.) *Psychological Stress and Psychopathology*, McGraw-Hill, New York, 179–217.

Antonovsky, A. (1987). *Unraveling the Mystery of Health*, Jossey-Bass, San Francisco.

Antonovsky, A. and Sagy, S. (1986). The development of sense of coherence and its impact on responses to stress situations, *Journal of Social Psychology*, **126**, 213–25.

Antonovsky, A. and Sourani, T. (1988). Family sense of coherence and family adaptation, *Journal of Marriage and the Family*, **50**, 79–92.

Appels, A., Jenkins, C. D. and Rosenman, R. H. (1982). Coronary-prone behavior in the Netherlands: A cross-cultural validation study, *Journal of Behavioral Medicine*, **5**, 83–90.

Baker, L. J., Dearborn, M., Hastings, J. E. and Hamberger, K. (1984). Type A behavior in women: A review, *Health Psychology*, **3**, 477–97.

Barefoot, J. C., Dahlstrom, W. G. and Williams, R. B. (1983). Hostility, CHD incidence and total mortality: A 25-year follow-up study of 255 physicians, *Psychosomatic Medicine*, **45**, 59–63.

Bass, C. (1984). Type A behavior: Recent developments, *Journal of Psychosomatic Research*, **28**, 371–378.

Beck, A. T. (1967). *Depression: Clinical, Experimental, and Theoretical Aspects*, Hoeber, New York.

Bergman, L. R. and Magnusson, D. (1986). Type A behavior: A longitudinal study from childhood to adulthood, *Psychosomatic Medicine*, **48**, 134–42.

Bhatia, K. and Golin, J. (1978). Role of locus of control in frustration-produced aggression', *Journal of Personality*, **46**, 364–65.

Blumenthal, J. A., Lane, J. D. and Williams, R. B. (1985). The inhibited power motive, Type A behavior, and patterns of cardiovascular response during the Structured Interview and Thematic Apperception Test, *Journal of Human Stress,* **11**, 82–89.

Booth-Kewley, S. and Friedman, H. S. (1987). Psychological predictions of heart disease: A quantitative review, *Psychological Bulletin,* **101**, 343–62.

Bortner, R. W. (1969). A short rating scale as a potential measure of pattern A behavior, *Journal of Chronic Diseases,* **22**, 87–91.

Brozek, J., Keys, A. and Blackburn, H. (1966). Personality differences between potential coronary and noncoronary subjects, *Annals of the New York Academy of Sciences,* **134**, 1057–64.

Brunson, B. I. and Matthews, K. A. (1981). The Type A coronary prone behavior pattern and reactions to uncontrollable events: An analysis of learned helplessness, *Journal of Personality and Social Psychology,* **40**, 906–18.

Burger, J. M. and Cooper, H. M. (1979). The desirability of control, *Motivation and Emotion,* **3**, 381–93.

Buss, A. H. and Durkee, A. (1957). An inventory for assessing different kinds of hostility, *Journal of Consulting Psychology,* **21**, 343–9.

Chesney, M. A., Black, G. W., Chadwick, J. H. and Rosenman, R. H. (1981). Psychological correlates of the Type A behavior patterns, *Journal of Behavioral Medicine,* **4**, 217–29.

Contrada, R. J., Wright, R. A. and Glass, D. C. (1985). Psychophysiological correlates of Type A behavior: Comments on Houston (1983) and Holmes (1983), *Journal of Research in Personality,* **19**, 12–30.

Costa, P. T. and McCrae, R. R. (1980). Influence of extraversion and neuroticism on subjective well being, *Journal of Personality and Social Psychology,* **38**, 668–78.

Costa, P. T. and McCrae, R. R. (1987). Neuroticism, somatic complaints, disease: Is the bark worse than the bite?, *Journal of Personality,* **55**, 301–16.

Costa, P. T. Jr., Fleg, J. L., McCrae, R. R. and Lakatta, E. G. (1982). Neuroticism, coronary artery disease and chest pain complaints: Cross-sectional and longitudinal studies, *Experimental Aging Research,* **8**, 37–44.

Costa, P. T., Zonderman, A. B., McCrae, R. R. and Williams, R. B. (1986a). Cynicism and paranoid alienation in the Cook and Medley HO Scale, *Psychomatic Medicine,* **48**, 283–5.

Costa, P. T., Jr., McCrae, R. R., Zonderman, A. B., Barbano, H. E., Lebowitz, B. and Larson, D. M. (1986b). Cross-sectional studies of personality in a national sample: 2. Stability in neuroticism, extraversion, and openness, *Psychology and Aging,* **1**, 144–9.

DeGood, D. E. (1975). Cognitive control factors in vascular stress responses, *Psychophysiology,* **12**, 299–401.

Dembroski, T. M. and Czajkowski, S. M. (1989). Historical and current developments in coronary-prone behavior. In A. W. Siegman and T. H. Dembroski (eds), *In Search of Coronary-Prone Behavior,* Erlbaum, Hillsdale, NJ, Chapter 2, pp. 21–39.

Dembroski, T. M., MacDougall, J. M., Williams, R. B., Haney, T. L. and Blumenthal, J. A. (1985). Components of Type A, hostility and anger-in: Results of angiographic findings, *Psychosomatic Medicine,* **4**, 219–33.

Dodd, N., Conti, M. B. and Sime, W. E. (1983). The convergence of questionnaire Type A measures and the Structured Interview, paper presented at the Annual Meeting of the Society of Behavioral Medicine, Baltimore, Maryland.

Doherty, W. J. (1983). Locus of control and marital interaction. In H. M. Lefcourt (ed.) *Research with the Locus of Control Construct*, Academic Press of New York, pp. 155–83.

Doherty, W. J. and Ryder, R. G. (1979). Locus of control, interpersonal trust, and assertive behavior among newlyweds, *Journal of Personality and Social Psychology*, **37**, 2212–20.

Dweck, C. S. (1975). The role of expectations and attributions in the alleviation of learned helplessness, *Journal of Personality and Social Psychology*, **31**, 674–85.

Eagly, A. H. and Steffen, V. J. (1986). Gender and aggressive behavior: A meta-analytic review of the social psychological literature, *Psychological Bulletin*, **100**, 309–30.

Eysenck, H. J. (1983). Stress, disease, and personality: The 'inoculation effect'. In C. L. Cooper (ed.) *Stress Research*, Wiley, Chichester, pp. 121–46.

Eysenck, H. J. and Eysenck, S. B. G. (1968). *Eysenck Personality Inventory*, Educational and Industrial Testing Service, San Diego, Calif.

Findley, M. J. and Cooper, H. M. (1983). Locus of control and academic achievement: A literature review, *Journal of Personality and Social Psychology*, **44**, 419–27.

Fitch, G. (1970). Effects of self-esteem, perceived performance, and choice on causal attribution, *Journal of Personality and Social Psychology*, **16**, 311–15.

Fodor, E. M. (1984). The power motive and reactivity to power stresses, *Journal of Personality and Social Psychology*, **47**, 853–9.

Fontana, A. F., Rosenberg, R. L., Kerns, R. D. and Marcus, J. L. (1984). Motivational links to the Type A behavior pattern, unpublished manuscript.

Fontana, A. F., Rosenberg, R. L., Marcus, J. L. and Kerns, R. D. (1987). Type A behavior pattern, inhibited power motivation, and activity inhibition, *Journal of Personality and Social Psychology*, **52**, 177–83.

Friedman, H. S. and Booth-Kewley, S. (1987a). The 'Disease-prone personality': A meta-analytic view of the construct, *American Psychologist*, **42**, 539–55.

Friedman, H. S. and Booth-Kewley, S. (1987b) Personality, Type A behavior and coronary heart disease: The role of emotional expression, *Journal of Personality and Social Psychology*, **53**, 783–92.

Friedman, H. S. and Booth-Kewley, S. (1988). Validity of the Type A construct: A reprise, *Psychological Bulletin*, **104**, 381–4.

Friedman, H. S., Hall, J. A. and Harris, M. J. (1985). Type A behavior, nonverbal expressive style, and health, *Journal of Personality and Social Psychology*, **48**, 1299–315.

Friedman, M. (1969). *Pathogenesis of Coronary Artery Disease*, McGraw-Hill, New York, NY.

Friedman, M. and Rosenman, R. H. (1974). *Type A Behavior and Your Heart*, Fawcett, Greenwich, CT.

Ganster, D. C. and Schaubroeck, J. (1990). Role stress and worker health: An extension of the plasticity hypothesis of self esteem, unpublished manuscript.

Ganster, D. C., Schaubroeck, J., Sime, W. E. and Mayes, B. T. (1991). The nomological validity of the Type A personality among employed adults, *Journal of Applied Psychology [Monograph]*, **76**, 143–68.

Glass, D. C. (1977). *Behavior Patterns, Stress, and Coronary Disease*, Erlbaum, Hillsdale, NJ.

Hall, E. R., Joesting, J. and Woods, M. J. (1977). Relationships among measures of LOC for black and white students, *Psychological Reports*, **40**, 59–62.

Harbin, T. J. (1989). The relationship between the Type A behavior pattern and physiological responsivity: A review, *Psychophysiology*, **26**, 110–19.

Haynes, S. G., Feinleib, M. and Kannel, W. B. (1980). The relationship of psychosocial factors to coronary heart disease in the Framingham study: III. Eight-year incidence of coronary heart disease, *American Journal of Epidemiology*, **III**, 37–58.

Haynes, S. G., Levine, S., Scotch, N., Feinleib, M. and Kannel, W. B. (1978). The relationship of psychosocial factors to coronary heart disease in the Framingham study: I. Methods and risk factors, *American Journal of Epidemiology*, **107**, 362–83.

Herman, S., Blumenthal, J. A., Black, G. M. and Chesney, M. A. (1981). Self-ratings of Type A (coronary-prone) adults. Do Type A's know they are Type A's?', *Psychosomatic medicine*, **43**, 405–14.

Hotard, S. R., McFatter, R. M., McWhirter, R. M. and Stegall, M. E. (1989). Interactive effects of extraversion, neuroticism, and social relationships on subjective well being, *Journal of Personality and Social Psychology*, **57**, 321–31.

Houston, B. K. (1972). Control over stress, locus of control, and response to stress, *Journal of Personality and Social Psychology*, **21**, 249–55.

Houston, B. K. (1983). Psychophysiological responsivity and the Type A behavior pattern, *Journal of Research in Personality*, **17**, 22–39.

Houston, B. K. (1986). Psychological variables and cardiovascular and neuroendocrine reactivity, in K. A. Matthews and Associates (eds), *Handbook of Stress, Reactivity, and Cardiovascular Disease*, Wiley, New York, pp. 207–30.

Howard, J. J., Cunningham, D. A. and Rechnitzer, P. A. (1986). Personality (hardiness) as a moderator of job stress and coronary risk in Type A individuals: A longitudinal study, *Journal of Behavioral Medicine*, **9**, 229–44.

Hubbs-Tait, L. and Blodgett, C. J. (1989). The mediating effects of self-esteem on coronary-prone behavior on problem solving and affect under law and high stress, *Journal of Human Stress*, **15**, 101–10.

Janisse, M. P. and Dyck, D. G. (1988). The Type A behavior pattern and coronary heart disease: Physiological and psychological dimensions. In M. P. Janisse (ed.) *Individual Differences, Stress, and Health Psychology*, Springer-Verlag, New York, pp. 57–71.

Jorgensen, R. J. and Houston, B. K. (1986). Family history of hypertension, personality patterns, and cardiovascular reactivity to stress, *Psychosomatic Medicine*, **48**, 102–16.

Kasl, S. V. (1978). Epidemiological contributions to the study of work stress. In C. Cooper and R. Payne (eds) *Stress at Work*, Wiley, Chichester.

Keenan, A. and McBairn, G. D. (1979). Effects of Type A behavior, intolerance of ambiguity, and locus of control on the relationship between role stress and work-related outcomes, *Journal of Occupational Psychology*, **52**, 277–85.

Keltikangas-Jarvinen, L. (1988). Similarity of Type A behavior in adolescents and their parents, *Journal of Social Psychology*, **128**, 97–104.

Kernis, M. H., Granneman, B. D. and Barclay, L. C. (1989). Stability and level of self-esteem as predictors of anger arousal and hostility, *Journal of Personality and Social Psychology*, **56**, 1013–22.

Kittel, F. Kornitzer, M., DeBacker, B., Dramaix, M., Sobolski, J., Degre, S. and Denolin, H. (1983). Type A in relation to job stress, social and bioclinical variables: The Belgian physical fitness study, *Journal of Human Stress*, **9**, 37–45.

Kobasa, S. C., Maddi, S. R. and Zola, M. A. (1983). Type A and hardiness, *Journal of Behavioral Medicine*, **6**, 41–51.

Kohn, M. L. (1969). *Class and Conformity: A Study in Values*, Dorsey Press, Homewood, Ill.

Kohn, M. L. and Schooler, C. (1969). Class, occupation, and orientation, *American Sociological Review*, **34**, 659–78.

Leikin, L. J. (1990). Type A behavior and health locus of control: Another view on Perloff et al. (1988), *British Journal of Medical Psychology,* **63**, 81–4.

Levenson, H. (1973). Multidimensional locus of control in psychiatric patients, *Journal of Consulting and Clinical Psychology,* **41**, 397–404.

Lundberg, U. (1980). Type A behavior and its relation to personality variables in Swedish male and female university students, *Scandinavian Journal of Psychology,* **21**, 133–8.

McClelland, D. C. (1975). *Power: The Inner Experiences,* Irvington, New York, NY.

McClelland, D. C. (1979). Inhibited power motivation and high blood pressure in men, *Journal of Abnormal Psychology,* **88**, 182–90.

McClelland, D. C. and Burnham, D. (1976). Power is the great motivator, *Harvard Business Review,* March/April, 100–11.

McClelland, D. C. and Jemmott, J. B. (1980). Power motivation, stress and physical illness, *Journal of Human Stress,* **6**, 6–15.

McClelland, D. C., Floor, E., Davidson, R. J. and Saron, C. (1985a). Stressed power motivation, sympathetic activation, immune function, and illness, *Advances,* **2**, 42–52.

McClelland, D. C., Ross, G. and Patel, V. (1985b). 'The Effect of an Academic Examination on Salivary Norepinephrine and Immunoglobulin Levels', *Journal of Human Stress,* **11**, 52–59.

MacDougall, J. M., Dembroski, T. M. and Musante, L. (1979). The structured interview and questionnaire methods of assessing coronary-prone behavior in male and female college students, *Journal of Behavioral Medicine,* **2**, 71–83.

Manuck, S. B., Craft, S. and Gold, K. J. (1978). Coronary-prone behavior pattern and cardiovascular response, *Psychophysiology,* **15**, 403–411.

Mason, A. and Blankenship, V. (1987). Power and affiliation motivation, stress, and abuse in intimate relationships, *Journal of Personality and Social Psychology,* **52**, 203–10.

Matthews, K. A. (1982) Psychological perspectives on the Type A behavior pattern, *Psychological Bulletin,* **91**, 293–323.

Matthews, K. A. (1985). Assessment of Type A behavior, anger, and hostility in epidemiological studies of cardiovascular disease. In K. A. Matthews and Associates (eds) *Measuring Psychological Variables in Epidemiologic Studies of Cardiovascular Disease,* Wiley, New York, pp. 461–73.

Matthews, K. A. and Haynes, S. G. (1986). Type A behavior patterns and coronary disease risk: Update and evaluation, *American Journal of Epidemiology,* **123**, 923–960.

Matthews, K. A. and Saal, F. E. (1978). The relationship of the coronary prone behavior pattern to achievement, power, and affiliation motives, *Psychosomatic Medicine,* **40**, 631–636.

Matthews, K. A., Jamison, J. W. and Cottington, E. M. (1985). Assessment of Type A, anger, and hostility: A review of scales through 1982. In A. M. Ostfeld and E. D. Eaker (eds) *Measuring Psychosocial Variables in Epidemiologic Studies of Cardiovascular Disease,* NIH Publication No. 85–2270, National Institute of Health, Bethesda, Maryland.

Matthews, K. A., Krantz, D. S., Dembroski, T. M. and MacDougall, J. M. (1982). Unique and common variance in structured interview and Jenkins Activity Survey measures of the Type A behavior pattern, *Journal of Personality and Social Psychology,* **42**, 303–13.

Mayes, B. T., Sime, W. E. and Ganster, D. C. (1984). Convergent validity of Type A behavior pattern scales and their ability to predict physiological responsiveness in a sample of female public employees, *Journal of Behavioral Medicine,* **7**, 83–108.

Moss, G. E., Dielman, T. E., Campanelli, P. C., Leech, S. L., Harlan, W. R., Van Harrison, R. and Horvath, W. J. (1986). Demographic correlates of SI assessments of type A behavior, *Psychosomatic Medicine*, **48**, 564–74.

Mossholder, K., Bedeian, A. and Armenakis, A. (1981). Role perceptions, satisfaction, and performance: Moderating effects of self-esteem and organizational level, *Organizational Behavior and Human Performance*, **28**, 224–34.

Murray, D. C. (1971). Talk, silence and anxiety, *Psychological Bulletin*, **75**, 244–60.

Musante, L., MacDougall, J. M., Dembroski, T. M. and Costa, P. T., Jr. (1989). Potential for hostility and dimensions of anger, *Health Psychology*, **8**, 343–54.

Musante, L., MacDougall, J. M., Dembroski, T. M. and Van Horn, A. E. (1983). Component analysis of the Type A coronary-prone behavior pattern in male and female college students, *Journal of Personality and Social Psychology*, **45**, 1104–17.

Novaco, R. W. (1975). *Anger Control: The Development and Evaluation of an Experimental Treatment*, Lexington/D.C. Health, Lexington, Mass.

Nowack, K. M. (1986). Type A hardiness and psychological distress, *Journal of Behavioral Medicine*, **9**, 537–48.

Nowack, K. M. and Sassenroth, T. (1980). Coronary-prone behavior, locus of control, and anxiety, *Psychological Reports*, **47**, 359–64.

Nowicki, S. and Segal, W. (1974). Perceived parental characteristics, LOC orientation, and behavioral correlates of LOC, *Development Psychology*, **10**, 33–7.

Pedersen, N. L., Plomin, R., McClearn, G. E. and Friberg, L. (1988). Neuroticism, extraversion, and related traits in adult twins reared apart and reared together, *Journal of Personality and Social Psychology*, **55**, 950–7.

Perloff, L., Yarnold, P. R. and Feltzer, B. (1988). Control theory and Type A behavior, *British Journal of Medical Psychology*, **61**, 365–8.

Pittner, M. S., Houston, B. K. and Spiridigliozzi, G. (1983). Control over stress, Type A behavior patterns, and response to stress, *Journal of Personality and Social Psychology*, **44**, 627–37.

Powell, A. and Vega, M. (1972). Correlates of adult LOC, *Psychological Reports*, **30**, 455–460.

Rahe, R. H., Hervig, L. and Rosenman, R. H. (1978). Heritability of Type A behavior, *Psychosomatic Medicine*, **40**, 478–81.

Rhodewalt, F. and Agustsdottir, S. (1984). On the relationship of hardiness to the Type A behavior pattern: Perception of live events versus coping with life events, *Journal of Research in Personality*, **18**, 212–23.

Rhodewalt, F. and Zone, J. B. (1989). Appraisal of life change, depression, and illness in hardy and nonhardy women, *Journal of Personality and Social Psychology*, **56**, 81–8.

Richert, A. J. (1981). Sex differences in relation of LOC and reported anxiety, *Psychological Reports*, **49**, 971–3.

Rosenberg, M. (1965). *Society and Adolescent Self-Image*, Princeton University Press, Princeton, NJ.

Rosenberg, M. (1979). *Conceiving the Self*, Basic Books, New York.

Rosenman, R. H. and Chesney, M. A. (1980). The relationship of Type A behavior pattern to coronary heart disease, *Activitas Nervosa Superior*, **22**, 1–45.

Rotter, J. B. (1966). Generalized expectancies for internal versus external control of reinforcement, *Psychological Monographs*, **80**, 1–609.

Ryckman, R. M. and Malikiosi, M. (1974). Differences in LOC orientation for members of selected occupations, *Psychological Reports*, **34**, 1222–6.

Ryckman, R. M. and Malikiosi, M. (1975). Relationships between LOC and chronological age, *Psychological Reports*, **36**, 655–8.

Scherwitz, L., Berton, K. and Leventhal, H. (1978). Type A behavior, self-involvement and cardiovascular response, *Psychosomatic Medicine*, **40**, 593–609.

Schmeid, L. A. and Lawler, K. A. (1986). Hardiness, Type A behavior, and the stress–illness relation in working women, *Journal of Personality and Social Psychology*, **51**, 1218–23.

Shekelle, R. B., Schoenberger, J. A. and Stamler, J. (1976). Correlates of the VAS Type A behavior pattern score, *Journal of Chronic Diseases*, **29**, 381–94.

Shekelle, R. B., Gale, M., Ostfeld, A. M. and Paul, O. (1983). Hostility, risk of coronary heart disease and mortality, *Psychosomatic Medicine*, **45**, 109–14.

Siegman, A. W. (1989). The Role of hostility, neuroticism, and speech style in coronary-artery disease. In A. W. Siegman and T. M. Dembroski (eds) *In Search of Coronary Prone Behavior*, Erlbaum, Hillsdale, NJ, pp. 65–90.

Siegman, A. W., Dembroski, T. M. and Ringel, N. (1987a). Components of hostility and severity of coronary artery disease, *Psychosomatic Medicine*, **49**, 127–35.

Siegman, A. W., Feldstein, S., Tommaso, C. T., Ringel, N. and Lating, J. (1987b). Expressive vocal behavior and the severity of coronary artery disease, *Psychosomatic Medicine*, **49**, 545–61.

Smith, T. W. and Frohm, K. D. (1985). What's so unhealthy about hostility? Construct validity and psychological correlates of the Cook and Medley HO Scale, *Healthy Psychology*, **4**, 503–20.

Smith, T. W., Houston, B. K. and Zurawski, R. M. (1983). The Framingham Type A Scale and anxiety, irrational beliefs, and self-control, *Journal of Human Stress*, **9**, 32–7.

Spence, J., Helmreich, R. and Stapp, J. (1975). Ratings of self and peers on sex role attributes and their relation to self-esteem and conceptions of masculinity and femininity, *Journal of Personality and Social Psychology*, **32**, 29–39.

Spielberger, C. O., Gorsuch, R. L. and Lushene, R. E. (1970). *Manual for the State–Trait Anxiety Inventory*, Consulting Psychologists Press, Palo Alto, Calif.

Spielberger, C. D., Jacobs, G. A., Russell, S. and Crane, R. S. (1983). Assessment of anger: The stale-trait anger scale. In J. N. Butcher and C. D. Spielberger (eds), *Advances in Personality Assessment*, Erlbaum, Hillsdale, NJ, Volume 2, pp. 52–76.

Sprafka, J. M., Folsom, A. R., Burke, G. L., Hahn, L. P. and Price, P. (1990). Type A behavior and its association with cardiovascular disease prevalence in Blacks and Whites: The Minnesota Heart Survey, *Journal of Behavioral Medicine*, **13**, 1–13.

Stewart, A. J. and Chester, N. L. (1982). Sex differences in human social motives. In A. J. Stewart (ed.) *Motivation and Society*, Jossey-Bass, San Francisco, pp. 172–218.

Strickland, B. L. R. (1978). Internal–external expectancies and health-related behaviors, *Journal of Consulting and Clinical Psychology*, **46**, 119–211.

Strube, M. J. (1985). Attributional style and the Type A coronary-prone behavior pattern, *Journal of Personality and Social Psychology*, **49**, 500–9.

Suls, J. and Sanders, G. S. (1988). Type A behavior as a general risk factor for physical disorder, *Journal of Behavioral Medicine*, **11**, 201–26.

Ursin, H., Mykletun, R., Tonder, O., Vaernes, R., Relling, G., Isaksen, R. and Murison, R. (1984). Psychological stress factors and concentrations of immunoglobulins and complement components in humans, *Scandinavian Journal of Psychology*, **25**, 340–47.

Waldron, I., Hickey, C., McPherson, A., Butensky, L., Gross, K., Overall, A., Schmader, A. and Wohlmuth, D. (1980). Type A behavior pattern: Relationship to variation in blood pressure, parental characteristics, and academic and social activities of students, *Journal of Human Stress*, **6**, 16–27.

Watson, D. and Pennebaker, J. W. (1989). Health complaints, stress, and distress: Exploring the central role of negative affectivity, *Psychological Review*, **96**, 234–54.

Watson, D. and Tellegen, A. (1985). Toward a concensual structure of mood, *Psychological Bulletin*, **98**, 219–35.

Weidman, J. C., Phelan, W. T. and Sullivan, M. A. (1972). The influence of educational attainment on self-evaluations of competence, *Sociology of Education*, **45**, 303–12.

Williams, R. B. (1989). Biological mechanisms mediating the relationship between behavior and coronary heart disease. In A. W. Siegman and T. M. Dembroski (eds) *In Search of Coronary-Prone Behavior*, Erlbaum, Hillsdale, NJ, pp. 195–207.

Woodall, K. L. and Matthews, K. A. (1989). Familial environment associated with Type A behaviors and psychophysiological responses to stress in children, *Health Psychology*, **8**, 403–26.

Yancey, J. M., Rigsby, L. and McCarthy, J. D. (1972). Social position and self-evaluation: The relative importance of race, *American Journal of Sociology*, **78**, 338–59.

Yarnold, P. R. and Grimm, L. G. (1986). Interpersonal dominance and coronary prone behavior, *Journal of Research in Personality*, **20**, 420–33.

Zeidner, M. (1990). Some demographic and health correlates of trait anger in Israeli adults, *Journal of Research in Personality*, **24**, 1–15.

Zika, S. and Chamberlain, K. (1987). Relations of hassles and personality to subjective well-being, *Journal of Personality and Social Psychology*, **53** 155–62.

Zuckerman, M. and Gerbasi, K. C. (1977). Dimensions of the I–E scale and their relationship to other personality variables, *Educational and Psychological Measurement*, **37**, 159–75.

Chapter 4

The Structural Sources of Salutogenic Strengths

Aaron Antonovsky, Ben-Gurion University of the Negev, Israel

SPECIFYING THE QUESTION

This chapter may seem "odd person out" in a volume concerned with individual differences. It is an attempt to open discussion of a question which has largely been ignored. Starting from the concept of individual differences, it asks: Where do some of those individual differences of concern in this volume come from? The point of departure is the personality characteristic of an individual, a characteristic which is known or believed to be linked to stressors, coping, and health. Taking this link for granted, we shall ask: What are its proximal and distal situational, structural, cultural, and historical origins?

Chapter 3 of my second book on the salutogenic model (Antonovsky, 1987) is devoted to a comparison between my construct of the sense of coherence and the work of others whom I saw as kindred spirits. I opened the chapter by saying that I no longer felt alone, as I had a decade earlier when my first book appeared (Antonovsky, 1979). But when I came to write Chapter 5, the sense of isolation returned. That chapter is devoted to the origins and development of the sense of coherence. Then, as now, silence prevailed on the subject of origins.

We forget that every social and psychological "independent" variable can also be dealt with as a dependent variable, and that the more powerful a concept, the more important it is to understand its origins. The individual researcher, devoted to the difficult study of the relations between variables A and B under conditions C_1, C_2, C_n, might be forgiven for not also studying the antecedents of A. As a collective enterprise, however, we cannot so easily be excused, any more than can those who study smoking and disease but disregard the tobacco lobby and agricultural subsidies, or study relaxation and health but ignore the pressures which lead a woman to work at two jobs, one

Personality and Stress: Individual Differences in the Stress Process. Edited by C.L. Cooper and R. Payne
© 1991 John Wiley & Sons Ltd

of which is unpaid. Just as life-styles originate somewhere, so do personality characteristics.

A decade ago, Sarason (1981, p. 827) scathingly wrote:

> . . . I have come to believe that from its inception a hundred years ago, American psychology has been quintessentially a psychology of the individual organism, a characteristic that however it may have been and is productive has severely and adversely affected psychology's contribution to human welfare. . . . The substance of psychology cannot be independent of the social order. It is not that it *should not* be independent but that it *cannot* be.

I think it fair to say that this charge can likewise be levelled at British and Continental psychology as well. Albee (1980), too, savages American psychiatry and psychology for continuing to use the medical model of the individual patient's sickness and disregarding the study of how the social structure makes people incompetent to cope with the stressors that are socially induced.

Whatever the reasons for the silence about social sources of strengths, it is the intention and hope of this chapter to place the issue on the agenda. Given the silence (though I do not claim to have read every word written about the concepts to be covered), much of what will be said is necessarily based on inference, speculation, and suggestion.

What I propose to do, then is to examine four stress and coping-linked personality constructs. I shall ask: How are the individual differences represented by each construct related to the social order? That is, I shall consider the explicit and implicit suggestions about social sources in the work about each construct, point to gaps, and add ideas of my own. The sections will thus not be parallel to each other. In the final section of the chapter, a brief attempt will be made to formulate a theoretically based integration of the disparate yet related ideas. I have selected the four on the basis, first, that they are all salutogenic, and then used four additional criteria, though here and there I must admit to having been a bit procrustean.

(1) *Salutogenesis:* In 1973, at a conference organized by Barbara and Bruce Dohrenwend, I made the first public statement of what I later came to call the salutogenic orientation (Antonovsky, 1974). When I started writing *Health, Stress and Coping* (Antonovsky, 1979), in which the **sense of coherence** construct was first formulated, Bandura's seminal paper on **self-efficacy** (1977) had not yet appeared. Kobasa's first paper on **hardiness** (1979) was unknown to me. True, Rotter's work on **locus of control** had appeared earlier (Rotter, 1966), but it had not yet made a strong impact on the study of the stress and coping process. It was not really until the mid-1980s that it became clear that a radically different mode of thinking about coping with life stressors was being crystalized. Instead of asking about the pathogens and failures in coping which led to disease, what was common to these four approaches was their

focus on explanations of successful resolution of stressors and maintenance of or return to health. They constitute a fitting response to Bronfenbrenner's (1986) critique of family research, whose

> predominant focus is on the ecologies of family disorganization and developmental disarray. Yet, for every study that documents the power of disruptive environments, there is a control group that testifies to the existence and unrealized potentials of ecologies that sustain and strengthen constructive processes in society, the family, and the self.
>
> (p. 738)

This focus on successful coping is the first and major criterion for selection of the constructs (in **bold** type), or salutogenic strengths, as the chapter title has it, to be discussed in this chapter.

(2) *Transactional:* The second criterion requires that the constructs discussed have their full potential meaning when they are understood *transactionally*. They do not refer to specific, overt coping styles. Rather, the behaviors to which these orientations lead are intimately linked with the nature of the stressor situation being confronted: its simplicity or complexity, its controllability, its time-limited or enduring character, the kinds of problems posed and their sources, and so on.

(3) *Generalized orientation:* The "nature" of the situation, however, always requires interpretation. This view has led me to specify a third criterion. The constructs discussed, I believe, refer to a *generalized* set of beliefs about oneself and about one's world, rather than to beliefs about specific situations or even domains. It is this set which shapes one's appraisal of a given stressor situation and one's resource-mobilization behavior in that situation.

(4) *Directness of contribution:* All four constructs share, in whole or in part, the thesis that being "high" on these personality orientations facilitates successful coping and thus contributes to health. Given the development of study of the stress process, which for decades focused on stressful life events and noxious stimuli, it was only natural that when the concept of coping was first introduced, it was understood largely as a buffer. In the face of a high stressor load, being high on X was seen as facilitative in the avoidance of disease. Yet I believe that a good case could be made for the argument that these personality orientations are directly, and not only conditionally, linked to the maintenance and improvement of health and health-inducing behavior.

(5) *Collective orientations:* Finally, and with an even greater stress on the potential exploitation of these constructs than was implied in presenting the fourth criterion, rather than as they have been used, I believe that they all lend themselves to application to collectives. That is, I think it makes sense, with all due awareness of the theoretical and methodological complications, to speak of high self-efficacy, high hardiness, and so on of a family or of any other social unit.

As we shall see below, the use of the word "procrustean" was not inadertent. Rotter's internal locus of control might be (mis)understood as a specific coping style, similar to Pearlin and Schooler's (1978) concept of mastery, rather than as transactional in character. Bandura might well object to the inclusion of his work using the generalizability criterion. Kobasa might be unhappy about my thought that hardiness could be an orientation of a collective. I have taken the liberty of extending the interpretation of these constructs in a spirit that I hope will be seen as an expression of esteem, trusting that I have not thereby introduced any distortions.

In sum, I have selected four constructs—self-efficacy (SE), locus of control (LOC), hardiness (HARD), and my own sense of coherence (SOC)—which, explicitly or at least potentially in my view, are generalized personality orientations which have been studied in relation to successful coping and salutogenic outcomes, are to be understood in transactional contexts, can make direct as well as buffering contributions to health, and can be applied to collectives as well as to individuals. With respect to each and, subsequently, with respect to all, I shall ask: What are the origins and patterns of development of these salutogenic strengths?

It is of interest to note that each of the authors concerned had a different point of departure. Bandura's dominant commitment was and is to the study of human task performance; health behaviors and health outcomes are simply one domain to which his theoretical model is applied and in which it can be tested. Rotter's point of departure was the attempt to formulate an empirically measurable construct of attribution of causality of events, embedded in a broader theory of behavior. Kobasa, with a strong background in theology and philosophy, started by asking "How does one come to live fully humanly?". My own earlier work focused on the link between social class and morbidity and mortality. But whatever the point of departure, we have all come to focus our research on a given core personality orientation.

It will not be my concern here to explicitly compare these orientations in any detail, but to study their origins and, in the end, search for commonality in these. What I mean by origins, however, must be sharpened and focused. As a sociologist, my primary concern is with the *structural* sources of personality dispositions, orientations, *Weltanschauungen*, ideologies, or whatever term one prefers to use that characterizes the constructs to be discussed. The psychologist might well prefer to concentrate on the nature of the particular, individual personal-historical experiences which shape such dispositions. I will not ignore this question. I will, though, seek to link these experiences with the sociocultural and historical contexts in which they are embedded.

The model which has here shaped my approach is found in the work of Melvin Kohn. As he put the general problem in a recent paper (1989), the point is not to psychologize social structure or to sociologize individual functioning, but "to draw *systematic linkages* between two valid levels of analysis"

(p. 31). Kohn is critical of psychologists, who seldom go beyond the immediately impinging environment in explaining behavior, and even more so of sociologists, who "act as if they thought that social institutions function without benefit of human participants" (p. 27). Below, I shall consider the substance of Kohn's model.

Though Kohn does use concepts like self-esteem and distress, his work is not concerned with the study of the stress process. But Pearlin, whose contributions to the field are well known, has recently issued a call in a very similar vein (1989). He systematically discusses how locations in a society's stratification systems, embeddedness in institutionalized roles, and cultural values, norms, aspirations, and interpretations are crucial in shaping the stressors to which one is exposed, how these are dealt with, and what outcomes result. Unfortunately, the briefest and weakest section of the paper is that which deals with coping behaviors, of greatest present interest.

Given this lengthy but, I believe, necessary introduction, we can now turn to the four constructs.

FOUR SALUTOGENIC STRENGTHS

Bandura's Self-Efficacy (SE)

> Perceived self-efficacy is defined as people's judgments of their capabilities to organize and execute courses of action required to attain designated types of performances.
>
> (Bandura, 1986, p. 391)

And elsewhere:

> Perceived self-efficacy is concerned with people's beliefs in their capabilities to mobilize the motivation, cognitive resources and courses of action needed to exercise control over task demands.
>
> (Bandura, 1988, p. 1)

Bandura's work is not often cited in the stress and coping literature. His primary commitment, in formulating and developing the SE construct, is to advance theoretical understanding of the principles governing human behavior related to task performance. He would, however, find it uninteresting to study, for example, the task of crossing a familiar street by most adults, a behavior which has become automatic and routinized. Crossing a street in downtown Cairo, however, or by children of different ages, is a different matter. In this sense, he is no less concerned with individual differences in coping with stressor situations than are those of us who more explicitly work in the stress field. In outcome terms, his research has been conducted with persons with phobias and other psychological problems, and with health behaviors such as smoking cessation. He is clearly committed to the view that enhancing a person's self-perceived capacities for successful task performances prevents stress and contributes to her or his health and well-being.

Bandura sees SE beliefs as symbolic representations which, in a generative process, integrate knowledge and skills and are translated into action. But if we are to consider the sources of these symbolic representations, we must be clear about their meaning. Over and over again in his writing one finds an insistence that the reference is to beliefs about one's capacity to perform well in engaging in a specific task. His view is perhaps best summed up in the following statement:

> Causal processes are best clarified by a microanalytic approach in which self-referent thought is measured in terms of particularized self-percepts of efficacy that may vary across activities and circumstances, rather than in terms of a global disposition assayed by an omnibus test.
>
> (Bandura, 1986, p. 396)

In a personal conversation in 1989, this view was reiterated, as he rejected the use of a published general self-efficacy scale (Sherer et al., 1982). As a guide to a varied and rich research program, concerned with very careful analysis of specific conditions which might affect the power of SE to predict behavior, there is justification for this approach. On the empirical level, one is also much more likely to find greater predictive power to specific behaviors of specific than of general SE measures.

Yet there is little doubt that Bandura is ambivalent about the matter of generalization. Immediately following the above quotation, he writes: "Measures of self-percepts must be tailored to the domain of psychological functioning being explored." We have, then, moved from task to domain. A few lines later: "Domain-linked assessments reveal the patterning and degree of generality of people's perceptions of their efficacy." And, if the reader will bear with one more quotation, on p. 399: "Once established, enhanced self-efficacy tends to generalize to other situations . . As a result, behavioral functioning may improve across a wide range of activities."

All of us have some hangups, some self-doubts, some self-perceived inefficacies. Rare is the person who sees her or himself as totally inefficacious. But by and large, I would suggest that most adults have arrived at some relatively stable generalized assessment of their level of SE. As I have made clear throughout my work, stressors are omnipresent in life, and most of these are "familiar", in that they arise from our familiar life situation. Of course there are the non-normative stressors—a 50 year old confronting unemployment for the first time in life because the plant closed, or losing a child in a traffic accident. But different non-normative stressors have happened before. One has already come to have an image of how efficacious one is in the face of such stressors.

Further, on theoretical grounds, it is difficult to imagine someone going through childhood and adolescence, confronting an extraordinarily wide variety of stressor situations, without coming to have a generalized SE. A close reading of Bandura's (1989) paper on the developmental processes of learning competencies in terms of social cognition theory, in which the SE construct is the central thread, suggests that he comes very close to agreement. Thus: "The stronger the instilled sense of coping self-efficacy, the bolder the behavior" (p. 23). "By reflecting on their varied experiences and on what they know, they can derive generic knowledge about themselves and the world around them" (p. 41). And "By the middle years, people settle into established routines that stabilize their self-appraised self-efficacy in the major areas of functioning. However, the stability is a shaky one because life does not remain static" (p. 47).

But whether one considers SE with respect to a specific task (running a mile in less than four minutes, a task which many of Bandura's and my generation will remember), or to a domain (mathematical competencies), or to a generalized capacity to cope well with life stressors, our question is: What are the sources of these symbolic representations, of the perception that one can indeed perform efficaciously? Bandura's meticulous research program has led him to formulate a set of principles which give a clear answer. Human beings, he posits, have five unique capacities: symbolizing, vicarious learning, forethought, self-regulation, and self-reflection. Using these capacities, one can come to achieve a high level of SE in four ways. The first and foremost way is that of performance attainments or enactive mastery, actually doing something competently. The three other major sources of SE information are through vicarious experiences (modeling), verbal persuasion and social influences, and physiological states (Bandura, 1986, pp. 399–401). In oversimplified terms, the more one actually experiences mastering a task, the more one observes others doing so, the more one is exposed to encouragement that one can do so, and the more one experiences internal states (not feeling fear, tension and visceral arousal) which facilitate performance, the stronger will one's SE be. Let us consider these four shapers of SE in terms of the sociocultural context.

Performance attainments

The most pertinent sociological concept in this respect, I suggest, is that of the power opportunity structure. There is no possibility of learning from a mastery experience if one is simply not allowed to engage in the experience by whoever or whatever is the gatekeeper to such experiences. Satchel Paige (a black baseball pitcher who is quoted by Bandura admiringly) could not have learned from personal experience how good a major league pitcher he could be in the pre-Jackie Robinson era. If a very limited admissions quota to medical school is imposed on women, it is impossible for most to learn directly that they can be good doctors. The exclusion of Jews from agriculture in Czarist Russia provided no opportunity for them to learn that they could be good farmers. These examples are particularly ironic, in view of what happened historically once the barriers were removed. The examples of continuing limited or non-existent opportunity structures, unhappily, can be multiplied, e.g. people who are HIV-positive or homosexuals are excluded from teaching.

This leads to a further point, relating to total inefficaciousness. The phrasing of the sentence above was intentional: I did not write "homosexuals are excluded . . .", but rather "people who are homosexuals . . .". We tend to forget that identification of the entire person with one characteristic, whatever its importance or centrality, is not limited to the familiar categories of race, gender, or ethnicity. It is often also applied to other characteristics. Thus, in a study entitled *The Making of Blind Men*, Scott (1969) analyzes how people with a very severe or complete limitation in the capacity to see physical objects in their close vicinity are transformed into "the blind". A terribly important but still only one characteristic of a person comes to identify the entire person.

This example takes us a step further. If Blacks or women or Jews have historically been excluded from many possible mastery experiences, they have not been excluded from many others, though these may of lesser social valuation. In the case of people who are blind, or have cognitive limitations, or a physical or psychiatric disability, or are elderly, they are often socially and *structurally* (i.e. with formal or informal institutionalized barriers) regarded as *in-valid*, as totally incompetent, and excluded from all opportunities. In Nazi Germany they became non-persons and destined for extermination. Rosow (1976, p. 464), discussing the elderly, referred to the roleless status, in which the status occupant is shorn of all effective resources and significant activities.

Labeling theory suggests the further invidious character of the process. Socially defined by the powers that be as incompetent, structurally barred from opportunities, the person herself or himself often arrives at the same self-definition. The process is one of institutionalization of trained incapacity. Even should, by some miracle, an opportunity arise to engage in a mastery experience, no attempt will be made to do so, because one has been trained in perceived self-inefficacy.

It is not appropriate here to analyze the sources of opportunity barriers or the origins of power differentials which make them possible. But surely to discuss mastery experiences only in terms of the extent to which a family encourages or discourages a child to ride a bicycle or the like is to trivialize the SE construct. Bandura does not do so, particularly with respect to gender (see 1986, p. 419; 1988, p. 17; 1989, pp. 23–7). Yet he does not even mention (other than a passing reference in 1986, p. 404) what for most sociologists is the crucial concept in discussing power and opportunity structures: social class.

This is not, however, just another example, important as it may be, of a social category which moderates opportunity for enactive experiences. Merton's classic paper on anomie (1957) focuses on the disjunction between culturally inculcated goals and the structured and legitimated means for goal achievement. Thus Americans of lower class position are taught the "American dream", but very few have Horatio Alger opportunities. In the present context, one must ask: What are the consequences for SE of such a disjunction? Would it not be reasonable to hypothesize that, at least for those who are not deviant, who continue to accept the goals and the legitimated means, the disjunction subjects lower class persons to a *generalized* debilitation of SE?

It is paradoxical that, despite my commitment to a salutogenic approach, this entire section has been cast in terms of structural limitations on opportunities for enactive mastery. It is as if I were implying: Remove the barriers and everyone will have all the mastery experiences she or he could wish for. Yet, as Bandura makes clear, particularly in his analysis of school structures that foster efficacy or inefficacy (1989, pp. 46–7), creating such opportunities is not a matter of happenstance. The British Empire had to be a real empire of power to allow males of the upper class to enjoy mastery experiences. Soldiers have to be well-equipped to defeat an enemy. Politicians have to have extensive financial resources to win office. Someone whom I love also has to love me. In other words, the mastery experience, as a source of information to build SE, is contingent not only on the absence of barriers to engage in a given activity, but on the availability of appropriate resources to be successful in that activity. Such resources are very often not only in one's own hands. A lovely and salutogenic case in point came to my attention just after writing the above: the wealthy Gilbert Kaplan, obsessed by the desire to conduct Mahler's second symphony, was able to hire the American Symphony Orchestra and rent Avery Fisher Hall. Of course, the successful experience, enhancing his task-specific high SE, was not only contingent upon his wealth. But without it?

One final point should be made. I have focused on the opportunities for mastery experiences created or closed by people's positions in the various stratification systems of a society, expressed in and reinforced by cultural definitions. On the more proximal level, and possibly with at least as great an impact, the sociologist would point to the institutionalized norms attached to social roles. A woman giving birth may be institutionally defined as subordinate to the obstetrician—or there may be a role reversal. A team of factory workers may have a fair degree of autonomy and decision-making power in organizing its part of the production process—or it may be subject to management decision straight down the line. In each case, the nature of the experience in terms of mastery and SE enhancement will be different.

Vicarious experiences (modeling)

"Seeing people similar to oneself", Bandura writes (1988, p. 8), "succeed by sustained effort raises observers' beliefs about their own eficacy." The similarity, he notes, need not be in characteristics which affect the performance, e.g. age, sex, or race (1986, p. 404). The use of reference group theory, I believe, would provide a more profund understanding of how vicarious experiences provide SE information.

Merton and Kitt's reanalysis of the Second World War *The American Soldier* data (1950) is a case in point. The original data seemed perplexing. Soldiers without any combat experience in outfits composed solely of soldiers like themselves had higher perceived SE (in our present terms) regarding "confidence in their ability 'to take charge of a group of men' in combat" than did those similarly without experience but who had been assigned as replacements in experienced outfits. (p. 72) Objectively, there is no reason for this to have been the case. Merton and Kitt propose that the explanation lies in considering the different reference groups or significant others of each group. The former compared themselves to the other green soldiers in their outfits, and did not find themselves wanting; the latter compared themselves to the combat veterans in their own outfits. The efficacy information received in the two cases is quite different.

Note that the analysis does not deal with who will perform better. SE beliefs can be illusory and even self-defeating. It may well be that the replacement troops, aware of their inadequacies, knowing that combat awaits them, and with a direct opportunity to learn from their experienced buddies, will perform better than those who have no learning opportunities.

My point is that the actor is always in a reference group situation, is always comparing her or his capability of performance with that of significant others. They are a constant source of efficacy information. But the problem then arises: how is the researcher, interested in prediction rather than in *post hoc* explanation, to know which reference groups are pertinent? Here too the answer lies in social structure, but at the meso level, for reference groups are neither macro, abstract social categories, nor micro, persons involved in the immediate situation. To put it simply, the performances of those with whom we associate in our daily lives *and* their relative statuses are guidelines for most of us most of the time for what we believe we can do.

Observation of successful performance by a superordinate does not convey effective information that one can do the same; it may even suggest the opposite. Analogously, one is influenced by the observed performances of peers and subordinates. The more specific the behavior under consideration, the less clear is the information, for different individuals perform concrete tasks at considerably different levels of efficacy. But the more general the domain, the more likely is one to sense that if even some of one's peers and certainly one's subordinates perform well, one can also do so. What remains to be added is that judgment as to who one's peers are is a social judgment. The inexperienced soldier in a replacement outfit who judged himself to be a peer with the veterans was likely to be quickly disabused of the notion. I am, in sum, proposing that the structural factor of power and status differentials in one's daily life is decisive in the extent and direction of the impact of vicarious experiences.

Verbal persuasion and social influence

Bandura emphasizes the decisive role of the credibility of those who seek to persuade one that one is capable of performing a task (1986, p. 406). How is one to judge the credibility of a persuader? This may be easy with respect to a specific task, when a persuader is an expert in the matter. But this brings us back to vicarious experience, for the expert is really telling one about her or his own experience. Consider, for example, a woman who has had a mastectomy and takes part in a self-help group. It is the vicarious experience which matters, and it is the peer comparative reference group character of the group which is decisive in conveying SE information. If, however, the other participants are far more educated, or have far more supportive husbands, or the means to have their children in a good day care center or hire a housekeeper, the information may well have a boomerang effect.

Reference groups also have a normative as well as a comparative function. Thus the message is: "You should, and not only can, successfully cope. This is what we expect of people like ourselves." Or, conversely, "People like us should not be able to do this". Thus the message perpetually reiterated in adult peer groups in Western societies is that of women's mechanical and men's emotional incompetence. Bandura and I are old enough to remember how well women performed as welders during the Second World War, and how quickly thereafter they again became "incompetent" at such tasks.

The crucial issue, then, with respect to social persuasions are the societal norms, conveyed by the mass media and reference groups, and backed by sanctions which can only be ignored at one's peril.

Physiological states

Emotional arousal (tension, fear, anger) expressed in visceral agitation may provide positive or negative SE information. At first glance, it would seem that these internal states are far removed from structural influences. Yet, if the crucial question is how one interprets the arousal, the link may not be far-fetched. Emotions bring the memory network into play. All of us have a history of emotions. If this history is one of consistent association between the emotion and coping success, arousal in the new situation is likely to be predictive of high SE. Which brings us back to one's history of mastery experiences and their structural determinants, which need not be repeated here.

We can, however, go a step further by referring to what has come to be known as the sociology of emotions. Lennon (1989) has discussed social norms that govern the appropriateness of emotions as well as shape emotion management. We feel, interpret, and handle certain emotions in certain situations in good measure because we are women or men, outsiders or insiders, and so on—i.e. we relate to the situation in terms of our social identity. Kemper (1978) has proposed a more specific hypothesis—namely, that power and status are the two core dimensions which characterize social relations. Emotions, both distressful and positive, result from real, anticipated, re-collected, or imagined outcomes of power and status relations. Thus, for example, he suggests that deficit of own power is the social relational condition which elicits fear or anxiety, whereas loss of status generates anger. Emotions, then, may be the proximal source of SE information. But these are grounded and to be understood in large part in terms of social origins and contexts.

I have written this extended discussion relating to Bandura's work because he has paid systematic attention to the sources of strengths. This will facilitate briefer discussions below. I must note, however, that his work is that of a psychologist. Moreover, he is primarily concerned with task-specific SE. I do not believe that there is anything I have written which is incongruent with his work. There is ample evidence, in his many references to historical-social contexts, that, had he written this section, he might well have done an even better job.

Rotter's Locus of Control (LOC)

IE [internal–external] beliefs are generalized expectancies that reflect the consistent individual differences among individuals in the degree to which they perceive contingencies or independence between their behavior and subsequent events.

(Strickland, 1989, p. 1)

If the person perceives that the event is contingent upon his own behavior or his own relatively permanent characteristics, we have termed this a belief in *internal control.*

(Rotter, 1966, p. 1)

LOC is probably the most-cited construct in psychology and the most often used in empirical studies. Bandura and Rotter would surely agree that there is an affinity between SE and LOC in theoretical origins. Similarly, though neither was formulated with respect to the stress process, both have been applied to coping, health, and well-being. They might agree that empirical associations between the two constructs would be found (i.e. positive correlations between high SE and internality). There is, however, one fundamental difference. Though both are concerned with predicting behavior, SE refers to beliefs about behavioral capacities; LOC refers to beliefs about the link between behavior and outcome. Further, Bandura's stress is on task-specific confidence expectancies. LOC, on the other hand, refers to more general and enduring, stable personality expectancies. (Rotter (1975) has, however, suggested that specific expectancies may, for specific situations with which one has had experience, which are not novel or ambiguous, be more important than a generalized belief. And Lefcourt (1981, p. 386) approves of the trend in more recent research toward specificity.) We have, then, competing hypotheses as to which set of beliefs is more powerful in predicting coping behavior, persistence, and successful resolution of stress. (For a comparative study on persistence, see Haines, McGrath and Pirot, 1980. For an attempt to develop a theoretical model of personal efficacy beliefs, including the two constructs as well as others, see Saltzer, 1982.) But both can legitimately be seen as referring to salutogenic strengths.

One searches in vain for any systematic analysis of the structural origins of an internal LOC, the belief that there is a causal relationship between one's own behavior and outcomes of reward and punishment. There is little doubt that the theory predicts that internals will do better at coping with stressors, though Rotter (1975, p. 61) very explicitly warns against thinking that internals are the "good guys". I cannot even begin to claim that I have covered the vast literature. But at least in Rotter's classic paper (1966), his clarifying 1975 paper, Lefcourt's three volumes (1976, 1981, 1983), Strickland's most recent review paper (1989), and other works I have reviewed, few indeed are the systematic references to the question of the structural sources of high internality.

Take, for example, Strickland, who has been, from her graduate student days with Rotter to the present, closely associated with, and a leading contributor to LOC theory and research. In preparing this chapter, I was pleased to encounter her statement "Nowicki and I were particularly interested in how children came to hold beliefs about the relationship of their behavior to various reinforcement outcomes" (1989, pp. 3–4). What follows is an account of the development of a children's I–E measure and the most impressive research findings to which it led. "Came to hold" is forgotten.

Nonetheless, here and there one finds references which I shall here try to organize and build upon. These will be considered under four headings: internality as a reflection of the objective situation; internality and culture; the concept of powerful others; and responsible vs. defensive internality.

The objective situation

There is a close relationship between the LOC and Seligman's (1975) concept of learned helplessness. Referring to the latter among Negroes, soldiers and concentration camp inmates, Lefcourt (1976, p. 21) writes ". . . helplessness, a perceived inability to affect one's fate meaningfully [i.e. low internal control—AA], is the natural response to deprivation and denigration". It may be natural and even functional in the short run, he notes, but it prevents one from a true assessment of the situation and what one can do, and "is a source of immature and poor coping behavior".

Our concern here is not with consequences but with sources. What can be inferred is that, as a *sine qua non*, high internality develops when objectively there are at least some degrees of freedom for effective action. When one's world is overwhelmingly controlled by hostile powerful others or arbitrariness and chance, as in the concentration camp or societies which generate a culture of poverty, then, because it is truly more functional in the long run too, one comes to have externalized beliefs. By ingratiating oneself with the powers that be, by seizing whatever scraps may by chance come one's way, one learns that such beliefs indeed facilitate survival.

I am not suggesting a linear correlation between options and internality. But in a world in which many fewer people are in Psych 101 classes than in situations of hunger, gulags, red guards, and civil wars, it is crucial to insist that a minimum of options are required to develop internality. In this respect, Beardslee's (1989) work is germane. True, he does not write of LOC in his studies of black civil rights workers, survivors of childhood cancer, and children of parents with affective disorders who were all "resilient individuals". But he does link his concept to "a sense of being effectual and in control of one's surroundings" (p. 267). Particularly the first of these groups had for many years lived in a social situation in which the margins were narrow—but they were there. Having personally known participants in ghetto uprisings and survivors of Auschwitz who have rebuilt their lives, people who, against all logic and reality, were internal, I would be the last to deny that there are always the extraordinarily courageous who are our heroes and give us hope for human dignity. But for the very great majority of us who are not heroes, without some minimal room for indeed affecting our fates, we are not likely to be internal. (I shall, subsequently, return to Beardslee's work. My concern here was to make the point of a minimal requirement of socially structured margins for the development of internality.)

The issue is further clarified if we start from Rotter's passing remark (1975, p. 64), made in his discussion of the distinction between defensive and passive external beliefs, that the latter "would clearly be the norm in more fatalistic cultures, such as Hindu or Moslem". In Nowicki and Duke's paper (1983, pp. 19–21), a series of cross-cultural studies are reviewed. Israeli Jewish children were found to be more internal than Israeli Arab children and than comparable American children; Chinese more external than Americans; South African Blacks more external and Whites more internal than Americans; in the US, Mexican-Americans and Native Americans (Indians) more external than Caucasians. The authors, however, primarily focus on the finding that, whatever the mean differences, "correlates of locus of control seem to be similar from group to group" (p. 21).

Can any structural pattern be discerned in such findings? It is helpful if we relate these findings to passing references in the Lefcourt (1983) volume to social class and race (p. 18), parental occupational and educational levels (p. 66), and own social class (p. 68), generally showing a direct relationship between class and internality. As Phares (1976, p. 44) put it: "We can probably safely assert that variations in I–E scale scores are related to differences in access to power or to the presence of social barriers to group mobility."

The suggestion, then, is that when the objective reality of people's lives is such that their fates are largely shaped by powerful others or by "chance", i.e. forces which are beyond their control and even their comprehension, they will come to see the world accurately, i.e. as externals. Dynamically, over time, this outlook becomes a self-fulfilling prophecy. No attempts are made to break the vicious circle. Interestingly, in the Nowicki and Duke paper cited above (1983), no link is made between the sociocultural differences reported and the consistent "correlates" of LOC: externality with maladjustment, lower achievement levels and powerlessness; internality with higher self-esteem, self-acceptance and other indicators of adaptive functioning.

To clarify, with respect to the reported study in a culture I know well. When Israeli Jewish children are found to be more internal than Israeli Arab children, and LOC is found to be related to the adjustment indicators, is it not plausible to suggest that *both* variables are functions of the respective majority and minority statuses of the two ethnic groups? Sociodemographic statuses, then, are not just troublesome variables to be held constant in analyses; they may provide the very clue to the development of internality.

Later in the same paper (pp. 35–6), in a brief section on antecedents of LOC, Nowicki and Duke write that most researchers "have assumed that such orientations are learned through children's continuous experience with their parents". They report a study showing that children's internality is associated with the parental behaviors of trust, consistency, nurturance, and autonomy. Another reported study pointed to the externality-fostering role of stressful life events of which sense cannot be made. But where do such parental behaviors and such inexplicable life events originate? They are, I suggest, not at all randomly distributed.

As a model for the required kind of analysis, I would propose turning to Kohn's work. (For the most useful and recent summaries, see Kohn, 1990 and Kohn et al., 1990.) This is not simply a methodological proposal as to how the structural origins of LOC should be studied. Kohn writes, it might be noted (1990, p. 51), that "These studies, almost all of them based on one or another variant of Rotter's (1966) conceptualization and index, are altogether consonant with my own and with other studies of job conditions and personality." In the course of a research program which has spanned more than a quarter of a century and three continents, Kohn has sought to study the links between location in a society's stratification system, the conditions under which people live and work, and values and self-concepts. More recently, he has sought to apply this analytic scheme in a historical context and dynamically in a life cycle perspective (Kohn et al., 1990). Kohn's point of departure is a person's location in the society's stratification systems. This, in good measure, shapes the nature of the work conditions of her or his daily life. The particular conditions which Kohn and his colleageus have found to be of crucial significance are substantive complexity, closeness of supervision, and routinization of tasks. These work conditions are subsumed under "exercising self-direction in work". These, in turn, shape such characteristics as intellectual flexibility and such values as autonomy. These values, finally, are translated to parental behavior. Lest the model be misunderstood as one of linear causality, he stresses that "the relationship between social structure and personality are mainly reciprocal" (1989, p. 27).

Internality and culture

Now let us return to Rotter's reference to "fatalistic" cultures. The concept is tempting. Unfortunately, it is seriously misleading and often ethnocentric. More important, I suggest that it unnecessarily vitiates the power of the LOC construct, which has the important advantage over other salutogenic constructs in that it has been widely applied cross-culturally. Some cultures which we would label "traditional" do indeed not only not foster but even castigate internality as we understand it in Western society. It is held to be an expression of hubris, doomed to the punishment foreseen both by the Greeks and by the friends of Job. Members of such cultures would react in horror to a culture which insists that one's fate is in one's own hands. Rotter himself has noted (1975, p. 61): "But there must also be a limit on personal control."

There are here, I believe, three significant implications about the macro-social sources of the kind of internality that would predict successful coping. First, what is most devastating to internality is not whether one's culture provides "traditional" rather than "modern" guides to behavior, but whether it provides clearcut guides. If there are clear, legitimate rules, then it is likely that I will believe that by following the rules, whatever their substance, things will work out well. If I don't know what to do, it is much less likely that I will anticipate contingency between behavior and outcome. Many traditional cultures do provide clear guides; they are in this sense supportive of internality.

Who makes the rules matters much less, as long as they are regarded as legitimate. Other cultures are more transitional, in which confusion, conflict, and uncertainty prevail. This may be the source of the data showing less internality in non-Western cultures. This understanding of internality may very well require revision of LOC scales, making them less culture-bound.

Second, as noted above, internality is likely to be nurtured in social contexts in which there is indeed room, objectively, for the individual to affect his or her environment and fate. Cultures tend to resort to magic, Malinowski has noted, when there is inadequate knowledge or instrumentality for control. Or, to put it another way, if internality is to be effective, it can only be in situations where what the individual does indeed can make a difference. Otherwise it is likely to boomerang, because it quickly leads to experiences of failure. Traditional cultures, alas, very often are resource-poor, and hence what their members do cannot very effectively affect their well-being.

The reference to traditional cultures raises a third significant issue which has not yet in any way been alluded to: a belief about *collective* behavior-outcome contingencies. There are dozens of LOC scales. As far as I have been able to discover, without exception they are intended to measure the *individual's* belief about his or her own behavior and outcome. This reflects the total theoretical commitment to the culture-boundedness of the concept. In many traditional cultures, the normative emphasis in task performance is on the collective. In this culture context, individual internality may be far less important in predicting both individual behavior and outcome, even for the individual, than "collective internality". The former, in such cases, makes no cultural sense. No wonder that such cultures do not foster internality as we understand it.

"Collective internality" may have diverse meanings. (For a more extended discussion of this complex issue, as applied to the sense of coherence, see Antonovsky, 1987, pp. 170–9; and Antonovsky and Sourani, 1988.) For present purposes, the important internal belief is "I believe that the behavior of the group of which I am a part will lead to the desired outcome". "Collective internality", however, is not a concept relevant only to traditional cultures. As Bandura (1986) writes in his discussion of collective efficacy, a discussion with no parallel in the LOC literature as far as I know, "People do not live their lives in social isolation. Many of the challenges and difficulties they face reflect group problems requiring sustained collective effort to produce any significant change." (p. 449) I would go further and suggest that even in the most individualistic, entrepreneurial societies, most of the major tasks in life—in interpersonal relations, in marriage, at work, and even in health matters—are collective tasks. How then, the question becomes, do people come to hold beliefs in collective internality (or collective SE)? Though Bandura and I have each discussed the concept, neither he nor I nor anyone else, to the best of my knowledge, has even begun to propose an answer. This leads me at this point to go no further on this issue.

The concept of powerful others

There is, however, a clear link between the question of culture and a central concept in the LOC literature: the meaning of "powerful others". Researchers, following Levenson (1981), have made the tripartite distinction between contingency attributions to self, powerful others, and chance. Levenson's point of departure was to distinguish

> between two types of external orientation—belief in the basic unordered and random nature of the world and belief in the basic order and predictability of the world, coupled with the expectancy that powerful others are in control. In the latter case there is a potential for control.
>
> (p. 15)

Examination of the eight item "powerful others" (P) scale Levenson developed indicates that the concept refers to belief in control of outcome by those with power who are at best uninterested in one's welfare. One must, then, adapt, manipulate, please, and ingratiate oneself with these people to achieve a desired outcome. No wonder that the P and C (Chance) scales are most often correlated; that females and blacks score higher (in most studies) on P; that paranoid patients score higher on P than neurotics or normal controls, as do long-term prisoners compared to those recently jailed.

True, Levenson does take note of the possible functional consequences of a high P score:

> For people whose perceptions of control by powerful others are realistic because of the nature of specific situations or cultural sanctions. . . . People who see the "system" or other individuals as controlling may attempt to change the system into one that would permit more individual, or personal, control.
>
> (p. 54)

Are there not, however, powerful others and powerful others? The sociological distinction between power and authority is relevant here. As I put it in an earlier discussion of the LOC construct (Antonovsky, 1979, p. 155), "The crucial question is whether . . . there is a serene belief that those in control have legitimate power and act in one's own interest." Such legitimacy can refer to all spheres of life, as with belief in a benevolent deity, or be functionally specific, such as with belief in a trusted physician. Neither Levenson nor others, to the best of my knowledge, make such a disctinction. Thus, searching for structural origins of internality is handicapped, for, given the dominant understanding of the LOC construct, we are blinded to the possibility of including in the search the origins of beliefs in benevolent, legitimate powerful others. Thus, for example, Levenson (1981, p. 27) reports positive relations between P scores and parental demanding, punishing, protective, and controlling behaviors. But suppose we had a B (benevolent) P scale; might we not find that high scores are both predictive of salutogenic outcomes and originate in quite different parental behaviors? One would, however, have to go one step further, differentiating between BP beliefs which cast one in permanent, dependent passive roles, and BP beliefs which have considerable room for growth, choice, responsibility, and active cooperation. There are, for example, some family structures, religions, and health care settings which, acknowledging that parents, God, or the doctor have special knowledge or authority, encourage proactive behavior. Growing up and living in such sociocultural settings might well foster strong BP beliefs which correlate positively with internality.

Responsive vs. defensive internality

As the point of departure in considering this issue, we turn to the discussion of health LOC as a dependent variable in Wallston and Wallston (1981), pp. 210–18). A study of persons with epilepsy with varying degrees of control led to the conclusion "that negative experiences over which there is little control are conducive to the development of high beliefs in external control . . . and low belief in internal control" (p. 211). A study of childbirth experiences in a hospital, i.e. a situation with low control, showed an increase in externality. Studies of various intervention programs designed to enhance internality and data on various known-groups analyses show mixed results. There is little help here in a quest for sources.

But there is one suggestion which may be useful in considering the final point of this section. As noted, the Wallstons refer to both negative experiences and little control leading to externality. They do not ask whether externality develops against the background of a history of negative experiences, a history of lack of control experiences, or both? This may be linked to Rotter's (1975, p. 64) above-noted distinction between defensive and passive (or congruent) externals. The former are those who endorse external items as defenses against failure; the latter, as an expression of lack of control.

But our interest is in internality. This brings us to Mirowsky and Ross's recent paper (1990). They tested the relative power of "defense" and "control" theory to predict depressive feelings. Or, as they ask: "Which is the cognitive foundation of emotional well-being—a sense of personal responsibility or a sense of self-justification?" (p. 71) In the present context, the question may be put: Does internality facilitate coping with stressors because it means taking credit for good outcomes while rejecting blame for unfortunate ones (defense), or does it do so because it expresses a willingness to assume responsibility, whatever the outcome (control)? What they found, in a probability sample of Illinois residents, was that "instrumentalists", who assume responsibility for success and for failure, are less depressed than those who feel an absence of control over good outcomes ("self-blamers"), over bad outcomes ("self-defenders"), or over both ("fatalists"). It is, then, the sense of control rather than the nature of the experience which matters.

What, then, are the sources of internality understood as a sense of responsibility (which term, I believe, more adequately reflects Mirowsky and Ross's discussion than control), as seeing contingency between one's own behavior and outcome, whether success or failure? A possible answer may be inferred from Rotter's remark (1975, p. 65) about the possibility of "an increased tendency toward defensive externality with increased age and time in the school system". The American school system is one which applies achievement measures consistently but marks on a curve, at least regarding subsequent admission to the better schools and universities. Demands are made of all, but by structured definition of the situation, some must fail and many are socially and self-defined as inferior.

This brings us back to Merton's (1957) discussion of anomie and social structure. Those defined as inferior can adapt to such a situation in various ways. They can drop out, relinquishing goals and means, becoming passive externals or fatalists, unless they become revolutionaries, with new goals and means. They can become self-defenders (= defensive externals), maintaining goals but adopting new means. Or they can become self-blamers (= defensive internals), ritually keeping means, but giving up achievement goals or, in Mirowsky and Ross's terms, taking blame for failure but not credit for success. But even the successes, in such a structured situation, need not become responsible instrumentalists, maintaining goals and means, seeing contingency between own behavior and outcome, because the danger of failure is always there! One alternative which can be the source of true, stable, and responsible internality can be a social situation which allows consistent success measured in terms of improvement on one's own past achievements. There are other cultural and structural alternatives, which await our exploration.

I have, in this discussion of LOC, found it necessary to clarify the nature of internality as a salutogenic strength in order to consider its sociocultural sources. I first noted that internality requires a minimum of socially structured options in the real world. But this generalization, if it is to be useful, requires translation and application within a detailed theoretical framework, a model of which is supplied by Kohn. Second, I pointed to the relationship between internality and culture, considering three issues: the difference between traditional and transitional cultures, between clear rules and confusion; the resource-poor character of most traditional cultures; and the concept of collective internality. Third, I suggested the possibility of studying what I called "benevolent powerful others" beliefs which may be no less salutogenic, provided they leave room for growth, choice, responsibility, and active cooperation. Finally, I made the distinction between responsible and defensive internality, suggesting that the former, the true salutogenic strength, is vitiated in a social structure which demands unending achievement as one of the ultimate values but marks on a curve. Implicit here is the question of values and meaning—which brings us to a consideration of the concept of hardiness.

Kobasa's Hardiness (HARD)

Three existential concepts appear especially relevant to this optimistic orientation: commitment, challenge, and control. These together comprise the personality style of stress-resistance, or hardiness. *Commitment* is the ability to believe in the truth, importance, and interest value of who one is and what one is doing . . . and thereby the tendency to involve oneself fully in the many situations of life . . . an overall sense of purpose. . . . From the perspective of *challenge*, much of the disruption associated with the occurrence of a stressful life event can be anticipated as an opportunity and incentive for personal growth . . . persons who welcome challenge . . . are characterized by an openness or cognitive flexibility and tolerance of ambiguity. . . . Persons with *control* seek explanations for why something is happening not simply in terms of others' actions or fate, but also with an emphasis on their own responsibility. . . . They feel capable of acting effectively on their own.

(Kobasa, 1982b, pp. 6–9, my emphasis)

Bandura and Rotter are not oblivious to the question of values, in two senses. First, the value of the outcome to the actor is included in equations predicting behavior. Second, inasmuch as high SE and internality foster health, and health is a good, these orientations are desirable. As we shall see, my own explicit view is that there is no relationship between the SOC and morality. For Kobasa, however, high HARD is not only valued because it is salutogenic. It is the very core of full humanity. Orr and Westman (1990), in their overall review of the HARD literature, give only a slight hint of the centrality of values in Kobasa's work when they refer (p. 64) to "this attractive blend". Unless this is understood, it would be difficult to consider the sources of HARD. I would even go further. If the philosophic roots of the HARD construct are ignored, one might well misinterpret Kobasa's work as an expression of American entrepreneurial, capitalistic values. (Unfortunately, Kobasa bears some responsibility for such misunderstanding. In the first version of the HARD scale, agreeing with the following items adds to one's *low* score on HARD: "The young owe the old complete economic security"; or "Public supported medical care is the right of everyone." Such items have subsequently been excluded.)

Orr and Westman (1990) conclude their comprehensive review by saying "We did not find any studies dealing with the development of hardiness, either naturally or through hardiness training" (p. 90). Nor, I might add, have I encountered any systematic theoretical discussion of sources. Once again, then, let me suggest implications on the basis of what has appeared. My point of departure, as suggested above, is the philosophical basis of the HARD construct. I will then discuss the transactional character of HARD in terms of situational contexts. Finally, I will consider the intriguing issue of temperament.

The philosophical basis

Those who have discussed or researched the HARD construct, including myself (see Antonovsky, 1987, pp. 35–8), make at most a passing reference to the existential theory of personality out of which the construct developed. Without at least some understanding of the theory, one tends to get caught up in secondary methodological discussions. Kobasa's commitment is to the personality theory of existential psychology which sees "the person as a biological, social, and psychological being whose primary task is the search for and establishment of meaning" (Kobasa and Maddi, 1977, p. 399). For present purposes, it seems to me that the construction of meaning is essential for survival as a human being. Without it one has no viable personality. Human existence is throughout a confrontation with alternatives, from the everyday problem of sorting potatoes (or choosing what clothes to wear), through selection of a mate or an occupation, to the great, ultimate questions such as how to remain human in Auschwitz (Frankl, 1963), or the confrontation with death. What is crucial is that human beings, in fact, to a greater or lesser extent, do search for meaning. This is what making decisions means. Every choice is, implicitly or explicitly, consciously or unconsciously, an attribution of meaning.

As Kobasa and Maddi (1977, pp. 405–6) point out, Binswanger goes beyond discrete decision-making, with his concept of fundamental meaning structure, defined as "the universal and unlearned human ability to perceive specific meanings in the world of events and to transcend any concrete situation on the basis of that attributed meaning." This allows a distinctive style and life direction of a person to emerge (Sartre's "fundamental project"), a style and direction which are dynamic, as one lives in constantly changing inner and outer worlds.

Freedom to choose recognizes both the realities of one's life and the possibility of what might be. If one insists on only the former, or chooses only to continue the past, or seeks to avoid decisions, the dangers of meaninglessness are strengthened. Through a constant, lifelong struggle, never completed, always accompanied by danger and anxiety, one can approach authentic being. The characteristics associated with authenticity are courage, a fascination with growth, the capacity to tolerate anxiety, assertiveness, subtlety and taste, intimacy, the setting of priorities, responsibility, communion, trust, and, above all, individuality.

From authenticity to HARD

In one paper, Kobasa (1982b) traces, albeit briefly, her translation of the existentialist concept of the authentic personality to the HARD construct and its application to health. Fascinated by the frequent phenomenon of persons subjected to a heavy stressor load and yet remaining healthy, and influenced by the personality-in-situation emphasis then emerging in psychology, she asserted that the existentialist concepts of commitment, control, and challenge, when integrated, could be a powerful explanatory variable. She regarded these as "inextricably intertwined", as "interlocking parts of an overall orientation or style of stress-resistance" (p. 9). On both empirical and theoretical grounds, however (see Orr and Westman, 1990, p. 69–72), this integration has been challenged. It is, then, important to look more closely at the theoretical roots of the three concepts.

The concept of *challenge* seems to be most closely related to the spirit of existentialism. It emphasizes the search for meaning, the orientation to the future, the zest involved in confronting choices, the ever-becoming. Perceptual search, however, as some existentialists were very deeply and painfully aware, can as easily lead to despair as turning one's back on search. Choices and decisions must be made. But if meaning is to be found in these choices, they must be made with genuine *commitment*. One chooses to not marry, to quit graduate school and paint, to join a political party. One could have chosen differently; the choice one did make may turn out to have been unwise, and confront one with the need for a new decision. If, however, the choice of singlehood, art, or activism does not become part of one's self-identity, if commitment is shallow, authenticity is forfeited.

The status of the third component of HARD, *control*, in the existentialist view of personality is less clear at first sight, particularly as originally operationalized by Kobasa using Rotter's LOC measure. It becomes clear when we consider that confronting a challenge and making a committed choice necessarily implies a willingness to assume responsibility for consequences of the choice. The notion of responsibility only makes sense if one assumes contingency between one's behavior and outcome. It is in this sense, and not in the sense of an arrogant belief in one's own near-omnipotence, that control is an essential part of the triad of an authentic personality. We can, now, start our own search for the sources of authenticity, having understood how HARD is a direct expression of the authentic person.

Becoming authentic

Kobasa and Maddi provide an account of the developmental process of becoming authentic (1977, assertions 10–16, pp. 414–19). The key capacities underlying the development of authenticity are symbolization, imagination, and judgment. One must first acquire "the rudiments of courage": a faith in oneself as capable of making choices, and consciousness "that persons construct their lives through decision-making and change." These also involve the capacity to tolerate the anxiety which always accompanies change.

An environment which has provided such rudiments allows the child to take part in satisfying psychological, social, and biological needs. (assertion #10) Authentic parenting encourages individuality. By learning to act "as a distinct and assertive person, the child is on his way to learning to be courageous, to tolerate anxiety, and to choose his future" (#11). But the child must also learn that freedom is not absolute, that there are limits to control (#12). Richness of experience, frustratingly negative as well as positive, in all three need spheres is essential (#13). Childhood is inherently a period of inauthenticity, because others have power over one. A repeated pattern of "independence training, richness of experience, respect for individuality, and imposed limits" makes emergence into a vigorous self-determined development possible by the time adolescence is reached, a spiral which continues throughout life (#14). Note that failure, for one with a sound basis for authenticity, need not be damaging, and can provide useful information (#15). The independence of adolescence and young adulthood does not guarantee authenticity. One passes through, first, a hedonistic, "aesthetic" phase, reveling in the intoxication of freedom of choice. But the party must soon end, for without commitment and discrimination, failure and emptiness are inevitable. One then passes through an "idealistic" phase, characterized by a sense of total commitment and control. Again, inevitable failure leads one to the possibility of an adult life-style which is truly authentic (#16). The rest of life, moreover, is a perpetual struggle to maintain authenticity.

Kobasa and Maddi have here given no clues as to the social and cultural contexts which determine the extent to which children, adolescents, and adults are encouraged to develop authenticity. Only subsequently (p. 429), discussing "institutionalization", do they mention Sartre's political activity and Laing's contention "that society will have to become more tolerant and supportive of deviant behavior if authentic being is to be possible for greater numbers of persons". In this context, they refer to bureaucratization, technical complexity, participatory democracy, and creative endeavor in dealing with social problems.

But in the last analysis, "The special message of the existential approach is that each person can construct the unique life he chooses" (p. 430). Really? Reading Kobasa and Maddi's account of the child-rearing practices and subsequent experiences which foster authenticity, I could not help but be sceptical. Do they indeed believe that each person can construct the unique life *she* chooses, given the powerful constraints to which the overwhelming number of females are subjected? Their reply, I would guess, would be that in real life no one can ever achieve full authenticity; that what they have written is a scientific analysis of the experiences requisite for authenticity, a yardstick against which reality is to be measured, an ideal type in the Weberian sense. Authenticity (and HARD) is a complex and dynamic continuum. They would say that maintenance and improvement of one's location on the continuum is, to the very end, always a matter of struggle, always requiring the exercise of the three key processes of symbolization, imagination, and judgment.

The above has been an account of the experiential conditions which foster HARD, with little clarification of the underlying structural and cultural contexts which foster them. Everything that has been said above in discussing Bandura and Rotter, I believe—the options offered by reality, power relations, role assignment, reference group orientations, cultural definitions, and so on—must no less be applied if we are to understand the sources of authenticity. It will, however, be helpful to turn to a second level of discussion, one more proximal to the HARD orientation.

HARD and the situational context

In specifying the criteria for the constructs to be discussed in this chapter, I noted that they all share a transactional character, a commitment to understanding behavior as an outcome of the interaction between a personality disposition and a situational context. Just what this means is clarified by Smith and Anderson's (1986) paper on the Type A behavior pattern (TABP). Previous work, they claim, has been mechanistic, in which challenging and demanding environments are seen as eliciting, in certain persons, the TABP. They propose going further. Type A people, they suggest, tend to look for or to create such situations; they tend to appraise situations in these terms when others might not do so; their behavior generates behavior in others. In sum, the Type A person is highly proactive in multiplying experiences which reinforce the predisposition.

The centrality of challenge in the HARD concept, the emphasis on the search for perpetual change and growth, lends itself even more to this view. Type A persons are often punished as a consequence of their behavior, which might lead to extinction. The more hardy persons tend to generate, foster, and maintain situations in which HARD is reinforced. This is certainly the case if the situation is rewarding. But even failure (punishment, sanction) is, for the hardy person, but a spur to further engagement in challenge, commitment, and control. "To him that hath, shall be given."

A second aspect of situational determinants of HARD is found in Kobasa's own work. In her study of lawyers (1982a), she points out that the myths about law schools and the image of lawyers conveyed in the mass media as well as in the profession tend to attract people who thrive on stressors, i.e. who are presumably high on HARD. (In passing, one cannot help but wonder what happened to the identification of authenticity with HARD.) The life of a lawyer, as she puts it elsewhere (1982b, p. 28) "may also serve to help lawyers develop stress-resistance resources like hardiness". On the other hand, she adds, "There are, in fact, things about the current Army's socialization practices, role expectations, and social climate [in the post-Vietnam period] which may hinder the development and practice of hardiness." And, discussing her studies of executives:

> Regardless of an executive's basic level of hardiness, actions that display control, commitment, and challenge are hard to come by in situations where exactly what the company wants and is willing to give are left unclarified.
>
> (p. 22)

In sum, persons already high on HARD are active in creating proximal and discrete, but also distal and more encompassing, structured situations which reinforce their HARD. At the same time, there are limits, and we all become involved, by choice, by happenstance, or by the realities of life, in marriages, occupations, communities, or societies which send messages with varying degrees of clarity: HARD is welcomed . . . or disdained. Once again, I would suggest, the question of power is central. How welcoming, or how disdaining, are the powers that be at whatever system level is under consideration?

Temperament

In a passing remark in an interview with her (Wood, 1987, p. 43), Kobasa mentions an issue generally ignored but well worth pursuing. "I believe", she says, "that one might find a particular temperament early in one's life that would help in the development of later hardiness." As anyone who is a parent (or, perhaps with a better vantage point, a grandparent) knows, some children, even in early infancy, seem to radiate proactiveness, exploring, and what might best be called resilience. Writing in the early 1980s, Garmezy (1983) predicted that "It is likely that the next decade will witness a significant growth in research that may pass under many banners: '*stress-resistance*,' '*ego-resilience*', '*protective factors*', '*invulnerability*' (p. 73). Personality dispositions in infancy and childhood are one source of resilience.

Let us, then, assume that there are indeed temperamental dispositions which are the basis of and foster HARD. Is not the crucial question: Do the family environments and structures, the stories read and the games played, the experiences in street, playground, and nursery schools, the video programs children see, the attitudes, values, and behaviors of sibling and significant adults, foster or debilitate the original dispositions? The original push cannot be ignored. But if a powerful understanding of the sources of HARD is to be developed, we must go beyond these general remarks, and discuss the specificities of temperamental dispositions, environmental experiences, and HARD.

We have, then, discussed three sources of HARD. Unquestionably, the emphasis is on the childhood experiences which foster the search for individuality and meaning, experiences which may be affected by initial temperament. Once the basis for a life of authenticity has been laid, one creates situations which reinforce HARD. But Kobasa does take note of occupational (and by extension, other) situations which may work in either direction. Specificities are unclear, but I believe a research agenda has been set.

Antonovsky's Sense of Coherence (SOC)

The sense of coherence is a global orientation that expresses the extent to which one has a pervasive, enduring though dynamic feeling of confidence that (1) the stimuli deriving from one's internal and external environments in the course of living are structured, predictable, and explicable [comprehensibility]; (2) the resources are available to one to meet the demands posed by these stimuli [manageability]; and (3) these demands are challenges, worthy of investment and engagement [meaningfulness].

(Antonovsky, 1987, p. 19)

I have elsewhere (Antonovsky, 1987, pp. 35–9) discussed the similarities and differences between Kobasa's work and my own. In the present context, Beardslee's recent paper on resilience (1989) can serve as a link between the two. He has, it will be recalled, studied black civil rights workers, survivors of childhood cancer, and children of parents with affective disorders who were all "resilient individuals". His central proposition is that "resilient individuals have a total organizing conceptualization of who they are and how they came to be" (p. 275). This allows them "self-understanding", the key to resilience, which is "among the higher level, complex, integrative ego functions" (p. 274). The three crucial dimensions of self-understanding are: an adequate cognitive appraisal of stressors over time; a realistic appraisal of the capacity for and the consequences of action; and engagement in actions in the world. Thus Beardslee, like Kobasa, emphasizes struggle and development. But he seems to differ from Kobasa in that the people he studies do not spend their lives looking for stressors (or challenges); their load is heavy enough. If they are fortunate, they have arrived at a stable self-understanding, though one tested in action and modified if necessary. Beardslee, Kobasa, and I, then, share the stress on the centrality of meaningfulness (=commitment = action) and the importance of manageability (= control = stressor and capacity appraisal). He and I, though, emphasize the explanatory and organizing framework (my "comprehensibility") which "eventually becomes a stable part of the individual's experience" (p. 268). This stands in tension, at least, if not in conflict with Kobasa's challenge.

Though Beardslee uses life history material, his paper "is not an examination of the etiology of self-understanding or of resiliency" (p. 275). In contrast to this and to the reviewed work of my three colleagues, I have published a systematic account of the development over the course of the life cycle of a strong SOC (1987, Ch. 5; see also Antonovsky, 1990 for the "history" of the SOC construct). Hence it need only be summarized here briefly. This is a theoretical statement, not yet tested by research. But because it is systematic, it is, I believe, subject to such testing.

Experiences leading to the SOC

A brief statement summarizes the origins of the SOC. (Quotations, unless otherwise noted, are from Antonovsky, 1987.) "Consistent experiences provide the basis for the comprehensibility component; a good load balance, for the manageability component; and . . . participation in shaping outcome, for the meaningfulness component." (p. 92) Let us clarify these terms, so as to avoid the misinterpretations I have frequently encountered.

Consistent experiences relate to the human need for stability. The same source, whether inner or outer, often sends different, surprising, and even contradictory messages simultaneously and certainly over time. Different sources bombard us with conflicting information. Rules are often vague or inconsistent. Facing this perpetual danger of chaos, the human being finds it difficult to make sense of her or his world, to know how to feel, think, or behave. There is, of course, the danger of maladaptive frozenness in an ever-changing world. But without rules, guidelines, criteria for setting priorities; without some significant thread of continuity between past, present, and future; without some degree of harmony, we are lost. Consistency does not mean identity. A string quartet does not have four violins or four clone players, nor are the first and second movements identical. But to make music, and for the listener to share it, there must be some integration and agreement about rules.

Load experiences are those which make demands upon us to act, to mobilize resources for task performance. Again, the source of the demand can be inner or outer. The demand can be comprehensible; we understand what is wanted. The question becomes: Do we believe that the resources at our disposal enable us to meet the demand? Note, not "I have the resources", the familiar theme of the SE, LOC, and HARD literature. The demands are very often on "us". And the important question, even when the demand is on "me", is whether "we"—I and all those on my side—have the resources. This is the problem of overload. No less important, however, is the problem of underload. Much as unused muscles atrophy, so do unused skills, capacities, and potentialities. Balanced load experiences, then, refer to a consistent history of being called upon (by one's inner self or by the world around one) to act in the manifold ways that utilize one's potential and are appropriate to the resources at one's disposal.

Experiences of participation in shaping outcome refer to the why of action, much as consistency refers to the what and load balance to the how. I can believe that I know what to do and that I can do it—but why should I? This motivational component of the SOC, meaningfulness, grows out of a history of life experiences in which

> we have taken part in choosing to undergo that experience, in judging whether the rules of the game are legitimate, and in solving the problems and tasks posed by the experience. When others decide everything for us . . . we are reduced to being objects. A world thus experienced as being indifferent to what we do comes to be seen as a world devoid of meaning.
>
> (p. 92)

Two points must be emphasized. First, note that I did not write "decided, controlled, chosen" but rather "taken part". The part may even be subsidiary, as in an experience shaped by child and parent, or worshipper and the deity. Second, it may be that for the adolescent worshippers of Ayn Rand, or even Kobasa's fully authentic persons, it is enough for the actor to decide that the activity chosen is worthy. For most of us, it is crucial that the activity be socially valued. The housewife, I wrote (p. 93), "has decision-making power with respect to process and product in a sphere that, in Western societies, is not held to be of much account".

Sources of SOC-enhancing experiences

The last sentence above expresses my approach to the question of sources. The psychologist, taking either a depth, life history, or a social-interactional approach, may ask: To what extent are the patterned life experiences of this individual characterized by consistency, load balance, and participation in socially valued decision-making? The anthropologist may use the same criteria in analyzing cultures and subcultures. And, further, those engaged in action, whether on the individual, group, institutional, or societal level, may use the same guidelines (assuming, of course, that they are persuaded about the cogency of the SOC well-being hypothesis). As a sociologist, my primary concern is at the structural level: To what extent do the institutionalized roles, from childhood through old age, shaped by the nature of the society in which they are rooted, facilitate such experiences? Needless to say, the different perspectives, using the same criteria, can only enrich one another.

Largely, though not exclusively, taking the structural approach, I have sought to consider the life cycle in terms of these three criteria (pp. 94–118). Rather than seek to compress these pages into a few lines, let me suggest the flavor by selected quotations, leaving the rest to the reader's imagination.

- [Rejecting an argument that there is inherent structure in the world for the child to discover] For the three-year-old left in the care of her somewhat older sibling while her mother is at work, playing in a dilapidated tenement dwelling, with a succession of "fathers", the "inherent structure" is not readily apparent.
- When parents reward (or punish) one kind of behavior, teachers another, playmates a third, and the mass media a fourth—sexual behavior is perhaps the most dramatic example in contemporary Western cultures—it is hard to be sanguine about the chances for consistent life experiences.
- But consider the boy who has grown up in a childhood of age-graded continuity in a pleasant upper middle-class suburb . . . A wide variety of challenging legitimate opportunities . . . experiments . . . are smilingly and tolerantly criticized . . . Reed College . . . Peace Corps . . . Harvard Law School.
- [Noting alternative cultural paths to a strong SOC] For the Mormon adolescent in Provo, the Jewish boy or girl in orthodox Williamsburg, or the Komsomol youngster in Kiev, life is a rich tapestry of myth, ritual, and models . . . For a large number of the world's adolescents, however . . . life is a constant reminder of a world that is alien, hostile, incomprehensible, and absurd . . . [There is] one further alternative: the world of fundamentalist apocalypse . . . A special ethic of redemption, self-sacrifice, and identification emerges . . . The experiences . . . are dramatically consistent, provide a load balance, and very much involve participation in socially valued decision making . . . They become the Bolshevik commissars and the yogi, the mullahs and the mafiosi, the police torturers and the professional terrorists—all, I am afraid, moving from an adolescent to an adult strong SOC.
- Not only does the housewife not "work"; when she does work . . . she most often works in a disvalued female job . . . economic dependence of the housewife on her husband . . . the cultural definition of the woman as serving the needs, sexual and otherwise, of her master.

And, at greater length, since I consider the adult work role the most decisive setting in shaping life experiences:

- involvement in enterprises culturally valued or regarded as heroic [World War II vs. Vietnam; the pioneering enterprise of Israeli kibbutzim] . . . "joy and pride in work" . . . [as] expressed in the resources (power, rewards, prestige) allocated by the society to the collectivity . . . [and] the individual worker . . . Discretionary freedom is . . . taken to refer to the decision latitude of the individual worker [but also] in the collective context of most work . . . one's voice in the overall production process . . . In most work settings we can only feel that we work well when we perceive that those with whom we are interdependent also work well . . . chronic or frequently repeated acute overload . . . we are seldom called on to exercise our abilities or to actualize our potentials . . . [Coser's] structured role complexity which is the counterpart to Kohn's concept of substantive job complexity . . . a work condition so obvious in its significance that we often tend to disregard it: job security [of the individual, the section and the enterprise] . . . the nature of social relations in the work group . . . shared values, a sense of group identification, and clear normative expectations.

Subsequently, I considered, in the same terms, the life experiences in adult nonoccupational roles. At times, such as with the roles of female, ethnic, or racial minority status, these may transcend the importance of the work role, though most often the two role sets reinforce each other. The chapter concludes with a discussion of the dynamics of the SOC in later adult years. Having evolved a strong SOC by one's thirties, I suggested, allows one to continue to choose and to create life experiences of consistency, load balance, and participation, maintaining its strength. On the other hand, I predicted that those with a weak SOC will continue to be subjected to debilitating experiences. The disparity between the two will, then, increase.

A note on values

Though marginal to the present inquiry, I find it essential to point to an important difference between the SOC on the one hand and SE, LOC, and HARD. They all share a prediction to a causal relationship with well-being and wise health behavior. There is little doubt, however, that being high on SE, responsible internality, and, above all, being authentic and high on HARD are seen by Bandura, Rotter, Kobasa, and their colleagues (as well as by myself) as desirable dispositions in and of themselves, over and above their functional consequences. I would even go so far as to suggest that they may even be seen as morally good. (In my more cynical moments, I cannot help but think that it is so nice that what is good and admirable is also good for the health.)

But consider the quotation above referring to commissars, mullahs, and terrorists. I have repeatedly said that there are many cultural roads to a strong SOC. Some of these I despise and hate. Others (such as religiosity) I can respect but would not accept for myself. There are many people who I see as lovely, but have a weak SOC; others, with a strong SOC, I cannot stand. Health is but one value, and not necessarily the supreme one. The structural realities which promote salutogenic strengths for some may well not be identical with, and may even contradict, the realities which foster such values as equality, compassion, solidarity, and freedom.

A BRIEF ATTEMPT AT INTEGRATION

In this final section, I will seek to use the hints, suggestions, ideas, and hypotheses advanced above in a perhaps audacious attempt at the beginning of a construction of a single intellectual scaffolding to answer the problem posed by the chapter title, a structure strong enough to hold the core of all four constructs with as little procrustean distortion as possible. If in doing so I misinterpret the work of others, my apologies.

I would like to suggest that the scaffold be built in terms of systems theory and its core idea, information processing.[1] In brief, the individual is seen (1) as a system linked to/isolated from suprasystems, (2) from which information/noise is received, (3) which messages are internally integrated/undeciphered,

(4) who sends information/noise to the suprasystems, (5) which provides feedback to/ignores the messages. It is, however, crucial to add, particularly in the present context, a further concept from systems theory applied to people. In this view, the human being is a self-organizing, variable-boundary, or autopoietic system. This refers to the capacity of human beings to transform themselves and their environments to a more complex level of integration. By presenting these five elements and autopoietic transformation, I believe that I will provide a framework within which the SE, LOC, HARD, and SOC constructs can comfortably be accommodated and which suggests a systematic understanding of their sources.

The Self and the Environment: Linkage vs. Isolation

Human history has known isolated monasteries and communes. But even Saint Anthony had visitors and visitations. Commune members buy petrol and read newspapers. Almost all of us very much live in the world. This is a basic assumption of all who deal with the stress process, so obvious that it most often goes unstated. We move on to the complex issues of information *processing*. Bandura assumes that tasks are continually set by the environment; Rotter, that events continually occur; I, that stressors are omnipresent. Even Kobasa takes for granted that we always face challenges (or burdens). These are not, however, simply facts of life. I suggest that such linkages are the *sine qua non*, the essential prerequisite for all salutogenic strengths. Of course there are also stimuli from the inner environment. We can, however, agree that developmentally, without bonding and attachment, there is no survival. In adulthood, a prophet in the wilderness, obeisant only to the inner voice or the voice of God, may be an admirable figure; she or he more often knows despair and suffering than well-being.

Do, however, all of us live in the world? The relevant cultural-structural questions, I suggest, are how a society defines deviance and the extent to which it incorporates, tolerates, or extrudes those it does define as deviant. The non-persons, the physically and emotionally disabled, the cognitively handicapped, the homeless, the isolated elderly, the stigmatized, have, to a considerable degree, no links to the world around them. Messages are simply not sent to them, other than "you do not really exist for us; you may be objects to be maltreated, exploited or even cared for, but you do not count". Note that I do not include minority groups, refugees, or immigrants, who often have a viable subculture and who do get messages from the broader system.

Environmental Input: Information vs. Noise

Let us assume that most of us are structurally linked to the world in which we live, that the environment does set demands upon us, that we have status and role sets, names recognized by others. The question then arises as to the substantive content of the messages. For the development and maintenance of a salutogenic strength, this content must have two qualities.

First, it must have some degree of clarity. A terrorizing environment, a suprasystem which sets inherently insoluble, simultaneously conflicting, or random, disconnected problems before one makes it impossible to know what to do. It is most important to note that these no-win situations, in which the messages are noise, include those which impose an overload of freedom and choice or, as Etzioni (in Geyer, 1982, p. 157) put it, one finds oneself caught in an invisible nylon set. A Stalinist, perpetual achievement, or ultimate consumer society (or their equivalents on lower system levels such as the corporation, the school, or the family), much as they differ in many important ways, have in common that the messages they transmit are noise (except to the commissars and the few successes).

Second, it is not enough that the messages contain information, not noise. The messages must contain content which allows a moderate degree of freedom and choice, which does not impose by brute illegitimate force. If the action demanded promises to be pleasant or benign, so much the better. It also may be aversive and painful: becoming toilet-trained; paying taxes; undergoing surgery; assignment to a combat outfit. Even in such experiences, the salutogenic strength is enhanced, if one recognizes the legitimacy of the demand and sees the alternative as making less sense.

The two crucial structural issues here are (1) power relations between the actor and the environment, and (2) the degree of cultural integration. The greater the power, the more one can take part in accepting or rejecting demands. The more the integration, the greater the ease in making sense of the messages. These are the core problems of minority groups, immigrant workers, lower clas persons, illiterates . . . and of women. To the degree that they cannot escape into a viable subculture, they are bombarded by noise and by brutal information.

Internal Processing: Integrating vs. Chaos

Many readers will have objected, reading the previous section, that what is noise for one is information for another; what is freedom of choice for one is overload for another. I would not digress to the complex problem of false consciousness, and I make no claim that the boundaries are sharp. Nonetheless, I do think that there can be some consensus that some messsages are noise (the work conditions in Modern Times) or imposed by brute force (a lynching or unemployment). I suspect that one must be a devout deconstructionist, have a great deal of power, or rarely have suffered to insist that all life is in the eyes of the beholder.

Salutogenic strengths, then, are contingent upon repeated experiences of linkage and benevolent (or legitimate aversive) information input from the suprasystems. Such input, however, must be processed by the system. At this point, one must recall that messages also issue from within the system. They may be equally unclear, contradictory, brutally compelling, or illegitimate. Whatever the source of the information, processing must go on before behavior eventuates. The information must be sorted out, translated, coded, and integrated. The problem is not only what to do with noise and brutal information, but how to order and give priorities to the massive complexities of even benevolent information which bombards us. To the extent that we succeed in doing so, our strengths are enhanced. An experience of chaos (note, not failure) debilitates.

Are these not intrapsychic, non-structural processes? Yes, but only in the immediate sense. Information is processed in the context of history, of memory. The past is used to confront the present and build the future. From infancy, we accumulate knowledge, norms, skills, appetites, rules, values—a self, if one wills. It is this self which responds to a demand. Social structure and culture enter the picture at this point in two ways.

First, the self has been shaped by socializing agencies. It is from them that we have learned a language which allows us to interpret the information, culling rules which allow us to set priorities, and directives which shape behavior. What must be stressed in the present context is that the greater the internal integrated complexity which has been developed, the greater the capacity to handle complex input. Second, the demands whose sources are social can be consonant to a greater or lesser extent with the self as it is at that point in our histories.

A word must be added at this point with regard to the processing of noise and brutal information. Frankl (1963) has insisted that even in Auschwitz one can survive another day and perhaps another day by isolating oneself from the broader environment and drawing meaning from one's inner self and by sharing a crust with another. As a temporary measure, it is feasible. Other helpful temporary measures are adaptive (not unconscious defense) mechanisms (Kroeber, 1963), or turning to the strengths of others. These capacities of strength, however, have been socially constructed in the past, and can be worn away by continued exposure to a destructive environment.

For salutogenic strengths to develop and be maintained, then, one must have grown up and continue to live in a sociocultural setting which has equipped one with a stable, complex, rich internal set of hardware and software—or, as Koestler has put it (Antonovsky, 1987, p. 26), a set of fixed rules and flexible strategies.

Output: Availability of Resources

Assume, then, that one has the capacity to integrate the information, to make emotional and cognitive sense of its complexities, to bear with the noise and brutal messages, and to formulate a plan of action. This does not yet guarantee a salutogenic-enhancing experience. The plan must be carried out, translated into behavior. All plans, to be carried out, require resources: motivational, emotional, cognitive, and instrumental; personal and social. Presumably the selection of a plan by the self has been shaped by its assessment of the resources at its disposal. But the existence of behavioral inhibitions, of the capacity for self-deception, of rigid commitments, and of misjudgment of external resources may well doom a plan of action to failure. These at first would seem to be questions of personal characteristics. But aside from the fact that these have been socially shaped in the past, an additional question of resources arises. The more time one has to consider alternative plans, the more one can make tentative forays into reality-testing, the more one can formulate congintency plans, the better the chances of success. In large measure, it is the environment which will determine the degrees of freedom available to the actor in the course of carrying out a plan.

Feedback: Responsiveness vs. Rejection

The problem of output is the exact counterpart of that of input. In order for an experience to be salutogenic, the environment must carefully regard the actor's existence and respond benevolently. Once one acts, sends messages to the environment, the crucial question is twofold: Does it listen? And does it respond in the anticipated, desired way? Information is defined as a message which makes a difference. One's message may fall on deaf ears. Who has not known a child's message to be unheard by the parent? A cry for help disregarded? A hospital structure which doesn't hear a patient? A homeless person who is not seen by anyone? The suffering of a minority group which is unheeded? The problem, then, is of the power in the hands of the actor to force the environment to attend. The problem, however, may not be one of communication, but of a refusal to accept the message.

Every such message imposes a demand on the environment, much as every input message does. It may be regarded as chaotic, incomprehensible. The rejection may be phrased in terms of values, seeing the behavior as illegitimate, inappropriate, or irrational. Or, finally, the demand may simply be seen as requiring too great a price. In the last analysis, the issue again is one of the relative power of the actor to compel the desired response.

This, then, is the model I propose be used to understand the sources of salutogenic strengths. The assumption has been that salutogenic experiences, from early childhood, slowly build up a salutogenic personality orientation. At each stage of the process, structural factors are decisive in determining whether the experience will indeed be salutogenic. This brings us to a crucial final point, which rests on the concept of autopoiesis. Once a stable strength has come into being, the human system is capable of a reorganization of self onto a higher level of complexity, more capable of proaction. Which brings us to what would require another essay: the possibility of reorganization of the environmental suprasystem. Lest this sound too abstract, the reader may think of the move from adolescence to adulthood; divorce and remarriage; the retirement of a family; the creation of an international community; or building a viable democratic society in Czechoslovakia.

I have suggested that systems theory could accommodate the SE, LOC, HARD, and SOC constructs, and advance understanding of the sources of these salutogenic strengths. Bandura, Rotter, Kobasa, and I would not be equally happy with this approach. Kobasa might be most attracted by autopoiesis; Bandura, by internal processing; Rotter, by information output; I, by system–suprassystem integration and feedback. These are, however, complementary emphases. None of us has the full answer. I have tried to learn from each, to take us a step forward toward this inherently unachievable answer.

NOTE

1 In writing this section, I have been influenced by several works unknown, I believe, to most stress researchers, which I would highly recommend: Geyer's (1982) study of de-alienation; Gardner's (1985) attempt at integrating developments in the cognitive sciences; Maturana and Varela's (1987) work on biological systems; and Katakis's (1990) discussion of the self-referential conceptual system. It is perhaps not accidental that an Israeli medical sociologist would bring the work of a Dutch sociologist, an American psychologist, a South American biologist-physicist team, and a Greek family therapist to the attention of mostly Anglo-Saxon readers.

REFERENCES

Albee, G. W. (1980). A competency model to replace the defect model. In L. A. Bond and J. C. Rosen (eds) *Competence and Coping during Adulthood*, University Press of New England, Hanover, NH, pp. 75–104.

Antonovsky, A. (1974). Conceptual and methodological problems in the study of resistance resources and stressful life events. In B. P. Dohrenwend and B. S. Dohrenwend (eds), Wiley, NY, pp. 245–58.

Antonovsky, A. (1979). *Health, Stress, and Coping*, Jossey-Bass, San Francisco.

Antonovsky, A. (1987). *Unraveling the Mystery of Health*, Jossey-Bass, San Francisco.

Antonovsky, A. (1990). A somewhat personal odyssey in studying the stress process, *Stress Medicine*, **6**, 71–80.

Antonovsky, A. and Sourani, T. (1988). Family sense of coherence and family adaptation, *Journal of Marriage and the Family*, **50**, 79–92.

Bandura, A. (1977). Self-efficacy: Toward a unifying theory of behavioral change, *Psychological Review*, **84**, 191–215.

Bandura, A. (1986). *Social Foundations of Thought and Action: A Social Cognitive Theory*, Prentice-Hall, Englewood Cliffs, NJ (Ch. 9, 'Self-Efficacy').

Bandura, A. (1988). Reflections on nonability determinants of competence. In J. Kolligan and R. J. Sternberg (eds) *Competence Considered: Perceptions of*

Competence and Incompetence Across the Life Span (offprint), Yale University Press, New Haven, pp. 1–36.

Bandura, A. (1989). Social cognitive theory, *Annals of Child Development*, **6**, 1–60.

Beardslee, W. R. (1989). The role of self-understanding in resilient individuals: The development of a perspective, *American Journal of Orthopsychiatry*, **59**, 266–78.

Bronfenbrenner, U. (1986). Ecology of the family as a context for human development: Research perspective, *Developmental Psychology*, **22**, 723–42.

Frankl, V. E. (1963). *Man's Search of Meaning: An Introduction to Logotherapy*, Washington Square Press, NY.

Gardner, H. (1985). *The Mind's New Science*, Basic Books, NY.

Garmezy, N. (1983). Stressors of childhood. In N. Garmezy and M. Rutter (eds) *Stress, Coping and Development in Children*, McGraw-Hill, NY, pp. 43–84.

Geyer, F. (1982). A General Systems approach to psychiatric and sociological de-alienation. In S. G. Shoham and A. Grahame (eds) *Alienation and Anomie Revisited*, Ramot Publishing, Tel Aviv, pp. 139–74.

Haines, P., McGrath, P. and Pirot, M. (1980). Expectations and persistence: An experimental comparison of Bandura and Rotter, *Social Behavior and Personality*, **8**, 193–201.

Katakis, C. (1990). The self-referential conceptual system: Towards an operational definition of subjectivity, *Systems Research*, **7**, 91–102.

Kemper, T. D. (1978). *A Social Interactional Theory of Emotions*, Wiley, NY.

Kobasa, S. C. (1979). Stressful life events, personality, and health, *Journal of Personality and Social Psychology*, **37**, 1–11.

Kobasa, S. C. (1982a). Commitment and coping in stress resistance among lawyers, *Journal of Personality and Social Psychology*, **42**, 707–17.

Kobasa, S. C. (1982b). The hardy personality: Toward a social psychology of stress and health. in J. Suls and G. Sanders (eds) *Social Psychology of Health and Illness*, Erlbaum, Hillsdale, NJ, pp. 3–33.

Kobasa, S. C. and Maddi, S. R. (1977). Existential personality theory. In R. Corsini (ed.) *Current Personality Theories*, T. F. Peacock, Itasca, Ill., pp. 399–466.

Kohn, M. L. (1989). Social structure and personality: A quintessentially sociological approach to social psychology, *Social Forces*, **68**, 26–33.

Kohn, M. (1990). Unresolved issues in the relationship between work and personality. In K. Erikson and S. P. Vallas (eds) *The Nature of Work: Sociological Perspectives*, Yale University Press, New Haven, pp. 36–68.

Kohn, M. L., Naoi, A., Slomczynski, K. M., Schoenbach, C. and Schooler, C. (1990). Position in the class structure and psychological functioning in the United States, Japan and Poland, *American Journal of Sociology*, **95**, 964–1008.

Kroeber, T. C. (1963). The coping functions of the ego mechanisms. In R. W. White (ed.) *The Study of Lives*, Aldine, Hawthorne, NY, pp. 178–99.

Lefcourt, H. M. (1976). *Locus of Control: Current Trends in Theory and Research*, Wiley, NY.

Lefcourt, H. M. (ed.) (1981). *Research with the Locus of Control Construct, Vol. 1: Assessment Methods*, Academic Press, NY.

Lefcourt, H. M. (ed.) (1983). *Research with the Locus of Control Construct, Vol. 2: Developments and Social Problems*, Academic Press, NY.

Lennon, M. C. (1989). Comment: The structural contexts of stress, *Journal of Health and Social Behavior*, **30**, 261–8.

Levenson, H. (1981). Differentiating among internality, powerful others, and chance. In H. M. Lefcourt (ed.) *Research with the Locus of Control Construct, Vol. 1: Assessment Methods*, Academic Press, NY, pp. 15–63.

Maturana, H. and Varela, F. (1987). *The Tree of Knowledge: The Biological Roots of Human Understanding*, New Science Library, Boston.

Merton, R. K. (1957). Social structure and anomie. In his *Social Theory and Social Structure*, Free Press, NY.

Merton, R. K. and Kitt, A. (1950). Contributions to the theory of reference group behavior. In R. K. Merton and P. F. Lazarsfeld (eds) *Continuities in Social Research*, Free Press, Glencoe, Ill., pp. 40–105.

Mirowsky, J. and Ross, C. E. (1990). Control or defense? Depression and the sense of control over good and bad outcomes, *Journal of Health and Social Behavior*, **31**, 71–86.

Nowicki, S. and Duke, M. P. (1983). The Nowicki–Strickland life-span locus of control scales: Construct validation. In H. M. Lefcourt (ed.) *Research with the Locus of Control Construct, Vol. 2*, Academic Press, NY, pp. 9–51.

Orr, E. and Westman, M. (1990). Does hardiness moderate stress and how?. In M. Rosenbaum (ed.) *Learned Resourcefulness: On Coping Skills, Self-control and Adaptive Behavior*, Springer, NY, pp. 64–94.

Pearlin, L. I. (1989). The sociological study of stress, *Journal of Health and Social Behavior*, **30**, 241–56.

Pearlin, L. I. and Schooler, C. (1978). The structure of coping, *Journal of Health and Social Behavior*, **19**, 2–21.

Phares, E. J. (1976). *Locus of Control in Personality*, General Learning, Morristown, NJ.

Rosow, I. (1976). Status and role change through the life span. In R. H. Binstock and E. Shanas (eds) *Handbook of Aging and the Social Sciences*, Van Nostrand, NY, pp. 457–82.

Rotter, J. B. (1966). Generalized expectancies for internal versus external control of reinforcement, *Psychological Monographs*, **80**, No. 1.

Rotter, J. B. (1975). Some problems and misconceptions related to the construct of internal versus external control of reinforcement, *Journal of Consulting and Clinical Psychology*, **43**, 56–67.

Saltzer, E. B. (1982). The relationship of personal efficacy beliefs to behavior, *British Journal of Social Psychology*, **21**, 213–21.

Sarason, S. (1981). An asocial psychology and a misdirected clinical psychology, *American Psychologist*, **36**, 827–36.

Scott, R. A. (1969). *The Making of Blind Men*, Russell Sage, NY.

Seligman, M. E. P. (1975). *Helplessness: On Depression, Development, and Death*, Freeman, San Francisco.

Sherer, M., Maddux, J. E., Mercandante, B., Prentice-Dunn, S., Jacobs, B. and Rogers, R. W. (1982). The self-efficacy scale: construction and validation, *Psychological Reports*, **51**, 663–71.

Smith, T. W. and Anderson, N. B. (1986). Models of personality and disease: An interactional approach to Type A behavior and cardiovascular risk, *Journal of Personality and Social Psychology*, **50**, 1166–73.

Strickland, B. R. (1989). Internal–external control expectancies: From *contingency* to *creativity*, *American Psychologist*, **44**, 1–12.

Wallston, B. S. and Wallston, K. A. (1981). Health locus of control scales. In H. M. Lefcourt (ed.) *Research with the Locus of Control Construct, Vol. 1: Assessment Methods*, Academic Press, NY, pp. 189–243.

Wood, C. (1987). Buffer of hardiness: An interview with Suzanne C. Ouellette Kobasa, *Advances, Institute for the Advancement of Health*, **4**(1), 37–45.

PART III

Major Personality and Individual-differences Variables

Chapter 5

Demographic Aspects of Stress

Rachel Jenkins, Institute of Psychiatry,
London, UK

INTRODUCTION

Demographic variations in rates of stress and stress outcomes are important because of the epidemiological clues they give us about the origins of stress and about protective factors. They are also important for practical reasons. For example, looking specifically at occupational stress, it is of practical significance to discover what effects may be anticipated from the influx of women into the workforce, from a predominantly older work-force and from a predominantly urban work-force.

Stress

The concept of stress is confused and ill-defined (Hinkle, 1973; Mason, 1975; Selye, 1975). It has been used historically both to describe an adverse force or influence external to the individual and to describe the internal state induced within the individual by the external adversity. The term is used here in its sense of external hardship, adversity and affliction (Oxford English Dictionary). Operationally, it includes both acute unpleasant life events and chronic social difficulties.

Life events have been demonstrated to precede physical and mental illness in vulnerable indivdiuals (Dohrenwend and Dohrenwend, 1974). However, interpretation of these findings is difficult despite complex methods of statistical analysis (e.g. Paykel et al., 1980; Brown, 1974; Tennant and Bebbington, 1978). It should always be borne in mind that the correlation coefficients between life events and mental illness are small (between 0.20 and 0.29).

Chronic social difficulties such as financial hardship, social isolation, migration and low social class have been shown to be associated with an increased prevalence of mental illness although the causal interpretation of these relationships is by no means clear (e.g. Liem and Liem, 1978).

Personality and Stress: Individual Differences in the Stress Process. Edited by C.L. Cooper and R. Payne
© 1991 John Wiley & Sons Ltd

Support

The concept of social support has been conceived as information leading the subject to believe that he or she is cared for and loved, to believe that he or she belongs to a network of communication and mutual obligation (Cobb, 1976). Such support is accessible to an individual through social ties to other individuals, groups and the larger community. Evidence of the effects of social support on health exists and has been extensively reviewed (e.g. Gore, 1978; House, 1981; Payne and Jones, 1987). Social support can affect normal growth, mortality, degenerative and infectious diseases and mental illness.

House (1981) has extended Cobb's definition of social support to include:

(1) emotional support (esteem, affection, trust, concern, listening);
(2) appraisal support (affirmation, feedback, social comparison) which is associated with information relevant to self-evaluation;
(3) informational support (advice, suggestion, directives, information); and
(4) instrumental support (aid in kind, money, labour, time, modifying environment).

The precise nature of the interaction between stress and support is in debate and remains unsolved. Two major alternatives have been identified. First, stressful life events may cause and precipitate illness while social support decreases the incidence of illness, and each acts independently of the other. Several studies (e.g. Andrews et al., 1978; Miller and Ingham, 1976) present evidence supporting this hypothesis that stress and support act in opposite directions and independently of each other. They find that good crisis support and coping behaviour do not have an interactive effect in reducing the impact of high life-event stress; instead, they are independently related to neurosis.

A second alternative is that social support may act by decreasing the likelihood of encountering stressful life events (e.g. Myers, Lindenthal and Pepper, 1971) or by decreasing the impact of life events (e.g. Kessler, 1979; Nuckolls, Cassel and Kaplan, 1972; Brown and Harris, 1978). Such an interactive effect has been widely discussed (e.g. Henderson, 1977) but significant methodological criticisms remain.

An additional effect which may complicate matters is that stressful life events may elicit social support which then protects against illness either in an independent or interactive fashion. Furthermore, the two major alternatives are by no means necessarily mutually exclusive. Research in this field has been bedevilled by methodological problems of measurement and research design. There are further confounding factors which need to be kept in mind. For example, the association between poor support and psychiatric morbidity may be exaggerated by neurotic people down-rating their social milieu, or it may be the consequence of long-term illness, with social support melting away in the face of prolonged neurotic behaviour. This underlines the need for prospective studies.

All the studies mentioned so far concentrate on the occurrence of psychological illness rather than on its course and outcome. The few studies that relate to prognosis demonstrate that social support plays a key role in outcome. (e.g. Mann, Jenkins and Belsey, 1981)

The Problem of Social Conditions to the Individual

It has long been argued that people react to their "life situations" or social conditions in terms of the meaning of these situations to them. (Hinkle, 1973) The individual's reaction to stress may depend upon the significance of the event to that person, his or her appraisal of the circumstances surrounding that event, his or her prior experience with that event and with symbolically related events. A number of studies have indicated the wide variability in the magnitude assigned to different events both by individuals and by groups of individuals (e.g. Americans or Japanese). Ratings of an event tend to differ between subjects who have experienced it and those who have not. Nevertheless, Holmes and Rahe's schedule is based on average ratings of events by a sample drawn from the general population. This approach has been extensively criticised, and it has been suggested that the subject's own ratings of the stressfulness of events he or she experienced should be used (Vinokur and Selzer, 1975; Hurst, Jenkins and Rose, 1978). It is likely that such subjective ratings are a better indicator of the possible impact of a stressful event than the assignment of an average score.

While it is recognised in the life-event literature that events may be desirable or undesirable (e.g. Myers et al., 1971), the implicit assumption in the literature in social support is that items deemed by the researcher to be supports are in fact supportive, e.g. family networks, although it is known that in some circumstances the presence of such close ties, with their consequent demands, may be deleterious to the prognosis of certain illnesses. It has been suggested that it is the quality of the supporting emotional relationships and their significance to the individual rather than the quantity of help available that is the principal determinant of effective crisis support (Henderson, 1977; Chan, 1977).

Stress Outcomes

Stress may have consequences for both illness itself and illness behaviours. It is crucial to make this distinction between the empirical notion of illness as the combination of observed symptoms and signs (measured by questionnaires and standardised interviews by appropriately trained personnel) and illness behaviour which comprises the actions taken by the individual on account of his or her illness, and which include the desire for therapy ("therapeutic concern") experienced by the individual and his or her social environment, and the "medical concern" experienced by the doctor. Illness behaviour therefore includes variables such as self-assessment of ill-health, general-practice consultations, consumption of over-the-counter medication, consumption of prescribed medication and sickness absence (both certified and uncertified).

Early studies of stress outcomes have tended to infer the presence of illness by measuring illness behaviours such as sickness absence. However, the relationship between illness and illness behaviour is not a direct one-to-one relationship, and it is now well known that many complex, social, cultural and demographic factors contribute to the causation of sickness absence besides illness *per se* (Johns and Nicholson, 1982). We therefore find that the demographic aspects of illness are not necessarily the same as the demographic aspects of illness behaviour.

Theoretical and Methodological Issues

In stress research the concepts of stress, coping and well-being are frequently confounded (Edwards and Cooper, 1988). The authors give the example in life-events research, where some "stressful" life events may also be construed as an inability to cope (e.g. divorce). Personal illness may be regarded as a stressful life event or as a health outcome. Furthermore, some definitions of stress, such as those which describe stress as a situation where demands exceed abilities (e.g. French, Rodgers and Cobb, 1974), confound stress with the inability to cope. It is therefore essential, in stress research, for authors to clearly present the theoretical model which they are investigating.

SEX DIFFERENCES

It has been argued that women, by virtue of the roles they occupy, experience more life events and chronic social stresses, and less social support than men, and that this differential exposure to risk factors explains women's greater vulnerability to depression.

Sex Differences in Social Stress

The empirical data available so far suggest that there is no difference in the rates at which men and women experience acute life events or adversity (Meyers et al., 1971; Dekker and Webb, 1974; Newman, 1975, Henderson et al., 1980; Markush and Favero, 1974). However, the possibility remains to be tested that women in general may experience more undesirable life events by virtue of their low socio-economic status overall (Myers, Lindenthal and Pepper, 1975), since there is much evidence that women in general enjoy lower status than men, both at home and at work, and frequently earn less even when in comparable jobs (Office of Population Censuses and Surveys, *Social Trends*). There is no evidence that life events have more impact on women than on men (Paykel, Prusoff and Uhlenhuth, 1971; Personn, 1980). However, there is evidence that women experience more chronic social stress than men. Radloff and Rae (1979) reported that women were more exposed than men to low education, low income, low occupational status, fewer leisure activities, and more current and recent physical illness.

Furthermore, there is evidence that men and women respond differently to the same number of stresses (e.g. Russo, 1985). In addition, there is ample evidence for sex differences in stress-induced physiological responses (e.g. Frankenhauser, 1983; Stoney, Davis and Matthew, 1985) and also for differences in the ways people cope cognitively, emotionally and behaviourally in response to stress.

According to Kessler, Price and Wartman (1985) gender differences in health are to a large extent attributable to differences in the appraisal of stresses and the selection of coping strategies.

Vingerhoets and Van Heck (1990) explored gender differences in coping and found that males preferred problem-focused coping strategies, planned and rational actions, positive thinking, personal growth and humour, daydreaming and fantasies. Women preferred emotion-focused coping solutions, self-blame, expression of emotions, seeking of social support and wishful thinking/emotionality. The same authors also found that men and women do not differ in terms of the amount of stressful events experienced.

Sex Differences in Social Support

There are few studies which specifically address the question of whether women experience less social support then men. Miller and Ingham (1976) found that causal, less intimate friends as well as intimates afforded protection from developing illness, and that "psychological symptom levels probably vary with social support even when there is no serious life event present". It is therefore apparent that contacts with colleagues at work may also be supportive to the individual, and it may be that the housewife often experiences relative isolation in the home, experiencing less frequent daily verbal exchanges with other individuals than does her counterpart in the office.

Henderson et al. (1979) found that males reported more availability of social integration than females, while females scored higher on the quality or adequacy of the social integration. Females scored more on availability of attachment than males, but there was no sex difference on the quality or adequacy of the attachment. It was the author's view that special attention should be paid to those social bonds which promote self-esteem—both the esteem of self in terms of appearance, abilities, competence and position in a dominance hierarchy, as well as the degree to which one believes one is lovable to others. The question is, therefore, whether such self-esteem is more likely to be derived from social integration within a group, while the extent to which one believes one is lovable may be obtained from both kinds of social bond. If the important aspects of self-esteem are more likely to be derived from social integration, then Henderson's finding that males reported quantitatively more availability of social integration than females may be of crucial significance to the question of whether women experience less social support than men. While females report a better quality of social integration, in terms of self-esteem thus engendered, quality may not make up for quantity. Henderson found that for minor psychiatric morbidity social integration had a stronger association with symptom level than did attachment for women. For men, the strength of the association of symptom level with social integration and with attachment was the same. Henderson concluded that "social bonds" appear to be related to morbidity in a manner independent of the challenge of adversity". While these primary questions afford some hope of elucidating the nature of the sex difference in the prevalence of minor psychiatric morbidity, it is clear that further work is required. In the mean time the evidence suggests that women do experience more chronic social stresses, e.g. low occupational status and low income, than men and also experience less availability of social integration—a factor with a strong negative association with minor psychiatric morbidity.

Brugha et al. (1990) found that the explained variance in recovery from depression due to social support was equal in men and women. But according to subset analyses, the aspects of personal relationships and perceived support that predict recovery in men and women appear to be different. In women, the significant predictors of recovery appeared to be the number of primary group members named and contacted, and satisfaction with social support, while in men it appeared to be living as married, and the number of non primary group social contacts named as acquaintances or friends.

Sex Differences in Illness

Men and women certainly differ in terms of the balance of role obligations in the occupational, marital and parental domain. If these distinctive role patterns are responsible for gender differences in health, it should be the case that where gender equality is achieved, gender differences in health should be reduced. Studies of men and women in similarly responsible and demanding jobs do seem to find a reduction in the substantially lower mortality rates among women (e.g. Detre et al., 1987). Jenkins (1985), in a study of young male and female executive officers, found that there was no sex difference in prevalence of minor psychiatric morbidity. Other studies of true homogeneous samples have found the same thing (e.g. Parker, 1979; Golin and Hartz, 1977; Hammen and Padesky, 1977).

A paradox which has attracted considerable attention ever since John Graunt, the founder demography, commented on it in his "Natural and political observations", published in 1662, is that while women attend doctors more often than men, their life expectancy is no less than that of men (indeed, is now about 8% longer). Graunt concluded that either the women were generally cured by their physicians or that the men suffered from untreated morbidity. In Western countries, where women's life expectancy is greater than men's, women are nonetheless reported to suffer more illness than men, are higher users of medical services and prescriptions, and take more time off work for sickness (Verbrugge, 1976; Nathanson, 1977; Wingard, 1984; Verbrugge, 1985; Strickland, 1988; Jenkins, 1985).

Table 5.1 illustrates this paradox with figures taken from UK sources. It can be seen that, while females' life expectancy in England and Wales exceeds that of men by six years, women consult general practitioners (GPs) more often than men, they take prescribed drugs more often than men, they take more frequent spells of sickness absence (although the total duration of the certified absence is not greater) and, despite attending out-patient facilities in roughly equal numbers, women are admitted to hospital more often than men. In general it can be said that women suffer more from psychological distress and minor somatic disorders, whereas men seem to be especially

Table 5.1   A comparison of life expectancy, certified sickness absence and use of health services for all disorders (physical and mental)

	Males	Females
Life expectancy [1] (years at age 0); England and Wales 1983–5	71.8	77.6
Hospital discharges[2] (rates per 1000); England and Wales 1985	101	110
Persons making use of out-patient[3] facilities (rates per 1000); GB 1984 in 3 months reference period	130	130
Persons making physician[4] visits in a 14-day reference period (rates per 1000); GB 1984	110	150
Persons (%) consulting a doctor[5] in last 14 days who obtained a prescription from the doctor; GB 1984	74%	74%
Persons (%) absent from work[6] because of sickness in a 7 day reference period; GB 1984	4.5%	5.1%

[1] Health and Personal Social Services Statistics for England 1987, p.14.
[2] Health and Personal Social Services Statistics for England 1987, p. 74.
[3] General Household Survey, p. 135.
[4] General Household Survey, p. 139.
[5] General Household Survey, p. 140.
[6] Central Statistical Office (1988) *Social trends 18*, London: HMSO: 74.

vulnerable to life-threatening diseases, e.g. myocardial infarction and cancer (e.g. Rice et al., 1984; Bush and Barrett-Connor, 1985).

Looking now at mental illness, GPs diagnose more episodes of mental illness in women than in men, women take more certified sickness absence for mental illness than do men (both in terms of frequency and duration) and women have more psychiatric admissions to hospital than do men. These comparisons are illustrated in Table 5.2. When specific diagnostic categories of mental illness are examined, using the International Classification of Diseases the picture becomes rather more subtle. Table 5.3 presents the general practice episode rates for psychiatric illness and the admission rates to

Table 5.2   A comparison of certified sickness absence and use of health service for mental disorders in men and woman

	Males	Females
Hospital admissions per[1] 100000 background population England and Wales	364	482
General practice episode rates [2] per 100000	3540	11270
Certified incapacity[3] for mental disorder 1985 { days	292000	198
{ spells	4512	3877

[1] Health and Personal Social Services Statistics, 1987, p. 130.
[2] Morbidity Statistics from General practice – Third National Morbidity Survey 1987, p. 196.
[3] Personal communication, Robert Chew, OHE, 1987.
Not all employed women are contributing to national insurance and hence included in the DHSS incapacity figures.

Table 5.3   Comparison of recorded episode rates of psychiatric illness in general practice and admission rates to psychiatric hospitals for the year 1982 in men and women (rates quoted per 100 000 population England and Wales)

IDD category	Episode rate recorded in general practice		All psychiatric admissions	
	M	F	M	F
All mental disorders 290–319	5540	11270	330	461
Senile and presenile dementia 290	10	30	27	46
Organic psychosis 291	10	10	2	1
Schizophrenia, schizoaffective and paranoid states 295–297	170	210	60	58
Affective psychosis 296	140	280	32	67
Other, and unspecified psychoses 292–4, 298, 299	60	100	24	36
Psychoneuroses 300	3210	8390	25	51
Personality disorders and sexual deviation 301–2, 307–9, 312–5	260	250	29	33
Alcoholism and drug dependency 303–4	260	140	17	41
Other psychiatric conditions 306, 310, 316	1750	3450	1	1
Mental retardation 317–9	40	40	1	1

Table 5.4 Explanations of sex differences in illness

A. Constitutional differences
(1) Genes
(2) Hormones
B. Environmental differences
(1) Social stress
(2) Social support
C. Sex role differences and their
(1) Interaction with constitution
(2) Interaction with environment
(3) Effect on reporting behaviour and diagnostic habit

---

psychiatric hospitals for the year 1972 by diagnosis and sex. Males predominate in the areas of alcoholism and personality disorders. Sex differences in reported rates of schizophrenia are negligible. However, for affective psychoses and the psychoneuroses, women predominate over men.

These sex differences in illness have been variously ascribed to a number of explanations which may be categorised as in Table 5.4.

These theories have been considered in relation to mental health in Jenkins (1985), who concluded that:

> Clearly the relative importance of each of these variables is likely to vary from illness to illness. For mental health, we now have evidence that both manic depressive psychosis and schizophrenia have a multifactorial aetiology, involving both genetic and environmental factors. Both diseases are so severe that sex differences in reporting behaviour and diagnostic habits have minimal impact on reported rates. However for minor psychiatric morbidity, the depressions and anxiety states, the evidence for a genetic aetiology is small. While there is evidence that changes in gonadal hormones are sometimes linked to mood changes, there is no direct evidence that reproductive physiology is responsible for women's excess of reported depression. The evidence for the importance of environmental stress and support in the aetiology of minor psychiatric morbidity is much stronger, although the variance explained by such factors is not large.

This chapter will therefore concentrate on environmental factors, rather than the biological factors of genes and hormones responsible for sex differences in illness. Sex differences in stress and support have already been discussed above. Differences in sex roles and their effects on health will be discussed below.

Sex Roles and Their Influence on Constitutional and Environmental Vulnerability to Illness, and on Reporting Behaviour

Sex roles and their interaction with constitution

It has been suggested that sex differences in the early upbringing and social environment of males and females place a permanent stamp on the phenotype of the individual, thus affecting constitutional vulnerability to psychiatric ill-ness in adult life (Chesler, 1971, 1972; Chodorow, 1974). The learned helpless-ness model proposes that helplessness is the salient characteristic of depression and that it results from learning that one's actions do not produce predictable responses (Seligman, 1975). Cochrane and Stopes (1980) aregued that women are traditionally more sheltered than boys, women have less initiative in selecting their spouses than do men, their life-styles face more disruption with the advent of children, and they have to follow their husbands geographically and socially. This relatively low ability to influence their en-vironment may make females more prone to "learned helplessness" than males.

Evidence certainly exists to support the notion of the sex stereotype belief about male and female abilities (Williams and Best, 1982), and the view that such stereotypes are influential in the development of male and female abil-ities (Rheingold and Cook, 1975). There is some evidence that stereotypical female abilities encourage low self-esteem, but how far this phenomenon accounts for the reported sex differences in the rate of illness has yet to be assessed.

Sex roles and their interaction with environment

Regardless of the influence of early environment, it has been suggested that sex differences in adult sex roles lead to men and women being differentially exposed to environmental risk factors. This is discussed below under Employ-ment and Marital Status.

Sex roles and their effect on reporting behaviour and diagnostic habits

This section examines the extent to which sex roles and sex stereotypes influ-ence the illness behaviour of men and women, and the diagnostic habits of physicians. Four major hypotheses are examined. First, it has been suggested that women's traditional sex role as homemaker is more compatible with adoption of the sick role (visiting a doctor, taking medication, spending time in bed) than is men's traditional sex role as breadwinner (Mechanic, 1965; Glaser, 1970). There is vigorous opposition to this view. Parsons and Fox (1952) suggested that the nature of a woman's household and family respon-sibility makes her illness more disturbing to family equilibrium than illness in her husband. Marcus and Seeman (1981) examined data from the Los An-geles Health Survey and demonstrated that role obligations do explain male–female differences in illness behaviour, but not in illness *per se.*

Second, it has been suggested that differences in sex stereotypes result in men and women being socialised into different patterns of perception of illness and help-seeking behaviour based on those stereotypes (Mechanic,

1964). There is speculation that women more readily translate diffuse feelings of psychological distress into conscious recognition of themselves as having emotional problems (Verbrugge, 1979).

Several studies have suggested that it is culturally acceptable for women to be expressive about their difficulties, while men are expected to bear their problems with greater self-control and to be reluctant to admit symptoms of distress (Komarovsky, 1946; Phillips and Segal, 1969; Cooperstock, 1971). Psychological studies have indicated that women are more likely than men to disclose intimate information about themselves, especially unpleasant feelings such as anxieties and worries (Horwitz, 1977; Briscoe, 1982). But this hypothesis was rejected by Clancy and Gove (1974) who presented data showing that the higher rates of symptoms reported by women reflect actual differences in symptoms and not the greater willingness of women to discuss their problems with others. Indeed, Clancy and Gove found that controlling for three forms of response bias (naysaying, perceived trait desirability and need for social approval) actually increased the difference between the sexes. Gove et al. (1976), on the other hand, found that controlling for response bias slightly diminished the differences between the sexes. Horwitz (1977) found that women in treatment were more likely than the men to recognise a psychiatric problem in themselves (although all were attending for psychiatric treatment), were more likely to discuss these problems with other people and were more likely to have entered treatment voluntarily. Horwitz suggested that, since women discuss their problems more often among themselves (presumably a culturally learned pattern of behaviour), then their problems are more visible both to themselves and to others, and they are more likely to gain information concerning useful courses of action to obtain help.

Kessler, Brown and Broman (1981) found that women were significantly more likely than men to report having a problem, but that there were no consistent sex differences in the perception that help was needed to deal with it. Kessler and his colleagues therefore took the view that women were more likely than men to move towards obtaining psychiatric treatment only at the beginning of the help-seeking process, i.e. at the stage of problem recognition.

Third, it has been suggested that, because sex stereotypes exist, the social consequences of expression of symptoms differ between the sexes. Phillips (1964) presented subjects with descriptions of behaviour in which the disturbed individual was described as either a male or a female. He found that men were rejected more than women for descriptions of the same behaviour. Phillips argued on the basis of his study that illness is stigmatising for men but not so for women, and that, therefore, women are more willing to report symptoms at interview and are more likely to seek professional help for them. Unfortunately, although the majority of doctors are male, Phillips used only women as raters. These findings have received support from the studies of Broverman et al. (1970), Coie, Pennington and Buckley (1974) and Hammen and Peters (1977), although Yamamoto and Disney (1967), using the same methods as Phillips (1964), failed to find differences in the rejection of disturbed individuals on the basis of their reported sex.

Fourth, it has been suggested that sex stereotypes affect the diagnostic habits of physicians. Broverman et al. (1970) provided an empirical demonstration of a double standard of mental health among clinicians, and this finding has been replicated by Nowacki and Poe (1973). However, as Zeldow (1978) pointed out, double standards of optimal mental health do not necessarily imply that a differential assessment of the assessment of psychiatric symptomatology alone elicits differential assessment (Lewitties, Mosell and Simmons, 1973; La Torre, 1975; Zeldow, 1976). However, Coie, Pennington and Buckley (1974) found that, although females in general were not perceived as more mentally ill than males, greater psychological disorder was attributed to females for aggressive behaviour than to males, while greater pathology was attributed to males for somatic complaints than to females.

Although Broverman et al. (1970) showed that both male and female clinicians endorsed a double standard of mental health, there is no evidence from recent studies that judges of either sex are partisan towards their own kind (Kosherak and Masling, 1972; Lewitties, Mosell and Simmons, 1973; Schlosberg and Pietrofesa, 1973; Werner and Block, 1975; Zeldow, 1975).

Wilhelm and Parker studied teachers in 1989, expecting social role differences to have emerged in that period. In fact, using social role questionnaires, they had not done so, and in fact there were no sex differences in depressive episodes (suggesting the irrelevance of biological factors in determining any sex difference).

EMPLOYMENT STATUS

Employment status is a variable where difficulties arise when comparisons are made between the sexes because of the traditional separation of men's and women's roles. Men's employment status may be classified as full-time or unemployed, with tiny proportions being either in part-time employment or as homemakers. Women's employment status on the other hand, may be classified as full-time employment, part-time employment, unemployed or housewives, or some combination of housewife and one of the preceding categories. This means that considerable care must be exercised in designing studies and drawing the relevant comparisons. It is also important to remember that housewives actively seeking work may not always register as unemployed.

Employment Status and Women's Health

Two opposing views are to be found in the literature. The first is that employment in women increases their role obligations (since they usually still retain much of their homemaking tasks, if not all of them, in addition to their paid employment), and that this may cause overload which predisposes the women to more ill-health than her housewife counterpart. The other view is that employment increases affiliation and that this extra social support is protective against morbidity. In addition, the extra role obligations make it less likely that such employed women will adopt the sick role.

Certainly the relative availability of domestic support may differ between working men and working women. Metcalfe's study of managers showed that 90 per cent of married women had a partner in full-time employment, whereas only 25 per cent of married men had a partner in full-time employment. If working women also have to fulfil a domestic role, then home may represent a loss of personal time for women, whereas for men, home is a place of refuge, a place to relax and recharge the batteries.

Reasons Why Women May Have More Stress than Men at Work

Freeman, Logan and McCoy (1989) listed various reasons why women may experience more stress than men in occupational settings:

(1) the circumstances under which women enter or re-enter the labour force, including those wherein the husband is unemployed and a financial crisis exists;
(2) poor work conditions in which racial or sexual discrimination exists;
(3) lack of co-operation of family members in helping the woman cope with increased role responsibilities;
(4) women's individual development;
(5) prior experiences in coping with conflicting role demands;
(6) amount of consensus between her and spouse about decision to work, extent of role sharing, and satisfaction with quality of time available for primary role responsibilities.

These variables also interact with each other, e.g. some women may experience stress because they feel guilty about the quality of time spent in the parental role, and may therefore be less effective in encouraging their children to share work responsibilities around the house.

The presence of role models in family or at work can help to demonstrate how to role share or how to protect time for oneself.

Baruch, Biener and Barnett (1987) suggested that non-employed women experience greater stress than do employed women, asserting that the homemaker role makes greater psychological demands and gives less opportunity for control than does the employment role. These greater demands, coupled with less control, are hypothesised to lead to greater stress. Nelson and Quick (1985) took the opposite view, that employed women experience greater stress than both unemployed women and men, because of several unique stressors faced by employed women. These factors include the interface of marriage and work, social isolation, discrimination and stereotyping. However social isolation, discrimination and stereotyping may be said to be even more prominent in the housewife role.

Do men and women experience and manifest stress in the same way? Jick and Mitz (1985) suggested that stress manifested in women via depression and other emotional discomforts while men experienced coronary heart disease, liver cirrhosis and so on. Nelson and Quick thought that women experienced both physical and psychological stress. Meanwhile, Deaux (1984) suggested that little variance has been accounted for by sex in most areas of psychology.

Martocchio and O'Leary (1989) reported a meta-analysis of 15 studies that examined sex differences in occupational stress. Contrary to previous qualitative literature reviews, these empirical results indicate that there are no sex differences in psychological and physiological stress in occupational settings. There was also no support found for the idea that men and women experience stress differently (i.e. psychologically versus physiologically).

Jick and Mitz (1985) have also suggested that psychological stress is perceived stress, and physiological stress is manifested stress. This seems much too simplistic. Psychological stress is also manifested stress. It seems better to proceed on the assumption that there is both physical and mental stress and both psychological and physiological manifested stress. Martocchio and O'Leary (1989) suggested, that the important question is whether there are sex differences within perceived stress and within manifested stress, not whether the type of stress acts as a moderator variable in the sex–stress relationship.

Employment Status and Physical Health

Waldron (1976) reviewed evidence that employed women have lower rates of coronary heart disease and report fewer physical symptoms and fewer disability days than housewives. Waldron found that women with medically treated hypertension were more likely to be housewives. But among women not taking antihypertensives, high blood pressure was more common for women employed full time. The author therefore suggested that women who are employed full time are more likely to develop high blood pressure, but women who are currently employed may actually have lower morbidity since people who become ill also tend to leave their jobs. This illustrates the problems of interpretation associated with the issue of selection into the different employed statuses.

Welch and Booth (1977) studied a sample of 500 urban married women with children, and found that wives employed for more than a year were healthier than wives employed for less than a year and also healthier than housewives. Poor marital relationships and the absence of preschool children increased the health advantage of long-term employed wives over those in the housewife category. The occupational status of wife and husband did not materially change these health differences. The finding, that married women who had recently taken jobs were among the least healthy, does not support the proposition that only healthier women take up outside employment.

Employment Status and Suicide

Cumming, Lazer and Chisholm (1975) compared the suicide rates of married employed women with housewives in British Columbia in 1961 to test the proposition that the costs of working (role conflict and role overload) outweigh the economic and affiliative benefits. The authors found that married women who are not in the labour force have an excessive rate of suicide compared with those in the labour force in all age groups except the under 25s and the over 65s. This was unlikely to be due to selection factors (i.e. those who were psychologically ill were unable to work) because in the early 1960s a large proportion of married women did not have paid employment.

Occupational Type and Stress

The classical study design in occupational medicine is to establish differences in morbidity and mortality by type of occupation and place of work, and then research for environmental agents in the work-place which might explain these differences. Kasl (1988) has listed the conditions which assist the working of this strategy:

(1) minimal self-selection into occupations (e.g. prior health status and personal characteristics);
(2) the ability to identify and quantify the type and extent of exposure;
(3) case finding should not rely on medical records which are biased by factors which influence seeking and receiving treatment, but should cover the whole population under stady without bias;
(4) latency between exposure and detection is short (this also requires latency between exposure and development of the disease to be short);
(5) the disease is rare and preferably unicausal.

When studying stress in people at work, such a strategy is less useful because it is rarely possible to satisfy the first and second conditions, and the fifth condition is impossible to satisfy as we know that stress outcomes are common and multicausal in origin. Furthermore, the third condition is costly to satisfy, since it precludes reliance on medical records of any kind, and uses epidmiological case finding techniques instead. Two well known large-scale studies of occupational stress which did rely on medical records are those of Colligan, Smith and Hurrell (1977) and Schuckit and Gunderson (1973). Colligan et al. used admission records of Tennessee community mental health centres to compare rates for 130 major occupations, using US census data for the state to provide the numerator for each occupation. Some of the occupations with high rates were health technicians, waiters and waitresses, practical nurses, inspectors and musicians. However, besides any stresses inherent in such occupations, most of those mentioned above also have a high rate of turnover, often associated with prior personality probelms and psychological difficulties.

Schuckit and Gunderson (1973) examined US navy records and calculated rates of first psychiatric hospitalisation (while in the Navy) by occupation. Kasl has suggested that within such a closed system, one would guess that the hospitalisation data would have fewer inherent weaknesses than the rates derived from the community mental health centres.

The study found that men in the jobs with high rates were older, of lower education, of lower social class origin and more likely to be divorced or single. Since these are the characteristics the men brought with them to the jobs, and since these are well established correlates of treated or untreated mental health problems, Kasl concluded that this whole approach only devised self-selection factors.

MARITAL STATUS, STRESS AND MENTAL ILLNESS

Gove's (1972) review of the literature concluded that married women have higher rates of mental illness than married men, but single men, the divorced and widowed have higher rates than their female counterparts. Gove suggested that being married is a less stressful and more satisfying experience for men than for women in Western society where traditionally the woman works for the husband, does the housework and looks after the children for him while the man goes out to work, associates with colleagues and earns money. Even if the married woman does work, Gove suggested that it was often in an intrinsically unsatisfying job. Other workers have subsequently recognised that the experience of marriage may differ among groups of different educational attainments and social expectations, and have found that variables such as social class, social isolation, poverty and the presence of children are important complicating factors.

Meile, Johnson and St Peter (1976) reviewed evidence that the marital role seems more stressful in lower class women where motherhood is viewed as more important than being a wife and companion but where, nonetheless, the children are perceived as problematic rather than gratifying, and are often more numerous, resulting in increasing confinement to the home, where the husband helps less with the home and the children, and is more likely to desert. In this group, employment is seen mainly in financial rather than social terms. Middle-class women are more likely to find motherhood gratifying, to report close friends, to find interesting employment and generally to participate in outside activities.

Meile et al. 1976 used educational attainment as an indicator of socioeconomic status rather than occupation of spouse because of the need for a comparable status indicator when comparing married with never married women, and employed women with housewives. They found that marital status and educational attainment interact in their relationship with mental disorder in women. In the low-education group, single women have less disorder than married women, whereas this difference is not found in the higher education groups. (The divorced, separated and widowed were excluded from this analysis.)

Pearlin and Johnson (1977) examined the conditions of poverty, social isolation and parenthood in relation to marital status and mental illness, and found that the unmarried were more likely to be under economic strain than the married, and that regardless of marital status, depression was directly associated with economic strain. Thus, economic hardship links marital status and depression by being more prevalent among the unmarried, and by being a condition predisposing people to depression. Their data also showed that the unmarried appear to be more vulnerable to the effects of economic hardship. Thus, severe economic strains are more heavily concentrated in the unmarried population and such strains take a greater psychological toll from the unmarried.

In a similar fashion, Pearlin and Johnson found that the unmarried were more likely to experience social isolation, and that the unmarried were more likely than the married to be depressed by equivalent conditions of isolation. In addition, they found that parenthood increased the prevalence of depression in the single but not in the married. Interestingly the authors found 18 single men with children and said that they were similar to their female counterparts in being "much more disposed to depression than are married men having the same parental responsibilities, and more depressed too than those men who are also single but free of these responsibilities". The authors concluded that about 70 per cent of the association between marital status and depression is attributable to the differential exposure and vulnerability of the unmarried to the life strains of economic hardship, social isolation and parenthood, and that the most important of these three factors is economic hardship.

In contrast to the preceding studies, Cochrane and Stopes-Roe (1980), in an English community survey of psychological symptoms, found that neither marital status nor the interaction between sex and marital status contributed to the variance in psychological symptoms.

Bebbington et al. (1981) found that in both sexes, the divorced, widowed and separated had a high prevalence of disorder. Single men had over twice the case rate of married men. By contrast, single women had less than one quarter the rate of married women and a lower rate than single men. Romars-Clarkson et al. (1988), in a random community sample of New Zealand women, found in contrast to previous studies (Grove, 1972; Brown and Harris, 1978; Bebbington et al. 1981; Surtees et al., 1983) that married, widowed women and mothers showed lower rates than the never married and childless women. The authors suggest that New Zealand gender roles which affirm the importance of homemaking and motherhood, and facilitate social contacts with mothers, explain this discrepancy with other studies, and reconfirm the importance of socio-cultural factors in community psychiatric disorder.

SOCIAL CLASS, STRESS AND MENTAL ILLNESS

People of lower social class are likely to encounter more adverse experiences and fewer supportive experiences, and to be less in control of their environment. One would therefore expect a high prevalence of minor affective disorders in people of lower social class. This relationship was demonstrated for both sexes by Srole et al. (1962) and in a number of subsequent studies reviewed by Dohrenwend and Dohrenwend (1969).

Brown and Harris (1978) found high rates of disorder in working-class women than in women of higher social class. Bagley (1973) reviewed mainly studies of patients admitted to hospital, and concluded that they suggested an association of higher class with manic depressive psychosis (MDP). However the admission rates for MDP in England and Wales did not vary much with social class except for a small excess in Class V (Bebbington, 1978).

Generally, Dohrenwend and Dohrenwend (1969) reviewed population studies and found that 20 out of 25 reported the highest rates in the lowest class. Of the more recent studies, some confirmed this finding (e.g. Brown and Harris, 1978; Cochrane and Stopes-Roe, 1980; Comstock and Helsing, 1976; Mellinger et al., 1974; Uhlenhuth et al., 1974; Warheit, Holzer and Schwab, 1973.

Bebbington et al. (1981) found a small association between class and morbidity which was not quite significant. Others have not (e.g. Brown et al., 1977; Hare and Shaw, 1965; Taylor and Chave, 1964).

AGE, STRESS AND MENTAL DISORDER

Leighton et al. (1963) found an increase in disorder with age in men in Stirling County, and Comstock and Helsing (1976) reported a similar association in both sexes in surveys in Kansas City and Washington County. However, there was no association of age with disorder in Stirling County women, or in either sex in Croydon (Hare and Shaw, 1965) and Alachua County (Warheit et al.,

1973). Benfari et al. (1972) found a decrease with age, as did Uhlenhuth et al. (1974). Comstock and Helsing (1976), after correcting for socio-economic factors in the Kansas City and Washington County surveys, also found that minor affective disorder decreased with age. However, this decrease could not then be explained in their study by reduction in the rate of life events.

Psychiatric case registers, dealing with referred patients, show a prevalence peak for reactive depression and, to a lesser extent for other neuroses, between ages 25 and 34, particularly in women (Wing and Bransby, 1970; Wing and Fryer, 1976). Bebbington et al. 1981 found no significant difference by age among men, but did find two peaks (at 25–34) and 45–54) among women.

RURAL/URBAN DIFFERENCES IN STRESS AND MENTAL DISORDER

Dohrenwend and Dohrenwend (1969, 1974) found that rates of psychiatric disorder are lower in rural than urban areas. Integration into a traditional way of life, with social, religious affiliation, seems to be related to a lower chance of developing depression (Brown and Prudo, 1981). Women on isolated Scottish islands experienced *fewer* of the severe life events, but rate of severe events involving illness and death was no different. Women in the Hebrides were more likely than women in London to develop depression following a death of someone close, and it is this which explains most of the association between death and onset of depression in the Hebrides (Prudo et al., 1981).

These findings support the contention of Rutter and Quinton (1977) that depression city women is more common because they experience different problems, i.e. inner city stresses. But this disadvantage is partly counteracted by the tendency of women in the Hebrides to become depressed more frequently following the death of close relatives and for such disorders to take a chronic course.

CONCLUSION

It is clear that the consideration of demograpic aspects of stress is highly complex and bedevilled by the various interpretations of the term. It has proved helpful in this brief review to separate "stress" into a consideration of life events, social supports, physical health outcomes and psychological health outcomes. Within this perspective, it seems that there are no sex differences in the experience of life events, but there are sex differences in the physiological responses to stress. Social support is equally effective in men and women in protecting from stress, but the significant components of support appear to differ between the sexes. Employment status, occupational status and marital status are all associated with variation in stress, and all interact with sex. However, they are gross structural variables, and it is the particular quality of the experiences that are associated with the role which are significant in supplying the medium through which environmental stress and support are encountered. Research methodology needs to be increasingly refined if we are to develop a more subtle understanding of demographic aspects of stress. Furthermore, we need to incorporate into our model of stress the notion of coping abilities, which inevitably modify the extent to which we expose ourselves to stress and obtain support from the environment.

REFERENCES

Andrews, G., Tennant, C., Hewson, D. and Vaillant, G. E. (1978). Life event stress, social support, coping style and risk of psychological impairment, *Journal of Nervous and Mental Disorders*, **166**, 307.

Bagley, C. (1973). Occupational class and symptoms of depression, *Social Science and Medicine*, **7**, 327–39.

Baruch, G. K., Biener, L. and Barnett, R. C. (1987). Women and gender on work and family stress, *American Psychologist*, **42**, 130–6.

Bebbington, P. E. (1978). The epidemiology of depressive disorder, *Culture, Medicine and Psychiatry*, **2**, 297–341.

Bebbington, P., Hurry, J., Tennant, G., Stuart, E. and Wing, J. R. (1981). Epidemiology of mental disorders in Camberwell, *Psychological Medicine*, **11**, 561–80.

Benfari, R. C., Belser, M., Leighton, A. H. and Mertens, C. (1972). Some dimensions of psychoneurotic behaviour in an urban sample, *Journal of Nervous and Mental Disorders*, **155**, 77–90.

Briscoe, M. (1982). *Sex differences in Psychological Well-being*, Psychological Medicine Monograph, Supplement 1, Cambridge, Cambridge University Press.

Broverman, I., Broverman, D., Clarkson, E., Rosenkranz, P., and Vogel, S. (1970). Sex role stereotype and clinical judgements of mental health, *Journal of Consulting and Clinical Psychology*, **34**, 1–7.

Brown, G. W. (1974). Meaning, measurement and stress of life events. In B. S. Dohrenwend and B. P. Dohrenwend (eds) *Stressful Life Events: Their Nature and Effects*, Wiley, New York.

Brown, G. W. and Harris, T. (1978). *Social Origins of Depression. A Study of Psychiatric Disorder in Woman*. London, Tavistock.

Brown, G. W. and Prudo, R. (1981). Psychiatric disorder in a rural and an urban population. I. Aetiology of depression, *Psychological Medicine*, **11**, 581–99.

Brown, G. W., Davidson, S., Harris, T., Maclean, U., Pollock, S. and Prudo, R. (1977). Psychiatric disorder in London and North Uist, *Social Science and Medicine*, **11**, 367–77.

Brugha, T. S., Bebbington, P. E., MacCarthy, B., Sturt, E., Wykes, T. and Potter, J. (1990). Gender, social support and recovery from depressive disorders: A prospective clinical study, *Psychological Medicine*, **20**, 147–56.

Bush, T. L. and Barrett-Connor, E. (1985). Non-contraceptive oestrogen used and cardiovascular disease, *Epidemiological Review*, **7**, 80–104.

Chan, K. B. (1977). Individual differences in reactions to stress and their personality and situational determinants: Some implications for community health, *Social Sciences Med.* **11**, 89.

Chesler, P. (1971). Patient and Patriarch: Women in the psychotherapeutic relationship. In V. Gornick and B. K. Moran (eds), *Women in Sexist Society*, New York, Basic Books.

Chesler, P. (1972). *Women and Madness*, London, Allen Lane.

Chodorow, N. (1974). Family structure and feminine personality, in M. Z. Rosaldo and L. Larnphere (eds) *Women, Culture and Society*, Stamford, Stamford University Press.

Clancy, K. and Gove, W. (1974). Sex differences in respondents' reports of psychiatric symtoms: an analysis of response bias, *American Sociological Review*, **80**, 205–16.

Cobb, S. (1976). Social support as a moderator of life stress, *Psychosomatic Medicine*, **38**, 300–14.

Cochrane, R. and Stopes, R. M. (1980). Factors affecting the distribution of psychological symptoms in urban areas of England, *Acta Psychiatrica Scandinavia*, **61**, 445–60.

Coie, J. D., Pennington, B. F. and Buckley, H. H. (1974). Effects of situational stress and sex roles on the attribution of psychological disorder, *Journal of Consulting and Clinical Psychology*, **42**, 559–68.

Colligan, M. J., Smith, M. J. and Hurrell, J. J. (1977). Occupational incidence rates of mental health disorders, *Journal of Human Stress*, 34–9.

Comstock, G. W. and Helsing, K. J. (1976). Symptoms of depression in two communities, *Psychological Medicine*, **6**, 551–63.

Cooperstock, R. (1971). Sex differences in the use of mood modifying drugs: an explanatory model, *Journal of Health and Social Behaviour*, **12**, 238–344.

Cumming, E., Lazer, C. and Chisholm, L. (1975). Suicide as an index of role strain among employed and not employed married women in British Columbia, *Canadian Review of Sociology and Anthropology*, **12**(4), 462–70.

Deaux, K. (1984). From individual differences to social categories: Analysis of a decade's research on gender, *American Psychologist*, **39**, 105–16.

Dekker, D. J. and Webb, J. T. (1974). Relationships of the social readjustment rating scale to psychiatric patient status, anxiety and social desirability, *Journal of Psychosomatic Research*, **18**, 1225–1230.

Detre, K. M., Feinleib, M., Matthews, R. A. and Kerr, B. W. (1987). The Federal Women's Study. In E. D. Ealer, B. Packard, N. K. Wenger, T. B. Clarkson and H. A. Tyroler (eds) *Coronary Heart Disease in Women*, Haymarker Doyma, New York, pp. 78–82.

Dohrenwend, B. P. and Dohrenwend, B. S. (1976). Sex differences and psychiatric disorders, *American Journal of Sociology*, **81**, 1447–54.

Dohrenwend, B. S. and Dohrenwend, B. P. (1969). *Social Status and Psychological Disorder: A Causal Enquiry*, Wiley, New York.

Dohrenwend, B. S. and Dohrenwend, B. P. (1974). *Stressful Life Events, Their Nature and Effects*, John Wiley, New York.

Edwards, J. R. and Cooper, C. I. (1988). Research in stress, coping and health: Theoretical and methodological issues, *Psychological Medicine*, **18**, 15–20.

Frankenhauser, M. (1983). The sympathetic – adrenal and pituitary – adrenal response to challenge: Comparison between the sexes. In T. M. Dembroski, T. H. Schmidt and G. Blumchen (eds) *Biobehavioral Basis of Cardiovascular Disease*, Karger, Basel, pp. 95–105.

Freeman, E. M., Logan, S., McCoy, R. (1989). Clinical Practice with Employed Women Social Casework, 413–20.

French, J. R. P., Rodgers, W. L. and Cobb, S. (1974). Adjustment as person–environment fit. In G. Coelho, D. Humburg and J. Adams (eds) *Coping and Adaptation*, Basic Books, New York, pp. 316–33.

Glaser, W. A. (1970). *Social Settings and Medical Organisation*, New York, Atherton Press.

Golin, S. and Hartz, M. A. (1977). A factor analysis of the Beck Depression Inventory in a mildly depressed pouplation, unpublished typescript from the University of Pittsburgh. Quoted in Parker (1979).

Gore, S. (1978). The effect of social support in moderating the health consequences of unemployment, *Journal of Health and Social Behaviour*, **19**, 157–65.

Gove, W. R. (1972). The relationship between sex roles, mental illness and marital status, *Social Forces*, **51**, 34–44.

Gove, W. R., McCorkel, J., Fain, T. and Hughes, M. D. (1976). Response bias in community surveys of mental illness: Systematic bias or random noise, *Social Science and Medicine*, **10**, 497–502.

Hammen, C. L. and Padesky, S. D. (1977). Sex differences in the expression of depressive responses on the Beck Depression Inventory, *Journal of Abnormal Psychology*, **86** (6), 609–14.

Hammen, C. L. and Peters, S. D. (1977). Differential response to male and female depressive reactions, *Journal of Consulting and Clinical Psychology*, **45**, 974–1001.

Hare, E. H. and Shaw, G. K. (1965). *Mental Health on a New Housing Estate: A Comparative Study of Health in Two Districts in Croydon*, Maudsley Monograph No. 12, Oxford University Press, London.

Henderson, A. S. (1977). The social network, support and neurosis. The function of attachment in adult life, *British Journal of Psychiatry*, **131**, 185.

Henderson, S., Byrne, D. G. and Duncan-Jones, P., Scott, R. and Adcock, S. (1980). Social relationships, adverstiy and neurosis: A study of associations in a general population sample, *British Journal of Psychiatry*, **136**, 574–83.

Henderson, S., Duncan-Jones, P., Byrne, D. G., Adcock, S. and Scott, R. (1979). Neurosis and social bands in an urban population, *Australian and New Zealand Journal of Psychiatry*, **13**, 121–5.

Hinkle, L. E. Jr. (1973). The concept of stress in the biological and social sciences, *Sci. Med. Man.*, **1**, 31.

Horwitz, A. (1977). The pathways into psychiatric treatemnt: Some differences between men and women, *Journal of Health and Social Behaviour*, **18**, 169–75.

House, J. S. (1981). *Work, Stress and Social Support*, Addison-Wesley, Reading, Massachusetts.

Hurst, M. W., Jenkins, C. D. and Rose, R. M. (1978). The assessment of life changes stress: A comparative and methodological inquiry, *Psychosom. Med.*, **40**, 126.

Jenkins, R. (1985). Sex differences in minor psychiatric morbidity *Psychological Medicine, Monograph Supplement No. 7*, pp. 1–53.

Jick, T. D. and Mitz, L. F. (1985). Sex differences in work stress, *Academy of Management Review*, **10**, 408–20.

Johns, G. and Nicholson, N. (1982). The meanings of absence: New strategies for theory and research. In B. M. Shaw and L. L. Cummings (eds), *Research in Organisational Behaviour*, Greenwich, CT, JA1 Press.

Kasl, S. V. (1978). Epidemiological contributions to the study of work stress. In C. L. Cooper and R. Payne (eds) *Stress at Work*, Wiley, New York.

Kasl, S. V. (1988). Epidemiological contributions to the study of work stress. In C. L. Cooper and R. Payne (eds), *Stress at Work*, New York, Wiley.

Kessler, R. C. (1979). Stress, social status and psychological distress, *J. Hlth Soc. Behav.*, **20**, 259.

Kessler, R. C., Brown, R. L. and Broman, C. L. (1981). Sex differences in psychiatric help-seeking: Evidence from four large scale surveys, *Journal of Health and Social Behaviour*, **22** 49–64.

Kessler, R. C., Price, R. H. and Wartman, C. B. (1985). Social factors in psychopathology, *Annual Review of Psychology*, **36**, 531–72.

Komarovsky, M. (1946). Cultural contradictions and sex roles, *American Journal of Sociology*, **52**, 184–9.

Kosherak, S. and Masling, J. (1972). Noblesse oblige effect: The interpretation of Rorschach responses as a function of ascribed social class, *Journal of Consulting and Clinical Psychology*, **39**, 415–19.

La Torre, R. A. (1975). Gender and age as factors toward those stigmatised as mentally ill, *Journal of Consulting and Clinical Psychology*, **43**, 97–8.

Leighton, D. C., Harding, J. C., Macklin, D. B., MacMillan, A. M., and Leighton, A. H. (1963). *The Character of Danger: Psychiatric Symptoms in Selected Communities. The Stirling County Study of Psychiatric Disorder and Sociocultural Environment Vol. 3*, New York, Basic Books.

Lewitties, D. J., Mosell, J. A. and Simmons, W. L. (1973). Sex role bias in clinical judgements based on Rorschach interpretations. In *Proceedings of the 81st Annual Convention of the American Psychological Association*, Vol. 8, pp. 495–6. Referred to in Zelcher, P. B. (1978). Sex differences in psychiatric evaluation and treatment, *Archives of General Psychiatry*, **35**, 89–93.

Liem, R. and Liem, J. (1978). Social class and mental illness reconsidered: The role of economic stress and social support, *J. Health Soc. Behaviour*, **19**, 139–56.

Mann, A. H., Jenkins, R. and Belsey, E. (1981). The twelve month outcome of patients with neurotic illness in general practice and their consultation pattern, *Psychological Medicine*, **11**, 535–50.

Marcus, A. C. and Seeman, T. E. (1981). Sex differences in health status: A re-examination of the nurturant role hypothesis, *American Sociological Review*, **46**, 119–23.

Markush, R. E. and Favero, R. (1974). Epidemilogic assessment of stressful life events, depressed mood, and psychophysiological symptoms. In B. S. Dohrenwend and B. P. Dohrenwend (eds) *Stressful Life Events: Their Nature and Effects*, Wiley, New York, pp. 171–90.

Martocchio, J. J. and O'Leary, A. M. (1989). Sex differences in occupational stress: A meta analytic review, *Journal of Applied Psychology*, **74**, 495–501.

Mason, J. W. (1975). A historical view of the stress field, *J. Hum Stress*, **1**, 37.

Mechanic, D. (1964). The influence of mothers on their children's health attitudes and behaviour, *Paediatrics*, **22**, 444–53.

Mechanic, D. (1965). Perceptions of parental responses to illness: A research note, *Journal of Health and Human Behaviour*, **6**, 253.

Meile, R. L., Johnson, D. R. and St Peter, L. (1976). Marital role, education, and mental disorder among women: Test of an interaction hypothesis, *Journal of Health and Social Behaviour*, **17**, 295–301.

Mellinger, G. D., Balter, M. B., Manheimer, D. I., Cisin, I. M. and Parry, H. J. (1978). Psychic distress, life crisis and the use of psychotherapeutic medicines, *Archives of General Psychiatry*, **35**, 1045–52.

Mellinger, G. D., Balter, M. B., Parry, H. J., Manheimer, D. I. and Cisin, I. H. (1974). An overview of psychotherapeutic drug use in the United States. In E. Josephson and E. Carroll (eds) *Drug Use: Epidemiological and Sociological Approaches*, Hemisphere, New York, pp. 333–6.

Miller, P. McC. and Ingham, J. G. (1976). Friends, confidants and symptoms, *Social Psychiatry*, **11**, 51–8.

Myers, J. K., Lindenthal, J. J. and Pepper, M. P. (1971). Life events and psychiatric impairment, *Journal of Nervous and Mental Disease*, **152**, 149–57.

Myers, J. K., Lindenthal, J. J. and Pepper, M. R. (1975). Life events, social integration and psychiatric symptomatology, *Journal of Health and Social Behaviour*, **16**, 421–7.

Nathanson, C. A. (1977). Sex, illness, and medical care: A review of data, theory and method, *Social Science and Medicine*, **11**, 13–25.

Nelson, D. L. and Quick, J. C. (1985). Professional women: Are distress and disease inevitable, *Academy of Management Review*, **10**, 206–18.

Newman, J. P. (1975). Sex differences in life problems and psychological distress, Master's Thesis, University of Wisconsin, Madison.

Nowacki, C. M. and Poe, C. A. (1973). The concept of mental health as related to sex of person perceived, *Journal of Consulting and Clinical Psychology*, **40**, 160.

Nuckolls, K. B., Cassell, J. and Kaplan, B. M. (1972). Psychosocial assets, life crises and the prognosis of pregnancy, *Am. J. Epidemiol.*, **95**, 431.

Parker, G. (1979). Sex differences in non-clinical depression: Review and assessment of previous studies, *Australian and New Zealand Journal of Psychiatry*, **13**, 127–32.

Parsons, T. and Fox, R. (1952). Illness, therapy and the modern urban American family, *Journal of Social Issues*, **8**(4), 31–44.

Paykel, E. S., Prusoff, B. A. and Uhlenhuth, E. H. (1971). Scaling of life events, *Archives of General Psychiatry*, **25**, 340–7.

Paykel, E. S., Emms, E. M., Fletcher, J. and Rassaby, E. S. (1980). Life events and social support in puerperal depression, *Br. J. Psychiat.*, **136**, 339.

Payne, R. L. and Jones, J. G. (1987). Measurement and Methodological Issues in Social Support. In S. V. Kasl and C. L. Cooper (eds) *Stress and Health: Issues in Research Methodology*, Wiley, Chichester, pp. 167–205.

Pearlin, L. I., and Johnson, J. S. (1977). Marital status, life strains and depression, *American Sociological Review*, **42**, 704–15.

Personn, G. (1980). Life event ratings in relation to sex and marital status in a 70 year old urban population, *Acta Psychiatrica Scandinavica*, **62**, 112–18.

Phillips, D. L. (1964). Rejection of the mentally ill: The influence of behaviour and sex, *American Sociological Review*, **29**, 679–87.

Phillips, D. L. and Segal, B. E. (1969). Sexual status and psychiatric symptoms, *American Sociological Review*, **34**, 58–72.

Prudo, R., Brown, G. W., Harris, T. and Dowlands, J. (1981). Psychiatric disorder in a rural and an urban population: 2. Sensitivity to loss, *Psychological Medicine*, **11**, 601–16.

Radloff, L. S. and Rae, D. S. (1979). Susceptibility and precipitating factors in depression: Sex differences and similarities, *Journal of Abnormal Psychology*, **88**, 174–81.

Rheingold, H. L. and Cook, K. V. (1975). The contents of boys' and girls' rooms as an index of parents behaviour, *Child Development*, **46**, 459–63.

Rice, D. P., Hing, E., Kavar, M. G. and Prager, K. (1984). Sex differences in disease risk. In E. B. Gold (ed.) *The Changing Risk of Disease in Women*, Collamore, Lexington, Mass., 1–24.

Romans-Clarkson, S. E., Watton, V. A., Herbison, G. P. and Mullen, P. E. (1988). Marriage, motherhood and psychiatric morbidity in New Zealand, *Psychological Medicine*, **18**, 983–90.

Russo, N. F. (ed.) (1985). *A Women's Mental Health Guide,* American Psychological Association, Washington D. C.

Rutter, M. and Quinton, D. (1977). Psychiatric disorder – ecological factors and concepts of causation. In H. McGurk (ed.) *Ecological Factors in Human Development,* North Holland, Amsterdam, 173–87.

Schlosberg, N. K. and Pietrofesa, J. J. (1973). Perspectives on counselling bias: Implications for counsellor education, *Counselling Psychology,* **4,** 44–54.

Schuckit, M. A. and Gunderson, E. K. E. (1973). Job stress and psychiatric illness in the US Navy, *J. Occup. Med.,* **15,** 884–7.

Seligman, M. E. P. (1975). *Helplessness: On Depression Development and Death,* San Francisco, W. H. Freeman.

Selye, H. (1975). Confusion and controversy in the stress field, *J. Hum. Stress,* **1,** 37.

Srole, L., Langner, T. S., Michael, S. T., Opler, M. K. and Rennie, R. A. C. (1962). *Mental Health in the Metropolis: The Midtown Manhattan Study,* New York, McGraw Hill.

Stoney, C. M., Davis, M. C. and Matthews, K. A. (1985). Sex differences in physiological responses to stress and in coronary heart disease: A causal link? *Psychophysiology,* **24,** 127–31.

Strickland, B. R. (1988). Sex related differences in health and illness, *Psychology of Women Quarterly,* **12,** 381–99.

Surtees, P. G., Ingham, G., Kreitman, N. B., Miller, P. McC. and Sashidharan, S. P. (1983). Psychiatric disorder in women from an Edinburgh community: Associations with demographic factors. *British Journal of Psychiatry,* **142,** 238–46.

Taylor, Lord and Chave, S. (1964). *Mental Health and Environment,* Longman Green, London.

Tennant, C. and Bebbington, P. (1978). The social causation of depression: A critique of the work of Brown and his colleagues, *Psychol. Med.,* **8,** 565.

Uhlenhuth, E. H., Lipmann, R. S., Balter, M. B. and Stern, M. (1974). Symptom intensity and life stress in the city, *Archives of General Psychiatry,* **31,** 759–64.

Verbrugge, L. M. (1979). Female illness rates and illness behaviour: Testing hypotheses about sex differences in health, *Women and Health,* **4,** 61–79.

Verbrugge, L. (1976). Sex differences in morbidity and mortality in the United States, *Social Biology,* **23,** 275–96.

Verbrugge, L. (1985). Gender and health: An update on hypotheses and evidence, *Journal of Health and Social Behaviour,* **26,** 156–82.

Vingerhoets, A. J. J. M. and Van Heck, G. L. (1990). Gender, coping and psychosomatic symptoms, *Psychological Medicine,* **20,** 125–35.

Vinokur, A. and Selzer, M. L. (1975). Desirable versus undesirable life events: Their relationship to stress and mental illness, *J. Personal. Soc. Psychol.,* **32,** 329.

Welch, S. and Booth, A. (1977). Employment and health among married women with children, *Sex Roles,* **3,** 385–97.

Waldron, I. (1976). Why do women live longer than men? Part I, *Journal of Human Stress,* **2,** 2–13.

Warheit, G. J., Holzer, C. E. and Schwab, J. J. (1973). An analysis of social class and racial differences in depressive symptomatology: A community study, *Journal of Health and Social Behaviour,* 14, 291–5.

Werner, P. D. and Block, J. (1975). Sex differences in the eyes of expert personality assessor: Unwarranted conclusions, *Journal of Personal Assessment,* **39,** 110–13.

Wilhelm, K. and Parker, G. (1989). Is sex necessarily a risk factor to depression?, *Psychological Medicine,* **19,** 401–14.

Williams, J. E. and Best, D. L. (1982). *Measuring Sex Sereotypes: A Thirty Nation Study,* London, Sage Publications.

Wing, J. K. and Bransby, E. R. (1970). *Psychiatric Case Registers,* DHSS Statistical Report Series, No. 8, HMSO, London.

Wing, J. K. and Fryer, S. T. (1976). *Psychiatric Services in Camberwell and Salford: Statistics from the Camberwell and Salford Psychiatric Registers 1964–1974,* MRC Social Psychiatry Unit, London.

Wingard, D. L. (1984). The sex differential in morbidity, mortality and life style, *Annual Review of Public Health,* **5**, 433–58.

Yamamoto, K. and Disney, H. (1967). Rejection of the mentally ill: A study of attitudes of student teachers, *Journal of Counselling Psychology,* **13**, 254–68.

Zeldow, P. B. (1975). Clinical judgement: A search for sex differences, *Psychology Reports,* **37**, 1135–42.

Zeldow, P. B. (1976). Effects of non-pathological sex role stereotypes on evaluations of psychiatric patients, *Journal of Consulting and Clinical Psychology,* **44**, 304.

Zeldow, P. B. (1978). Sex differences in psychiatric evaluation and treatment: An empirical review, *Archives of General Psychiatry,* **35**, 89–93.

Chapter 6

Locus of Control, Job Demands, and Health

Joseph J. Hurrell, Jr. and Lawrence R. Murphy, National Institute for Occupational Safety and Health, Ohio, USA

While virtually all job stress theories "acknowledge" some influence of personality characteristics, traits, or dispositions on the relationship between job demands and worker health, there is little consensus regarding the significance of these individual-difference variables or the mechanisms by which they exert their influence. This chapter will examine the contribution of the disposition known as locus of control beliefs (more simply called locus of control) to the job demands/worker health relationship. Locus of control refers to the generalized belief that events in life are controlled either by one's own actions (an internal orientation) or by outside forces (an external orientation). For the purposes of this chapter, "worker health" is interpreted in its broadest sense, encompassing a wide variety of adverse physical and affective responses.

Before beginning our review, some "words of caution" are in order. First, as much of the literature reviewed in this chapter comes from the ever growing body of "stress" literature, it is difficult to avoid the confusion associated with term "stress". In some of the studies discussed below, stress refers to a demanding stimulus condition; while in others, stress refers to a negative response to demanding circumstances. We have attempted to avoid confusion by using the term "stressor" to refer to demanding conditions, and by specifying the nature of the individual's response to demanding conditions, instead of the global term "stress". Second, locus of control is currently one of the most studied variables in psychology. However, relatively few locus of control studies have been conducted in work settings, and only a limited number of these are concerned with work demands and their health-related outcomes. Hence, some of the literature reviewed in this chapter comes from beyond the job stress arena, and the extent to which the results generalize to organizational settings and actual workers (as opposed to college students) is questionable.

Personality and Stress: Individual Differences in the Stress Process. Edited by C.L. Cooper and R. Payne
Published 1991 by John Wiley & Sons Ltd

Finally, since personality characteristics, traits, or dispositions are nearly always studied individually, it is easy to lose sight of the multidimensional and interactive nature of personality. The reader should bear in mind that locus of control is enmeshed in a complex matrix of dispositions whose interrelationships are largely unknown.

THE LOCUS OF CONTROL CONSTRUCT

The construct of locus of control is conceptually rooted in Rotter's (1954) social learning theory, which maintains that behavior in a specific situation is a function of expectancy and reinforcement value. Julian Rotter and his colleagues at Ohio State University formulated the locus of control construct to explain the failure of people to respond in a predictable manner to reinforcement (Phares, 1976; Rotter, 1990). People, according to Rotter (1966), can be differentiated on the basis of their "generalized expectancy" concerning internal and external control of reinforcement. If an individual perceives reinforcement to be contingent upon their own actions (i.e. has an internal orientation), then positive or negative reinforcement will strengthen or weaken the behavior. If, on the other hand, the individual believes that reinforcement is externally controlled by chance, fate, or powerful others, then reinforcement will not strengthen or weaken the behavior. Rotter (1966) believed that expectancy for control was a global characteristic, which is "relatively" stable over time and across situations.

To measure the construct, Rotter (1966) developed the Internal–External (I–E) Scale which has been the assessment instrument of choice in locus of control investigations. This instrument had its origins in the scales developed by Phares (1955) and James (1957) and consists of 23 locus of control items and six filler items in a forced-choice format. Factor-analytic studies of the I–E Scale have reported an unstable factor structure across various samples (e.g. Collins, 1974; Gurin et al., 1969; Nowicki, 1976), raising doubts concerning the unidimensionality of the I–E Scale and, perhaps more importantly, the generality of the locus of control construct. Mirels (1970), for example, found two factors (personal control and social system control), while Gurin, Gurin and Morrison (1978) found three factors (personal efficacy, control ideology, and political control. Levenson (1973), speculating that a person who believes in chance control of reinforcement is cognitively and behaviorally different from a person who is low in internality, developed a three-dimensional index which assesses the extent to which individuals believe their lives are under their own control, under the control of powerful others, or controlled by chance or fate.

Apart from concerns regarding unidimensionality of the construct, doubts have been raised about the stability or trait-like nature of locus of control beliefs (for a partial review, see Lefcourt, 1981). For example, Rodin (1986) has shown that people tend to adopt a more external orientation with age, while work by O'Brien and Kabanoff (1979) suggests that certain life experiences (e.g. unemployment) may result in a more external orientation. Endler and Edwards (1978) and Reid, Haas and Hawkins (1977) also have demonstrated that people who display an internal orientation in some situations may display an external orientation in other situations.

To add to the confusion, the I–E Scale may not only measure beliefs about control of events in a person's life, but also the tendency to use defensive maneuvers (Houston, 1972) and to display anxiety (Spector, 1982). Internal individuals, for example, have been found to score higher on the MMPI Denial scale (Tudor, 1970) and the I–E scale has been shown to be correlated with measures of anxiety (see Joe, 1971; Archer, 1979). Hersch and Scheibe (1967) also have suggested that I–E Scale scores reflect more than the view of the world as controlling. That is, one may view the world as controlling and malevolent or as controlling and benevolent. Inspection of the scales' external items suggests that they may be more affected by a malevolent than a benevolent view.

In response to these concerns, Rotter (1975, 1990) has argued that users of the I–E Scale have not fully understood the theory in which the construct is embedded. Indeed, much of the recent research on locus of control has not been linked to the social learning theory that spawned it. The theory, clearly, does not specify independent, fixed traits, faculties, or types. Rather, the reinforcement value and the characteristics of the situation need to be taken into account for accurate prediction. Specifically, generalized expectancy involves the learning theory principles of generalization and gradients of generalization (Rotter, 1990). Numerous authors, according to Rotter (1990), have mistakenly concluded that the concept had no generality because some specificity could be demonstrated. Generality and specificity, in Rotter's view (1990), should be considered a ". . . matter of degree not kind" (p. 490).

Rotter (1975) has also acknowledged that while generalized assessments concerning locus of control are appropriate in many studies, domain-specific measures may be required in others. Phares (1976) has likewise called for the development of domain-specific measures. As yet, however, only a limited number of standardized domain-specific indices have been offered. Most notably, Wallston and Wallston (1982) have developed the Multidimensional Health Locus of Control Scale, which includes Internal, Chance, and Powerful Others scales specific to the health domain, and Spector (1988) has recently published a 16-item measure of generalized control beliefs in work settings.

LOCUS OF CONTROL AND HEALTH

In a recent review of the literature linking control at work to organizationally relevant outcomes, Ganster and Fusilier (1989) concluded that:

> ... controlled studies with subjects ranging from rats to college sophomores all support the basic validity of the proposition that control beliefs can lessen the experienced stressfulness, and perhaps the negative physiological effects of exposure to threatening events.

Indeed, one of the most consistent and widespread findings in the locus of control literature is the association between belief in external control and self-reports of ill-health. These ill-health reports include higher levels of distress, negative affect, dissatisfaction, perceived stress, and poor adjustment (see Kasl, 1989). With few exceptions, similarly consistent results are found in studies conducted in the occupational arena. Here, externals have been shown to report more burnout (Glogow, 1986; McIntyre, 1984), job dissatisfaction (Spector, 1982), stress (Halpin, Harris and Halpin, 1985; Kyriacou and Sutcliffe, 1979; Lester, 1982), alienation (Korman, Wittig-Berman and Lang, 1981), and lower self-esteem (Lester, 1986).

Despite the consistency of results, evidence from the studies cited above is difficult to interpret. As Kasl (1989) has noted: (a) there may be conceptual overlap between the health and locus of control measures, (b) a single dispositional factor such as negative affectivity (Watson and Clark, 1984) may be present, (c) the directionality of causality is ambiguous, and (d) the association may be due to the influence of an underlying stable trait (such as defensiveness or anxiety).

Moreover, studies directly linking locus of control to health outcomes have generally been cross-sectional in nature and have used global self-ratings of health status. There are notable exceptions. Palinkas, Stern and Holbrook (1986), for example, examined the medical service records of 2724 enlisted Navy men who volunteered, were screened and accepted for winter-over duty in Antarctica. At an average follow-up time of 5.4 years, individuals with an internal locus of control (characterized by scores on the FIRO-B Control-Expressed scale) were found to be at significantly reduced risk of long-term disease incidence. Work by Kobasa, Maddi and Kahn (1982) also offers prospective support for a link between locus of control and ill-health. In this five-year study of 259 executives, it was found that a "hardy" personality disposition (one component of which is an internal locus of control) was prospectively linked to fewer reported illnesses and symptoms.

LINKAGES BETWEEN LOCUS OF CONTROL, JOB DEMANDS, AND HEALTH

Exposure to Occupational Stressors

Locus of control could influence exposure to particular job demands through vocational decisions, which place workers in work environments having different characteristics. Evidence that locus of control is not uniformly distributed across occupations seems to support this contention. For example, Friedrich (1988) found that locus of control was associated with job aspirations and expectations among college students, such that externals had lower expectations for satisfaction and greater discrepancies between what they would like in a job and what they actually expected to get. Similarly, Sztaba and Colwill (1988) found that undergraduates in training for managerial jobs had lower scores on Powerful Others and Luck locus of control scales than those in training for clerical jobs. Among adult women, those who chose careers have been found to have higher internal locus of control scores than those who chose to be homemakers (Mellinger and Erdwins, 1985). Finally, Kapalka and Lachenmeyer (1988) found that workers in supervisory leadership jobs had higher internal locus of control scores that those in nonsupervisory jobs.

Occupational differences in the distribution of internals and externals could be due to vocational choice, as suggested above, or exposure to the job environment. Just as the work environment is thought to be instrumental in the development of the Type A behavior pattern (Margolis et al., 1983), it is conceivable that long-term exposure to certain job conditions (e.g. machine-pacing) influences control perceptions. In this regard, Doherty and Baldwin (1985), in a prospective study of four cohorts from the National Longitudinal Surveys, found that both young and old female cohorts displayed a shift toward externality in locus of control beliefs from the 1960s to the 1970s, but no changes were found for males. The authors speculated that social constraints on females meeting their goals in the labor force were responsible for the shift in locus of control.

Finally, occupational differences in locus of control beliefs could be due to workers moving or "drifting" into certain occupations, as a result of health concerns, desire for advancement, or job dissatisfaction. In a recent study of health care personnel (Marino and White, 1985), internals in highly controlled environments were found to experience more distress than externals. Seemingly, experiencing more distress could prompt internals to seek out less structured work environments.

Perceptions of Control at Work

The degree of control an individual has, or perceives he or she has, over job demands (or stressors) has been demonstrated to be a salient dimension in determining the psychological and physiological impact of those demands (see Sauter, Hurrell and Cooper, 1989). In theory, locus of control beliefs should act as a dispositional antecedent to perceptions of control at work and thus indirectly impact health status. However, evidence for this relationship is sparse. Spector's (1982) review of the locus of control literature as it relates to behavior in organizations suggests that locus of control may affect some work-related control perceptions. Internals appear to have higher expectancies about the relationship between effort and job performance, and between performance and rewards (Broeding, 1975; Evans, 1974; Kimmons and Greenhaus, 1976; Lied and Pritchard, 1976; Szilagyi and Sims, 1975). Moreover, Kimmons and Greenhaus (1976) found a relationship between internal locus of control and perceived job autonomy. This relationship was not supported, however, in a study by Frost and Wilson (1983). There appears to be little empirical evidence to suggest that internals are more likely to perceive greater control over other work processes.

It is noteworthy that researchers studying general life stress (e.g. Dohrenwend and Martin, 1979; Sandler and Lakey, 1982; Nelson and Cohen, 1983) have concluded that control perceptions are more a function of stable event properties than subjects' dispositional characteristics. Nelson and Cohen (1983), in a longitudinal study of 192 college students, found controllability perceptions of the 57 life events on the Life Experiences Survey (Sarason, Johnson and Siegel, 1978) to be unrelated to subjects' I–E Scale scores.

Locus of Control as Moderator

A limited number of studies have examined the moderating effects of locus of control on the job stressor/ill-health relationship. In general, the underlying premise of these studies is that individuals who define stressors as controllable will be more likely to attempt to cope with them via problem-focused actions, and thereby experience fewer negative health effects. Krause and Stryker (1984) analyzed data from the 1969 and 1971 panels of the National Longitudinal Survey of Middle-aged Men and found that those with an internal orientation, who scored high on a composite index of job- and economic-related stressors, reported less psychophysiological distress than externals scoring high on the composite job stressor index. Interestingly, moderate externals were found to be most vulnerable to stressor-related health effects. With regard to specific job stressors, Keenan and McBain (1979) found that role ambiguity was significantly associated with high tension at work in middle managers classified as externals on the I–E Scale. A similar moderating effect of the role ambiguity/distress relationship was reported by Arney (1988) in a study of secondary school teachers. Fusilier, Ganster and Mayes (1987) found that, among police officers, role conflict was more strongly related to somatic complaints for externals than internals. In a study of mid-level managerial personnel in a large manufacturing firm, Abdel-Halim (1980) found a locus of control moderating effect on the relationship between role ambiguity and job satisfaction. As hypothesized, externals reported more job satisfaction under low, rather than high, ambiguity. However, conflicting results have been reported. Batlis (1980), for example, found no evidence for a moderating effect of locus of control on the relationship between role ambiguity or role conflict and job satisfaction among supermarket department managers. In a laboratory simulation study, Perrewe (1986) reported that locus of control among college students (as measured by Levenson's 1973 scale) did not interact with perceived demands to affect either task satisfaction or psychological anxiety. High externals, however, did show the strongest negative relationship between perceived demands and satisfaction.

Several studies in the non-occupational arena (e.g. Houston 1972; Watson and Baumol, 1967) have suggested that psychological distress may result when beliefs about locus of control and perceived freedom to take action are incongruent. Limited support for such a premise can be found in studies conducted in the occupational arena. In the Marino and White (1985) study cited earlier, locus of control was found to moderate the effects of one of four types of mechanistic structural characteristics of the work environment on workload-related stress. Specifically, internals reported more stress in response to jobs involving adherence to specific operating procedures. Also Eskew and Riche (1982), using a laboratory simulation of an inspection task, found that internals made fewer false alarms when working under self-paced as opposed to machine-paced conditions. Sims and Szilagyi (1976) reported that the autonomy/work satisfaction correlation among 766 medical center employees was actually higher for externals than for internals.

On the other hand, Kimmons and Greenhaus (1976) found no moderating effect of locus of control on the relationship between autonomy and satisfaction among managers. Likewise, Lang and Markowitz (1989) found no locus of control moderating effect on the relationship between perceived lack of job opportunity and job-related distress among liberal arts Ph.D.s.

Locus of control has been shown to moderate the relationship between job satisfaction, turnover, and turnover intentions. Blau (1987), for example, using a sample of 119 nurses, found that internals (as measured by Levenson's (1973) Chance scale) showed significantly stronger negative relationships than externals between two facets of satisfaction (pay and promotion) and withdrawal cognitions and turnover. Internals also showed a stronger positive relationship than externals between withdrawal cognitions and turnover. Using a sample of 192 hospital employees, Griffeth and Hom (1988) found that internals (as measured by the I–E Scale) were more likely to use the future attainment of valued outcomes from their present job than the current level of job satisfaction when deciding to terminate employment. Externals were more influenced by their current level of job satisfaction when deciding whether to quit or stay, rather than the future of attainment of valued outcomes. A study of Storms and Spector (1987) of 160 mental health facility employees also suggests that externals are more likely than internals to respond to "organizational frustration" with counter-productive behaviors (e.g. the intention to quit). This finding is consistent with several laboratory studies

(Brissett and Nowicki, 1973; Butterfield, 1964) which found that internals react to frustrating experimental tasks more constructively, and with fewer interfering responses, such as aggression and self-blame. However, Lang and Markowitz (1989), using 98 academics as subjects and Joe's (1974) abbreviated version of the I–E Scale as a measure of locus of control, found no moderator effects on the relationship between perceived lack of job opportunities and career change decisions.

The moderator studies reviewed above have generally treated locus of control as an independent, stable trait, and have not considered the potential influence of other personality characteristics. By contrast, Arsenault and Dolan (1983) examined the concomitant moderating effects of locus of control and the competitive, hard-driving Type A personality style among 1200 Quebec hospital employees. The results indicated that non-Type A's (both internal and external) showed the most deterioration in qualitative performance when exposed to job context stressors (e.g. role ambiguity, role conflict, skill underutilization). By comparison, Type A externals showed relatively lower, but significantly negative, responses to job context stressors, whereas Type A internals appeared not to respond to these types of stressors. Interestingly, both Type A internals and non-Type A externals manifested greater absenteeism in response to job context stressors. The authors speculated that among Type A internals, absenteeism was related to active avoidance, whereas among non-Type A externals absenteeism was related to passive avoidance. Apparently, for the Type A internal, the threat of losing control and the threat of inhibition of action leads to an aggressive getaway. On the other hand, non-Type A externals, lacking competitiveness and feeling their lives controlled by external forces, react to job context stressors with a passive flight strategy.

Specific Moderating Mechanisms

Coping

It is generally assumed that the dynamics behind the moderating effects of locus of control on health-related outcomes involve the use of more effective coping behavior by those with an internal locus of control. Externals are thought to experience more adverse health outcomes because they define events in their lives as outside of their control, and believe that their actions will have little influence on the stressors. Few studies, however, have examined specific differences in coping styles between internals and externals. Anderson's (1977) study of small business owners after a severe flood suggests that internals utilize more task-centered coping behaviors and fewer emotion-centred coping behaviors. Likewise, Strentz and Auerbach (1988) found that internals engaged in less emotion-focused coping than externals in response to a simulated abduction. Parkes (1984), in a natural experiment involving female student nurses, examined relationships between locus of control, three types of coping processes (General Coping, Direct Coping, and Suppression), and the appraisal (in terms of importance and controllability) of recalled stressful episodes. The results showed interactions between locus of control and appraisal for each of the measures. Overall, the results were consistent with the prediction that the relations between locus of control and coping would be mediated by subjective perceptions of situational characteristics. On the General Coping measure, internals and externals differed in their approach to situations that they evaluated in a relatively clear-cut manner, that is, situations they "could change" or "must accept". Faced with these clear-cut appraisals, internals discriminated the specific nature of the demands and focused their coping efforts on a limited number of appropriate strategies. Internals also showed higher levels of overall Direct Coping. Of greater interest, for internals, both Direct Coping and Suppression were related to appraisal, whereas for externals this was not the case. Specifically, in situations appraised as amenable to change, internals reported high levels of Direct Coping and low levels of Suppression, whereas externals reported high levels of Suppression and low levels of Direct Coping.

It is important to bear in mind that, in contrast to stressors in other life areas (e.g. parenting), workplace stressors may be less likely to be under the control of the individual (Pearlin and Schooler, 1978). Examples here include workload, workpace, autonomy, lack of participation in decision-making, deadlines, role conflict/ambiguity, and shiftwork, among others (Holt, 1982). In view of data showing that problem-focused coping (i.e. direct action to reduce/eliminate the stressors) is ineffective when the stressor is uncontrollable (Caplan, Naidu and Tripathi, 1984; Felton, Revenson and Hinrichsen, 1984), an internal locus of control may be of questionable benefit to individuals in certain work settings (Menagham and Merves, 1984; Needle, Griffin and Svendsen, 1981; Pearlin and Schooler, 1978). Internals may not experience less distress (through their attempts to control workplace stressors), as has been found in nonwork life areas. In the Krause and Stryker (1984) study described earlier, extreme internals were found to fare no better than extreme or moderate externals upon exposure to uncontrollable stressors such as unemployment, age discrimination, inability to keep up the job pace, and increased job pressure. Moreover, at least one study reported *increases* in distress among workers who attempted to alter or control stressful work conditions (Howard, Rechnitzer and Cunningham, 1975). The most efficient strategies for reducing distress in work settings, it seems, are those which increase the distance between the worker and the problem, or which are emotion-focused or palliative (Murphy, 1985). Neither of the latter strategies would be typically employed by persons with an internal locus of control.

Social support

Studies in both the life- and job-stress arenas have suggested that an interaction between locus and control and social support may help clarify the stress-moderating effects of locus of control. Sandler and Lakey (1982) and Lefcourt, Martin and Saleh (1984) reported significant interactions between negative life events and social support in predicting psychological distress among internals but not among externals. Studies in the occupational arena tend to support these results. Fusilier et al. (1987), for example, reported significant three-way interactions among role demands, locus of control and social support in predicting depression and somatic complaints among police officers and firefighters. Interpretation of these three-way interactions suggested that locus of control and social support jointly determine how workers respond to job stressors. A recent study by Cummins (1989), using employed university business administration students, found a similar significant three-way interaction between job stress (work-related hassles), social support, and locus of control on job satisfaction. Social support appeared to buffer the effects of job stress, but only for internals and only when the support was work-related.

Data from a longitudinal study of older adults (Krause, 1987) indicate that social support may buffer the effects of stress (specifically life stress) by bolstering locus of control beliefs. However, the study also suggested that the effects of social support are limited. There appears to be a threshold for the effects of support; beyond a certain point, increased support erodes feelings of internality. Work by Caldwell, Pearson and Chin (1987) suggests that gender may be an important factor in determining the moderating effects of locus of control and social support on the stress/ill-health relationship. In this study of college men and women, the relationships between social support and psychological adjustment varied depending on which social support measure was used, which psychological adjustment measure was used, in addition to locus of control beliefs and gender. Locus of control beliefs did not affect the impact of stress on symptom formation for women, but it did have an effect for men. Internal men were more likely to develop psychosomatic health symptoms when exposed to stressors, whereas external men were more likely to become depressed. Social support had the least effect on adjustment among external men.

SUMMARY AND DIRECTIONS FOR FUTURE RESEARCH

The studies reviewed in this chapter do not present a clear picture of the relationship between locus of control beliefs and job demands/health outcomes. While multiple studies were found which supported various relationships between these variables, conflicting results were also found which prevent definitive conclusions. As noted earlier, even where the research literature has produced consistent findings, such as the relationship between externality and ill-health (usually without reference to occupational factors), the meaning of the relationship is obscured by confounding influences (see Kasl, 1989).

Methodological problems in locus of control studies also hinder firm conclusions. One problem is the criteria for classifying individuals as internals or externals. Most studies treated locus of control as a continuous variable and never address the criterion issue. Of those studies which classified individuals as internal or external, most chose to split the sample at the mean or the median. Several problems come to mind using this type of cutoff score. First, the distribution of locus of control in the working population is not 50–50; internals probably outnumber externals. Using a median or mean split results in misclassifications of some (many?) internals and externals, thus introducing unnecessary variability into analyses of group differences. Second, because most studies use only a sample of the working population, potential bias is introduced because the distribution of locus of control in the sample may not resemble that in the population. This bias would be exacerbated if locus of control beliefs differed substantially by occupation. Finally, unless the response rate or participation rate in a study is 100%, still more bias will be introduced to the extent that locus of control beliefs influence participation rates. It is not unreasonable to hypothesize greater participation rates among internals than externals.

The concerns listed above are not academic. As noted earlier, Krause and Stryker (1984) demonstrated the utility of a four-fold classification of locus of control, which contained extreme and moderate, internals and externals. These results highlight yet an another potential problem: locus of control may not influence health in a linear fashion. The use of linear modeling techniques in locus of control studies may be inappropriate and underestimate the relationships between locus of control and psychological health outcomes.

The paucity of studies evaluating locus of control in the context of occupational factors is also problematic. Additional research is needed (1) to determine the stability of the locus of control construct, and (2) to identify the path through which locus of control influences worker health. Components of this path should include (a) the interaction of locus of control with other traits of the worker and characteristics of the work environment, and (b) reciprocal effects of work environment factors and locus of control beliefs.

Figure 6.1 shows the major paths through which locus of control beliefs are thought to influence the relationship between job demands and health and is presented to facilitate discussion of future research needs in this area. While each path is shown as unidirectional, some of the paths are likely to be bidirectional in nature (i.e. reciprocal effects).

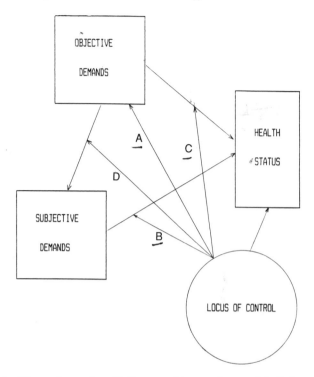

Figure 6.1   The major paths of influence of locus of control beliefs

Path A in Figure 6.1 denotes the direct and indirect effects of locus of control on objective stressors, primarily via vocational choice. Few studies have examined the influence of locus of control on vocational choice, and such data may help explain some of the conflicting results regarding locus of control/health relationships, especially when different occupations are studied. A related issue is the relationship of locus of control to occupational mobility and turnover intentions,

Paths B and C in Figure 6.1 depict the moderating effects of individual coping behaviors on the job demands/ill-health relationship. Of concern here is the extent to which internals utilize more, different, and/or more effective coping strategies or behaviors when faced with objective or perceived job demands. Other factors which should be assessed in this context include situational (and occupational) specificity, stage of career development, and concurrent stressful life events.

Path D represents the effects of locus of control beliefs upon perceptions of the objective work environment. Very little is currently known about this potential path of influence, but as we have suggested, its influence may be substantial. While one might assume that locus of control has a direct effect on perceptions of control at work, there is only limited empirical support for this assumption. Clearly there is a need for some rather fundamental research which examines the relationship between locus of control and job perceptions. The question of whether internals and externals differ in their perceptions of specific objective job demands needs to be assessed. The effects of acute and chronic exposure to various job conditions on locus of control beliefs are largely unknown. Future studies which incorporate measures of related individual dispositions (e.g. defensiveness and anxiety) and domain-specific measures of locus of control should produce less ambiguous results.

REFERENCES

Abdel-Halim, A. A. (1980). Effects of person–job compatibility on managerial reactions to role ambiguity, *Organizational Behavior and Human Performance*, **26**, 193–211.

Anderson, C. R. (1977). Locus of control, coping behaviors, and performance in a stress setting: a longitudinal study, *Journal of Applied Psychology*, **62**, 446–51.

Archer, R. P. (1979). Relationships between locus of control and anxiety, *Journal of Personality Assessment*, **43**, 617–26.

Arney, L. K. (1988). Effects of personality–environment fit on job stress, *Educational and Psychological Research*, **8**, 1–18.

Arsenault, A. and Dolan, S. (1983). The role of personality, occupation and organization in understanding the relationship between job stress, performance and absenteeism, *Journal of Occupational Psychology*, **56**, 227–40.

Batlis, C. C. (1980). Job involvement and locus of control as moderators of control-perception/individual-outcome relationships, *Psychological Reports*, **46**, 111–19.

Blau, G. J. (1987). Locus of control as a potential moderator of the turnover process, *Journal of Occupational Psychology*, **60**, 21–9.

Brissett, M. and Nowicki, S., Jr. (1973). Internal versus external control of reinforcement and reaction to frustration, *Journal of Personality and Social Psychology*, **25**, 35–44.

Broeding, L. A. (1975). Relationship of internal–external control to work motivation and performance in an expectancy model, *Journal of Applied Psychology*, **60**, 65–70.

Butterfield, E. C. (1964). Locus of control, test anxiety, reactions to frustration, and achievement attitudes, *Journal of Personality*, **32**, 355–70.

Caldwell, R. A., Pearson, J. L. and Chin, R. J. (1987). Stress-moderating effects: Social support in the context of gender and locus of control, *Personality and Social Psychology Bulletin*, **13**, 5–17.

Caplan, R. D., Naidu, L. K. and Tripathi, R. C. (1984). Coping and defense: constellations and components, *Journal of Health and Social Behavior*, **25**, 303–20.

Collins, B. (1974). Four components of the Rotter internal–external scale, *Journal of Pesonality and Social Psychology*, **29**, 381–91.

Cummins, R. (1989). Locus of control and social support: Clarifiers of the relationship between job stress and job satisfaction, *Journal of Applied Social Psychology*, **19**, 772–88.

Doherty, W. J. and Baldwin, C. (1985). Shifts and stability and locus of control during the 1970s: Divergence of the sexes, *Journal of Personality and Social Psychology*, **48**, 1048–53.

Dohrenwend, B. S. and Martin, J. L. (1979). Personal vs. situational determination of anticipation and control or the occurrence of stressful events, *American Journal of Community Psychology*, **7**, 453–68.

Endler, N. S. and Edwards, J. (1978). Person by treatment interaction in personality research. In L. A. Pervin and M. Lewis (eds) *Perspectives in Interactional Psychology*, Plenum, New York, pp. 141–70.

Eskew, R. T., Jr. and Riche, C. V., Jr. (1982). Pacing and locus of control in quality of control inspection, *Human Factors*, **24**, 411–15.

Evans, M. G. (1974). Extensions of a path–goal theory of motivation, *Journal of Applied Psychology*, **59**, 172–8.

Felton, B. J., Revenson, T. A. and Hinrichsen, G. A. (1984). Stress and coping in the explanation of psychological adjustment among chronically ill adults, *Social Science and Medicine*, **18**, 889–98.

Friedrich, J. R. (1988). The influence of locus of control on students' aspirations, expectations and information preferences for summer work, *Journal of College Student Development*, **29**, 335–9.

Frost, T. F. and Wilson, H. G. (1983). Effects of locus of control and A-A personality type on job satisfaction within the health care field, *Psychological Reports*, **53**, 399–405.

Fusilier, M. R., Ganster, D. C. and Mays, B. T. (1987). Effects of social support, role stress, and locus of control on health, *Journal of Management*, **13**, 517–28.

Ganster, D. C. and Fusilier, M. R. (1989). Control in the workplace. In C. Cooper and I. Robertson (eds), *International Review of Industrial and Organizational Psychology*, John Wiley, Chichester.

Glogow, E. (1986). Research note: Burnout and locus of control, *Public Personnel Management*, **15**, 79–83.

Griffeth, R. W. and Hom, P. W. (1988). Locus of control and delay of gratification as moderators of employee turnover, *Journal of Applied Social Psychology*, **18**, 1318–33.

Gurin, P., Gurin, G. and Morrison, B. M. (1978). Personal and ideological aspects of internal and external control, *Social Psychology*, **41**, 275–95.

Gurin, P., Gurin, G., Lao, R. C. and Beattie, M. (1969). Internal–external control in the motivational dynamics of Negro youth, *Journal of Social Issues*, **25**, 29–53.

Halpin, G., Harris, K. and Halpin, G. (1985). Teacher stress as related to locus of control, sex, and age, *Journal of Experimental Education*, **53**, 136–40.

Hersch, P. D. and Scheibe, K. E. (1967). Reliability and validity of internal–external control as a personality dimension, *Journal of Consulting Psychology*, **31**, 609–13.

Holt, R. R. (1982). Occupational stress. In L. Goldberger and S. Breznitz (eds) *Handbook of Stress*, Free Press, New York.

Houston, B. K. (1972). Control over stress, locus of control, and response to stress, *Journal of Personality and Stress*, **21**, 249–55.

Howard, J. H., Rechnitzer, R. A. and Cunningham, D. A. (1975). Coping with job tension—effective and ineffective methods, *Public Personnel Management*, **4**, 317–26.

James, W. H. (1957). Internal versus external control of reinforcement as a basic variable in learning theory, unpublished doctoral dissertation, Ohio State University.

Joe, V. C. (1971). Review of the internal–external control construct as a personality variable, *Psychological Reports*, **28**, 619–40.

Joe, V. C. (1974). Perceived personal control and attributions of causality, *Perceptual and Motor Skills*, **38**, 329–339.

Kapalka, G. M. and Lachenmeyer, J. R. (1988). Sex-role flexibility, locus of control and occupational status, *Sex Roles*, **19**, 417–27.

Kasl, S. V. (1989). An epidemiological perspective on the role of control in health. In S. L. Sauter, J. J. Hurrell, Jr. and C. L. Cooper (eds) *Job Control and Worker Health*, Wiley, Chichester, pp. 161–89.

Keenan, A. and McBain, G. D. M. (1979). Effects of Type A behavior, intolerance to ambiguity and locus of control on the relationship between role stress outcomes, *Journal of Occupational Psychology*, **52**, 277–85.

Kimmons, G. and Greenhaus, J. H. (1976). Relationship between locus of control and reactions of employees to work characteristics, *Psychological Reports*, **39**, 815–20.

Kobasa, S. C., Maddi, S. R. and Kahn, S. (1982). Hardiness and health: A prospective study, *Journal of Personality and Social Psychology*, **42**, 168–77.

Korman, A. K., Wittig-Berman, U. and Lang, D. (1981). Career success and personal failure: Alienation in professionals and managers, *Academy of Management Journal*, **24**, 342–60.

Krause, N. (1987). Understanding the stress process: Linking social support with locus of control beliefs, *Journal of Gerontology*, **42**, 589–93.

Krause, N. and Stryker, S. (1984). Stress and well-being: The buffering role of locus of control beliefs, *Social Science and Medicine*, **18**, 783–90.

Kyriacou, C. and Sutcliffe, J. (1979). A note on teacher stress and locus of control, *Journal of Occupational Psychology*, **52**, 227–8.

Lang, D. and Markowitz, M. (1989). Individual-difference predictors of felt stress among academics seriously considering career change, *Work and Stress*, **3**, 305–14.

Lazarus, R. (1966). *Psychological Stress and the Coping Process*, McGraw-Hill, New York.

Lefcourt, H. M. (ed.) (1981). *Research with the Locus of Control Construct: Vol. 1 Assessment Methods*, Academic Press, New York.

Lefcourt, H. M., Martin, R. A. and Saleh, W. E. (1984). Locus of control and social support: Interactive moderators of stress, *Journal of Personality and Social Psychology*, **47**, 378–89.

Lester, D. (1982). Perceived stress in police officers and beliefs in locus of control, *Journal of Applied Psychology*, **107**, 157–8.

Lester, D. (1986). Subjective stress and self-esteem of police officers, *Perceptual and Motor Skills*, **63**, 1334.

Levenson, H. (1973). Multidimensional locus of control in psychiatric patients, *Journal of Consulting and Clinical Psychology*, **41**, 397–404.

Lied, T. R. and Pritchard, R. D. (1976). Relationships between personality variables and components of the expectancy-valence model, *Journal of Applied Psychology*, **61**, 4631-7.

McIntyre, T. C. (1984). The relationship between teacher locus of control and burnout, *British Journal of Educational Psychology*, **54**, 235–8.

Margolis, L. H., McLeroy, K. R., Runyan, C. W. and Kaplan, B. H. (1983). Type A behavior: An ecological approach, *Journal of Behavioral Medicine*, **6**, 245–58.

Marino, K. E. and White, S. E. (1985). Departmental structure, locus of control, and job stress: The effects of a moderator, *Journal of Applied Psychology*, **70**, 782–84.

Mellinger, J. C. and Erdwins, C. J. (1985). Personality correlates of age and life roles in adult women, *Psychology of Women Quarterly*, **9**, 503–14.

Menagham, E. G. and Merves, E. S. (1984). Coping with occupational problems: The limits of individual efforts, *Journal of Health and Social Behavior*, **25**, 405–23.

Mirels, H. (1970). Dimensions of internal vs external control, *Journal of Consulting and Clinical Psychology*, **34**, 226–8.

Murphy, L. R. (1985). Individual coping strategies. In C. L. Cooper and M. J. Smith (eds) *Job Stress and Blue Collar Work*, John Wiley, Chichester.

Needle, R., Griffin, T. and Svendsen, R. (1981). Occupational stress: Coping and health problem of teachers, *Journal of School Health*, **51**, 175–81.

Nelson, D. W. and Cohen, L. H. (1983). Locus of control and control perceptions and the relationship between life stress and psychological disorders, *American Journal of Community Psychology*, **11**, 705–22.

Nowicki, S. (1976). Factor structure of locus of control in children, *Journal of Genetic Psychology*, **29**, 13–17.

O'Brien, G. E. and Kabanoff, B. (1979). Comparison of unemployed and employed workers on work values, locus of control, and health variables, *Australian Psychologist*, **14**, 143–54.

Palinkas, L., Stern, M. J. and Holbrook, T. L. (1986). *A Longitudinal Study of Personality and Disease Incidence among Antarctic Winter-Over Volunteers*, Report No. 86–25, Naval Health Research Center, San Diego, Calif.

Parkes, K. R. (1984). Locus of control, cognitive appraisal, and coping in stressful episodes, *Journal of Personality and Social Psychology*, **46**, 655–68.

Pearlin, L. I. and Schooler, C. (1978). The structure of coping, *Journal of Health and Social Behavior*, **19**, 2–21.

Perrewe, P. L. (1986). Locus of control and activity level as moderators in the quantitative job demands-satisfaction/psychological anxiety relationship: An experimental analysis, *Journal of Applied Social Psychology*, **16**, 620–32.

Phares, E. J. (1955). Changes in expectancy in skill and chance situations, unpublished doctoral dissertation, Ohio State University.

Phares, E. J. (1976). *Locus of Control in Personality*, General Learning Press, Morristown, NJ.

Reid, D. W., Haas, G. and Hawkins, D. (1977). Locus of desired control and positive self-concept of the elderly, *Journal of Gerontology*, **32**, 441–50.

Rodin, J. (1986). Health control and aging. In M. M. Baltes and P. B. Baltes (eds) *Aging and the Psychology of Control*, Erlbaum, Hillsdale, NJ, pp. 139–65.

Rotter, J. B. (1954). *Social Learning and Clinical Psychology*, Prentice-Hall, Englewood Cliffs, NJ.

Rotter, J. B. (1966). Generalized expectancies for internal versus external control of reinforcement, *Psychological Monographs*, **80**, 1–28.

Rotter, J. B. (1975). Some problems and misconceptions related to the construct of internal versus external control of reinforcement, *Journal of Consulting and Clinical Psychology*, **43**, 56–67.

Rotter, J. B. (1990). Internal versus external control of reinforcement, *American Psychologist*, **45**, 489–93.

Sandler, I. N. and Lakey, B. (1982). Locus of control as a stress moderator: the role of control perceptions and social support, *American Journal of Community Psychology*, **10**, 260–71.

Sarason, I., Johnson, J. and Siegel, J. (1978). Assessing the impact of life changes: Development of Life Experiences Survey, *Journal of Consulting and Clinical Psychology*, **46**, 932–46.

Sauter, S. L., Hurrell, J. J., Jr. and Cooper, C. L. (eds) (1989). *Job Control and Worker Health*, Wiley, Chichester.

Sims, H. P., Jr. and Szilagyi, A. D. (1976). Job characteristics relationships: Individual and structural moderators, *Organizational Behavior and Human Performance*, **17**, 211–30.

Spector, P. E. (1982). Behavior in organizations as a function of employee's locus of control, *Psychological Bulletin*, **91**, 482–97.

Spector, P. E. (1986). Perceived control by employees: A meta-analysis of studies concerning autonomy and participation at work, *Human Relations*, **39**, 1005–16.

Spector, P. E. (1988). Development of the work locus of control scale, *Journal of Occupational Psychology*, **61**, 335–40.

Storms, P. L. and Spector, P. E. (1987). Relationships of organizational frustration with reported behavioural reactions: The moderating effect of locus of control, *Journal of Occupational Psychology*, **60**, 227–34.

Strentz, T. and Auerbach, S. M. (1988). Adjustment to the stress of simulated captivity – effects of emotion-focused versus problem-focused preparation on hostages in differing in locus of control, *Journal of Personality and Social Psychology*, **55**, 652–60.

Szilagyi, A. A. and Sims, H. P., Jr. (1975). Locus of control and expectancies across multiple occupational levels, *Journal of Applied Psychology*, **60**, 638–40.

Sztaba, T. and Colwill, N. L. (1988). Secretarial and management students: Attitudes, attributes and career choice considerations, *Sex Roles*, **19**, 651–65.

Thompson, S. C. (1981). Will it hurt less if I can control it? A complex answer to a simple question, *Psychological Bulletin*, **90**, 89–101.

Tudor, T. (1970). The concept of repression: The results of two experimental paradigms, unpublished doctoral dissertation, University of Texas.

Wallston, K. A. and Wallston, B. S. (1982). Who is responsible for your health? The construct of health locus of control. In G. S. Sanders and J. Suils (eds) *Social Psychology of Health and Illness*, Earlbaum, Hillsdale, NJ, pp. 65–9.

Watson, D. and Baumol, E. (1967). Effects of locus of control and expectation of future control upon present performance, *Journal of Pesonality and Social Psychology*, **6**, 212–15.

Watson, D. and Clark, L. A. (1984). Negative affectivity: The disposition to experience aversive emotional states, *Psychological Bulletin*, **96**, 465–90.

Chapter 7

The Measurement of Type A Behavior Pattern: An Assessment of Criterion-oriented Validity, Content Validity, and Construct Validity

Jeffrey R. Edwards, University of Virginia, USA

During the past 30 years, Type-A behavior pattern (TABP) has maintained a central position in research into individual differences and stress. TABP was initially identified by Friedman and Rosenman (1959), who noted that patients with more severe coronary heart disease (CHD) tended to exhibit excessive speed, impatience, time urgency, competitiveness, achievement striving, aggressiveness, and hostility. These initial observations stimulated several large-scale epidemiological studies, which generally supported the role of TABP in the development of CHD (French-Belgian Collaborative Group, 1982; Haynes, Feinleib and Kannel, 1980; Jenkins, Rosenman and Zyzanski, 1974; Rosenman et al., 1975). However, more recent studies have challenged the conclusiveness of these findings, with results varying considerably depending upon the method of measuring TABP (Booth-Kewley and Friedman, 1987; Matthews, 1988).

The inconsistent relationship between TABP and CHD, combined with the apparent dependence of this relationship on method of measurement, suggests that the validity of TABP measures should be seriously examined. Of the many measures that have been proposed, the most widely used are the Structured Interview (SI; Rosenman, 1978; Rosenman et al., 1964), the Jenkins Activity Survey (JAS; Jenkins, Rosenman and Friedman, 1967; Jenkins, Zyzanski and Rosenman, 1979a), the Framingham scale (Haynes et al., 1978b), and the Bortner scale (Bortner, 1969). Several excellent reviews of these measures are available (e.g. Dembroski, 1978; Fekken and Holden, 1988; Jenkins, 1978; Matthews, 1983, 1985; O'Looney, 1984; Powell, 1987), but these reviews tend to emphasize a rather limited set of psychometric

Personality and Stress: Individual Differences in the Stress Process. Edited by C.L. Cooper and R. Payne
© 1991 John Wiley & Sons Ltd

properties, such as convergence, test–retest reliability, and ability to predict CHD. Though these properties are important, they represent only a subset of the criteria traditionally considered in measurement validation (Cronbach, 1971; Cronbach and Meehl, 1955; Nunnally, 1978). Hence, there is currently no comprehensive review of the validity of the SI, JAS, Framingham, and Bortner, making it difficult to conclusively evaluate these measures and identify areas for improvement.

The purpose of this chapter is to critically evaluate the validity of the SI, JAS, Framingham, and Bortner. This evaluation will focus on three traditional forms of validity, including criterion-oriented validity, content validity, and construct validity (Cronbach, 1971; Cronbach and Meehl, 1955; Nunnally, 1978). First, a brief summary of the SI, JAS, Framingham, and Bortner will be provided. Next, each form of validity will be defined, followed by a review of relevant evidence. The chapter will conclude with recommendations for the use and development of TABP measures.

OVERVIEW OF THE SI, JAS, FRAMINGHAM, AND BORTNER

The SI was the first measure of TABP used in empirical research (Rosenman, 1978; Rosenman et al., 1964). Though the SI content and protocol have varied somewhat over time (Scherwitz, 1988), the central features have remained essentially the same, consisting of approximately 30 questions concerning characteristic behaviors and responses to challenging and frustrating situations. These questions are augmented by the pacing and mannerisms of the interviewer, which are intended to elicit behaviors characteristic of TABP. The interviewer records not only the content of the responses, but also the manner in which they are given, focusing primarily on speech stylistics and motor behavior. The standard scoring protocol for the SI yields an overall TABP rating, expressed as a simple A/B dichotomy or a four- or five-point classification. Component rating systems for the SI have also been developed, one yielding separate scores for seven speech stylistic and answer content dimensions (Dembroski et al., 1978), and another yielding scores for five dimensions that combine speech stylistics and answer content (Matthews et al., 1977).

The JAS was developed in an effort to duplicate the SI classification with a self-report measure (Jenkins et al., 1967). The current adult version of the JAS (form C; Jenkins, Zyzanski and Rosenman, 1979) consists of 52 multiple-choice items describing a variety of behaviors, such as competitive drive, speed, time pressure, and job involvement. The standard JAS scoring procedure recodes and sums subsets of the original 52 items to yield a 21-item global TABP scale (JAS-AB) and three component scales, including the 21-item speed and impatience scale (JAS-S), the 24-item job involvement scale (JAS-J), and the 20-item hard-driving and competitive scale (JAS-H). To maintain consistency with the SI, Framingham, and Bortner, the following review will focus on the global TABP scale of the JAS. Properties of the JAS component measures will be discussed as they pertain to the evaluation of the global measures.

The Framingham scale consists of 10 multiple-choice items drawn from a 300-item inventory administered in the Framingham study (Haynes et al., 1978b). The items comprising the Framingham focus primarily on time pressure, competitive drive, and, to a lesser extent, speed and impatience. Six items concern these factors as they generally exist, and four items focus specifically on reactions to work. The standard scoring procedure consists of converting each response to the same scale and averaging, yielding a total score ranging from zero to one. A six-item version of the Framingham has also been created by dropping the four work-related items, which reportedly increases its agreement with the SI (Chesney et al., 1981).

The Bortner scale (Bortner, 1969) consists of 14 bipolar items, with descriptors intended to reflect Type A and Type B behavior placed at opposte ends of each continuum. Respondents place a vertical mark through a 1.5 inch line separating the two descriptors, with scores generated by measuring the distance of the mark from the Type B descriptor. Later versions have adopted a numerical response format, consisting of an 11-point scale centered at zero and ascending to five in both directions (Cooper and Marshall, 1979; Edwards, Baglioni and Cooper, 1990c). Bortner (1969) also constructed a seven-item scale by selecting items that independently contributed to the prediction of SI classifications in multivariate analyses. A weighted version of the seven-item scale has also been proposed (Bortner, 1969), with weights derived from a multiple regression of the SI on the items forming the scale.

The following evaluation of the SI, JAS, Framingham, and Bortner will focus on criterion-oriented validity, content validity, and construct validity (Cronbach, 1971; Cronbach and Meehl, 1955; Nunnally, 1978). Taken together, these forms of validity comprise a set of complementary standards for measurement evaluation (Nunnally, 1978). For some measures, certain forms of validity may receive greater emphasis, depending upon the purpose of the measure. For example, criterion-oriented validity is emphasized if a measure is intended to predict another variable, whereas content validity is emphasized if it is intended to represent a specified universe of content, and construct validity is emphasized if it is intended to tap an underlying psychological phenomenon. Despite these distinctions, most measures are intended to fulfill all three of these functions to varying degrees. This is certainly true of TABP measures, which are intended to predict CHD, represent the domain of behaviors and characteristics comprising TABP, and reflect underlying psychological phenomena (e.g. competitiveness, hostility, impatience).

CRITERION-ORIENTED VALIDITY

Perhaps the most commonly invoked standard for the evaluation of TABP measures is criterion-oriented validity. Criterion-oriented validity refers to the relationship between the measure of interest and another measure, the latter being referred to as the criterion (Carmines and Zeller, 1979; Cronbach and Meehl, 1955). Criterion-oriented validity is emphasized when the purpose of a measure is to predict some phenomenon of theretical or practical importance that is external to the measure itself (Nunnally, 1978). Two forms of criterion-oriented validity include predictive validity, where the measure of interest is adminstered before the criterion measure, and concurrent validity, where the measure of interest and the criterion measure are administered at the same time (Cronbach and Meehl, 1955). For both forms, evidence for validity is provided by, and only by, the correlation between the criterion measure and the measure of interest (Nunnally, 1978).

Criterion-oriented validation in TABP research has focused primarily on correspondence with the SI and CHD (i.e. angina pectoris, myocardial infarction, sudden cardiac death). The SI has acquired the status of a criterion because it was developed by the originators of the TABP construct (Rosenman et al., 1964) and is more consistently related to CHD than other TABP measures, particularly those relying exclusively on self-reports (Booth-Kewley and Friedman, 1987; Matthews, 1988). This has led some investigators to select and evaluate items for self-report TABP measures based primarily on their agreement with the SI (e.g. Bortner, 1969; Jenkins et al., 1967). Other investigators have taken a more extreme position, claiming that the SI *defines* TABP, and that lack of agreement between the SI and another measure implicates the latter but not the former (e.g. O'Looney, 1984; O'Looney, Harding and Eiser, 1985). Extreme operationalism such as this presumes that the SI is a perfect (i.e. error-free) indicator of TABP, which is inconsistent with evidence regarding its reliability (Scherwitz, 1989). Furthermore, since the SI and other TABP measures are intended to reflect the same construct, lack of correspondence implicates the validity of each measure involved (Campbell, 1960; Campbell and Fiske, 1959). For these reasons, evidence regarding the relationship between the SI and other TABP measures should be interpreted in terms of convergent validity, not criterion-oriented validity. This evidence is reviewed later, when the convergence of the SI, JAS, Framingham, and Bortner is considered.

Unlike the SI, CHD is a readily defensible criterion for the validation of TABP measures, given that the original intent of these measures was to predict CHD prevalence and incidence. Because several excellent reviews regarding the relationship between TABP and CHD are available (e.g. Booth-Kewley and Friedman, 1987; Cooper, Detre and Weiss, 1981; Jenkins,

1983; Matthews, 1988; Matthews and Haynes, 1986; Siegel, 1984), this evidence will be only briefly summarized here.

Concurrent Validity

Evidence regarding concurrent validity is provided by cross-sectional studies of TABP and CHD prevalence. Initial evidence for the concurrent validity of the SI was provided by the Western Collaborative Group Study (WCGS; Rosenman et al., 1964; Rosenman et al., 1975), which found that, compared to Type B's, Type A's were more than twice as likely to exhibit symptoms of CHD (i.e. angina pectoris, myocardial infarction). These results were replicated in subsequent studies (e.g. Caffrey, 1970; Keith, Lown and Stare,. 1965), though more recent evidence is somewhat less consistent (Booth-Kewley and Friedman, 1987). The WCGS also provided initial evidence for the concurrent validity of the JAS, indicating higher scores among respondents with evidence of myocardial infarction (Jenkins et al., 19781b). Subsequent studies have generally yielded similar results (e.g. DeBacker et al., 1983; Shekelle, Schoenberger and Stamler, 1976).

Evidence for the concurrent validity of the Framingham and Bortner is weaker than that for the SI and JAS. The primary evidence for the Framingham was presented by Haynes et al. (1978a), who found positive relationships with myocardial infarction among men aged 45–64, angina among men aged 65 or older, and both angina and total CHD among women aged 45–64. Evidence for the concurrent validity of the Bortner has been mixed. Johnston, Cook and Shaper (1987) found a higher prevalence of CHD among men with higher Bortner scores, and Heller (1979) found that patients with myocardial infarction had higher Bortner scores than matched controls. In contrast, two major population studies (French–Belgian Collaborative Group, 1982; Koskenvuo et al., 1988) found no relationship between CHD prevalence and either the full or seven-item version of the Bortner.

Predictive Validity

The predictive validity of TABP measures has been given much greater credence than concurrent validity, given the superiority of prospective studies over cross-sectional studies in establishing a causal relationship between TABP and CHD (Matthews, 1988). The predictive validity of the SI was first examined in the WCGS, which found that, among men initially free from CHD symptoms, those who were categorized as Type A were more than twice as likely to develop CHD after 8.5 years than those categorized as Type B (Rosenman et al., 1975). In contrast, more recent studies have not been supportive (e.g. Shekelle et al., 1985). However, because some elements of the SI procedure have varied (Scherwitz, 1988), it is difficult to attribute these inconsistent results to variation in the SI or to weaknesses in the predictive validity of its core elements. The predictive validity of the JAS was also initially demonstrated in the WCGS, which found that the JAS A/B classification was related to CHD incidence over a four-year period (Jenkins et al., 1974). Though some studies have replicated these findings (DeBacker et al., 1983), others have not (Cohen and Reed, 1985), particularly those examining high-risk populations (e.g. Case et al., 1985; Shekelle et al., 1985).

The predictive validity of the Framingham was initially demonstrated by Haynes et al. (1980), who found a positive relationship between the Framingham and subsequent development of total CHD and angina for women aged 45–64 and total CHD and myocardial infarction for white-collar men aged 45–64. Follow-up analyses by Haynes and Feinleib (1982) corroborated these findings, but more recent analyses found significant relationships only for angina (Eaker, Abbott and Kannel, 1989). The predictive validity of the Bortner was supported by the French–Belgian Collaborative Group (1982), who found significant relationships with total CHD and marginally significant relationships with myocardial infarction and angina. However, later prospective studies using both the full and the seven-item version of the Bortner have found no relationship with CHD (Johnston et al., 1987; Koskenvuo et al., 1988).

Taken together, evidence for concurrent validity is fairly strong for the SI and JAS, limited but supportive for the Framingham, and mixed for the Bortner. Evidence for predictive validity is inconsistent for all measures, though the SI has fared notably better than the JAS, Framingham, and Bortner. This evidence has led some to conclude that the SI is the only valid measure of TABP, and that self-report measures (including the JAS, Framingham, and Bortner) should be avoided (e.g. Dembroski and Czajkowski, 1989; O'Looney et al., 1985; Rosenman, 1978). Such conclusions are unwarranted, because sole reliance on the SI introduces mono-operation bias (Cook and Campbell, 1979), which completely confounds trait and method variance, thereby preventing unambiguous interpretation of observed relationships (Yarnold and Bryant, 1988). Furthermore, criterion-oriented validity provides insufficient basis to either accept or reject a measure, for two reasons. First, because it is determined entirely by the relationship between the criterion and the measure of interest, criterion-oriented validity indicates nothing about the meaning of the measure itself (Nunnally, 1978). As a result, it is impossible to attribute the observed relationship to the construct of interest or to correlated but conceptually distinct constructs. Second, criterion-oriented validity is influenced not only by the properties of the measure of interest, but also by the properties of the criterion measure and the strength of the relationship between their respective underlying constructs. Without independent evidence regarding the latter two factors, the correlation between the criterion and the measure of interest cannot be unambiguously interpreted. This ambiguity is partially avoided when multiple measures are correlated with the same criterion within a single study (e.g. Shekelle et al., 1985), which effectively holds constant the properties of the criterion measure. However, unless the construct represented by the measures being evaluated is also held constant, results will remain ambiguous. This condition is not met by the measures considered here, which represent different aspects of TABP (Edwards, Baglioni and Cooper, 1990a; Matthews, 1983; Matthews et al., 1982). In sum, available evidence appears to provide the strongest support for the criterion-oriented validity of the SI, particularly in terms of predictive validity. However, due to its inherent ambiguities, this evidence is insufficient to draw firm conclusions regarding the relative utility of these measures.

CONTENT VALIDITY

Content validity, defined as the degree to which a measure adequately represents a specified domain of content (Carimes and Zeller, 1979; Cronbach and Meehl, 1955), is at issue when the purpose of the measure is to directly reflect some attribute (Nunnally, 1978). Content validity is achieved by clearly defining the intended domain of content, generating items that convincingly represent this domain, and combining these items into a measure (Nunnally, 1978). As this procedure suggests, establishing content validity rests mainly on "appeals to reason" regarding the adequacy with which the domain of content has been sampled and represented in a measure (Nunnally, 1978, p. 93). Content validity should be distinguished from face validity, which relies on *post hoc* assessments of whether a measure "looks like" it reflects the intended attribute (Carmines and Zeller, 1979). In this sense, face validation represents an inductive process, whereas content validation represents a deductive process (Cronbach and Meehl, 1955).

Of the three forms of validity considered here, content validity is perhaps the most difficult to verify, given the absence of specific guidelines for its evaluation (Carmines and Zeller, 1979), and the rather sparse documentation regarding the origins of the SI, JAS, Framingham, and Bortner. This situation is not unusual, as the process of creating a measure is often iterative and intuitive, making thorough scientific description somewhat difficult. Nonetheless, information regarding the content validity of the SI, JAS, Framingham, and Bortner may be gleaned from the definitions of TABP underlying these measures and available descriptions of the procedures used to derive and combine their constituent items.

The definition of TABP underlying the SI consists of several major components, including competitiveness, an intensive drive to achieve poorly defined goals, a desire for recognition and advancement, involvement in multiple activities subject to time restrictions, habitual acceleration of mental and physical activities, heightened mental and physical alertness, and aggressive, hostile feelings (Friedman and Rosenman, 1959; Rosenman et al., 1964; Rosenman, Swan and Carmelli,1988). The SI was constructed by generating multiple items representing these components and selecting those that, combined with certain modes of delivery, best elicited verbal and behavioral manifestations of TABP in predisposed subjects. However, there is no specific formula for combining the resulting responses and observations to yield overall TABP classifications (Scherwitz, 1989), though the greatest weight is apparently given to speech stylistics (Dembroski and Czajkowski, 1989). From this, it appears that the items and procedures comprising the SI were indeed selected to represent the domain of TABP, but because it is unclear how interviewers integrate the resulting information, the content validity of the global TABP classification yielded by the SI is in question.

Like the SI, the definition of TABP underlying the JAS emphasizes multiple components, including competitiveness, achievement striving, aggressiveness, haste, impatience, restlessness, hyperalertness, explosive speech, muscular tension, external time pressures, challenging responsibility, and job commitment (Jenkins et al., 1979). However, the items comprising the JAS were not generated from this domain of content, but instead were adapted from questions asked in the SI (Jenkins et al., 1967; Jenkins et al., 1979). Successive revisions retained items that best predicted TABP classifications based on the SI (Jenkins et al., 1971a) or earlier versions of the JAS itself (Jenkins, 1978). The procedure used to combine the JAS items also raises concerns, because several items with similar content are assigned opposite weights, effectively canceling their contribution to the overall scale score (Edwards et al., 1990a). Hence, the JAS was apparently not constructed to represent the domain of content indicated by its associated definition, and the procedure used to combine its items dilutes their contribution to the overall scale score. Taken together, this evidence suggests that the content validity of the JAS is weak at best.

Descriptions of the origins of the Bortner and Framingham are less thorough than those for the SI and JAS. Bortner (1969) defined TABP in terms of competitive drive, ambition, and time urgency. However, the procedure used to generate the Bortner items is not described, other than indicating that they were thought to represent contrasting Type A and Type B behaviors. As a result, there is too little information available to adequately evaluate the content validity of the Bortner. The definition underlying the Framingham involves aggressiveness, ambition, competitive drive, impatience, chronic time urgency, and a high need for achievement (Haynes et al., 1978b; Haynes et al., 1980). To construct the scale, three experts screened a pool of 300 items compiled by Levine and Scotch, selecting those that measured "behavior patterns initially conceptualized in the design of the questionnaire" (Haynes et al., 1978b, p. 364). This *post hoc* interpretation suggests that the

Framingham items were chosen on the basis of face validity rather than generated to represent the defined domain of TABP, as required for content validity.

In sum, available evidence provides little support for the content validity of the SI, JAS, Framingham, and Bortner. As a result, there is little *a priori* basis for determining what these measures actually represent. Given this, it is perhaps not surprising that the appropriate interpretation of these measures has generated considerable debate (Matthews, 1983). Such debates could be largely circumvented by emphasizing content validity in the initial design of TABP measures. However, the development of content valid TABP measures is currently impeded by two obstacles. First, the definition of TABP itself has been broad, vague, and inconsistent, encompassing a wide variety of cognitive, affective, and behavioral components (Friedman and Booth-Kewley, 1987; Rosenman et al., 1988). Without a clear, concise definition of TABP, it is impossible to generate items that convincingly represent its domain of content. Second, there has been a traditional emphasis on global TABP measures, which collapse conceptually distinct TABP components into a single index. By design, these measures offer no clear interpretation, because the distinct content domains represented by different TABP components will be reflected to varying degrees for each respondent, depending on the specific pattern of responses obtained. These obstacles may be overcome by clearly defining each component comprising TABP, generating items that convincingly represent these content domains, and combining these items into separate measures for each component of interest.

CONSTRUCT VALIDITY

Construct validity refers to the correspondence between the conceptual definition of a variable and the operational procedure used to represent that variable (Cronbach and Meehl, 1955; Nunnally, 1978; Schwab, 1980). As this implies, construct validity is at issue when the purpose of a measure is to reflect an unobserved phenomenon of theoretical or practical interest (i.e. a construct). Two types of construct validity may be distinguished, including trait validity and nomological validity (Campbell, 1960). Trait validity is demonstrated, in part, by convergence between the measure of interest and other measures intended to reflect the same construct. Convergence with measures sharing the same method demonstrates reliability, whereas convergence with measures using different methods represents convergent validity (Campbell and Fiske, 1959). Evidence for trait validity is also provided by discriminant validity, meaning the divergence of the measure of interest from measures of conceptually distinct constructs (Campbell, 1960; Campbell and Fiske, 1959). Nomological validity is established by demonstrating that the measure of interest exhibits relationships with measures of other constructs in accordance with relevant theory (Carmines and Zeller, 1979; Cronbach and Meehl, 1955). Nomological validity is related to discriminant validity and criterion-oriented validity, in that each examines the relationship between the measure of interest and other measures. However, discriminant validity essentially requires higher correlations with measures of the same construct than with measures of other constructs (Campbell and Fiske, 1959), whereas nomological validity demands a specific pattern of relationships that conforms to theoretical predictions (Cronbach and Meehl, 1955). Nomological validity is also distinct from criterion-oriented validity, in that the latter presumes the validity of the criterion measure, whereas the former treats all measures as fallible indicators of their associated underlying constructs (Cronbach and Meehl, 1955; Campbell, 1960).

Trait Validity

Trait validity may be evaluated by examining evidence for reliability, convergent validity, and discriminant validity. These properties provide complementary information, and each is necessary but not sufficient to establish trait validity. Evidence for these properties as they pertain to the SI, JAS, Framingham, and Bortner is summarized below.

Reliability

Reliability provides a direct numerical estimate of trait validity, indicating the proportion of variance in a measure attributable to its associated underlying construct (Nunnally, 1978). Studies of the reliability of the SI, JAS, Framingham, and Bortner have focused primarily on test–retest reliability rather than estimates based on internal consistency, such as Cronbach's alpha (Cronbach, 1951) and its derivatives (Nunnally, 1978). For the SI, two types of test–retest reliability have been reported, based on a single interviewer rating either the same taped interview twice or the same subjects on two separate occasions (Dembroski, 1978; Powell, 1987). Agreement using the same taped interview has reached 74% for the dichotomous SI classification and 57% for the four-level classification (Keith et al., 1965). Agreement for the same subjects on different occasions has ranged from 67% to 80% for the dichotomous classification (Carmelli, Rosenman and Chesney, 1987; Jenkins et al., 1968). Early reports of the test–retest reliability of the JAS are misleading, because they actually compared scores obtained from successive revisions, some of which shared only a small core of items (Jenkins et al., 1971a; Jenkins et al., 1974). Studies using the same version have found test–retest reliabilities ranging from .54 to .82 (Carmelli et al., 1987; Jenkins et al., 1979; Johnston and Shaper, 1983). The test–retest reliability of A/B classifications based on the Framingham has ranged from 57% to 80% (Matthews and

Haynes, 1986). Finally, test–retest reliabilities for the Bortner have ranged from .68 to .84 for the full 14-item version (Bass, 1984; Johnston and Shaper, 1983; Pichot et al., 1977) and from .72 to .74 for the seven-item version (Price, 1979).

Though test–retest reliability has often been emphasized in the evaluation of TABP measures, there are several reasons why it yields ambiguous information. First, test–retest reliability presumes the stability of the underlying construct. This cannot be verified in TABP research, since the only evidence for the stability of TABP is provided by the test–retest reliability studies themselves. Any variation in the underlying construct will lower test–retest correlations, thereby biasing reliability estimates downward. (Obviously, this criticism does not apply to test–retest reliability estimates based on the same interviewer rating the same taped SI on different occasions.) Second, the proportion of true score variance in a measure is reduced by factors other than random measurement error, such as specific item variance and method variance (Lord and Novick, 1968). Because these sources of variance are stable over time, they tend to inflate test–retest reliability estimates. Studies suggest that these sources of variance are appreciable in the SI, JAS, Framingham, and Bortner (Edwards et al., 1990a; Matthews et al., 1982; Mayes, Sime and Ganster, 1984; Scherwitz, 1989). Third, experience with a measure on one occasion may affect responses to that measure on subsequent occasions (Nunnally, 1978). This may involve repeating guesses, habitual response styles, or striving for consistency, each of which would inflate reliability estimates. Finally, the estimation of reliability as derived from the domain sampling model is strictly a function of the correlation among the items comprising a measure (Nunnally, 1978). Even if these correlations are essentially zero (indicating no true score variance), each item may correlate with itself over time, yielding a nonzero reliability estimate.

Studies of the SI have also used interrater agreement to represent reliability. Agreement has ranged from 65% to 98% for the dichotomous classification and from 64% to 84% for the four-level classification (Powell, 1987; Scherwitz, 1989). Unfortunately, these findings provide an inflated view of reliability, because they do not control for chance agreement (Cohen, 1960; Matthews, 1982). Furthermore, interviewers in TABP studies often compare observations and criteria, which enhances agreement without necessarily increasing correspondence with the construct of interest (Scherwitz, 1989). These criticisms aside, it is debatable whether interrater agreement reflects the reliability of the SI itself, because SI ratings reflect behaviors of the interviewer as well as the interviewee (Howland and Siegman, 1982). As a result, interrater agreement may represent the similarity of the interviewers rather than the proportion of true score variance in the interview.

Due to these problems, estimates representing test–retest reliability and interrater agreement should generally be avoided in favor of estimates based on internal consistency (Nunnally, 1978). Unfortunately, few studies have examined the reliability of the SI, JAS, Framingham, and Bortner in this manner. The internal consistency reliability of the SI is particularly elusive, because the correlations among the facets that interviewers consider in deriving an overall classification are difficult to determine. To overcome this, several investigators have used correlations among scores obtained from the Dembroski et al. (1978) component rating system to estimate reliability. For example, Mayes et al. (1984) reported a reliability of .90 for a continuous SI score. The present author obtained a reliability estimate of .88 based on component correlations reported by Dembroski et al. (1978). Though these estimates are acceptably high, it should be emphasized that they pertain to a score representing the sum of the component ratings, *not* the SI classifications as they are typically generated.

In contrast to the SI, the internal consistency reliability of the JAS, Framingham, and Bortner can be readily estimated. Jenkins et al. (1979) reported that the reliability of the JAS has ranged from .83 to .85. However, Mayes et al. (1984) noted that these estimates were based on test–retest and item-total correlations rather than inter-item correlations (as required by alpha) and, therefore, were inflated. Estimates based on alpha have been much lower, ranging from .29 to .56 (Edwards and Baglioni, 1991; Edwards et al., 1990a; Lee, King and King, 1987; Mayes et al., 1984; O'Looney and Harding, 1985; Shipper et al., 1986). However, Edwards et al. (1990a) found that alpha increased to .71 after reversing items that yielded negative loadings in a single-factor measurement model of the JAS. Examinations of item content indicated that these reversals corrected apparent inconsistencies embedded in the recommended JAS scoring procedure. O'Looney and Harding (1985) found increases of similar magnitude after reversing items with negative item-total correlations. The Framingham has yielded internal consistency reliability estimates ranging from .54 to .71 (Edwards and Baglioni, 1991; Edwards et al., 1990a; Haynes et al., 1978b; Lee et al., 1987; O'Looney and Harding, 1985), and the Bortner has yielded estimates ranging from .50 to .75 (Bortner, 1969; Edwards and Baglioni, 1991; Edwards et al., 1990a, 1990c; Edwards, Baglioni and Cooper, 1990b; Mayes et al., 1984; Ray and Bozek, 1980).

In sum, test–retest reliabilities for the SI, JAS, Framingham, and Bortner are fairly high, and interrater agreement for the SI has been apparently adequate. However, these results yield ambiguous information regarding the proportion of true score variance in these measures, which is better reflected by estimates based on internal consistency. The few studies that have used this approach suggest that the reliability of the SI is acceptable, whereas the reliabilities of the JAS, Framingham, and Bortner are marginal at best.

Nonetheless, these estimates should be interpreted with caution, because they do not correspond to the SI classification as it is typically generated, and they assume that the SI, JAS, Framingham, and Bortner are unidimensional (Nunnally, 1978). Several studies indicate that this assumption is violated for each of these measures (Begley and Boyd, 1985; Edwards et al., 1990a; Johnston and Shaper, 1983; Matthews et al., 1977; Musantel et al., 1983; Pichot et al., 1977).

Convergent validity

Convergent validity concerns the relationships among different measures of the same underlying construct. The most direct evidence for the convergent valdity of the SI, JAS, Framingham, and Bortner is represented by their intercorrelations, since these measures are each intended to reflect global TABP. It may be argued that the relationships among the JAS, Framingham, and Bortner represent reliability, given that each of these measures is self-report. Despite this general similarity, there are several specific methodological distinctions among these measures, most notably length and response format. Therefore, the relationships among these measures will be interpreted in terms of convergent validity. Correlations between global TABP measures and measures of specific TABP components are also informative, provided the component is included in the conceptualization of TABP underlying the global measure in question.

As indicated earlier, the relationship between the SI and other TABP measures has typically been considered evidence for concurrent validity, based on the belief that the SI is the "gold standard" for TABP measures (Dembroski and Czajkowski, 1989; O'Looney, Harding and Eiser, 1985; Powell, 1987; Rosenman et al., 1988). However, because the SI is a fallible indicator of TABP (Scherwitz, 1989), this evidence is more appropriately interpreted in terms of convergent validity. Correlations between the SI and JAS have varied widely, ranging from .10 to .63 (Appels, Jenkins and Rosenman, 1982; Carmelli et al., 1987; Chesney et al., 1981; Herbertt, 1983; MacDougall, Dembroski and Musante, 1979; Matthews et al., 1982; Matthews and Saal, 1978; Mayes et al., 1984; Rahe, Hervig and Rosenman, 1978; Scherwitz, Berton and Leventhal, 1977). The SI has demonstrated weak positive relationships with the Framingham (Byrne et al., 1985; Haynes et al., 1980), with correlations ranging from .20 to .37 (Chesney et al., 1981; MacDougall et al., 1979). Correlations between the SI and Bortner have also been weak (Byrne et al., 1985), ranging from .25 to .45 (Bortner, 1969; Herbertt, 1983; Mayes et al., 1984).

Relationships among the JAS, Framingham, and Bortner have been somewhat higher than relationships between these measures and the SI. For example, correlations between the JAS and Framingham have ranged from .51

to .62 (Byrne et al., 1985; Edwards and Baglioni, 1991; Edwards et al., 1990a; Haynes et al., 1980; Lee et al., 1987; Smith and O'Keeffe, 1985). The Bortner has demonstrated correlations ranging from .33 to .71 with the JAS (Byrne et al., 1985; Edwards and Baglioni, 1991; Edwards et al., 1990a; Herbertt, 1983; Herbertt and Innes, 1982; Johnston and Shaper, 1983; Mayes et al., 1984). Finally, correlations between the Framingham and Bortner have ranged from .31 to .61 (Byrne et al., 1985; Edwards and Baglioni, 1991; Edwards et al., 1990a; Flannery and Bowen, 1986).

The modest relationships among the SI, JAS, Framingham, and Bortner provide rather weak support for convergent validity. This evidence has led some to conclude that these measures reflect different aspects of TABP (Matthews, 1982). Examinations of the content of these measures provide some support for this conclusion (Edwards, 1990a; Matthews, 1983). However, an alternative explanation for these weak relationships is attenuation due to measurement error. Given the modest reliability estimates yielded by these measures, correlations of greater magnitude cannot be reasonably expected (Nunnally, 1978). The effects of measurement error were demonstrated by Edwards et al. 1990a), who found that, after correcting for attenuation, the correlations among the JAS, Framingham, and Bortner exceeded .80. A third explanation is that these measures contain multiple dimensions, some of which are shared across measures, and others which are unique to each measure. Collapsing these dimensions within each measure will obviously limit the resulting intercorrelations. This was also demonstrated by Edwards et al. (1990a), who found that the correlations among the components shared by the JAS, Framingham, and Bortner were significantly higher than the correlations among the components unique to each measure. Though analogous analyses for the SI were not found, evidence concerning its measurement error (Scherwitz, 1989) and multidimensionality (Matthews et al., 1977) suggests that similar results would be obtained. Hence, the modest relationships among the SI, JAS, Framingham, and Bortner apparently reflect not only differences in underlying constructs, but also measurement error and overlap among only a subset of the components comprising each measure.

As indicated earlier, correlations between global TABP measures and measures of TABP components provide suggestive evidence for convergent validity, provided these components are included within the conceptualization of TABP underlying the global measure. The most abundant evidence of this type involves the S, J, and H scales from the JAS. Correlations between the SI and these scales have been rather low, ranging from .08 to .39 (Chesney et al., 1981; Herbertt, 1983; MacDougall et al., 1979; Matthews and Saal, 1978; Mayes et al., 1984; Rahe et al., 1978). Correlations between the JAS-AB and the S, J, and H scales have ranged from .15 to .67 (Byrne et al., 1985; Edwards et al., 1990a; Herbertt, 1983; Jenkins et al., 1979; Mayes et al., 1984). Correlations for the Framingham have ranged from .17 to .64 (Byrne et al., 1985;

Edwards et al., 1990a; Haynes et al., 1980; Lee et al., 1987; Smith and O'Keeffe, 1985), and correlations for the Bortner have ranged from .14 to .59 (Byrne et al., 1985; Edwards et al., 1990a; Herbertt, 1983; Herbertt and Innes, 1982; Johnston and Shaper, 1983; Mayes et al., 1984). For the JAS-AB, Bortner, and Framingham, correlations with the JAS-S are typically stronger than those with the JAS-H, which in turn are stronger than those with the JAS-J.

Relationships with other measures of TABP components have also been examined (Matthews, 1982). For example, Rahe et al. (1978) found tha the SI was positively related to speed, impulsiveness, dominance, aggression, and achievement. Similarly, Herman et al. (1981) found positive relationships with aggressiveness, assertiveness, speed, energy level, dominance, impatience, irritability, and tension, but not ambition or persistence. Chesney et al. (1981) found that the SI was related to aggression, achievement, dominance, and impulsiveness. Subsequent studies have yielded similar results, indicating positive relationships with speed, anger, aggression, need for achievement, need for power, and job involvement (Blumenthal, Lane and Williams, 1985; Blumenthal, O'Toole and Haney, 1984; Byrne et al., 1985; Ganster et al., 1991; Mayes et al., 1984).

Numerous studies have examined the relationship between the JAS and measures of various TABP components. In general, these studies indicate positive relationships with speed, activity level, impulsivity, dominance, anger, and, in some cases, need for achievement, but not hostility, aggression, or intolerance (Byrne et al., 1985; Dimsdale et al., 1978; Irvine et al., 1982; Jenkins et al., 1979; Matthews, 1982; Mayes et al., 1984). The Framingham has been positively related to speed, ambition, workload, anger, and need for achievement (Byrne et al., 1985; Haynes et al., 1979b; Smith, Houston and Zurawski, 1983). The Bortner has been positively related to speed, anger, and the overt expression of emotions (Bass, 1984; Bass and Akhras, 1987; Boekeloo, Mamon and Ewart, 1987; Byrne et al., 1985; Lee et al., 1987; Mayes et al., 1984), but not hostility (Koskenvuo et al., 1988).

Overall, the pattern of results reviewed above provides fairly strong support for the convergent validity of the SI and JAS. Evidence for the Framingham and Bortner is supportive but too sparse to permit firm conclusions. However, it should be noted that relationships between global TABP measures and TABP component measures provide ambiguous information regarding convergent validity, because it is impossible to attribute the observed relationships to the common construct, conceptually distinct but correlated constructs, or both. Furthermore, as indicated in the following section, relationships with these components are often not appreciably stronger than those with variables not included within the conceptualization of TABP. It should also be noted that evidence involving the JAS subscales is potentially misleading, because these measures contain multiple dimensions and substantial measurement error (Edwards et al., 1990a; Mayes et al., 1984). Furthermore, the JAS-AB shares several items with each JAS subscale, which artificially inflates evidence for its convergent validity. Hence, though the SI, JAS, Framingham, and Bortner generally exhibit the expected relationships with TABP component measures, this evidence provides only tenuous support for convergent validity.

Discriminant validity

The discriminant validity of the SI, JAS, Framingham, and Bortner is demonstrated primarily by stronger relationships among these measures than with measures of conceptually distinct constructs. Given the broad conceptualization of TABP (Friedman and Booth-Kewley, 1987), the identification of constructs that should *not* correlate with the SI, JAS, Framingham, and Bortner is somewhat of a challenge. However, examining the original conceptualization of TABP reveals an explicit distinction from psychopathology (i.e. anxiety, neuroticism, depression) (Rosenman et al., 1988). Therefore, evidence involving relationships with these constructs will be used to assess discriminant validity.

In most studies, the SI has demonstrated weak or nonsignificant relationships with psychopathology (e.g. Byrne et al., 1985; Caffrey, 1979; Chesney et al., 1981; Ganster et al., 1991; Matthews, 1982; Mayes et al., 1984; Suls and Wan, 1989). Because these relationships are typically smaller in magnitude than those between the SI and other TABP measures, they provide support for discriminant validity. In contrast, significant relationships with psychopathology have been found for the JAS (Byrne et al., 1985; Chesney et al., 1981; Dimsdale et al., 1978; Edwards and Baglioni, 1991), the Framingham (Byrne et al., 1985; Chesney et al., 1981; Edwards and Baglioni, 1991; Haynes et al., 1978b; Smith et al., 1983; Smith and O'Keeffe, 1985), and the Bortner (Bass, 1984; Bass and Akhras, 1987; Byrne et al., 1985; Edwards and Baglioni, 1991; Edwards et al., 1990c) (for a review, see Suls and Wan, 1989). However, for each of these measures, these relationships are generally smaller in magnitude than those with other TABP measures, providing some support for discriminant validity.

The preceding evidence provides modest support for the discriminant validity of the SI, JAS, Framingham, and Bortner. However, this evidence permits only tentative conclusions, for several reasons. First, no studies have reported whether the correlations among the SI, JAS, Framingham, and Bortner were *significantly* higher than those with conceptually distinct constructs. *Post hoc* analyses of results reported by Edwards and Baglioni (1991) indicate that the correlations among the JAS, Framingham, and Bortner were, in fact, significantly higher than those between these measures and anxiety and depression. Similar analyses based on other studies would allow stronger statements regarding discriminant validity. Second, evidence for the discriminant validity of the SI is based on self-report measures, which differ in method from the SI. Consequently, the small relationships between the SI and measures of psychopathology may be partly attributable to differences in method. Third, much of the evidence upon which the preceding evaluation is based was drawn from different studies, with some reporting the correlations among the SI, JAS, Framingham, and Bortner, and others reporting the relationships between these measures and psychopathology. If the former studies contain relatively fewer methodological weaknesses than the latter studies, then evidence for discriminant validity would be artifactual. Finally, the preceding evaluation focused exclusively on constructs comprising psychopathology. This approach was adopted to maintain manageable scope, and because these constructs are among the few that are consistently considered distinct from TABP. However, additional evidence reveals that the measures reviewed here often demonstrate relationships with variables not explicitly included in their conceptualization. For example, relationships have been found between the SI and autonomy, exhibition, sociability, self-confidence, extroversion, stress, and dissatisfaction (Rosenman et al., 1988). Similarly, the JAS has been related to sociability, flexibility, and femininity (Jenkins et al., 1979). For both measures, these relationships are of similar magnitude as those with measures of their constituent TABP components. As this illustrates, a comprehensive assessment of the discriminant validity of the SI, JAS, Framingham, and Bortner would require low correlations with a broad set of constructs that are distinct from their underlying conceptualizations.

Nomological validity

The nomological validity of the SI, JAS, Framingham, and Bortner is evidenced by relationships with the hypothesized antecedents and consequences of TABP. Theoretical discussions of TABP antecedents consistently emphasize the interaction of situation and person factors (Smith, 1989). In most cases, situation factors have included challenge and threats to control (Glass, 1977; Matthews, 1982; Rosenman et al., 1988). Person factors have not been clearly specified, other than indicating that TABP emerges among "susceptible" individuals (Dembroski and Czajkowski, 1989; Matthews, 1982) or invoking descriptors that are part of TABP itself, such as impatience, competitiveness, potential for hostility, and poorly defined goals. Because the person factors indicating susceptibility to TABP have not been adequately specified, they will not be considered in the following assessment. Consequences of TABP have focused mainly on factors that presumably mediate the relationship between TABP and CHD, most notably physiological reactivity (Contrada, Wright and Glass, 1985; Houston, 1983, 1986; Krantz and Manuck, 1984; Suls and Sanders, 1989). Of course, CHD is part of the nomological network of

TABP, constituting its consequence of greatest interest. However, this evidence was summarized in terms of predictive validity and, hence, will not be repeated here. Furthermore, though the relationship between TABP and CHD has been examined extensively, the mechanisms mediating this relationship have not been determined (Matthews, 1982). It is the explication of these mechanisms that will enhance the nomological network surrounding TABP. Hence, the following discussion of nomological validity will characterize antecedents of TABP in terms of challenge and threats to control, and consequences in terms of physiological reactivity.

As indicated above, the most widely emphasized antecedents of TABP include challenge and threats to control. One stimulus often used to present these antecedents is the SI itself, which is designed to challenge and frustrate the interviewee (Rosenman, 1978). However, reactions to the SI do not allow inferences regarding its nomological validity, because these reactions must be assumed *a priori* in order to generate TABP classifications. That is, it would be tautological to classify respondents based on their reactions to the SI, and subsequently use these same classifications to identify facets of the SI that elicit TABP. Rather, the assessment of nomological validity requires the examination of responses to situations external to the measurement of TABP itself.

Situations required for the assessment of nomological validity have been created in laboratory experiments examining the differential responses of Type A's and Type B's to challenge or threats to control. Available evidence indicates that Type A's classified by the SI respond to lack of control by exhibiting irritability, hostility, and increased rate of behavior (Matthews, 1982; Rosenman et al., 1988). Similar results have emerged for Type A's classified by the JAS, who exhibit greater aggression and achievement striving in response to frustration and lack of control than Type-B's (Carver and Glass, 1978; Glass, 1977). Unfortunately, no studies using the Framingham or Bortner to classify subjects could be located. Hence, evidence regarding the SI and JAS indicates that, compared to Type B's, Type A's are more likely to respond to challenge and threats to control with behaviors characteristic of TABP.

Numerous studies have examined the effects of TABP on physiological reactivity. Studies classifying subjects using the SI have found greater elevations in systolic blood pressure, catecholamines, and heart rate for Type A's, particularly in response to frustrating, difficult, and moderately competitive situations (Contrada et al., 1985; Houston, 1983, 1986; Matthews, 1982; Suls and Sanders, 1989). Type A's measured by the JAS have demonstrated greater elevations in systolic blood pressure and catecholamines in response to similar situations, but these effects have been much less consistent than those for the SI (Contrada et al., 1985; Houston, 1983, 1986; Matthews, 1982). Limited evidence indicates no relationship with physiological reactivity for either the Bortner or Framingham (Dembroski et al., 1979; MacDougall et al., 1981; Price and Clarke, 1978).

Overall, the available evidence provides moderate support for the nomological validity of the SI and similar but weaker support for the JAS. Subjects classified using either measure have exhibited the predicted manifestations of TABP in response to challenge or threats to control. Differences in physiological reactivity have also been found for both measures, though evidence for the SI is more consistent than for the JAS. The limited evidence available regarding the nomological validity of the Framingham and Bortner is not supportive. However, two limitations regarding the preceding evidence should be considered. First, studies of the relationship between TABP and physiological reactivity were intended to illuminate the relationship between TABP and CHD. However, current evidence is inadequate to establish or deny the necessary link between physiological reactivity and CHD (Contrada et al., 1985; Krantz and Manuck, 1984; Matthews, 1982). As a result, evidence regarding the relationship between measures of TABP and physiological reactivity provides only suggestive support for nomological validity. Second, the situational and individual factors typically described as predictors of TABP overlap considerably with the concept of TABP itself. This was mentioned earlier in reference to person factors, which often include poorly defined goals, competitiveness, impatience, potential for hostility, and other components of TABP. Similarly, situation factors involving challenge and threats to control overlap with TABP components, such as time pressure and the presence of multiple deadlines. The overlap between TABP and its presumed situation and person antecedents creates a confound, which artificially inflates their interrelationships and provides little basis for enhancing the nomological validity of TABP measures. It would be far more meaningful and informative to separate TABP into its constituent components and examine the causal relationships among these components implied by theoretical discussions of TABP (e.g. Smith, 1989).

CONCLUSIONS AND DIRECTIONS FOR FUTURE RESEARCH

Based on the preceding evidence, several tentative conclusions regarding the validity of the SI, JAS, Framingham, and Bortner seem warranted. Evidence for criterion-oriented validity is fairly strong for the SI, mixed for the JAS and Bortner, and limited but supportive for the Framingham. For each measure, evidence for concurrent validity is stronger than for predictive validity, with only the SI demonstrating acceptable predictive validity across studies (Booth-Kewley and Friedman, 1987; Matthews, 1988). In contrast, none of the four measures reviewed evidenced adequate content validity, primarily due to the lack of emphasis on the domain sampling approach in their initial development. Evidence for construct validity has varied, depending on the psychometric property under consideration. Reliability estimates for the SI have been quite high, but these estimates pertain to a linear combination of its components, *not* the global SI classification as it is typically used. Reliabilities for the JAS, Framingham, and Bortner have been low, due to measurement error, multidimensionality, and, in the case of the JAS, apparent reversals in the recommended scoring protocol. Evidence for convergent validity has been weak, though the relationships among the JAS, Framingham, and Bortner are somewhat stronger than those between these measures and the SI. Apparently, these weak relationships are attributable not only to differences in underlying constructs, but also measurement error and multidimensionality. Evidence for discriminant validity appears somewhat stronger for the SI than for the JAS, Framingham, or Bortner, though limitations in this evidence prevent firm conclusions. Finally, nomological validity appears stronger for the SI than for the JAS, but too little evidence is available to adequately evaluate the Framingham and Bortner. Taking all validity criteria into consideration, it appears that the SI is the most valid of the four TABP measures reviewed. Comparisons among the JAS, Framingham, and Bortner reveal relative strengths and weaknesses in certain areas, but none of these measures clearly dominates the others. Despite these comparisons, it should be emphasized that *none* of these measures has demonstrated acceptable validity across all criteria considered here.

Though the SI, JAS, Framingham, and Bortner have generated a massive volume of research, available evidence allows only tentative conclusions regarding their validity, for two main reasons. First, studies of these measures have focused primarily on their relationships with CHD and, to a lesser extent, with one another. Though informative, these studies provide evidence only for criterion-oriented and convergent validity. Evidence for other forms of validity is rather sparse and must be gleaned from studies that, in most cases, were not explicitly designed to provide such information. Second, the multidimensionality of the SI, JAS, Framingham, and Bortner repeatedly emerges as an obstacle to evaluating their validity. This is primarily because relationships involving these measures cannot be unambiguously attributed to specific TABP components (cf. Burt, 1976). As a result, evidence concerning concurrent, predictive, convergent, discriminant, and nomological validity offers no clear interpretation. Evidence for reliability is also ambiguous, because it cannot be determined which subsets of components are responsible for inter-item correlations. Furthermore, reliability estimation assumes unidimensional measurement (Nunnally, 1978), which is clearly violated by global TABP measures. Multidimensionality also makes content validity difficult to establish, because combining items that represent heterogeneous content domains allows no clear interpretation of the resulting measure. Unless multidimensional measures of TABP are avoided, it will remain difficult, if not impossible, to establish their validity (cf. Cronbach and Meehl, 1955; Gerbing and Anderson, 1988; Hunter and Gerbing, 1982; Nunnally, 1978).

The preceding discussion suggests several recommendations for the development and evaluation of TABP measures. First, measures of global TABP should be abandoned in favor of measures of TABP components. Several measures of TABP components are already available, most notably the S, J, and H scales from the JAS (Jenkins et al., 1979; Zyzanski and Jenkins, 1970), components derived from SI rating systems (Dembroski et al., 1978; Matthews et al., 1977), and measures of hostility and related constructs, such as the Buss–Durkee Hostility Inventory (Buss and Durkee, 1957) and the hostility scales derived from the Minnesota Multiphasic Personality Inventory (MMPI) (Cook and Medley, 1954). However, an examination of these measures reveals many of the same problems as those associated with global TABP measures, most notably multidimensionality. For example, though they purport to measure distinct TABP components, the S, J, and H scales from the JAS actually contain multiple dimensions (Edwards et al., 1990a). Similar evidence has emerged for the Buss–Durkee and Cook–Medley hostility measures (Costa et al., 1986; Siegman, Dembroski and Ringel, 1987; Smith and Frohm, 1985). These problems may be largely avoided by applying procedures for the development of unidimensional measures, such as ensuring internal consistency, external consistency, and homogeneity of content (Danes and Mann, 1984; Gerbing and Anderson, 1988; Hattie, 1985; Hunter and Gerbing, 1982).

A second recommendation is to adopt a more systematic and comprehensive approach to the validation of TABP measures. To enhance content validity, this approach should begin by clearly defining the constellation of components comprising TABP, followed by generating items that convincingly represent these components and combining these items into separate component measures (Nunnally, 1978). Ideally, the content validity of these measures should be confirmed by asking a panel of judges to classify the items according to their proposed definitions and retaining those items that are consistently placed in their appropriate categories. Next, confirmatory techniques, such as confirmatory factor analysis (CFA), should be used to ensure unidimensionality, using product rules for internal and external consistency and independence of measurement errors as criteria (Joreskog and Sorbom, 1988; Lord and Novick, 1968; Hunter and Gerbing, 1982). These analyses should be followed by assessments of reliability, convergent validity, and discriminant validity. Reliability should be evaluated using alpha, omega (which provides less stringent assumptions than alpha—see Greene and Carmines, 1980; Heise and Bohrnstedt, 1970; Smith, 1974), and CFA. Convergent and discriminant validity can also be assessed using CFA by contrasting the hypothesized multifactor measurement model with various competing models (e.g. a single factor model), and by formal analyses of multitrait multimethod matrices (Schmitt and Stults, 1986). Once these properties have been adequately demonstrated, it is then appropriate to examine the hypothesized relationships between the resulting measures and measures of other constructs, including CHD. The order of these procedures is critical, as it is necessary to establish content and construct validity before substantive relationships can be readily interpreted (Schwab, 1980). This order has not been followed in TABP research, where the relationship between a proposed TABP measure and CHD is typically examined before the validity of the measure has been demonstrated, yielding ambiguous and potentially misleading results.

Proponents of interview approaches to the measurement of TABP may argue that relying on observables avoids the need to consider construct validation. However, like any behavior, the behaviors comprising TABP are never precisely repeated. Instead, the interviewer must examine patterns and similarities from repeated observations and infer a general theme. It is the regularity embodied in these themes, not the behaviors themselves, that is the major concern in identifying TABP. Furthermore, this regularity is dependent upon underlying values, thoughts, and approaches to interpersonal relationships that are manifested behaviorally in appropriate situation (Rosenman et al., 1988). Like all constructs, these phenomena are unobservable and, as such, require a construct validation approach for their measurement (Hunter, 1980).

A third recommendation is to explicitly model the interactions and relationships among TABP components (Edwards and Baglioni, 1991). As indicated earlier, most conceptual discussions of TABP indicate that the behaviors comprising TABP occur when susceptible individuals encounter situations characterized by challenge and threats to control (Dembroski and Czajkowski, 1989; Glass, 1977; Matthews, 1982; Rosenman et al., 1988). This implies an underlying causal model in which person and situation factors interact to generate emotional and behavioral manifestations of TABP. However, most empirical TABP research has adopted a trait approach, essentially ignoring situational attributes (Smith, 1989). Furthermore, most studies have employed global measures, making it impossible to detect interactions and relationships among TABP components. Studies that do use component measures typically focus on their direct effects, with no attempt to examine their interactions or decompose their intercorrelations to identify indirect effects. By explicitly examining component interactions and relationships, it will be possible to verify and elaborate fundamental theoretical assumptions underlying TABP, which would contribute substantially to research in this area (Contrada et al., 1985; Fekken and Holden, 1988).

In sum, the SI, JAS, Framingham, and Bortner have yet to demonstrate adequate criterion-oriented, content, and construct validity. This is primarily because their development has emphasized a limited set of evaluation criteria.

most often convergence and ability to predict CHD. Though emphasizing a broader set of criteria is desirable, it is unlikely that these measures are capable of demonstrating adequate validity, due to their inherent multidimensionality. To overcome these problems, global TABP measures should be abandoned in favor of separate measures of TABP components. By developing these measures using appropraite validation procedures and explicitly modeling their interactions and interrelationships, our understanding of the determinants, nature, and consequences of TABP will be considerably enhanced.

REFERENCES

Appels, A., Jenkins, C. D. and Rosenman, R. H. (1982). Coronary-prone behavior in the Netherlands: A cross-cultural validation study, *Journal of Behavioral Medicine,* **5**, 83–90.

Bass, C. (1984). Type A behavior in patients with chest pain: Test–retest reliability and psychometric correlation of the Bortner scale, *Journal of Psychosomatic Research,* **28**, 289–300.

Bass, C. and Akhras, F. (1987). Physical and psychological correlates of severe heart disease in men, *Psychological Medicine,* **17**, 695–703.

Begley, T. M. and Boyd, D. P. (1985). The relationship of the Jenkins Activity Survey to Type A behavior among business executives, *Journal of Vocational Behavior,* **27**, 316–28.

Blumenthal, J. A., Lane, T. D. and Williams, R. B. (1985). The inhibited power motive, Type A behavior, and patterns of cardiovascular response during the Structured Interview and Thematic Apperception Test, *Journal of Human Stress,* **11**, 82–92.

Blumenthal, J. A., O'Toole, L. C. and Haney, T. (1984). Behavioral assessment of the Type A behavior pattern, *Psychosomatic Medicine,* **46**, 415–23.

Boekeloo, B. O., Mamon, J. A. and Ewart, C. K. (1987). Identifying coronary-prone behavior in adolescents using the Bortner self-rating scale, *Journal of Chronic Diseases,* **40**, 785–93.

Booth-Kewley, S. and Friedman, H. S. (1987). Psychological predictors of heart disease: A quantitative review, *Psychological Bulletin,* **101**, 343–62.

Bortner, R. W. (1969). A short rating scale as a potential measure of pattern A behavior, *Journal of Chronic Diseases,* **22**, 87–91.

Burt, R. S. (1976). Interpretational confounding of unobserved variables in structural equation models, *Sociological Methods and Research,* **5**, 3–52.

Buss, A. H. and Durkee, A. (1957). An inventory for assessing different kinds of hostility, *Journal of Consulting Psychology,* **21**, 343–9.,

Byrne, D. G., Rosenman, R. H., Schiller, E. and Chesney, M. A. (1985). Consistency and variation among instruments purporting to measure the Type A Behavior Pattern, *Psychosomatic Medicine,* **47**, 242–61.

Caffrey, B. (1970). A multivariate analysis of sociopsychological factors in monks with myocardial infarctions, *American Journal of Public Health,* **60**, 452–8.

Campbell, D. T. (1960). Recommendations for APA test standards regarding construct, trait, or discriminant validity, *American Psychologist,* **15**, 546–53.

Campbell, D. T. and Fiske, D. W. (1959). Convergent and discriminant validation by the multitrait-multimethod matrix, *Psychological Bulletin,* **56**, 81–105.

Carmelli, D., Rosenman, R. H. and Chesney, M. A. (1987). Stability of the Type A Structured Interview and related questionnaires in a 10 year follow-up of an adult cohort of twins, *Journal of Behavioral Medicine,* **10,** 513–25.

Carmines, E. G. and Zeller, R. A. (1979). *Reliability and Validity Assessment,* Sage, Beverly Hills.

Carver, C. S. and Glass, D. C. (1978). Coronary-prone behavior pattern and interpersonal aggression, *Journal of Personality and Social Psychology,* **36,** 361–6.

Case, R. B., Heller, S. S., Case, N. B. and Moss, A. J. (1985). Type A behavior and survival after acute myocardial infarction, *New England Journal of Medicine,* **312,** 737–41.

Chesney, M. A., Black, G. W., Chadwick, J. H. and Rosenman, R. H. (1981). Psychological correlates of the Type A behavior pattern, *Journal of Behavioral Medicine,* **4,** 217–29.

Cohen, J. (1960). A coefficient of agreement for nominal scales, *Educational and Psychological Measurement,* **20,** 37–46.

Cohen, J. B. and Reed, D. (1985). The Type A behavior pattern and coronary heart disease among Japanese men in Hawaii, *Journal of Behavioral Medicine,* **8,** 343–52.

Contrada, R. J., Wright, R. A. and Glass, D. C. (1985). Psychophysiologic correlates of Type A behavior: Comments on Houston (1983) and Holmes (1983), *Journal of Research in Personality,* **19,** 12–30.

Cook, T. D. and Campbell, D. T. (1979). *Quasi-experimentation: Design and Analysis Issues for Field Settings,* Houghton Mifflin Company, Boston.

Cook, W. W. and Medley, D. M. (1954). Proposed hostility and pharisaic-virtue scales for the MMPI, *Journal of Applied Psychology,* **38,** 414–18.

Cooper, C. L. and Marshall, J. (1979). *Executives under Pressure: A Psychological Study,* Praeger, New York.

Cooper, T., Detre, T. and Weiss, S. M. (1981). Coronary prone behavior pattern and coronary heart disease: A critical review, *Circulation,* **63,** 1199–215.

Costa, P. T., Zonderman, A. B., McCrae, R. R. and Williams, R. B. (1986). Cynicism and paranoid alienation in the Cook and Medley HO scale, *Psychosomatic Medicine,* **48,** 283–5.

Cronbach, L. J. (1951). Coefficient alpha and the internal structure of tests, *Psychometrika,* **16,** 297–334.

Cronbach, L. J. (1971). Test validation. In R. L. Thorndike (ed.) *Educational Measurement* (2nd edn), Washington, D.C., American Council on Education, pp. 443–507.

Cronbach, L. J. and Meehl, P. C. (1955). Construct validity in psychological tests, *Psychological Bulletin,* **52,** 281–302.

Danes, J. E. and Mann, O. K. (1984). Unidimensional measurement and structural equation models with latent variables, *Journal of Business Research,* **12,** 337–52.

DeBacker, G., Kornitzer, M., Kittel, F. and Dramaix, M. (1983). Behavior, stress, and psychosocial traits as risk factors, *Preventive Medicine,* **12,** 32–6.

Dembroski, T. M. (1978). Reliability and validity of procedures used to assess coronary prone behavior. In T. Dembroski, S. Weiss, J. Shields, S. G. Haynes and M. Feinleib (eds) *Coronary Prone Behavior,* Springer-Verlag, New York, pp. 95–106.

Dembroski, T. M. and Czajkowski, S. M. (1989). Historical and current developments in coronary-prone behavior. In A. W. Siegman and T. M. Dembroski (eds), *In Search of Coronary-prone Behavior: Beyond Type A,* Erlbaum, Hillsdale, NJ, pp. 21–39.

Dembroski, T., MacDougall, J., Herd, J. A. and Shields, J. L. (1979). Effects of level of challenge on pressor and heart responses in Type A and B subjects, *Journal of Applied Social Psychology,* **9,** 209–28.

Dembroski, T. M., MacDougall, J. M., Shields, J. L., Petitto, J. and Lushene, R. (1978). Components of the Type A coronary-prone behavior pattern and cardiovascular responses to psychomotor performance challenge, *Journal of Behavioral Medicine,* **1**, 159–76.

Dimsdale, J., Hackett, T., Block, P. and Hutter, A. (1978). Emotional correlates of Type A behavior pattern, *Psychosomatic Medicine,* **40**, 580–3.

Eaker, E. D., Abbott, R. D. and Kannel, W. B. (1989). Frequency of uncomplicated angina pectoris in type A compared with type B persons (the Framingham study), *American Journal of Cardiology,* **63**, 1042–45.

Edwards, J. R. and Baglioni, A. J. (1991). The relationship between Type-A behavior pattern and mental and physical symptoms: A comparison of global and component measures, *Journal of Applied Psychology,* **76**, 276–90.

Edwards, J. R., Baglioni, A. J. and Cooper, C. L. (1990a). Examining the relationships among self-report measures of Type-A behavior pattern: The effects of dimensionality, measurement error, and differences in underlying constructs. *Journal of Applied Psychology,* **75**, 440–54.

Edwards, J. R., Baglioni, A. J. and Cooper, C. L. (1990b). The psychometric properties of the Bortner Type-A scale. *British Journal of Psychology,* **81**, 315–33.

Edwards, J. R., Baglioni, A. J. and Cooper, C. L. (1990c). Stress, Type-A, coping, and psychologcial and physical symptoms: A multi-sample test of alternative models, *Human Relations,* **43**, 919–56.

Fekken, G. C. and Holden, R. R. (1988). Jenkins Activity Survey. In D. J. Keyser and R. C. Sweetland (eds), *Test Critiques* (Vol. 7), The Psychological Corporation, San Antonio, TX, pp. 264–76.

Flannery, R. B. and Bowen, M. A. (1986). Concordance in the Framingham and Bortner Type A behavior scales: Preliminary inquiry, *Psychological Reports,* **59**, 294.

French–Belgian Collaborative Group (1982). Ischemic heart disease and psychological patterns, *Advances in Cardiology,* **29**, 25–31.

Friedman, H. S. and Booth-Kewley, S. (1987). The "disease-prone" personality: A meta-analytic review of the construct, *American Psychologist,* **42**, 539–55.

Friedman, M. and Rosenman, R. H. (1959). Association of specific overt behavior pattern with increases in blood cholesterol, blood clotting time, incidence of arcus senilis and clinical coronary artery disease, *Journal of the American Medical Association,* **169**, 1286–96.

Ganster, D. C., Schaubroeck, J. M., Sime, W. E. and Mayes, B. T. (1991). The nomological validity of the Type A personality among employed adults. *Journal of Applied Psychology,* **76**, 143–168.

Gerbing, D. W., and Anderson, J. C. (1988). An updated paradigm for scale development incorporating unidimensionality and its assessment, *Journal of Marketing Research,* **25**, 186–92.

Glass, D. C. (1977). *Behavior Patterns, Stress, and Coronary Disease,* Lawrence Erlbaum, Hillsdale, NJ.

Greene, V. L. and Carmines, E. G. (1980). Assessing the reliability of linear composites. In K. F. Schuessler (ed.) *Sociological Methodology 1980,* Jossey-Bass, San Francisco, pp. 160–75.

Hattie, J. (1985). Methodology review: Assessing unidimensionality of tests and items, *Applied Psychological Measurement,* **9**, 139–64.

Haynes, S. G. and Feinleib. M. (1982). Type A behavior and the incidence of coronary heart disease in the Framingham study, *Advances in Cardiology,* **29**, 85–95.

Haynes, S. G., Feinleib, M. and Kannel, W. B. (1980). The relationship of psychosocial factors to coronary heart disease in the Framingham study: III. Eight-year incidence of coronary heart disease, *American Journal of Epidemiology*, **111**, 37–58.

Haynes, S. G., Feinleib, M., Levine, S., Scotch, N. and Kannel, W. B. (1978a). The relationship of psychosocial factors to coronary heart disease in the Framingham study: II. Prevalence of coronary heart disease, *American Journal of Epidemiology*, **107**, 384–402.

Haynes, S. G., Levine, S., Scotch, N., Feinleib, M. and Kannel, W. B. (1987b). The relationship of psychosocial factors to coronary heart disease in the Framingham study: I. Methods and risk factors, *American Journal of Epidemiology*, **107**, 362–83.

Heise, D. R. and Bohrnstedt, G. W. (1970). Validity, invalidity, and reliability. In E. F. Borgatta and G. W. Bohrnstedt (eds) *Sociological Methodology*, Jossey-Bass, San Francisco, pp. 104–29.

Heller, R. F. (1979). Type A behaviour and coronary heart disease, *British Medical Journal*, **2**, 368.

Herbertt, R. M. (1983). A critical evaluation of some commonly-employed methods for the assessment of Type A coronary-prone behavior, *Personality and Individual Differences*, **4**, 451–6.

Herbertt, R. M. and Innes, J. M. (1982). Type A coronary-prone behavior pattern, self-consciousness, and self-monitoring: A questionnaire study, *Perceptual and Motor Skills*, **55**, 471–8.

Herman, S., Blumenthal, J. A., Black, G. M. and Chesney, M. A. (1981). Self-ratings of Type A (coronary prone) adults: Do Type A's know they are Type A's?, *Psychosomatic Medicine*, **43**, 405–13.

Houston, B. K. (1983). Psychophysiological responsivity and the type A behavior pattern, *Journal of Research in Personality*, **17**, 22–39.

Houston, B. K. (1986). Psychological variables and cardiovascular and neuro-endocrine reactivity. In K. A. Matthews, S. M. Weiss, T. Detre, T. M. Dembroski, B. Falkner, S. B. Manuck and R. B. Williams (eds) *Handbook of Stress, Reactivity, and Cardiovascular disease*, Wiley, New York, pp. 207–29.

Howland, E. W. and Siegman, A. W. (1982). Toward the automated measurement of the type A behavior pattern, *Journal of Behavioral Medicine*, **5**, 37–54.

Hunter, J. E. (1980). Construct validity and validity generalization. In *Construct Validity in Psychological Measurement*, Educational Testing Service, Princeton, NJ, pp. 119–29.

Hunter, J. E. and Gerbing, D. W. (1982). Unidimensional measurement, second order factor analysis, and causal models. In B. M. Staw and L. L. Cummings (eds) *Research in Organizational Behavior*, JAI Press, Greenwich, CT, pp. 267–320.

Irvine, J., Lyle, R. and Allon, R. (1982). Type A personality as psychopathology: Personality correlates and an abbreviated scoring system, *Journal of Psychosomatic Research*, **26**, 183–9.

Jenkins, C. D. (1978). A comparative review of the interview and questionnaire methods in the assessment of the coronary-prone behavior pattern. In T. M. Dembroski, S. M. Weiss, J. L. Shields, S. G. Haynes and M. Feinleib (eds) *Coronary-prone Behavior*, Springer-Verlag, New York, pp. 71–88.

Jenkins, C. D. (1983). Psychosocial and behavioral factors. In N. M. Kaplan and J. Stamler (eds) *Prevention of Coronary Heart Disease: Practical Management of the Risk Factors*, Philadelphia, PA, W. B. Saunders, Co., pp. 98–112.

Jenkins, C. D., Rosenman, R. H. and Friedman, M. (1967). Development of an objective psychological test for the determination of the coronary-prone patterns in employed men, *Journal of Chronic Disease*, **20**, 371–9.

Jenkins, C. D., Rosenman, R. H. and Friedman, M. (1968). Replicability of rating the coronary-prone behavior pattern, *British Journal of Preventive and Social Medicine*, **22**, 16–22.

Jenkins, C. D., Rosenman, R. H. and Zyzanski, S. J. (1974). Prediction of clinical coronary heart disease by a test for the coronary-prone behavior pattern, *New England Journal of Medicine*, **290**, 1271–5.

Jenkins, C. D., Zyzanski, S. J., and Rosenman, R. H. (1971a). Progress toward validation of a computer-scored test for the Type A behavior pattern, *Psychosomatic Medicine*, **33**, 193–202.

Jenkins, C. D., Zyzanski, S. J. and Rosenman, R. H. (1979). *Jenkins Activity Survey Manual*, Psychological Corporation, New York.

Jenkins, C. D., Zyuzanski, S. J., Rosenman, R. H. and Cleveland, G. L. (1971b). Association of coronary-prone behavior scores with recurrence of coronary heart disease, *Journal of Chronic Diseases*, **24**, 601–11.

Johnston, D. W., and Shaper, A. G. (1983). Type A behavior in British men: Reliability and intercorrelation of two measures, *Journal of Chronic Diseases*, **36**, 203–7.

Johnston, D. W., Cook, D. G. and Shaper, A. G. (1987). Type A behaviour and ischaemic heart disease in middle aged British men, *British Medical Journal*, **295**, 86–9.

Joreskog, K. G. and Sorbom, D. (1988). *LISREL VII*, SPSS Inc, Chicago.

Keith, R. A., Lown, B. and Stare, F. J. (1965). Coronary heart disease and behavior patterns, *Psychosomatic Medicine*, **27**, 424–34.

Koskenvuo, M., Kaprio, J., Rose, R. J., Kesaniemik, A., Sarna, S., Heikkila, K. and Langinvainio, H. (1988). Hostility as a risk factor for mortality and ischemic heart disease in men, *Psychosomatic Medicine*, **50**, 330–40.

Krantz, D. S. and Manuck, S. B. (1984). Acute psychophysiologic reactivity and risk of cardiovascular disease: A review and methodological critique, *Psychological Bulletin*, **96**, 435–64.

Lee, D., King, D. and King, L. (1987). Measurement of the Type A behavior pattern by self-report questionnaire: Several perspectives on validity, *Educational and Psychological Measurement*, **47**, 409–23.

Lord, F. M. and Novick, M. R. (1968). *Statistical Theories of Mental Test Scores*, Addison-Wesley, Reading, Mass.

MacDougall, J. M., Dembroski, T. M. and Krantz, D. S. (1981). Effects of types of challenge on pressor and heart rate responses in Type A and B women, *Psychophysiology*, **18**, 1–9.

MacDougall, J. M., Dembroski, T. M. and Musante, L. (1979). The structured interview and questionnaire methods of assessing coronary-prone behavior pattern in male and female college students, *Journal of Behavioral Medicine*, **2**, 71–83.

Matthews, K. A. (1982). Psychological perspectives on the Type-A behavior pattern, *Psychological Bulletin*, **91**, 293–333.

Matthews, K. A. (1983). Assessment issues in coronary-prone behavior. In T. M. Dembroski, T. H. Schmidt and G. Blumchen (eds) *Biobehavioral Bases of Coronary Heart Disease*, Karker, New York, pp. 62–78.

Matthews, K. A. (1985). Assessment of Type A, anger, and hostility in epidemiologic studies of cardiovascular disease. In A. Ostfield and E. Eaker (eds) *Proceedings of the NHLBI Workshop on Measuring Psychosocial Variables in Epidemiologic Studies of Cardiovascular Disease*, NIH Publication No. 85-2270, National Institutes of Health, Bethesda, MD, pp. 153–83.

Matthews, K. A. (1988). Coronary heart disease and Type A behaviors: Update on and alternative to the Booth-Kewley and Friedman (1987) quantitative review, *Psychological Bulletin*, **104**, 373–80

Matthews, K. A. and Haynes, S. G. (1986). Type A behavior pattern and coronary disease risk: Update and critical evaluation, *American Journal of Epidemiology*, **123**, 923–60.

Matthews, K. A. and Saal, F. E. (1978). Relationship of the Type A coronary-prone behavior pattern to achievement, power, and affilitation motives, *Psychosomatic Medicine*, **40**, 731–36.

Matthews, K. A., Glass, D. C., Rosenman, R. H. and Bortner, R. W. (1977). Competitive drive Pattern A, and coronary heart disease: A further analysis of some data from the Western Collaborative Group Study, *Journal of Chronic Diseases*, **30**, 489–98.

Matthews, K. A., Krantz, D. S., Dembroski, T. M. and MacDougall, J. M. (1982). Unique and common variance in structured interview and Jenkins Activity Survey measures of the Type A behavior pattern, *Journal of Personality and Social Psychology*, **42**, 303–13.

Mayes, B. T., Sime, W. E. and Ganster, D. C. (1984). Convergent validity of Type A behavior pattern scales and their ability to predict physiological responsiveness in a sample of female public employees, *Journal of Behavioral Medicine*, **7**, 83–108.

Musante, L., MacDougall, J. M., Dembroski, T. M. and Van Horn, A. E. (1983). Component analysis of the Type A coronary-prone behavior pattern in male and female college students, *Journal of Personality and Social Psychology*, **45**, 104–17.

Nunnally, J. C. (1978). *Psychometric Theory*, McGraw-Hill, New York.

O'Looney, B. A. (1984). The assessment of Type A behavior and the prediction of coronary heart disease: A review, *Current Psychological Research and Reviews*, **Winter**, 63–84.

O'Looney, B. A. and Harding, C. M. (1985). A psychometric investigation of two measures of Type A behavior in a British sample, *Journal of Chronic Diseases*, **38**, 841–8.

O'Looney, B. A., Harding, C. M. and Eiser, J. R. (1985). Is there a substitute for structured interview assessments of Type A behaviour?, *British Journal of Medical Psychology*, **58**, 343–50.

Pichot, P., De Bonis, M., Somogyi, M., Degre-Coustry, C., Kittel-Bossuit, F., Rustin-Vandenhende, R. M., Dramaix, M. and Bernet, A. (1977). Etude metrologique d'une batterie de tests destinee a l'étude des facteurs psychologiques en épidémiologie cardio-vasculaire, *International Review of Applied Psychology*, **26**, 11–19.

Powell, L. H. (1987). Issues in the measurement of the Type A behaviour pattern. In S. V. Kasl and C. L. Cooper (eds) *Stress and Health: Issues in Research Methodology*, John Wiley, Chichester, pp. 231–82.

Price, K. P. (1979). Reliability of assessment of the coronary-prone behavior with special reference to the Bortner rating scale, *Journal of Psychosomatic Research*, **23**, 45–7.

Price, K. P. and Clarke, L. K. (1978). Behavioral and psychophysiological correlates of the coronary-prone personality: New data and unanswered questions, *Journal of Psychosomatic Research*, **22**, 409–17.

Rahe, R. H., Hervig, L. and Rosenman, R. H. (1978). The heritability of Type A behavior, *Psychosomatic Medicine*, **40**, 478–86.

Ray, J. J. and Bozek, R. (1980). Dissecting the A–B personality type, *British Journal of Medical Psychology*, **53**, 181–6.

Rosenman, R. H. (1978). The interview method of assessment of the coronary-prone behavior pattern. In T. M. Dembroski, S. M. Weiss, J. L. Shields, S. G. Haynes and M. Feinleib (eds) *Coronary-prone Behavior*, Springer-Verlag, New York, pp. 55–69.

Rosenman, R. H., Swan, G. E. and Carmelli, D. (1988). Definition, assessment, and evolution of the Type A behavior pattern. In B. K. Houston and C. R. Snyder (eds) *Type A behavior pattern: Current trends and future directions,* Wiley, New York, pp. 8–31.

Rosenman, R. H., Brand, R. J., Jenkins, C. D., Friedman, M., Straus, R. and Wurm, M. (1975). Coronary heart disease in the Western Collaborative Group Study: Final follow-up experience of 8½ years, *Journal of the American Medical Association*, **233**, 872–7.

Rosenman, R. H., Friedman, M., Strauss, R., Wurm, M., Kositchek, R., Hahn, W. and Werthessen, N. T. (1964). A predictive study of coronary heart disease: The Western Collaborative Group Study, *Journal of the American Medical Association*, **189**, 15–26.

Scherwitz, L. (1988). Interviewer behaviors in the Western Collaborative Group Study and the Multiple Risk Factor Intervention Trial structured interviews. In B. K. Houston and C. R. Snyder (eds) *Type A Behavior Pattern: Research, Theory, and Intervention*, Wiley, New York, pp. 32–50.

Scherwitz, L. (1989). Type A behavior assessment in the structured interview: Review, critique, and recommendations. In A. W. Siegman and T. M. Dembroski (eds) *In Search of Coronary-Prone Behavior: Beyond Type A*, Plenum Press, New York, pp. 117–47.

Scherwitz, L., Berton, K., and Leventhal, H. (1977). Type A assessment and interaction in the behavior pattern interview, *Psychosomatic Medicine*, **39**, 229–40.

Schmitt, N. and Stults, D. M. (1986). Methodology review: Analysis of multitrait-multimethod matrices, *Applied Psychological Measurement*, **10**, 1–22.

Schwab, D. P. (1980). Construct validity in organizational behavior. In L. L. Cummings and B. M. Staw (eds) *Research in Organizational Behavior* (Vol. 2), JAI Press, Greenwich, CT, pp. 3–43.

Shekelle, R. B., Schoenberger, J. A. and Stamler, J. (1976). Correlates of the JAS Type A behavior pattern score, *Journal of Chronic Diseases*, **29**, 381–94.

Shekelle, R. B., Hulley, S. B., Neaton, J. D., Billings, J. H., Borhani, N. O., Gerace, T. A., Jacobs, D. R., Lasser, N. L., Mittlemark, M. B. and Stamler, J. (1985). The MRFIT behavioral study. II. Type A behavior and incidence of coronary heart disease, *American Journal of Epidemiology*, **122**, 559–70.

Shipper, F., Kreitner, R., Reif, W. E. and Lewis, K. E. (1986). A study of four psychometric proeprties of the Jenkins Activity Survey type A scale with suggested modifications and validation, *Educational and Psychological Measurement*, **46**, 551–64.

Siegel, J. M. (1984). Type A behavior: Epidemiological foundations and public health implications, *Annual Review of Public Health*, **5**, 343–67.

Siegman, A. W., Dembroski, T. M. and Ringel, N. (1987). Components of hostility and the severity of coronary artery disease, *Psychosomatic Medicine*, **49**, 127–35.

Smith, K. W. (1974). On estimating the reliability of composite indexes through factor analysis, *Sociological Methods and Research*, **2**, 485–510.

Smith, T. W. (1989). Interactions, transactions, and the Type A pattern: Additional avenues in the search for coronary-prone behavior. In A. W. Siegman and T. M. Dembroski (eds) *In Search of Coronary-prone Behavior: Beyond Type A*, Erlbaum, Hillsdale, NJ, pp. 91–116.

Smith, T. W. and Frohm, K. D. (1985). What's so unhealthy about hostility? Construct validity and psychosocial correlates of the Cook and Medley Ho scale, *Health Psychology,* **4**, 503–20.

Smith, T. W. and O'Keefe, J. L. (1985). The inequivalence of self-reports of Type A behavior: Differential relationships of the Jenkins Activity Survey and the Framingham scale with affect, stress, and control, *Motivation and Emotion,* **9**, 299–311.

Smith, T. W., Houston, B. K. and Zurawski, R. M. (1983). The Framingham Type A Scale and anxiety, irrational beliefs, and self-control, *Journal of Human Stress,* **8**, 32–7.

Suls, J. and Sanders, G. S. (1989). Why do some behavioral styles place people at coronary risk? In A. W. Siegman and T. M. Dembroski (eds) *In Search of Coronary-prone Behavior: Beyond Type A,* Erlbaum, Hillsdale, NJ, pp. 1–20.

Suls, J. and Wan, C. K. (1989). The relation between Type A behavior and chronic emotional distress: A meta-analysis, *Journal of Personality and Social Psychology,* **57**, 503–12.

Yarnold, P. R. and Bryant, F. B. (1988). A note on measuremnt issues in Type A research: Let's not throw out the baby with the bath water, *Journal of Personality Assessment,* **52**, 410–19.

Zyzanski, S. J. and Jenkins, C. D. (1970). Basic dimensions within the coronary-prone behaviour pattern, *Journal of Chronic Diseases,* **22**, 781–95.

Chapter 8

Individual Differences in Cognition and the Stress Process

Roy Payne, University of Manchester, UK

The aim of this chapter is to consider how differences in cognitive functioning may influence people's experience and behaviour at different stages of the stress process. Following Pearlin et al. (1981) it is assumed that "There is probably a general agreement that stress refers to a response of the orgnism to conditions that, consciously or unconsciously, are experienced as noxious" (p. 341). Whether the experience is conscious or unconscious, stress is *a process* that occurs over time. Much of the literature on stress and cognition is based on studies of people exposed to short-term/acute stress in experimental situations. These are often conceptualised within a <u>Human Information Processing (HIP) framework</u> and have shed light on cognitive processes such as <u>attentional selectivity</u> and <u>memory allied</u> to differences in intelligence and cognitive style (Hockey, 1990).

I now wish to contrast experimental work with job stress, and marital stress where the conditions producing the stress are chronic and potentially damaging to physical and psychological well-being. While they differ in time and implications the underlying nature of the *stress process* remains very similar: the person perceives the environment and makes judgements about its implications, decides what to do about things, and then plans and executes actions to bring about a change in the situation. The plans may involve changing the situation, changing oneself or, of course, doing both. And taking no action is still an action which has consequences. These actions, or inactions, lead to consequences which reset the process of perception, cognitive evaluation based on affective reactions, and actions and so on. Alfred Kuhn (1974) labels these three processes as <u>Detector,</u> <u>Selecto</u>r and <u>Effecto</u>r and uses this framework to construct a model for explaining behaviour in social systems generally. Lazarus (1966) is well known for his distinctions between Primary Appraisal, Secondary Appraisal and Coping Behaviours. For the moment I

Personality and Stress: Individual Differences in the Stress Process. Edited by C.L. Cooper and R. Payne
© 1991 John Wiley & Sons Ltd

just wish to emphasise that, whether stress is acute or chronic, these three processes take place and they involve cognitive activity.

The different phases may even involve different kinds of cognitive processes, or the same processes to different degrees, but before examining this I wish to consider whether there are different kinds of cognitive individual differences which might lead different individuals to think and act differently at these phases of the stress process.

COGNITIVE ABILITIES AND COGNITIVE STYLES

It is simplest to think of cognitive abilities in relationship to the study of intelligence. It has traditionally been argued that there is a general factor of intelligence (g) which is composed of seven Primary Mental Abilities: spatial abilities, perceptual abilities, numerical, verbal relations, words, memory and inductive ability. Tests have been developed to measure each of these and they intercorrelate highly across the general population but any particular individual may be much better at some than others. An obvious absentee from this list is creative thinking. Guilford (1967) put this and much more into a cognitive classification. Guilford proposed three underlying categories: Mental Operations, Content and Products.

There were five sorts of mental operation which included divergent (creative thinking), four types of content (e.g. figural and semantic and six types of products (e.g. units, classes, relations, systems). This produced 120 types of cognitive activity and Guilford claims to have produced tests which measure 90 of them.

Both interest in and research on intelligence has been boosted in the last 15 years by the efforts of Robert Sternberg who has published dozens of papers and many books on the topic. In *Beyond I.Q.* (1985) he describes his triarchic theory of human intelligence. Figure 8.1 outlines the main concepts relating to each component of the triarchic theory. Sternberg argues that the componential subtheory integrates much of the research that has been carried out in traditional psychometric testing. Thus it explains fluid ability (general intelligence) and crystallised ability (abilities derived from specific kinds of experience such as mechanical ability) and the processes that lead to enhancement of both. Sternberg would accept that we have many good tests of these abilities, though the theory shows scope for improving them further.

There are far fewer tests of the other two kinds of intelligence proposed in the experiential subtheory and the contextual subtheory. Sternberg is at pains to point out that his theory attempts to explain intelligent (and less intelligent) human behaviour, not intelligence *per se* (i.e. intelligence as an attribute possessed by an individual). This concern with behaviour in the world is what led Sternberg to focus on the experience of the individual trying to deal with new elements of the environment including the strategy of

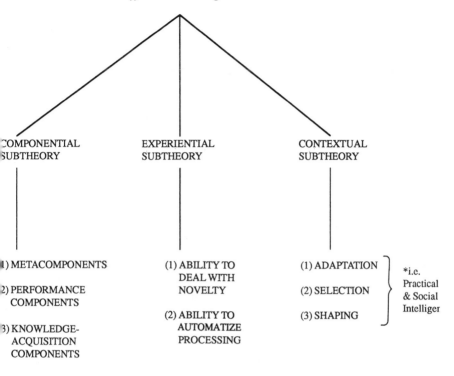

*My minor modification

Figure 8.1   Sternberg's triarchic theory of intelligence. Reproduced by permission from R.J. Sternberg (1985). *Beyond IQ*, Cambridge University Press, p. 320.

automating processing to release capacity for dealing with that novelty. This is what necessitated the development of the experiential subtheory.

Sternberg also recognises the importance of the experience offered by different environments and the practical and social intelligence these different contexts develop. Following this reasoning, Sternberg argues that it is the failure to take into account the tacit knowledge derived from contextual experience, and the creative thinking stimulated by novelty in the environment (experiential subtheory), that explains why traditional tests of intelligence only account for 10–25% of the variance in measures of success, achievement, adjustment to life's demands. While agreeing with this and believing that the figure from most studies is closer to 10% than 25% of accountable variance (see also Ghiselli, 1966 and Austin and Hanisch, 1990) it may be worth reminding ourselves that no other single variable predicts any more successfully.

Since cognitive abilities are multidimensional there is a need to consider how some of those dimensions relate to the stress process. As Sternberg's theory is the most recent, and is manageable in size, I propose to use it as a framework for understanding cognitive ability and stress. Sternberg's summary definition of intelligence appears on page 128 of *Beyond I.Q.*:

> Intelligence is the mental capability of emitting contextually appropriate behaviour at those regions in the experiential continuum that involve response to novelty or automization of information processing as a function of metacomponents, performance components, and knowledge-acquisition components.

For the sake of simplicity I would like to interpret this to mean that contextual intelligence involves the processes detailed in the two subtheories experiential and componential. That is, the intelligent behaviour involved in the adaptation, selection and shaping of environments outlined in Figure 8.1 relating to the contextual subtheory is dependent on the mental processes described in the other two subtheories. It is individual differences in these processes that influence the nature of adaptation, and ideally one should consider how each of them might affect adaptation to stressful environments. The sheer complexity of such a task prevents attempting it in the space available. I will therefore limit my attention to what Sternberg describes as the *content* of the implicit theory of contextual intelligence.

The conceptual specification of these skills of intelligent behaviour has been generated from studies of ordinary peoples' theories of what constitutes intelligent behaviour. Analyses of the responses of 476 Americans produced three constellations of behaviour which they regarded as indicating intelligent responses to the problems of living. They were:

(1) *Practical problem-solving ability*—reasons logically and well, identifies connections among ideas, sees all aspects of a problem, keeps an open mind, responds thoughtfully to others' ideas, sizes up situations well, gets to the heart of problems, interprets information accurately, makes good decisions, goes to original sources of basic information, poses problems in an optimal way, is a good source of ideas, perceives implied assumptions and conclusions, listens to all sides of an argument and deals with problems resourcefully.

(2) *Verbal ability*—speaks clearly and articulately, is verbally fluent, converses well, is knowledgeable about a particular field, studies hard, reads with comprehension, reads widely, deals effectively with people, writes without difficulty, sets time aside for reading, displays a good vocabulary, accepts social norms and tries new things.

(3) *Social competence*—accepts others for what they are, admits mistakes, displays interest in the world at large, is on time for appointments, has a social conscience, thinks before speaking and doing, displays curiosity

does not make snap judgements, makes fair judgements, assesses well the relevance of the information to a problem at hand, is sensitive to other peoples' needs and desires, is frank and honest with self and others, and displays interest in the immediate environment.

There is almost certainly empirical, as well as conceptual, overlap between these categories, and all of them involve action and effort as well as cognitive skills, though the actions and the effort are guided by cognitions, and the quality of the actions and the energy behind the efforts are to some extent dependent on differences in cognitive skills and abilities. Despite accepting that people high on verbal ability are more likely to be socially competent and therefore better at solving *practical* problems, I wish to consider these three components of practical and social intelligence separately. Figure 8.2 presents them in matrix form with the three stages of the stress process. I now wish to speculate how differences in these cognitive abilities might interact with the different phases of the stress process.

Before tackling this it is worth reminding ourselves that good measures of these forms of intelligence have not yet been developed and that hard, scientific evidence that might support the suggestions I am about to make is not easy to find. Sternberg (1985) makes this point: ". . . the most critical need in ability testing to-day is to develop measures that are more sensitive to real-world kinds of intelligence" (p. 311). A further important point is that different stressors will interact differently with (a) the stress process and (b) the cognitive abilities. Threat of mugging or rape (a physical threat?) provides a very different stressor from one of job failure due to being unable to cope with the complexity of the task (a cognitive stressor), and both are very different from losing a loved one (an emotional threat). These labels over-simplify, but I hope they convey the point that the threat/stress itself affects

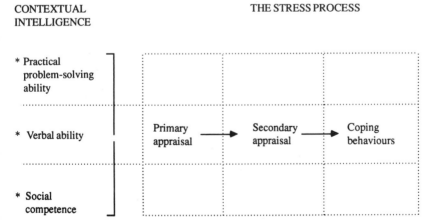

Figure 8.2   A framework for exploring contextual intelligence and the stress process

the stress process, and that affects the relevance of different cognitive skills. If Sternberg finds ability tests wanting I can only say that our ability to classify and measure situations is considerably less well developed.

In completing the matrix described in Figure 8.2, I have assumed the stress-ful situation involves a person who has been promoted to a new position and is failing to perform the work to the satisfaction of the boss, the subordinates and themselves. Demands exceed capacities. I shall further contrast and com-pare hypothetical individuals who are high versus low on the three aspects of practical intelligence defined above: problem-solving, verbal ability and social competence.

AN ILLUSTRATION OF THE INTERACTION BETWEEN CONTEXTUAL INTELLIGENCE AND THE 3 PHASES OF THE STRESS PROCESS

The Primary Appraisal process involves the person in deciding what a situa-tion or event means to them. It is essentially a cognitive process in which the individual decides whether the situation involves *harm or loss, threat* or *chal-lenge.* In the situation above I have determined it involves at least threat, and possibly loss (of job, income, self-esteem and so on). The individual with first-class problem-solving skills, even though stressed, is more likely to have accu-rately diagnosed the causes of the stress, particularly situational causes. This is because they will have collected information, examined it from different view-points, reasoned about the causes and the theoretical plausibility of the pro-posals generated.

The capacity to do this effectively would be further enhanced if the person was also high on social competence for they would have been able to talk to people sensitively and to get them to share uncomfortable facts. They would be honest with themselves as well as others and capable of arranging the meetings required to generate this information.

During these discussions the person of high verbal ability would enhance the possibility of discovering the "truth" of the situation. Their high verbal ability would enable them to read about work stress and cope with such concepts as role ambiguity, role overload and the difference between intra-personal stress and interpersonal stress (Kahn et al., 1964). These skills would undoubtedly help them to "understand" the causes of environmental stress. In sum, high contextual intelligence enhances the person's ability to under-stand why there is stress, and to be able to explain why it is occurring. Such people are much less likely to misperceive the situation and thus create stress from phantasising about their situation.

The person of low problem-solving skills will be much less inclined to collect information, to analyse the situation so that they might understand why they are stressed, and more inclined to accept other peoples' analyses of what is happening without criticising those analyses carefully. They will be less capable of generating alternative viewpoints and explanations and because of their greater reliance on intuition they may completely misperceive the psycho-socio dynamics of the situation. Thus they may conclude that their difficulties are due to their own shortcomings when they may really be due to the inadequacies of the management information system, or poor training and instruction.

Their poorer verbal ability makes it more difficult for them to discuss the situation with others, or to understand the nuances of the discussions if they do take place. Similarly, their disinclination to search for written information about job stress decreases the likelihood of them attempting a conceptual analysis of the situation. Indeed, even if they do try and work from conceptual frameworks they have greater difficulty in accurately translating their own situation into the language of the models. Since much of social competence depends on verbal ability too, they are again lacking the skills which might enable them to get help from others that might lead to a better understanding of the situation that is causing their distress. In complex social organisations which depend heavily on written and verbal communication the person deprived of these abilities is at much greater risk of regularly getting things wrong. The negative reinforcement that will generally follow such failures will only exacerbate the problem as Seligman argues in his description of "learned helplessness" (Seligman, 1975).

In this first stage of the stress process (primary appraisal) the person has decided whether the situation is benign, threatening or offering an opportunity. Situations such as job promotion can be both threatening and fulfilling at the same time (Folkman, 1984), but in the case above I determined it was threatening and I have suggested how differences in contextual intelligence might influence the accuracy of that judgement. It is possible that differences in cognitive abilities lead to differences in emotional experience: common phrases such as "ignorance is bliss" imply this possibility. I have assumed that both of our hypothetical individuals felt threatened. The difference between them lies in (a) the absolute levels of the difference between demands and capacity that might lead to stress and (b) the likelihood of them accurately interpreting the situation so that there is good cause to feel stressed.

Having identified they are stressed the Lazarus model proposes a *secondary appraisal* process where the person evaluates their capacities and resources against the demands of the situation, and asks, "How will my capacities and resources enable me to reduce or remove this threat (or exploit this opportunity)?" Resources include social, physical/material and knowledge-based factors as well as the person's intellectual, cognitive, emotional and conative resources. How will individual differences in contextual intelligence influence secondary appraisal?

As already suggested the person high on practical problem-solving ability, verbal ability and social competence will have used both written and social sources of information to understand what is causing the situation to be stressful. Their problem-solving capacity will enable them to generate options about how to change themselves, or their environment, or both. They will be able to evaluate the various options and calculate the odds that one will be more successful than another. They will probably be able to estimate the long-run consequences of the different options and decide which gives the better solution in the long term.

Their high verbal ability permits them to share their thoughts with other people in an efficient and effective manner so that they can rehearse their ideas about the differences between the options they have generated. They are also flexible in their thinking so that they may change their minds about their preferred strategies if they are convinced of the superior value of another person's solution. Their social competence decreases the likelihood of their being influenced by the status of the other person for they can argue well for their own ideas, and feel able to reject those of others while not causing them offence.

Being high on social competence they can also make good use of people around them and obtain their support both emotionally and in providing resources that may help to change the stressors in the situation. Above all, they are more likely to find a solution and implement it in a way that does not build up long-term resentment and thus long-term stress.

In sum, the person of high contextual intelligence can juggle the world inside their own heads, and can then share those jugglings with others so as to find quality solutions that are acceptable to the people affected by them. This all enhances the likelihood of success, and decreases the likelihood of developing a negative view of self through frequent failure.

The poor problem-solver is prone not to fully analyse the situation, to adopt the first decent looking solution that comes along, whether or not they have the capacities and resources to implement it effectively. Being socially incompetent they have far fewer people to consult, and because of their poor verbal ability they may fail to communicate the situation accurately even if they find someone. This lack of sharing and mentally rehearsing their tactics decreases the chances of anticipating the consequences of the tactics. Instead of helping to resolve the problem they risk exacerbating it by upsetting people close to them. Such failures increase frustration, which can increase anxiety in themselves and others so that this leads to more stress. In a sense problem-solving itself is stressful for such people and they avoid putting in the systematic effort required at secondary appraisal. As Hamlet observes, ". . . there is nothing either good or bad but thinking makes it so" (Act II, Scene 2). This combination of poor problem-solving, incapacity to mobilise social knowledge and tendency to generate social hostility heightens the risk of choosing a solution which is suboptimal and unworkable.

The *Coping* phase of the stress process is where the workability of the secondary appraisals is tested. According to Lazarus and Launier (1978) "Coping" refers to cognitive and behavioural efforts to master, reduce or tolerate the internal and/or external demands that are created in a stressful transaction. It is worth noting that this definition implies nothing about the success of the coping, but merely describes the nature of the attempts to cope. The simplest categorisation that is widely used also derives from Lazarus (Folkman and Lazarus, 1980) distinguishing between *emotion-focused* coping and *problem-focused* coping. Stone and Neale (1984) studied how people cope with daily problems and developed eight types of coping: distraction, situation redefinition, direct action, catharsis, acceptance, social support, relaxation and religion. For simplicity I will refer only to Lazarus's two-fold category.

Despite its title, emotion-focused coping involves much cognitive activity. Examples of emotion-focused coping are: looking for a silver lining, trying to forget or deny a situation, relying on someone's sympathetic support. They are, of course, cognitive strategies for changing internal emotions. The conscious or subconscious process that precedes them is the secondary appraisal, and this form of coping appears to be more common for problems which are analysed/intuited to be difficult to change. McCrae (1984) also found that the nature of the stressor influences coping: faith, fatalism and the expression of feelings were more often used to cope with loss, while threat produced coping responses of wishful thinking, faith and fatalism. Challenging adversities led to greater use of problem-focused coping.

The relationship between contextual intelligence and the use of emotion-focused coping is not necessarily a strong one. There is no obvious reason why people of all levels of contextual intelligence will not find emotion-focused coping strategies useful in some situations. It might be that those less skilled at contextual intelligence will use it more frequently because they will appraise more situations as ones they can do little about. Widger, Knudson and Rorer's (1980) study found that less intelligent people preferred more intuitive styles of problem-solving. There is some indirect evidence for a weak relationship between problem-solving ability and use of emotion-focused coping in that Anderson (1977) found external locus of control to be associated with use of emotion-focused coping, and externality has negative correlations with both intelligence and level of education (Lefcourt, 1976). Jerusalem and Schwarzer (1989) report a negative correlation of – 0.31 between emotion-focused coping and problem-focused coping, suggesting that people who prefer the latter tend to rely on it more frequently, and vice versa.

A much stronger relationship exists between practical problem-solving intelligence, social competence and verbal ability since all are dependent on the cognitive abilities that make up general intelligence. It is tautological to claim that high practical problem-solving ability is likely to lead to greater success in using problem-solving coping. Since success is likely to lead to the repetition of the behaviour then *frequency* of use of problem-focused coping is also likely to be associated with the capacity to use it. As has already been pointed out, high verbal ability is not only used at secondary appraisal to generate options and their consequences, but it enables implementation of the strategy. It provides the basis of successful persuasion and negotiation which are key elements in the management of transitions (Fisher and Cooper, 1991).

This verbal ability complements the sensitivity to people and environment that forms part of social competence which is vital to successful implementation. High social competence also involves the capacity to be frank and open with others, thus generating the valid information that Argyris and Schon (1974) demonstrate as being necessary, if not sufficient, for what they call "double-loop learning": i.e. the capacity to change the standards/values that guide behaviour—to be open, non-defensive, risk-taking, trusting and seeking win–win outcomes and so on. Since social competence is also argued to consist of flexibility, admitting mistakes, making fair judgements and showing a social conscience there is a possibility that those very high on this skill are genuinely double-loop learners, and can change the standards by which they judge the success of their coping efforts.

Those individuals who lack these three skills of practical intelligence will have a hard time in pursuing problem-solving coping, particularly if it involves dealing with social systems. The example chosen here, of dealing with a promotion in a complex organization, would make heavy demands on social competence and verbal ability even if the solution chosen at secondary appraisal were a good one. Communication is at the heart of the successful implementation of social change and lacking the skills of high social competence could still undermine what might be a technically sophisticated solution, as Lewin pointed out many years ago (Lewin, 1947).

This inductive tour of the matrix in Figure 8.2 was to demonstrate the possibility of relating types of cognitive abilities to the stress process. While tests of all three types of intelligence exist they tend to pick up limited aspects of each ability, and they are particularly poor at testing real-life situations, as Sternberg (1985) points out. Few studies of stress have actually examined the whole process. Those that have, tend to be clinically orientated and do not focus particularly well on the kinds of cognitive skills identified by Sternberg, though it would be naive to assume that they say nothing about any of them. Few stress studies actually address the different phases of the coping process either, and even fewer (perhaps none) have systematically related the two frameworks.

Several points seem worth making. First, that conceptual classifications oversimplify and create boundaries that inhibit in-depth understanding of what happens to particular people in real life. This applies both to Sternberg's categories where we have seen that there are close connections between practical problem-solving ability, verbal ability and social competence. It also applies to the division of the stress process into primary and secondary appraisal and coping. These divisions are not easy to sustain in real-life situations and the empirical evidence to support phase models in the literature on stress and unemployment is only slightly encouraging (Fryer and Payne, 1986).

This said, the advantages of such an analytical framework are that it facilitates attempts to provide generalizations of the kind attempted and it can be used as a useful starting point for the examination of individual cases/transactions. Second, if the above inductions are more or less correct it could be argued that individual differences in these capacities probably matter least in the primary appraisal process, and most in the coping process. That is, that cognitive factors are less important than feelings when a person is trying to decide if they are threatened or not. And practical problem-solving, verbal ability and social competence are most crucial in implementing solutions. The secondary appraisal might be poorly done, but all can be rescued if one has the capacity to learn, persuade, communicate and change course. These are what ultimately influence the effectiveness of coping.

The third point is that people of lower contextual intelligence suffer most in complex social situations where their social incompetence hinders them in accurate identification of stressors and implementation of appropriate actions.

The reader will undoubtedly be asking themselves, "What evidence is there that cognitive abilities influence the stress process?". It is relatively rare to find studies of stress that have included measures of cognitive ability. If one accepts that education and/or job level/social class can be used as substitutes for cognitive ability then the data base becomes larger. Measures of IQ do correlate positively with all of these, and they all intercorrelate amongst themselves, though all the correlations are only modest in size. In a large study of over 13 000 people involved in project TALENT, Austin and Hanisch (1990) quote correlations of just over 0.4 between verbal and mathematical ability and social class. They further showed that these abilities were good predictors of occupational attainment 11 years after the abilities were measured. Fletcher (1988) reviews the evidence on the relationship between social class and health and demonstrates convincingly that both physical and mental health are related to social class. Health is poorest in the lower social classes. It would be risky to claim that these differences are just due to differences in cognitive abilities, but it is highly likely that they do help in the ways outlined above.

Given that the average validity coefficient between ability tests and both training and job performance measures are about 0.3 (Ghiselli, 1966), however, it would be unwise to conclude that ability has any greater effects on the experience of stress and its management. Since ability has only low correlations with most other individual-difference variables, this might still be an important contribution to both the prediction and understanding of the stress process.

One of the few bodies of work that has studied intelligence and stress is that of Fiedler and Garcia (1987). They call their work "Cognitive Resource Theory" and as Vecchio (1990) points out much remains controversial about it, and Vecchio's own experimental study found little support for the theory. The main hypotheses are in some ways in conflict with the inductive reasoning above. One possible reason for this is that the hypotheses relate to the performance of groups for which the leader is responsible rather than the adjustment/performance of the leader *per se*. The main hypotheses of relevance are:

(1) If a leader is under stress, leader intellectual abilities will be diverted from the task so there will be no correlation between leader's intelligence and group performance.
(2) When under stress, a leader's job-relevant experience (rather than intellectual ability) will correlate with group performance.
(3) The correlation of leader intelligence and group performance will be higher when the group is supportive of the leader.

Vecchio points out that the theory ignores the effects of stress on subordinate behaviour and that the subordinates' behaviour might have a much greater influence on group performance than the leader's behaviour. The attempt to construct theories that define the conditions under which cognitive abilities help or hinder performance must, however, be applauded as they will encourage stress researchers more generally to include these variables in their studies.

Since intelligence does predict both training and performance within most kinds of occupations (managers, clerks, supervisors and so on—Ghiselli, 1966) it would seem clever people cope better on average, so theories that predict the conditions under which intellectual ability becomes a handicap are likely to be fruitful ones to follow, since there is plenty of variance that remains unaccounted for. Vecchio also refers to Sternberg's call to develop and use ability tests that are more ability specific and rooted in everyday activities.

To sum up. There is an *a priori* case for arguing that cognitive abilities influence the experience of everyday stress and the way people deal with it. Empirical investigations of this kind are relatively rare in the literature though the evidence is strong enough to suggest that cognitive abilities may be just as important as other individual difference variables in predicting and explaining stress.

It remains for us to consider the role of cognitive style.

COGNITIVE STYLE

Hockey (1990) differentiates style from ability by defining ability as being inferred from performance on cognitive tests, and style as being the manner in which tests are completed. While style undoubtedly has to do with manner, most theorists would regard this as an over-narrow definition. In the *Dictionary of Personality and Social Psychology* (Harré and Lamb, 1983) it is defined as "an individual's characteristic and consistent manner of processing and organizing what he sees and thinks about". Since some individuals process information faster than others such a definition would include the concept of "speed", but speed is a major component of ability too. McKenna (1984) has argued that many of the results found with a cognitive-style variable called field dependence–independence (Witkin et al., 1962) actually disappear if the effect of general intelligence is controlled, because this style correlates strongly with intelligence (cognitive ability). It seems unsurprising that ability correlates with style—this is surely true of other skills such as dancing or gymnastics. The theoretical and practical issue is whether style adds to our undersanding of coping behaviour, and perhaps to prediction too.

Hockey (1990) criticises measures of cognitive style because they have only modest test–retest correlations (about 0.6 for the Embedded Figures Test used to assess field independence). Style measures also tend not to correlate well with tests which supposedly measure the same style. Third, Hockey claims it is difficult to find convincing empirical evidence to support the distinction between performance (ability) and style. Despite this Hockey and others continue to use the concept, and Hockey refers to Widger's findings on the relationship between ability and style. Widger et al. (1980) found that high ability individuals showed a preference for using an analytical approach to information/problem-solving, but they could use a more global (intuitive) approach if the task needed it. Less able individuals are much more stuck with a global, holistic, diffuse approach to understanding information and using it to solve everyday problems. Hockey is implying, of course, that analysing information and problems requires the ability to hold information in memory, to abstract and juggle with ideas that are drawn from experience, and/or the ability to generate new ideas or solutions: i.e. the ability to manage strategic thinking.

Perhaps the important distinction to be made between ability and style concerns people's preferences for organising and using information. One of the best developed frameworks with this conceptual approach is the Myers–Briggs typology of thinking styles which are measured by the Myers–Briggs Type Indicator (Myers and McCaulley, 1985).

THE MYERS–BRIGGS TYPE INDICATOR (MBTI)

The MBTI is based on Carl Jung's theory of Psychological Types (Jung, 1921). It consists of four dimensions though each dimension is usually dichotomised. The four dimensions and the typological definitions of each dichotomy are:

PREFERENCE	MEANING
Extraversion vs. Introversion (EI)	Preference for focusing on the External world vs. world of Ideas.
Sensing vs. Intuition (SN)	Preference to rely on direct senses rather than global intuition in perceiving the world.
Thinking vs. Feeling (TF)	Preference to rely on rational thinking vs. feeling when deciding what to do and think.
Judgement vs. Perception (JP)	Preference for dealing with outer world through judging (by using T and F processes) rather than perceiving (using S and N processes).

The preference for EI is described as an *Attitude*. SN and TF are described as *Processes* and the JP preference is described as *Style*. Since JP or style refers to a preference for using the other processes one might have assumed some correlation between measures of them. The MBTI, however, measures all four dimensions and they are more or less independent though there are moderate correlations between JP and SN (0.38) and JP and TF (0.23) (N = 56 000). If each of the four dimensions is dichotomised this produces 16 possible types: e.g. INTJ, ENTJ, ESTP, ENFJ and so on.

People's preferences are partly determined genetically and partly by experience, but Jung proposed that it was important for people to develop their most natural preferences. Attempting to develop all eight of the qualities would lead to poor development in all of them and a "primitive mentality". Development requires:

- development of excellence in the favourite dominant process;
- adequate but not equal development of the auxiliary preferences;
- eventual admission of the least developed processes to conscious, purposeful use in the service of the dominant processes;
- use of each function for the tasks for which they are best fitted.

While the MBTI manual cautions that, "Type theory seems simple, but it is in fact rich and complex" (Myers and McCaulley, 1985, p. 19), the central concern it has with the way people search for and process information (SN and TF) makes it a typology of direct relevance for the notion of cognitive style.

There are clearly parallels with other classifications. The distinctions between left-brain and right-brain (Mintzberg, 1976) information processing (logical vs. intuitive: explicit vs. implicit) are not dissimilar to ST vs. NF preferences. Field dependence–independence is not unlike preferences for extraversion, sensing vs. introversion, intuition. The MBTI manual contains hundreds of correlations relating the four dimensions of the MBTI to other personality measures. None of them are obviously measures of cognitive style directly though some have a flavour of that sort. Thus the Practical Outlook scale of the Omnibus Personality Inventory correlates strongly with Sensing and Judging (0.67 and 0.41 respectively). The Complexity scale of the same inventory correlates 0.62 with Intuition and 0.55 with Perception. The Imaginative scale of Cattel's 16PF (Cattell, Eber and Tatsuoka, 1970) correlates 0.33 with Intuition. Intolerance of Ambiguity (Budner, 1962) correlates with preference for Sensing (0.47).

While I suggested earlier that cognitive ability might well be correlated with style because speed of processing information might well affect the way one prefers to organise and use the information, there is little evidence of MBTI correlating with measures of intelligence. The minor exception to this is that SN tends to correlate positively with intelligence, and the effect is larger if the IQ test is verbal rather than numerical. Intuitive types tend to be more intelligent, and the correlation is about 0.3. There is a smaller correlation with JP where those with a preference for perception tend to be more intelligent ($r =$ approx. 0.18). This may be partly due to the correlation between JP and SN. The internal reliability and test–retest reliability for MBTI are as good as for most tests of this kind, and there is considerable evidence for the test's validity in the MBTI Manual. As already suggested, its theoretical nature implies it is very much about what might be called information processing style.

The manual for the MBTI contains no references to studies on stress, though the bibliography held by the Centre for Applications of Psychological Type produced three. It does seem worthwhile, however, to repeat the format used to speculate on the effect of cognitive ability on the stress process. A way to do this is to consider all 16 of the MBTI types. Since space prevents that I will choose two contrasting types.

As the two processes (SN and TF) are the key cognitive variables, I will use them as the key contrast, and control for the other two types by keeping to (a) introverts and (b) to judging types. The pair to contrast becomes ISTJ and INFJ.

CHARACTERISTICS OF ISTJ AND INFJ TYPES

Introverts are concerned much more with their inner world. They are interested in the clarity of concepts and ideas, reliance on enduring ideas rather than transitory events and situations; they like privacy and quietness to allow them to reflect and abstract. The judging preference leads to a concern to make decisions, seek closure, plan, organise and so on and is to some extent in conflict with the introvertive attitude.

Combining these with a preference for Sensing and Thinking adds:

> *Sensing*: Because the senses can bring to awareness only what is occurring in the present moment, persons oriented towards sensing perception tend to focus on the immediate experience and often develop characteristics associated with this awareness such as enjoying the present moment, realism, acute powers of observation, memory for details and practicality.
>
> (Myers and McCaulley, 1985, p. 13)

Thinking: relies on cause and effect and impersonality. Thinking types develop analytical abilities, objectivity, concern with justice and fairness, criticality and time orientations which can span the past through to the future. ISTJs then are serious, logical, practical, difficult to divert from their own goals, reliable, organised and dependable. Their cognitive styles will be orientated to seeking information, analysing it, checking its accuracy, organising it, drawing a workable conclusion and planning how to implement it. Other people's views will not be allowed to interfere with a rational and well thought out conclusion, unless they are obviously superior to their own.

In contrast intuitive and feeling preferences bring: *Intuition*—perception by way of the unconscious:

> Persons oriented towards intuitive perception may become so intent on pursuing possibilities that they may overlook actualities. They may develop characteristics that can follow from emphasis on intuition and become imaginative, theoretical, abstract, future oriented or creative.
>
> (p. 12)

In combination with introversion it can produce dreamers. *Feeling*—relies on guiding decisions and action by personal values and/or an understanding of group values/culture. Feeling people are concerned with others rather than technology or systems, they need affiliation and show warmth, strive for cohesiveness and try and perpetuate traditional values and beliefs. The INFJ person, then, is concerned with the common good, committed, conscientious and clear about their own values. Their natural introversion is overcome when issues of values draw them into action. The cognitive style of INFJs is reflective, relying on impressions and intuitions with quick rejections of facts and arguments that conflict with valued positions and beliefs. They are likely to look for information which supports their predisposition rather than be analytical and dispassionate; they will be guided by what "feels right".

ISTJ AND THE STRESS PROCESS

In the Primary Appraisal phase of the stress process the individual is faced with deciding what the situation means for them: is it threatening, stressful, benign or a stimulating opportunity? Since ST types suppress and distrust feelings it may be that the level of stress/threat has to become quite high before it gets through their sensing/rational filters. This may be particularly true for introverted people who are less likely to pay attention to the outside world. Kahn et al. (1964) found introverts more prone to withdraw from situations of conflict and ambiguity. If the ISTJ person does eventually acknowledge threat then they will have collected and organised the information necessary for them to understand the nature of the stress and the causes of it. This will be particularly true if the causes lie more in technical systems than in the interpersonal world. Since introverts tend to be intrapunitive and blame themselves the IST combination does create difficulties in quickly determining whether the environment is threatening.

The ISTJ person's strengths would appear to be much more relevant to the requirements of Secondary Appraisal. The task here is to construct explanations, assess resources and decide how the resources can be deployed to remove the threat. The combination of sensing and thinking and the security of a judgemental orientation will be powerful aids for doing this task well. Once again, they are much more likely to fail where the situations are ambiguous, complex and multi-causal ("wicked systems") for their rationality and commitment to plans can make them inflexible and insensitive to the changing forces in complex systems.

At the Coping Phase their plans and analyses will be thorough, and well organised. If things work out as they planned they will cope very well. ISTJs tend to be well respected for their virtues and if they need to persuade other people to help them implement their plans then these qualities will usually carry others along with them. The MBTI manual shows the ST combination to be prevalent among managerial and business people and to be strongly associated with economic values as measured by the Allport, Vernon and Lindzey (1960) scales. The occupations which have high percentages of people with the ISTJ profile are dentists, police supervisors, police in general, auditors, accountants and technicians. Most of these reflect occupations where there are structured systems.

Introverted STJs are particularly vulnerable to the demands of coping with complex, social systems. The difficulties they have in understanding feelings and values which are unlike their own means they will have difficulty in communicating, negotiating and persuading people who are different from them. Being introverted, their lower concern with the external world makes them less motivated to commit themselves to interfering in situations which they find confusing and confounding. If they do get involved their cognitive preferences are a poor match for the situation and failure is only likely to exacerbate the situation. The counselling requirements for ISTJs are listed by Myers and McCaulley as helping them to create alternatives, exploring the environment, shaking their sense of reality, developing social skills, sensitizing them to feelings and to the grounds of their own judgements.

INFJs AND THE COPING PROCESS

This combination is likely to make people very sensitive to how things are affecting them, though the introversion might make them more concerned with self than the outside world. Their concerns with others' feelings, however, probably makes this more likely if the stressors are from the physical world or from technical systems rather than people. If anything, they may be oversensitive to others, blame themselves and be stress-prone as a result. Their problem in Primary Appraisal is not to be aware of threat, harm and so on but to distinguish the importance of the threats. Since they are not inclined to go out and check the facts, develop explanatory frameworks and test hypotheses, they can be victims of their own imaginations. The fact that they are strong on judgement does help to balance their preference for NF processes as they will tend to have a secure set of values which helps them to determine real threats from fantasies.

In Secondary Appraisal the ability to use intuition and sensitivity to feelings increases the possibility of developing creative solutions to problems. The feelings orientation makes this particularly likely when solving interpersonal relationships, but intuition is capable of producing novel solutions to many kings of problems. NF types do less well at developing the plans and allocating resources that the creative solutions may require. They have a strong tendency not to want to be swayed by unpleasant or inconvenient obstacles (the facts). Their confidence in what Lindblom (1959) called the "Science of muddling through" is high, and sometimes misplaced. The low interest in the outside world and in facts also makes them poor at time management and time scheduling. Their plans are often unrealistic and overambitious and the failure to achieve targets and deadlines means people can lose confidence in them.

When it comes to Coping, the NF processes make such people good at working with others because they listen both to their own feelings and those of others. Because they do not construct elaborate plans to which they get strongly committed, they can be flexible and adaptable within their own value system. Being high on J can make this narrower than it might be for someone with a high P style. They are also better able to make adjustments to their own feelings and expectations so can use many of the coping techniques that Lazarus would define as "emotion-focused" coping. Being introverts they are more likely to do this than make strong efforts to change the world and remove the stress that way.

These weaknesses come out in the strategies that counsellors use to help INFJs: checking facts, constructing models, helping them to discover their own solutions to problems, setting realistic deadlines, sensitising them to the processing preferences of other types who are different from them, and helping them to value explanation and understanding as well as insight. The professions that have attracted INFJs are clergy, physicians, teachers of English and arts subjects, media specialists, marketing personnel and social scientists (Myers and McCaulley, 1985).

It is not difficult to see that there is conceptual and practical overlap between the MBTI and the two coping strategies identified by Lazarus. High NF contains emotion-focused coping and high STs would undoubtedly be capable of using problem-focused coping. The advantage of the MBTI over the Lazarus categories is that it is rooted in an elaborated theoretical framework that describes the processes characteristic of the types, and that it is much richer for adding in the dimensions of EI and JP. There is also a large body of research on the MBTI measure itself which provides an excellent foundation for using it in studies of stress and coping. It certainly comes closest to the notion of cognitive style implied in the definition quoted above.

SUMMARY AND CONCLUSION

Sternberg's work indicates there is a need to develop measures of cognitive abilities that are capable of assessing individual differences in dealing with real-world problems. The stress literature has tended to avoid doing studies which recognise that stress is a process that takes place over time (Depue and Monroe, 1986) and the analyses presented above do suggest that cognitive capacities act differentially at different parts of the process. While the distinction between capacity and style has been used for many years there is a need to develop this area conceptually. MBTI seems one sensible way to develop the concept of cognitive style and since it appears to be independent of cognitive capacity (unlike field dependence) there seems to be considerable scope for studies that combine the two. It seems unlikely that capacity and style will not interact in complex ways themselves. Indeed, the single most obvious finding in this chapter is how few studies there are that relate cognitive variables to real-world stress.

The size of the challenge can be estimated if one merely set out to explore the interactions for the MBTI, for five levels of intelligence and the three phases of the coping process for the same set of stressors (e.g. job promotion). This produces 240 conditions. What the population of stressors is must be unknowable, but this at least gives some idea of our ignorance in this area.

Hopefully, we shall not be demotivated by this challenge, for as Wittgenstein observes: "In order to draw a limit to thinking, we should have to be able to think both sides of this limit." (Preface to the *Tractacus Logico-philosophicus*)

REFERENCES

Allport, G. W., Vernon, P. E. and Lindzey, G. (1960). *Study of Values: A Scale for Measuring the Dominant Interests in Personality* (3rd edn), Houghton Mifflin, Boston.

Anderson, C. R. (1977). Locus of control, coping behaviors and performance in a stress setting: A longitudinal study, *Journal of Applied Psychology,* **62**, 446–51.

Argyris, C. and Schon, D. A. (1974). *Improving Professional Practice*, Jossey-Bass, San Francisco.

Austin, J. T. and Hanisch, K. A. (1990). Occupational attainment as a function of abilities and interests: A longitudinal analysis using project TALENT data, *Journal of Applied Psychology,* **75**(1), 77–86.

Budner, S. (1962) Intolerance of ambiguity as a personality variable, *Journal of Personality,* **8**(3), 181–7.

Cattell, R. B., Eber, H. W. and Tatsuoka, M. M. (1970). *Handbook for the Sixteen Personality Factor Questionnaire* (16 PF), Institute for Personality and Ability Testing, Champaign, Ill.

Depue, R. A. and Monroe, S. M. (1986). Conceptualization and measurement of human disorder in life stress research: The problem of chronic disturbance, *Psychological Bulletin,* **99**(1), 36–51.

Fiedler, F. E. and Garcia, J. E. (1987). *New Approaches to Effective Leadership: Cognitive Resources and Organizational Performance*, Wiley, New York.

Fisher, S. and Cooper, C. L. (1991). *On The Move: The Psychology of Change and Transition*, Wiley, New York.

Fletcher, B. (1988). The epidemiology of occupational stress. In C. L. Cooper and R. Payne (eds) *Causes, Coping and Consequences of Stress at Work*, John Wiley, London, pp. 3–50.

Folkman, S. (1984). Personal control and coping processes: A theoretical analysis, *Journal of Personality and Social Psychology,* **46**(4), 839–52.

Folkman, S. and Lazarus, R. S. (1980). An analysis of coping in a middle-aged community sample, *Journal of Health and Social Behavior,* **21**, 219–39.

Fryer, D. M. and Payne, R. L. (1986). Being unemployed: A review of the literature on the psychological experience of unemployment. In C. L. Cooper and I. Robertson (eds) *International Review of Industrial and Organisational Psychology*, John Wiley, London, pp. 235–78.

Ghiselli, E. E. (1966). *The Validity of Occupational Aptitude Tests*, New York, Wiley.

Guilford, J. P. (1967). *The Nature of Human Intelligence*, McGraw-Hill, New York.

Harré, R. and Lamb, R. (1983). (eds) *The Dictionary of Personality and Social Psychology*, Blackwell, Oxford.

Hockey, G. R. J. (1990). Styles, skills and strategies: Cognitive variability and its implications for the role of mental models in HCI. In D. Ackermann and M. J. Tauber (eds) *Mental Models and Human–Computer Interaction 1*, North Holland, Elsevier Science Publishers B.V., pp. 113–29.

Jerusalem, M. and Schwarzer, R. (1989). Anxiety and self-concept as antecedents of stress and coping: A longitudinal study with German and Turkish adolescents, *Personality and Individual Differences,* **10**, 785–92.

Jung, C. G. (1971). *Psychological Types* (H.G. Baynes, Trans. revised by R. F. C. Hull), Vol. 6 of *The Collected Works of C. J. Jung*, Princeton University Press, Princeton, NJ (original work published in 1921).

Kahn, R. L., Wolfe, D. M., Quinn, R. P., Snoeck, J. D. and Rosenthal, R. A. (1964). *Organizational Stress: Studies in Role Conflict and Ambiguity*, Wiley, New York.

Kuhn, A. (1974). *The Logic of Social Systems*, Jossey-Bass, San Francisco.

Lazarus, R. S. (1966). *Psychological Stress and the Coping Process*, McGraw-Hill, New York.

Lazarus, R. S. and Launier, R. (1978). Stress-related transactions between person and environment. In L. A. Pervin and M. Lewis (eds) *Perspectives in Interactional Psychology*, Plenum, New York, pp. 287–327.

Lefcourt, H. M. (1976). *Locus of Control: Current Trends in Theory and Research*, Halstead, New York.

Lewin, K. (1947). Frontiers in group dynamics, *Human Relations*, **1**, 5–41.

Lindblom, C. E. (1959). The science of muddling through, *Public Administration Review*, **19**, 79–88.

McCrae, R. R. (1984). Situational determinants of coping responses: Loss, threat and challenge, *Journal of Personality and Social Psychology*, **46**(4), 919–28.

McKenna, F. (1984). Measures of field dependence: Cognitive style or cognitive ability? *Journal of Personality and Social Psychology*, **47**, 593–603.

Mintzberg, H. (1976). Planning on the left side, managing on the right, *Harvard Business Review*, **July–August**.

Myers, I. B. and McCaulley, M. H. (1985). *A Guide to the Development and Use of the Myers–Briggs Type Indicator*, Consulting Psychologists Press, California.

Pearlin, L. I., Lieberman, M. A., Menaghan, E. G. and Mullan, J. T. (1981). The Stress Process, *Journal of Health and Social Behavior*, **22**, 337–56.

Seligman, M. E. P. (1975). *Helplessness*, W. H. Freeman, San Francisco.

Sternberg, R. J. (1985). *Beyond I.Q.* Cambridge University Press, Cambridge.

Sternberg, R. J. and Turner, M. E. (1981). Components of syllogistic reasoning, *Acta Psychologica*, **41**, 37–55.

Stone, A. A. and Neale, J. M. (1984). New measure of daily coping: Development and preliminary results, *Journal of Personality and Social Psychology*, **46**(4), 892–906.

Vecchio, R. P. (1990). Theoretical and empirical examination of cognitive resource theory, *Journal of Applied Psychology*, **75**(2), 141–7.

Widger, T. A., Knudson, R. M. and Rorer, L. G. (1980). Convergent and discriminant validity of measures of cognitive style and abilities, *Journal of Personality and Social Psychology*, **39**, 116–29.

Witkin, H. A., Dijk, R. B., Faterson, H. F., Goodenough, D. R. and Karp, S. A. (1962). *Psychological Differentiation: Studies of Development*, Wiley, New York.

PART IV

Coping, Personality and Individual Differences

Chapter 9

Psychological Coping, Individual Differences and Physiological Stress Responses

Andrew Steptoe, University of London, UK

INTRODUCTION

The response to stressful encounters involves not only changes at the cognitive, affective and behavioural levels, but also a wide range of physiological adjustments. The activation of psychophysiological response system influences the competence with which we adapt to life's challenges. There are two major reasons why studies of physiological responses are valuable. The first is that many of the links between stress and illness are mediated by psychophysiological pathways. Alterations of autonomic, endocrine and immune function reflect processes that are of direct relevance to the aetiology and maintenance of disease. Second, physiological parameters can function as objective markers of stress responses. Much of the research linking stress with mental or self-reported physical health is plagued by problems of measurement contamination, leading to the identification of spurious associations between life stress and well-being (Schroeder and Costa, 1984; Watson and Pennebaker, 1989). Physiological markers provide objective evidence for the impact of stress and individual differences.

This chapter therefore focuses on psychological coping and individual differences as they relate to physiological responses and health outcomes. A growing research literature in this area points to the conclusion that from the psychophysiological perspective, there is no such thing as completely effective coping. An individual with a particular temperament or personality will not invariably be more successful in adapting to threats and challenges than another. Coping behaviours have different physiological correlates, so that there are costs as well as benefits in terms of neuroendocrine, autonomic and

Personality and Stress: Individual Differences in the Stress Process. Edited by C.L. Cooper and R. Payne
© 1991 John Wiley & Sons Ltd

immune activation. The delineation of these patterns will help us to identify the most appropriate coping behaviours for adaptation to different situations.

THE ORGANISATION OF PHYSIOLOGICAL STRESS RESPONSES

A wide range of neuroendocrine, autonomic and immune parameters are involved in the response to stress (see Steptoe, 1990). Table 9.1 summarises those that are most commonly measured in human stress research. They include autonomic, neuroendocrine and immune parameters, together with indices of activity in specific physiological systems such as the circulation and gut. The list is not exhaustive, and more parameters will be added as measurement techniques are refined.

Faced with such a bewildering array of physiological responses, it is not surprising that psychobiologists have searched for the organising principles that underlie the pattern of change. The responses are organised hierarchically through a series of basic pathways. Primary roles are played by the

Table 9.1   Physiological parameters measured in human stress studies

Musculoskeletal Parameters	Muscle tension, Breathing patterns
Neuroendocrine Parameters	Corticosteroids (Cortisol, Mineralocorticoids, Urinary metabolites)
	Catecholamines (Adrenaline, Noradrenaline)
	β-endorphin, Testosterone, Prolactin, Growth hormone, Insulin
Cardiovascular Measures	Heart rate, Cardiac arrhythmias
	Cardiac output, Stroke volume, Myocardial contractility, Pulse transit time
	Blood pressure, Total peripheral resistance
	Regional blood flow—muscle, skin
	Coronary blood flow, transient myocardial ischaemia
	Renal blood flow, Glomerular filtration rate, Sodium excretion
	Platelet aggregation and adhesion
	Sympathetic nerve activity (microneurography)
Electrodermal Parameters	Skin conductance, Skin potential, Sweat gland counts
Gastrointestinal Tract	Salivation, Gastrointestinal transit time, Electrogastrogram
Fat Metabolism	Total cholesterol, Cholesterol fractions, Triglycerides, Free fatty acids, Blood glucose levels
Immune-Related Parameters	Immunoglobulins—IgA, IgE, IgG, IgM
	Lymphocyte subsets
	Natural killer cell activity
	Mitogen-induced lymphocyte proliferation
	Antigen titres to latent Epstein-Barr virus

pituitary–adrenocortical axis (leading to the release of corticosteroids) and the sympathetic-adrenomedullary system (leading to sympathetic discharge and the release of catecholamines). Other responses emerge through the activation of these pathways. Hence many of the cardiovascular adjustments result from sympathetic nervous system activation coupled with the release of catecholamines from the adrenal medulla. Lipid metabolism and the release of stored energy supplies is stimulated by glucocorticoids and catecholamines, while the disturbances in cellular and humorally mediated immune function are caused in part through activation of corticosteroid and autonomic pathways.

Theoretical understanding in this field was dominated for many years by Selye's (1936) notion of the stress response as a non-specific pattern of physiological activation, adapted to defend the biological integrity of the organism. Selye hypothesised that the stress response could be elicited by any stimulus independent of its quality, and identified the pituitary–adrenocortical axis as the key mechanism. The physiological response would protect the individual in the short term by mobilising stored energy supplies, preparing for physical work and maintaining homeostasis. In the long term, deleterious effects of sustained activation might emerge (the so-called diseases of adaptation). This theory has an appealing biological plausibility. Unfortunately, studies over the last quarter of a century have discredited the concept of a non-specific physiological stress response, and the idea that the short-term biological response to stress is purely protective. These arguments are detailed elsewhere (see Munck, Guyre and Holbrook, 1984; Dantzer and Kelley, 1989). Here, it is relevant to highlight three points:

(1) The physiological response to stress is not "non-specific", but is patterned according to the emotional demands and behavioural responses elicited in the situation. For instance, a distinction can be drawn between active efforts to cope with stress and passive withdrawal (Henry, 1976). Active coping is accompanied by catecholamine release and sympathetic nervous system activation, while passive withdrawal is linked more closely to corticosteroid secretion. This difference is discussed in more detail later in this chapter. Patterns of greater subtlety can be identified when the interaction between individual predispositions and specific situations are taken into account. For instance, recent studies indicate that the sympathetic nervous system and catecholamines from the adrenal medulla may show different contours of response, and that there is even patterning of the sympathetic responses governing vasoconstriction in different tissues (Freyschuss et al., 1988).

(2) The notion that the physiological stress response is adaptive in the short term is hard to reconcile with the anti-inflammatory and immunosuppressive effects of glucocorticoids, since it implies that the most effective way

of protecting against stress is to suppress a major natural defence mechanism. Munck et al., (1984) have suggested that instead of being mobilised as a direct protective response, glucocorticoids have a regulatory function, protecting against overshoot of other defence systems. This process may be so effective as to lead to weakening rather than strengthening of the organism's biological defences.

(3) The conventional notion that peripheral physiological changes are secondary to central nervous system activation during stress may be misleading in the light of evidence concerning the bidirectional traffic between central and peripheral systems. This is apparent both in neuroendocrine parameters and in the peptide messengers released by the immune system. For example, the cytokine interleukin-1, produced by peripheral macrophages and monocytes in response to infection, co-ordinates central and peripheral responses, stimulating a range of behavioural effects (fatigue, sickness, loss of appetite and so on). It has been argued that this is part of an organised biobehavioural response system which optimises the role of fever in combatting infections (Dantzer, in press). This raises intriguing questions about the associations that have been observed between depression and immunosuppression following events such as bereavement (e.g. Stein, Keller and Schleifer, 1985). It has been supposed that a depressed state may lead to immunosuppression. It is however plausible that cytokines released from immune tissue reinforce negative mood changes and depressive symptoms. The conclusion must be that physiological responses are not biological epiphenomena to a basic cognitive-behavioural stress process. Rather, they are intrinsically involved in the mechanism of coping and adaptation.

PERSONALITY AND PSYCHOLOGICAL COPING

The emphasis of this chapter is on the relationships between physiological stress responses and psychological factors such as coping and personality. The premise is that individual differences are relevant to stress responses in so far as they modulate the way in which people cope with environmental demands. Coping responses arise through an interaction between situational factors and personal predispositions or habits. My intention is therefore to identify the psychobiological correlates of different coping responses, and to examine the way in which psychological coping affects physiological adaptation to stressful encounters.

Views about the importance of personality and coping to the stress process are quite diverse. On the one hand, some authors imply that the influence of personality is ubiquitous. Friedman (1990) states that "a strong case can be made for an independent causal role of personality in the progression (and probably in the development) of disease" (p. 8). Many hypotheses about the mechanisms linking personality with health focus on individual differences in coping having an impact on physiological stress responses (Suls and Rittenhouse, 1990). On the other hand, a recent review by Cohen and Edwards (1989) asserted that there is "little convincing evidence for personality factors operating as stress buffers" (p. 236). Cohen and Edwards argue that a stress-buffering role can only be identified when the effects of the individual-difference measure are studied both under high and low (or no) stress conditions. Otherwise, it is not possible to distinguish interactive (or buffering) processes from the main effects of personality or coping on outcome. This argument enabled Cohen and Edwards to dismiss much of the research literature. For example, they imply that only one published study has examined the stress-buffering role of active and avoidant coping styles (p. 264). However, their conclusion is certainly not true of investigations that have involved physiological responses as endpoints, since these studies rarely omit baseline or control conditions against which reactions to mental stress are assessed. A stress buffering effect can therefore be shown if a difference in the magnitude of stress responses between groups varying on the personality or coping measure is found, coupled with a lack of differences under baseline or control conditions. The psychophysiological literature was not reviewed by Cohen and Edwards (1989) and this led them to an inappropriately negative conclusion, and unwarranted generalisations from a subset of clinical and field studies to the research on personality, coping and stress at large.

The relationship between psychological coping and personality is also controversial. McCrae and Costa (1986) have argued that coping responses are epiphenomena of personality, with no causal status independent of personality. The alternative perspective (which is espoused here) is that personality and other individual differences influence the person's tendency to mobilise particular coping responses when confronted with stressful situations. I would suggest that coping is more immediately relevant to stressful encounters than personality for two major reasons.

First, personality factors may be influential only at certain phases of the coping process. The psychological coping strategy that an individual adopts is determined in part by personality, but other factors such as the social and cultural context are important. Situational factors and the nature of the stressful encounter are also highly significant. This is apparent in many field studies of stress and coping where, despite personality differences, most people attempt to cope with similar events in similar ways (e.g. Folkman and Lazarus, 1985; Bolger, 1990). There is an interaction between situational and individual preferences, and this was clearly illustrated in Averill and Rosenn's (1972) experimental study of anticipatory coping. The study concerned the behaviour of volunteers in the few minutes preceding the administration of electric shock, the exact timing of which was uncertain. Participants were allowed to listen to distracting music, or to monitor an auditory tone which changed in pitch to a warning tone just before shock. Subjects monitoring the tone were therefore given forewarning of the shock, while those preferring to distract themselves with music did not know when the shock would occur. In addition, half the participants were able to avoid shock by pressing a button during the short period between the warning tone and shock; obviously, this was only possible if the subject tracked the tone rather than music channel. The remaining subjects were not able to avoid.

The proportion of subjects who spent most of the time either monitoring or distracting is summarised in Table 9.2. It can be seen that at low shock intensities, 50% of the avoidance group and 30% of the no-avoidance group monitored the warning tone. At high shock intensities, the proportion of the avoidance group who monitored the warning tone rose to 70%, indicating how the situation impels people towards vigilant coping behaviour. Interestingly, however, 30% of the avoidance group continued to listen to music, even though by doing so they lost the opportunity to switch off the shock. For them, it would appear that the distress associated with being vigilant outweighed the stress of having an electric shock. It is also notable that nearly 50% of the no-avoidance group adopted a vigilant strategy, even though they could not prevent or avoid the aversive experience. Although later studies have shown some discrepancies with these results, they remain vivid demonstrations of the power of individual preferences to shape coping behaviours (Miller, 1979; Evans, Phillips and Fearn, 1984).

The second reason for examining coping rather than personality is that the same coping strategy may be used by individuals who differ in personality. For example, anxious people have a bias towards attending to the threatening aspects of a situation. This bias may be pre-attentive (outside conscious awareness), as has been shown in a number of cognitive psychological experiments on anxious and non-anxious individuals (see Eysenck, 1989). However, attention to threat and information seeking may be characteristic of a more general dimension of coping (illustrated in Table 9.2), described as vigilance versus avoidance, or monitoring versus blunting (Roth and Cohen, 1986; Miller, 1987). This dimension is independent of anxiety (Steptoe and O'Sullivan, 1986). Hence, personality measures may not adequately characterise the coping responses elicited in stressful environments.

Table 9.2   Coping behaviour during anticipation of shock: Percentage of subjects in each group showing vigilance or distraction

	Avoidance group		No-avoidance group	
	Vigilance	Distraction	Vigilance	Distraction
Low Shock Intensity	50	50	30	70
High Shock Intensity	70	30	45	55

From Averill and Rosenn, 1972

The Taxonomy of Psychological Coping

Scientific studies of psychological coping have suffered from variations in the use of the term. This confusion extends to the colloquial usage of "coping", which may refer either to contending with and encountering challenges, or to dealing effectively and successfully managing the situation. Is coping the same as effective coping? A body of thought stemming primarily from animal studies has tended to use coping in the sense of effective responding, suggesting that since the (teleological) biological purpose of coping is to reduce threats to survival, coping *is* the process of successful adaptation (Levine, 1983). However, an alternative tradition has developed over recent years in which coping is viewed as a multifaceted phenomenon involving a range of responses, not all of which may be adaptive (see Lazarus and Folkman, 1984). In this sense, coping can be defined as a set of responses mobilised in an effort to manage the situation. These responses may not necessarily be successful, in that adaptation in the stress measures under investigation may be less complete than for subjects engaging different coping responses.

The issue that lies at the heart of this distinction is what criterion can be used to decide whether coping is adaptive and successful or not. The definition of coping as successful adaptation has largely emerged from studies on neuroendocrine markers. Levine, for example, has concluded that "it would appear essential that coping mechanisms should have as their major consequence the reduction of continued hypersecretion of neuroendocrine systems" (1983, p. 18). This view is consistent with the finding that corticosteroid levels in the blood diminish as animals and humans gain mastery over threatening events by learning appropriate behavioural responses (e.g. Feldman and Brown, 1976; Ursin, Baade and Levin, 1978). Unfortunately, the difficulty with this model of coping as successful adaptation is that reduced responding in one biological system may be coupled with increased activation of other parameters (see Steptoe, 1989). A good example is the phenomenon of shock-induced "boxing" in rodents. Rats administered uncontrollable shock show large corticosteroid responses. But when they are placed in pairs during shock, they tend to stand up on their hind legs and "box". This behaviour is associated with decreased corticosterone, suggesting that the passive helplessness of solitary shock is transformed by the presence of a partner, and that boxing is an adaptive coping behaviour with beneficial consequences (Conner, Vernikos-Danellis and Levine, 1971). However, Mormède and co-workers (1984) have shown that rats shocked in pairs show stronger activation of the sympathetic-adrenomedullary system than animals shocked alone, indicating that this form of psychological coping has arousing effects on some physiological parameters.

If coping is seen as a range of responses brought into play in an effort to manage a stressful encounter, what are the coping responses and how are they organised? Several different schemes for understanding coping have been proposed. Cohen (1987) argued that five coping modes can be distinguished: information-seeking, taking direct action, inhibition of action, intrapsychic processes and turning to others for support. Factor analyses of the Ways of Coping scale devised by Lazarus and co-workers has led to the identification of coping factors such as problem-focused coping, seeking social support, distancing or threat minimisation, wishful thinking, self-blame, positive appraisal and growth (Lazarus and Folkman, 1984; Vitaliano et al., 1985). Billings and Moos (1981) distinguished active-cognitive, active-behavioural and avoidance responses, with a further distinction between problem and emotional focus. Investigators such as Carver and co-workers (1989) have devised coping measures on a rational basis, distinguishing a number of problem-focused coping responses such as active coping, planning, suppression of competing activities and restraint, and emotion-focused strategies such as ventilating emotion, behavioural disengagement, mental disengagement, positive reinterpretation, denial and acceptance. Other researchers have emphasised broader distinctions such as vigilant versus avoidant strategies (Roth and Cohen, 1986), or responses that lead to engagement versus disengagement with the problem or the emotions it evokes (Tobin et al., 1989). Yet another research tradition stems from the notion that coping responses involving denial, distancing or repression are almost by definition inaccessible to conscious awareness, so will not be accurately detected by direct questions or self-report (Ursin, Olff and Godaert, in press).

Faced with this complexity, and the limits of current knowledge relating coping with psychophysiological processes, it may be more useful to consider broad dimensions rather than very subtle patterns. A basic distinction that runs through many investigations is between coping responses designed to deal with the problem and those aimed at managing the associated emotion. It is also commonly agreed that coping can take place at both the behavioural and cognitive levels. This leads to classification into the four forms of coping shown in Figure 9.1. Of course, these forms of coping are not independent. Behavioural responses are inevitably associated with cognitions, and some methods of coping (such as information-seeking) may have an impact on the problem while simultaneously ameliorating the emotion. Nevertheless, this classification has the merit of simplicity. For illustrative purposes, some of the specific strategies identified in the literature have been inserted into the plan, with a general distinction being drawn between engagement (approach or confrontation) and disengagement (withdrawal) during coping (after Tobin et al., 1989). The later sections of this chapter will attempt to tease out what is known about the physiological and health correlates of these coping responses. The overview will not be exhaustive, but will rather concentrate on those areas in which a persuasive body of knowledge is developing.

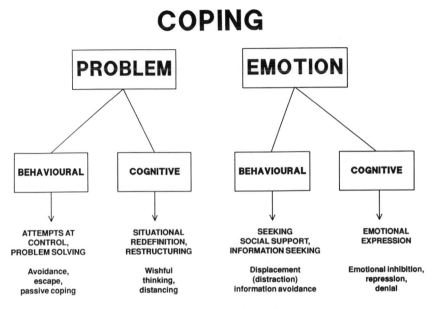

Figure 9.1   A classification of psychological coping, with specific responses tentatively allocated according to their form (behavioural or cognitive) and primary focus (problem or emotion). Responses leading to engagement are shown in upper case, while those associated with disengagement are shown in lower case

PROBLEM-FOCUSED BEHAVIOURAL COPING

Problem-focused behavioural coping responses are overt actions intended to deal directly with the situation. The most intensively investigated are active problem solving, attempts at control, avoidance, and withdrawal or escape from the situation. The effects of behavioural control, lack of control and loss of control over aversive events have been studied extensively in animals and humans (for detailed reviews see Steptoe and Appels, 1989). In animals, control has been studied with one animal able to control or escape shock through a simple behavioural response, while its yoked partner is unable to control the stressor. These experiments have shown widespread benefits of behavioural control, with animals in uncontrollable conditions showing poorer behavioural performance, reduced food consumption and weight loss, increased plasma corticosterone, gastric lesions, neurochemical changes in the brain, stress-induced analgesia and a variety of immune-related deficits, including increased susceptibility to malignancy, decreased mitogen-induced lymphocyte proliferation and decreased cytotoxic activity in natural killer cells (see Steptoe, 1990). In human experimental studies, uncontrollable aversive conditions can lead to greater self-reported stress, electrodermal and pituitary-adrenocortical responses, compared with controllable conditions (e.g. Breier et al., 1987). The motivational deficits and mood suppression associated with lack of control have been linked with depression in the learned helplessness model (Seligman, 1975), and clinical studies of depression imply that loss events are particularly significant in the aetiology of depression (Brown and Harris, 1978). Karasek (1979) has argued that health and productivity at work are also strongly influenced by control over decisions regarding work organisation.

Unfortunately, the simple notion that behavioural control over stressful events is beneficial, and that lack of control is damaging, cannot be sustained. Several lines of research indicate that the pattern is more complex.

(1) At the physiological level, there has been difficulty in replicating some of the findings. For example, the observation that uncontrollable shock leads to particularly impressive deficits in lymphocyte function has not been replicated in several studies (Maier and Laudenslager, 1988). In addition, it would appear that not all branches of the immune system respond in the same fashion. Mormède and co-workers (1988) found that splenocyte responses to mitogens were suppressed in animals exposed to uncontrollable compared with controllable shock, but that antibody responses were more effective in the uncontrollable condition.

(2) At the psychological level, several points have complicated the hypothesis that uncontrollability leads to disturbances in motivational, cognitive and emotional responses. Abramson, Seligman and Teasdale (1978) have argued that the negative effects of lack of control depend not so much on the uncontrollability of events, as on the attributions people make concerning the causes of events. Bandura (1977) has pointed out the need to distinguish outcome expectations (the perception of a relationship between one's behaviour and the outcome) from efficacy expectations (the belief people have that they can perform a relevant behaviour). Thus, people may fail to control or give up trying to control a situation because they believe their actions will have no influence on an unresponsive environment, or because they believe they do not have the capability to perform the correct behaviour. There are also circumstances in which people prefer not to exert control, either because doing so has costs that are worse than the negative event itself, or because they may perceive the desired outcome as more likely when they relinquish control (Burger, 1989).

(3) A number of studies have shown that physiological responses may actually be more pronounced in controllable than uncontrollable conditions (see Steptoe, 1983). This depends on the effort required to exert control. When the response required for controlling an aversive environment is complex or difficult, and when the outcome is uncertain, heightened physiological activation mediated through sympathetic nervous stimulation may be recorded. Thus, higher levels of blood pressure and heart

rate have been measured under controllable than under uncontrollable conditions, when subjects were actively engaged in effortful behavioural responses or active problem solving.

This evidence has converged on the hypothesis that the effects of control lie on a more general dimension of behavioural coping. Control in situations that are perceived as easy to master lies at an intermediate point, and is associated with only modest physiological responses. At one extreme lies active or effortful behavioural coping, in which vigorous steps are taken by the person to master the environment. Active behavioural coping has been linked in humans with cardiovascular changes such as increased heart rate and blood pressure, heightened muscle tension and increases in effort, concentration and anxiety (Solomon, Holmes and McCaul, 1980; Lovallo et al., 1985). Situations perceived as controllable may elicit active behavioural coping, but only if control is difficult to achieve, and the person elects to confront the problem in a direct fashion. At the other extreme is passive coping, when the person withdraws, tolerating the aversive environment inertly without taking any steps to change the situation. Passive coping is particularly likely when events are perceived as uncontrollable, and it is associated with heightened pituitary–adrenocortical activity, and possibly with immune suppression (Koolhaas and Bohus, 1989).

Personality Factors Underlying Active and Passive Coping

It will be evident from this discussion that different forms of problem-focused behavioural coping are associated with distinct patterns of physiological response. The probability that a person will engage each coping response depends on situational factors (whether the problem is perceived as amenable to solution) and efficacy expectations. For example, active behavioural coping is typically elicited in the laboratory by asking a subject to solve difficult mental problems, possibly with a financial incentive, or with social pressure induced by being told that other people find such tasks easy. Large sympathoadrenal responses are frequently found in this situation. However, it is possible that the subject will give up the challenge, believing that he or she is not going to succeed, so might as well not even try. Under these circumstances, sympathetically mediated physiological responses will not be prominent.

Several personality or behavioural dispositions may be associated with active and passive coping, including locus of control, hardiness, self-esteem and the tendency to self-handicapping behaviour. Some of these are discussed elsewhere in this volume. Two other factors may be particularly related to the outcome and efficacy expectations that a person brings to bear on a stressful encounter. The general orientation towards positive outcome expectations (i.e. beliefs that matters will turn out well) is synonymous with optimism, and the dimension of optimism versus pessimism is influential on coping responses. Scheier and Carver (1985) have argued that optimists may cope better with stressful encounters because they take effective action and engage in sensible forward planning. Certainly optimists report mobilising more problem-focused coping responses than pessimists in potentially controllable situations, and also take more actions to relieve their symptoms when they are ill (Scheier, Weintraub and Carver, 1986; Lin and Peterson, 1990). In a long-term follow-up study, Peterson, Seligman and Vaillant (1988) reported that a pessimistic explanatory style in youth was associated with poor physical health in later years. Whether or not this was due to more effective coping with stress is unknown, since no life stress measures were recorded, but it is plausible that physiological stress responses were responsible.

The other underlying dimension that may be relevant is self-efficacy, or beliefs that the person has the skills or competence to master the situation. Litt (1988) has reviewed evidence showing that perceived self-efficacy is associated with stress tolerance, particularly in relation to pain. A fascinating study by Bandura and colleagues (1988) suggested that low self-efficacy leads to activation of opioid mechanisms under stress, whereas this pathway is not activated in people with high self-efficacy and competence in their ability to cope. It has also been found that self-efficacy in coping with stress is a modulator of immune function, with greater immunocompetence in subjects with high self-efficacy (Weidenfeld et al., 1990). If perceived self-efficacy generalises from specific situations to broader beliefs in coping competence, it may induce appropriate use of behavioural problem-focused coping skills.

PROBLEM–FOCUSED COGNITIVE COPING

Coping responses performed at the cognitive level that are directed towards dealing with the problem tend to involve attempts to manage the way in which stressful events are perceived. Lazarus (1966) has coined the term "cognitive appraisal" to denote the fashion in which people interpret events or situations that are potentially stressful. Among cognitive appraisal strategies are selective attention to positive aspects of the situation, redefining events in a non-threatening fashion or perceiving experiences as opportunities for personal growth rather than as tragedies. Cognitive appraisals may have little influence in the face of major disasters or acute life events (Hobfoll, 1988). They may nevertheless be important in other situations, such as helping people cope with medical interventions like surgery or unpleasant diagnostic procedures, since there may be little that people can do directly to ameliorate these problems. The influence of cognitive appraisal on physiological responses was first investigated by Lazarus (1966) in a series of experiments in which volunteers watched unpleasant films under different instructional conditions. Instructions to redefine the film in non-threatening ways (for instance, by intellectualising or by denying the reality of the scenes depicted) were associated with reduced autonomic reactions compared with control conditions. Some of these effects have proved difficult to replicate in subsequent experiments (Steptoe and Vögele, 1986). Nevertheless, the general principle that cognitive redefinition may blunt physiological stress responses has been sustained.

Cognitive coping strategies are especially relevant to pain. Leventhal and co-workers (1979) conducted a study assessing distress during the cold pressor test, in which volunteers immersed their hands in freezing water. Distress was reduced when subjects were instructed to attend closely to the sensations they were experiencing. The efficacy of this strategy was attributed to the use of a cognitive schema rather than an emotional schema for processing the experience. More broadly, Turk, Meichenbaum and Genest (1983) have suggested several methods of situational definition that can be helpful in the management of clinical pain. These include "imaginative inattention", when the subject imagines a scene which is incompatible with pain; "imaginative transformation", when the sensations are relabelled perhaps as numbness or a dull ache; "somatisation", when the person learns to think about the sensations in a detached way, as if they belonged to someone else's body; and "transformation of context", in which the sensation is imagined in another setting, perhaps as a wound heroically received in battle.

The adaptive utility of positive appraisal and confrontation has attracted considerable attention following the studies of survival in breast cancer patients reported by Greer, Morris and Pettingale (1979). These investigators assessed the coping responses of women with breast cancer three months after surgery. Women who coped with the experience by showing a fighting spirit, or denied the illness, were more likely to have survived without recurrence than those who showed stoic acceptance or helplessness and hopelessness. Fighting spirit was defined as an optimistic attitude coupled with a search for information about cancer. Unfortunately, the effects of these coping responses on cancer progression have yet to be replicated consistently in other samples (Fox, 1988). Fighting spirit and denial cannot be viewed as purely cognitive coping responses, since they may have behavioural consequences such as attention to diet or healthy life-styles. Future studies of this topic will need to take account of the growing evidence that the immune changes related to cancer may themselves cause affective symptoms. Nevertheless, it does appear that positive thinking is associated with better psychological adjustment to cancer, and longitudinal studies suggest that this pattern of coping is not secondary but is causally related to mood and a sense of well-being (Filipp et al., 1990). Taylor's (1983) theory of cognitive adaptation, developed through studies of cancer patients, is centered around the tasks of searching for meaning in events, restoring belief in control over one's life and efforts at enhancing self-esteem (frequently through social comparisons). A

recent study of a group-based programme of problem-solving, health education, relaxation and social support in patients with malignant melanomas
showed that subjects in the intervention group reported improved mood together with greater use of active expressive and positive coping strategies, and
less passivity and resignation (Fawzy et al., 1990a). These responses were
accompanied by beneficial changes in various immune parameters (Fawzy et
al., 1990b).

EMOTION-FOCUSED BEHAVIOURAL COPING

The behaviours that fall into this category are diverse, but are all assumed to
share the aim of ameliorating the emotional impact of aversive events. Both
animals and humans engage in a number of responses that ethologists would
classify as displacement activities. These are behaviours irrelevant to the
situation that emerge when there is conflict or when ongoing responses are
thwarted. In animals, the performance of displacement activities may lead to
reductions in plasma corticosteroid concentrations which would not occur in
their absence. Other parameters such as catecholamines may be unaffected or
even increased, reflecting once again the patterning of physiological stress
responses (Dantzer, 1989).

Less is known about displacement activities in humans, but they include a
variety of trivial behaviours such as nail biting, leg swinging and bruxism.
There is also a range of behaviours that show some resemblance to displace-
ments, except that they have a more prominent intentional component. These
are the habitual activities that increase in times of stress. Many of these may
have negative effects on health, as in the case of increased smoking or alcohol
consumption (e.g. Conway et al., 1981). Others have positive health consequences. A good example is vigorous physical exercise, which some people
carry out when under stress, and which may help them to cope more effectively (Steptoe et al., 1989).

Two other forms of emotional coping behaviour bear discussion in rather
more detail, since there is growing literature about their relevance to
physiological stress responses.

Information-seeking and Avoidance

Individuals differ in the extent to which they seek out information related to
threatening events. Some people are vigilant, finding out as much as possible
about the nature and consequences of events, while others avoid information
at the behavioural level, and divert their attention away from threatening
knowledge. Numerous laboratory experiments have been carried out, either
observing natural variations in this coping dimension, or else deliberately
contrasting vigilant and avoidant strategies through experimental manip-

ulation (for reviews, see Suls and Fletcher, 1985; Miller and Birnbaum, 1989). The general pattern to emerge is that in acute settings, avoidance leads to smaller physiological responses and less distress than attention or information-seeking. For example, Miller (1979) showed that monitoring a warning signal in an experimental shock paradigm was associated with higher skin conductance levels and more non-specific electrodermal responses than was distraction. However in the longer term, the situation may be reversed, with attention or vigilance being more adaptive psychophysiologically. Somewhat similar findings have emerged in clinical settings, with information-seeking leading to more distress during investigative medical procedures than does avoidance, while long-term adjustment to illness is more effective in information-seekers (e.g. Phipps and Zinn, 1986). The explanation for this pattern may be that in the short term, vigilance leads to unnecessary worry, heightened attention to minor symptoms and excessive curtailment of activity. But with chronic illness or long-term problems, information-seeking may be more adaptive since the person may engage in appropriate behaviours and self-care. For instance, Felton and Revenson (1984) found that information-seeking was associated with more positive moods than was avoidant coping in patients with mixed chronic illness. Depression in medical patients is correlated with avoidant coping behaviours (Rosenberg et al., 1987). Moos and colleagues (1990) have shown that among elderly problem drinkers, avoidant coping is coupled with depression and physical symptoms. Poor adherence to treatment has been observed in diabetic adolescents who have a preference for avoidant coping and the ventilation of emotional distress (Hansen et al., 1989).

Information-seeking has been placed here in the category of an emotion-focused coping behaviour. Clearly this is not the whole story, since information-seeking may have practical consequences in facilitating problem solving. For example, a person deciding between two courses of action in a stressful situation might benefit from information about the likely outcome and risks of each option. However, information-seeking and avoidance are relevant to stressful encounters even in the absence of the possibility of influencing the course of events. As was seen in Averill and Rosenn's (1972) study (Table 9.2), many people elected to monitor the information channel even though they were in the no-avoidance condition. Accurate information may increase predictability and anticipatory preparation for unpleasant events. Under these circumstances, information is pursued for the emotional relief it confers.

Seeking Social Support

Another form of coping which is primarily aimed at the regulation of emotional responses is the effort people make to recruit social support when under stress. A large literature has developed over the past two decades concerning relationships between social support and health (see Cohen and Syme, 1985; House et al., 1988). Effects on physical and psychological morbidity are unequivocal. What is less certain is the mechanism responsible, and whether social support and social networks are directly related to health, or have a role in buffering the effects of life stress. Cohen and Wills (1985) have argued that direct or main effects of social support (irrespective of life events of chronic stress) tend to emerge when support is assessed in terms of integration within social networks. Such studies are typically conducted within an epidemiological framework, and involve the measurement of social network size and density. Buffering effects in the face of life stress are more commonly identified when measurements focus on the perceived availability and adequacy of social resources. Social support is not an objective characteristic of the social environment, but is intimately dependent on coping behaviours that provide cues about what support is wanted or needed in stressful situations (Dunkel-Schetter et al., 1987).

Research involving physiological measures is beginning to provide insight into the mechanisms through which social support may influence health. Several studies have assessed immune function, and have observed immune suppression among people with poor social support (Thomas et al., 1985; Levy et al., 1990). For example, Kiecolt-Glaser and her colleagues (1984, 1987, 1988) have shown reduced mitogen-induced lymphocyte proliferation and immune activation to latent Epstein Barr virus in students who are lonely, and in adults with disrupted marriages and personal relationships. A study of the spouses of cancer patients, selected as being under severe stress, found that immune function was disturbed in those who perceived low social support (Baron et al., 1990). Many of these studies appear to show that poor social supports have a direct effect on immune function irrespective of concurrent life stress, although the distinction is often difficult to make—after all, the attempt to cope by recruiting social support that fails to materialise may itself constitute a major stressor.

By contrast, a buffering effect of social support on cardiovascular reactivity has been observed experimentally by Kamarck, Manuck and Jennings (1990). Blood pressure and heart rate responses were recorded from female students while they performed demanding mental tasks either alone or in the presence of a female friend. No differences in baseline levels were observed, so social support did not have a direct effect on cardiovascular function. However, responses to tasks were smaller in the group who had a friend present. Cardiovascular reactions to mental arithmetic are shown in Figure 9.2, and clearly indicate a substantial buffering effect on blood pressure and heart rate levels.

These studies therefore indicate that social support may have both direct and buffering effects on physiological processes that may influence health. Differences between findings probably relate to the specific situation in which patterns are investigated. It should also be pointed out that although people

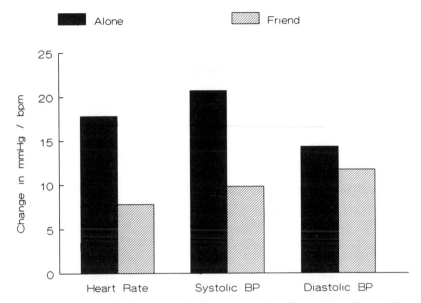

Figure 9.2   Increases in heart rate (in beats per minute), and systolic and diastolic blood pressure (in mmHg) in response to mental arithmetic, in volunteers who carried out the task either alone, or in the presence of a friend. From Kamarck et al., 1990

may seek social support primarily to help with emotional adjustment, other effects are also present. Social contacts can provide material support such as the provision of services and resources, and informational support in giving advice and opinions about how to cope with the event. Some studies indicate that these types of social contact are at least as important as non-specific emotional support (e.g. Seeman and Syme, 1987). These variations in the nature and meaning of social support must also be taken into account in trying to understand associations with physiological stress responses.

EMOTION-FOCUSED COGNITIVE COPING

The final category of coping response defined in Figure 9.1 concerns the way in which people manage the emotion aroused in stressful encounters at a cognitive level. The active engagement and expression of appropriate affect is thought to promote effective emotional processing of stressful material (Rachman, 1980). There are in addition a variety of coping strategies that lead to disengagement with emotions, including emotional inhibition, repression, defensive avoidance and denial. Many of the latter group of coping responses involve a disassociation of cognition from concomitant feelings, with the result that the individual may not acknowledge or experience distress (Haan, 1977). There has been a long tradition in psychosomatic medicine suggesting that inadequate or inappropriate recognition and ventilation of emotions may be maladaptive. This has been difficult to prove, since such responses may be hard to measure with conventional self-report procedures. Fortunately, there have been important developments both in the measurement of emotional inhibition and expression, and in studies of physiological correlates. The resultant pattern of findings is complex, with emotional inhibition or disengagement being damaging in some circumstances, but adaptive in others, depending on the nature of the situation and the physiological responses being assessed.

Voluntary Disclosure and Physiological Responses

A series of studies have addressed the issue of emotional inhibition by setting people tasks in which their disclosure of emotionally charged material is assessed. Pennebaker, Kiecolt-Glaser and Glaser (1988) asked subjects either to write about very traumatic experiences or neutral material on four occasions. Blood samples were taken and immune function measured through mitogen-induced lymphocyte proliferation. Subjects in the traumatic experience writing group were found to have superior immune function, particularly in those who were judged not to have held back stressful material. A similar pattern was reported by Esterling and co-workers (1990), who showed that subjects who are non-disclosers have poorer control over latent Epstein Barr virus. When asked to recount traumatic experiences, people who inhibit emotions produce higher skin conductance levels than those who disclose, suggesting the inhibition also leads to autonomic activation (Pennebaker, Hughes and O'Heeron, 1987).

Repressive Coping Responses

The second approach to emotional inhibition was developed by Weinberger, Schwartz and Davidson (1979). These investigators were concerned with distinguishing genuinely low anxious subjects from people who repressed negative emotions. They did this by administering anxiety measures along with the Marlowe Crowne Social Desirability scale, which can be seen as an index of defensive avoidance of social disapproval. Genuinely low anxious people are those with low anxiety and low social desirability scores, while repressors have low anxiety but high social desirability scores. Weinberger et al. (1979) found that students with a repressive coping style showed greater autonomic responses during a phrase association task than did low anxious subjects, while those with high anxiety ratings were generally intermediate in their reactivity. This pattern was confirmed by Asendorpf and Scherer (1983), who also demonstrated through analysis of facial expressions that repressors manifest high levels of anxiety expression. Blood pressure reactions to mental stress tests are also larger in repressors than in other groups (King et al., 1990).

Denial: Adaptive or Maladaptive?

The literature outlined in the last sections links failures to acknowledge and express feelings with heightened physiological stress responses. At the same time, there is evidence that denial may be adaptive and associated with smaller physiological responses than acknowledgement of feelings (see Breznitz, 1983). Some of this research has already been outlined in relation to information-seeking versus avoidance, while the benefits of denial among breast cancer patients observed by Greer et al. (1979) have been confirmed by Dean and Surtees (1989). A recent study of patients admitted to a coronary care unit found that individuals with high denial scores experienced fewer episodes of angina, required fewer nitroglycerine drips and reached a stable medical condition more rapidly than did non-deniers (Levenson et al., 1989). Patients with cancer who show repressive coping with distress report fewer side-effects of treatment than do other patients (Ward, Leventhal and Love, 1988).

How are these findings to be reconciled? It seems possible that denial and emotional inhibition or repression are rather different coping responses. While denial is associated with specific illnesses, repression is concerned with broader issues of self-presentation and defensiveness. Denial may therefore share many of the properties of the avoidant coping responses discussed in an earlier section. In addition, the match between coping response and information obtained about the stressful event needs to be taken into account. There is evidence from studies of cardiac patients that a mismatch between repressive coping and high information may be particularly damaging to later social and medical functioning (Shaw et al., 1985).

Cardiovascular Disease and the Inhibition of Anger and Hostility

Another area in which there are definite inconsistencies can be found in studies of the relationship between cardiovascular disease and the expression or inhibition of hostile feelings. Research implicating the experience and expression of hostiliy in disease risk has emerged through a re-evaluation of the association between coronary heart disease and Type A behaviour (Williams and Barefoot, 1988). The decade since 1980 witnessed repeated failures to observe robust correlations between Type A behaviour and coronary heart disease, both in US and European samples (e.g. Ragland and Brand, 1988; Appels et al., 1987). In seeking for an explanation, it has been argued that the hostility component of the Type A behaviour pattern is the crucial factor, and that people showing greater potential for hostility, cynical hostility or aggressive responding are at peculiar risk (e.g. Dembroski et al., 1989).

A number of psychophysiological studies have shown that subjects who express their anger, and those who display cynical hostility, react with greater cardiovascular responses to mental stress than do people without these characteristics (Suarez and Williams, 1989; Goldstein et al., 1989). But it is not possible simply to conclude that the expression of hostile emotion is maladaptive as far as these physiological parameters is concerned. A parallel literature has implicated the suppression of hostile emotion in the face of stressful situations as relevant to cardiovascular hyperreactivity and the aetiology of essential hypertension. Once again, the position is supported by epidemiological surveys coupled with laboratory studies. For instance, one study of factory workers found that job stress was related to the prevalence of hypertension but only among people who suppressed anger (Cottington et al.,1986). Julius and co-workers (1986) reported a prospective study in which suppression of anger was assessed through responses to hypothetical scenarios of unjustified criticism. Suppression of anger predicted mortality among hypertensives over the 12-year follow-up period. In the laboratory, anger inhibition has been linked with exaggerated blood pressure reactivity (Holroyd and Gorkin, 1983; Jorgensen and Houston, 1986).

Two factors may help to clarify the origins of this discrepancy. The first is that anger inhibition and hostility expression are not two poles of the same dimension, but are separate properties. This is endorsed by a number of factor analyses which show that the two constructs load on distinct factors (Suarez and Williams, 1990; Vögele and Steptoe, in press). It is therefore perfectly feasible for a person to inhibit anger when under stress, but also to show inappropriate emotional expression. Second, it may be that anger inhibition is only important for health when it is coupled with biological risk for cardiovascular disease. This possibility was tested in a recent physiological study carried out in the author's laboratory (Vögele and Steptoe, in press). Young adults at high and low biological risk for hypertension were selected on the basis of high and low "normal" blood pressure. A number of psychological measures were administered, and the scores subjected to factor analysis. Two factors emerged: an "anxious emotional inhibition" factor, comprising of scores on measures of trait anxiety, anger inhibition and tendency to self-concealment, and an "anger experience and expression" factor consisting of measures of trait anger and overt anger expression or anger-out. The interesting result to emerge was that although both psychological factors related cardiovascular reactivity with mental stress, only the inhibition factor interacted with biological risk. Results for systolic blood pressure are shown in Figure 9.3, and indicate that anxious emotional inhibition had no influence over the magnitude of reactions to mental arithmetic and a frustrating mirror drawing task in the low biological risk groups. However, in the high biological risk group, more pronounced reactions were observed among the high emotional inhibitors. Future work on this problem will need to take account of the subtle complexity of associations between biological constraints, patterns of emotional coping and situational factors.

CONCLUSIONS

This chapter on individual differences and stress physiology has concentrated on the autonomic, endocrine and immunological correlates of cognitive and behavioural coping responses. This emphasis was chosen partly because many important individual-difference parameters (such as hardiness, locus of control and Type A behaviour) are the topics of other chapters. In addition, it has been argued that psychological coping is the proximal process through which more sustained individual differences affect physiological responses to stressful encounters. The classification of coping responses outlined in Figure 9.1 should not be taken as a rigid framework, but rather as a heuristic device through which to organise a complex but exciting matrix of experimental and clinical observations.

The conclusions to be drawn from this review can be simply stated. First,

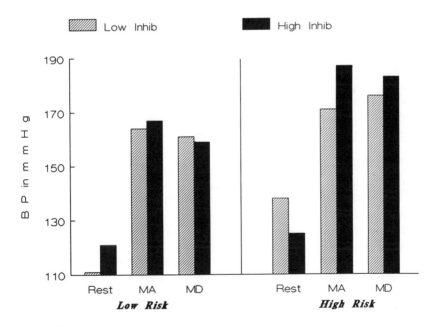

Figure 9.3   Systolic blood pressure at rest and during performance of mental arithmetic (MA) and mirror drawing (MD) tasks, in subjects at low and high biological risk for hypertension, divided into groups high and low on the "anxious emotional inhibition" psychological coping factor. From Vögele and Steptoe, in press

different coping responses have different physiological correlates. It is simplistic, therefore, to assume that certain patterns of psychological response will invariably be adaptive. All coping responses have physiological costs as well as benefits. The question of whether or not coping is successful depends on the physiological processes that are most significant in the particular case. For instance, it is possible that for a patient with severe coronary artery disease who has to deal with difficult decisions at work, coping responses that attenuate potentially life-threatening sympathetic nervous system activation and vulnerability to ventricular fibrillation will be most valuable (Verrier, 1987). On the other hand, a patient undergoing major surgery may be particularly susceptible to infection (Watkins and Salo, 1982). Coping responses that ameliorate immunosuppression and heightened cortisol levels in the blood would therefore be desirable. The adaptive coping responses in these two situations may be quite different. This conclusion echoes Lazarus's (1990) sentiments based on the psychological literature that "the functional value of the coping process can seldom if ever be divorced from the context in which it occurs" (p. 105).

Second, it is apparent that coping responses and their physiological outcomes are invariably products of an interaction between situational factors and individual predispositions. Individual differences are particularly significant in ambiguous situations, or when the most effective approach to stress management is uncertain owing to the fact that different types of outcome assume greater or lesser salience for each person. The experiment outlined in Table 9.2 is a good illustration, since it appears that the anticipatory distress associated with monitoring a warning signal is sufficiently aversive for some people that they prefer to distract, even though by doing so they forgo the opportunity for shock avoidance. Some of the individual differences relevant to particular coping responses were described earlier, with optimism and self-efficacy being seen as especially important for active behavioural coping. One might also add that coping responses such as wishful thinking and self-blame are characteristic of neurotic individuals (Bolger, 1990). The coping responses associated with different emotions are currently the subject of intensive research (Folkman and Lazarus, 1988; Manstead and Tetlock, 1989). It is likely that much more will be known about salient individual differences in the next few years.

Finally, it should be emphasised that the psychophysiological literature has contributed solid evidence linking individual differences in coping with successful or unsuccessful biological adaptation. By measuring the processes that are likely to mediate between stress and disease, studies of physiological responses can provide important evidence for the role of personality and other individual differences in the maintenance of health. It should not however be concluded that all associations between psychological stress and ill-health are mediated through physiological stress mechanisms.

Psychological stress also affects a number of behaviours that carry a health risk, including substance abuse (Brown, 1989), smoking and difficulty in stopping smoking (Epstein and Perkins, 1988; Cohen and Lichtenstein, 1990), alcohol intake (Gottheil et al., 1987) and increased dietary fat intake (McCann et al., 1990). These behaviours may themselves account for changes in health status independently of any psychophysiological process. A complete understanding of links between personality, coping and health therefore requires consideration of both behavioural and physiological mediating responses.

REFERENCES

Abramson, L. Y., Seligman, M. E. P. and Teasdale, J. D. (1978). Learned helplessness in humans: Critique and reformulation, *Journal of Abnormal Psychology*, **87**, 49–74.

Appels, A., Mulder, P., Van't Hof, M., Jenkins, B. D., Van Houten, J. and Tam, F. (1987). A prospective study of the Jenkins Activity Survey as a risk indictor for coronary heart disease in The Netherlands, *Journal of Chronic Disease*, **40**, 959–65.

Asendorpf, J. B. and Scherer, K. R. (1983). The discrepant repressor: Differentiation between low anxiety, high anxiety, and repression of anxiety by autonomic-facial-verbal patterns of behavior, *Journal of Personality and Social Psychology*, **45**, 334–46.

Averill, J. R. and Rosenn, N. (1972). Vigilant and non-vigilant coping strategies and psychophysiological stress reactions during anticipation of electric shock, *Journal of Personality and Social Psychology*, **23**, 128–41.

Bandura, A. (1977). Self-efficacy: Toward a unifying theory of behavioral change, *Psychological Review*, **84**, 191–215.

Bandura, A., Cioffi, D., Taylor, C. B. and Brouillard, M. E. (1988). Perceived self-efficacy in coping with cognitive stressors and opioid activation, *Journal of Personality and Social Psychology*, **55**, 479–88.

Baron, R. S., Cutrona, C. E., Hicklin, D., Russell, D. W. and Lubaroff, D. M. (1990). Social support and immune function among spouses of cancer patients, *Journal of Personality and Social Psychology*, **59**, 344–52.

Billings, A. G. and Moos, R. H. (1981). The role of coping responses and social resources in attenuating the stress of life events, *Journal of Behavioral Medicine*, **4**, 139–57.

Bolger, N. (1990). Coping as a personality process: A prospective study, *Journal of Personality and Social Psychology*, **59**, 525–37.

Breier, A., Albus, M., Picker, D., Zahn, T. P., Wolkowitz, O. M. and Paul, S. M. (1987). Controllable and uncontrollable stress in humans: Alterations in mood and neuroendocrine and psychophysiological functions, *American Journal of Psychiatry*, **144**, 1419–25.

Breznitz, S. (ed.) (1983). *The Denial of Stress,* International Universities Press, New York.

Brown, G. and Harris, T. (1978). *Social Origins of Depression*, Tavistock, London.

Brown, S. A. (1989). Life events of adolescence in relation to personal and parental substance abuse, *American Journal of Psychiatry*, **146**, 484–9.

Burger, J. N. (1989). Negative reactions to increases in perceived control, *Journal of Personality and Social Psychology*, **56**, 246–56.

Carver, C. S., Scheier, M. F. and Weintraub, J. K. (1989). Assessing coping strategies: A theoretically based approach, *Journal of Personality and Social Psychology*, **56**, 267–83.

Cohen, F. (1987). Measurement of coping. In S. V. Kasl and C. L. Cooper (eds) *Stress and Health: Issues in Research Methodology*, John Wiley, Chichester, pp. 283–305.

Cohen, S. and Edwards, J. R. (1989). Personality characteristics as moderators of the relationship between stress and disorder. In R. W. J. Neufeld (ed.) *Advances in the Investigation of Psychological Stress*, Wiley-Interscience, New York, pp. 235–83.

Cohen, S. and Lichtenstein, E. (1990). Perceived stress, quitting smoking, and smoking relapse, *Health Psychology*, **9**, 466–78.

Cohen, S. and Syme, S. L. (eds) (1985). *Social Support and Health*, Academic Press, New York.

Cohen, S. and Wills, T. A. (1985). Stress, social support and the buffering hypothesis, *Psychological Bulletin*, **98**, 310–57.

Connor, R. L., Vernikos-Danellis, J. and Levine, D. (1971). Stress, fighting and neuro-endocrine function, *Nature*, **234**, 564–6.

Conway, T. L., Vickers, R. R., Ward, H. W. and Rahe, R. H. (1981). Occupational stress and variation in cigarette, coffee and alcohol consumption, *Journal of Health and Social Behavior*, **22**, 155–65.

Cottington, E. M., Matthews, K. A., Talbot, D. and Kuller, L. H. (1986). Occupational stress, suppressed anger, and hypertension, *Psychosomatic Medicine*, **48**, 249–60.

Dantzer, R. (1989). Neuroendocrine correlates of control and coping. In A. Steptoe and A. Appels (eds) *Stress Personal Control, and Health*, John Wiley, Chichester, pp. 277–94.

Dantzer, R. (in press). Stress and disease: A psychobiological perspective, *Annals of Behavioral Medicine*.

Dantzer, R. and Kelley, K. W. (1989). Stress and immunity: An integrated view of the relationship between the brain and the immune system, *Lifescience*, **44**, 1995–2008.

Dean, C. and Surtees, P. G. (1989). Do psychological factors predict patient survival in breast cancer?, *Journal of Psychosomatic Research*, **33**, 561–9.

Dembroski, T. M., MacDougall, J. M., Costa, P. T. and Grandits, G. A. (1989). Components of hostility as predictors of sudden death and myocardial infarction in the Multiple Risk Factor Intervention Trial, *Psychosomatic Medicine*, **51**, 514–22.

Dunkel-Schetter, C., Folkman, S. and Lazarus, R. S. (1987). Correlates of social support receipt, *Journal of Personality and Social Psychology*, **53**, 71–80.

Epstein, L. H. and Perkins, K. A. (1988). Smoking, stress, and coronary heart disease, *Journal of Consulting and Clinical Psychology*, **56**, 342–9.

Esterling, B. A., Antoni, M. H., Kumar, M. and Schneiderman, N. (1990). Emotional repression, stress disclosure responses, and Epstein Barr viral capsid antigen titers, *Psychosomatic Medicine*, **52**, 397–441.

Evans, P. D., Phillips, K. C. and Fearn, J. (1984). On choosing to make aversive events predictable or unpredictable: Some behavioural and psychophysiological findings, *British Journal of Psychology*, **75**, 377–91.

Eysenck, M. W. (1989). Personality, stress arousal, and cognitive processes in stress transactions. In R. W. J. Neufeld (ed.) *Advances in the Investigation of Psychological Stress*, Wiley-Interscience, New York, pp. 133–60.

Fawzy, F. I., Cousins, N., Fawzy, N. W., Kemeny, M. E., Elashoff, R. and Morton, M. B. (1990a). A structured psychiatric intervention for cancer patients. I. Changes over time in methods of coping and affective disturbance, *Archives of General Psychiatry*, **47**, 720–5.

Fawzy, F. I., Kemeny, M. E., Fawzy, N. W., Elashoff, R., Morton, M. B., Cousins, N. and Fahey, J. L. (1990b). A structured psychiatric intervention for cancer patients. II. Changes over time in immunological measures, *Archives of General Psychiatry*, **47**, 729–35.

Feldman, J. and Brown, G. (1976). Endocrine responses to electric shock and avoidance conditioning in the rhesus monkey: Cortisol and growth hormone, *Psychoneuroendocrinology*, **1**, 231–42.

Felton, B. J. and Revenson, T. A. (1984). Coping with chronic illness: A study of illness controllability and the influence of coping strategies on psychological adjustment, *Journal of Consulting and Clinical Psychology*, **52**, 343–53.

Filipp, S. H., Klauer, T., Freudenberg, E. and Ferring, D. (1990). The regulation of subjective well-being in cancer patients: An analysis of coping effectiveness, *Psychology and Health*, **4**, 305–17.

Folkman, S. and Lazarus, R. S. (1985). If it changes it must be a process: A study of emotion and coping during three stages of a college examination, *Journal of Personality and Social Psychology*, **48**, 150–70.

Folkman, S. and Lazarus, R. S. (1988). Coping as a mediator of emotion, *Journal of Personality and Social Psychology*, **54**, 466–75.

Fox, B. H. (1988). Epidemiologic aspects of stress, aging, cancer and the immune system, *Annals of the New York Academy of Sciences*, **521**, 16–28.

Freyschuss, U., Hjemdahl, P., Juhlin-Dannfelt, A. and Linde, B. (1988). Cardiovascular and sympathoadrenal responses to mental stress: Influence of β-blockade, *American Journal of Physiology*, **255**, H1443-H1451.

Friedman, H. S. (1990). Personality and disease: Overview, review, and preview. In H. S. Friedman (ed.) *Personality and Disease*, Wiley-Interscience, New York, pp. 3–13.

Goldstein, H. S., Edelberg, R., Meier, C. F. and Davis, L. (1989). Relationship of expressed anger to forearm muscle vascular resistance, *Journal of Psychosomatic Research*, **33**, 497–504.

Gottheil, E., Druley, K., Paschko, S. and Weinstein, S. (eds) (1987). *Stress and Addiction*, Brunner/Mazel, New York.

Greer, S., Morris, T. and Pettingale, K. W. (1979). Psychological response to breast cancer: Effect on outcome, *Lancet*, **II**, 785–7.

Haan, N. (1977). *Coping and Defending: Processes of Self-Environment Organization*, Academic Press, New York.

Hanson, C. L., Cigrang, J. A., Harris, M. A., Carle, D. L., Relyea, G. and Burghen, G. A. (1989). Coping styles in youths with insulin-dependent diabetes mellitus, *Journal of Consulting and Clinical Psychology*, **57**, 644–51.

Henry, J. P. (1976). Mechanisms of psychosomatic disease in animals, *Advances in Vetinary Science and Comparative Medicine*, **20**, 115–45.

Hobfoll, S. (1988). *The Ecology of Stress*, Hemisphere, New York.

Holroyd, K. A. and Gorkin, L. (1983). Young adults at risk for hypertension: Effects of family history and anger management in determining responses to interpersonal conflict, *Journal of Psychosomatic Research*, **27**, 131–8.

House, J. S., Landis, A. R. and Umberson, D. (1988). Social relationships and health, *Science*, **241**, 540–4.

Jorgensen, R. S. and Houston, B. K. (1986). Family history of hypertension, personality patterns, and cardiovascular reactivity to stress, *Psychosomatic Medicine*, **48**, 102–17.

Julius, M., Harburg, E., Cottington, E. M. and Johnson, E. H. (1986). Anger-coping types, blood pressure, and all-cause mortality: A follow-up in Tecumseh-Michigan (1971–1983), *American Journal of Epidemiology*, **124**, 220–33.

Kamarck, T. W., Manuck, S. B. and Jennings, J. R. (1990). Social support reduces cardiovascular reactivity to psychological challenge: A laboratory model, *Psychosomatic Medicine*, **52**, 42–58.

Karasek, R. A. (1979). Job demands, job decision latitude and mental strain: Implications for job redesign, *Administrative Science Quarterly*, **24**, 258–308.

Kiecolt-Glaser, J. K., Speicher, C. E., Holliday, J. E. and Glaser, R. (1984). Stress and the transformation of lymphocytes by Epstein-Barr virus, *Journal of Behavioral Medicine*, **7**, 1–12.

Kiecolt-Glaser, J. K., Fisher, L. D., Ogrocki, P., Stout, J. C., Speicher, C. E. and Glaser, R. (1987). Marital quality, marital disruption, and immune function, *Psychosomatic Medicine*, **49**, 13–34.

Kiecolt-Glaser, J. K., Kennedy, S., Malkoff, S., Fisher, L., Speicher, C. E. and Glaser, R. (1988). Marital discord and immunity in males, *Psychosomatic Medicine*, **50**, 213–21.

King, A. C., Taylor, C. B., Allbright, C. A. and Haskell, W. L. (1990). The relationship between repressive and defensive coping styles and blood pressure responses in healthy middle-aged men and women, *Journal of Psychosomatic Research*, **34**, 461–71.

Koolhaas, J. and Bohus, B. (1989). Social control in relation to neuroendocrine and immunological responses. In A. Steptoe and A. Appels (eds) *Stress, Personal Control and Health*, Wiley, Chichester, pp. 295–305.

Lazarus, R. S. (1966). *Psychological Stress and the Coping Process*, McGraw-Hill, New York.

Lazarus, R. S. (1990). Stress, coping and illness. In H. S. Friedman (ed.) *Personality and Disease*, Wiley-Interscience, New York, pp. 97–120.

Lazarus, R. S. and Folkman, S. (1984). *Stress, Coping and Appraisal*, Springer-Verlag, New York.

Levenson, J. L., Mishra, A., Hamer, R. M. and Hastillo, A. (1989). Denial and medical outcome in unstable angina, *Psychosomatic Medicine*, **51**, 27–35.

Leventhal, H., Brown, D., Shacham, S. and Engquist, G. (1979). Effects of preparatory information about sensations, threat of pain, and attention on cold pressor distress, *Journal of Personality and Social Psychology*, **37**, 688–714.

Levine, S. (1983). Coping: An overview. In H. Ursin and R. Murison (eds) *Biological and Psychological Basis of Pychosomatic Disease*, Pergamon, Oxford, pp. 15–26.

Levy, S. M., Herberman, R. B., Whiteside, T., Sanzo, K., Lee, J. and Kirkwood, J. (1990). Perceived social support and tumor estrogen/progesterone receptor status as predictors of natural killer cell activity in breast cancer patients, *Psychosomatic Medicine*, **52**, 73–85.

Lin, E. H. and Peterson, C. (1990). Pessimistic explanatory style and response to illness, *Behaviour Research and Therapy*, **28**, 243–8.

Litt, M. D. (1988). Cognitive mediators of stressful experience: Self-efficacy and perceived control, *Cognitive Therapy and Research*, **12**, 241–60.

Lovallo, W. R., Wilson, M. F., Pincomb, G. A., Edwards, G. L., Tompkins, P. and Brackett, D. J. (1985). Activation patterns to aversive stimulation in man: Passive exposure versus effort to control, *Psychophysiology*, **22**, 283–91.

McCann, B. S., Warnick, R. and Knopp, R. H. (1990). Changes in plasma lipids and dietary intake accompanying shifts in perceived workload and stress, *Psychosomatic Medicine*, **52**, 97–108.

McCrae, R. R. and Costa, P. T. (1986). Personality, coping and coping effectiveness in an adult sample, *Journal of Personality*, **54**, 385–405.

Maier, S. F. and Laudenslager, M. L. (1988). Inescapable shock, shock controllability, and mitogen stimulated lymphocyte proliferation, *Brain, Behavior and Immunology*, **2**, 87–91.

Manstead, A. S. R. and Tetlock, P. E. (1989). Cognitive appraisals and emotional experience: Further evidence, *Cognition and Emotion*, **3**, 225–40.

Miller, S. M. (1979). Controllability and human stress: Method, evidence and theory, *Behaviour Research and Therapy*, **17**, 287–304.

Miller, S. M. (1987). Monitoring and blunting: Validation of a questionnaire to assess styles of information-seeking under threat, *Journal of Personality and Social Psychology*, **52**, 345–53.

Miller, S. M. and Birnbaum, A. (1989). When to whistle while you work: Towards a cognitive social learning approach to coping and health. In S. L. Sauter, J. J. Hurrell and C. L. Cooper (eds) *Job Control and Worker Health*, Wiley, Chichester, pp. 237–51.

Moos, R. H., Brennan, P. L., Fondacaro, M. R. and Moos, B. S. (1990). Approach and avoidance coping responses among older problem and nonproblem drinkers, *Psychology and Aging*, **5**, 31–40.

Mormède, P., Dantzer, R., Michaud, B., Kelley, K. W. and Le Moal, M. (1988). Influence of stressor predictability and behavioral control on lymphocyte reactivity, antibody response and neuroendocrine activation in rats, *Physiology and Behavior*, **43**, 577–83.

Mormède, P., Dantzer, R., Montpied, P., Bluthé, R. M., Laplante, E. and Le Moal, M. (1984). Influence of shock-induced fighting and social factors on pituitary–adrenal activity, prolactin and catecholamine synthesising enzymes in rats, *Physiology and Behavior*, **32**, 723–9.

Munck, A., Guyre, P. M. and Holbrook, N. J. (1984). Physiological functions of glucocorticoids in stress and their relation to pharmacological actions, *Endocrine Review*, **5**, 25–44.

Pennebaker, J. W., Hughes, C. F. and O'Heeron, R. C. (1987). The psychophysiology of confession: Linking inhibitory and psychosomatic processes, *Journal of Personality and Social Psychology*, **52**, 781–93.

Pennebaker, J. W., Kiecolt-Glaser, J. K. and Glaser, R. (1988). Disclosure of traumas and immune function: Health implications for psychotherapy, *Journal of Consulting and Clinical Psychology*, **56**, 239–45.

Peterson, C., Seligman, M. E. P. and Vaillant, G. E. (1988). Pessimistic explanatory style is a risk factor for physical illness: A 35 year longitudinal study, *Journal of Personality and Social Psychology*, **55**, 23–7.

Phipps, S. and Zinn, A. B. (1986). Psychological response to amniocentesis: II. Effects of coping style, *American Journal of Medical Genetics*, **25**, 143–8.

Rachman, S. J. (1980). Emotional processing, *Behaviour Research and Therapy*, **18**, 51–60.

Ragland, D. R. and Brand, R. J. (1988). Coronary heart disease mortality in the Western Collaborative Group Study: Follow-up experience of 22 years, *American Journal of Epidemiology*, **127**, 462–75.

Rosenberg, S. J., Peterson, R. A. and Hayes, J. R. (1987). Coping behaviour among depressed and nondepressed medical inpatients, *Journal of Psychosomatic Research*, **31**, 653–8.

Roth, F. and Cohen, L. J. (1986). Approach, avoidance and coping with stress, *American Psychologist*, **41**, 813–19.

Scheier, M. F. and Carver, C. S. (1985). Optimism, coping, and health: Assessment and implications of generalised outcome expectancies, *Health Psychology*, **4**, 219–43.

Scheier, M. F., Weintraub, J. K. and Carver, C. S. (1986). Coping with stress: Divergent strategies of optimists and pessimists, *Journal of Personality and Social Psychology,* **51**, 1257–64.

Schroeder, D. H. and Costa, P. T. (1984). Influence of life event stress on physical illness: Substantive effects or methodological flaws?, *Journal of Personality and Social Psychology,* **46**, 853–63.

Seeman, T. E. and Syme, S. L. (1987). Social networks and coronary artery disease: A comparison of the structure and function of social relations as predictors of disease, *Psychosomatic Medicine,* **49**, 341–54.

Seligman, M. E. P. (1975). *Helplessness: On Depression, Development and Death,* Freeman, San Francisco.

Selye, H. (1936). A syndrome produced by diverse nocuous agents, *Nature,* **138**, 32.

Shaw, R. E., Cohen, F., Doyle, B. and Palesky, J. (1985). The impact of denial and repressive style on information gain and rehabilitation outcomes in myocardial infarction patients, *Psychosomatic Medicine,* **47**, 262–73.

Solomon, S., Holmes, D. S. and McCaul, K. D. (1980). Behavioral control over aversive events: Does control that requires effort reduce anxiety and physiological arousal?, *Journal of Personality and Social Psychology,* **39**, 729–36.

Stein, M., Keller, S. E. and Schleifer, S. J. (1985). Stress and immunomodulation: The role of depression and neuroendocrine function, *Journal of Immunology,* **135**, 827–33s.

Steptoe, A. (1983). Stress, helplessness and control: The implications of laboratory studies, *Journal of Psychosomatic Research,* **27**, 361–7.

Steptoe, A. (1989). Coping and psychophysiological reactions. *Advances in Behaviour Research and Therapy,* **11**, 259–70.

Steptoe, A. (1990). Psychobiological stress responses. In M. Johnston and L. Wallace (eds) *Stress and Medical Procedures,* Oxford University Press, Oxford, pp. 3–24.

Steptoe, A. and Appels, A. (eds) (1989). *Stress, Personal Control and Health,* Wiley, Chichester.

Steptoe, A. and O'Sullivan, J. (1986). Monitoring and blunting coping styles in women prior to surgery, *British Journal of Clinical Psychology,* **25**, 143–4.

Steptoe, A. and Vögele, C. (1986). Are stress responses influenced by cognitive appraisal? An experimental comparison of coping strategies, *British Journal of Psychology,* **77**, 243–55.

Steptoe, A., Edwards, S., Moses, J. and Matthews, A. (1989). The effects of exercise training on mood and perceived coping ability in anxious adults from the general population, *Journal of Psychosomatic Research,* **33**, 537–47.

Suarez, E. C. and Williams, R. B. (1989). Situational determinants of cardiovascular and emotional reactivity in high and low hostile men, *Psychosomatic Medicine,* **51**, 404–18.

Suarez, E. C. and Williams, R. B. (1990). The relationships between dimensions of hostility and cardiovascular reactivity as a function of task characteristics, *Psychosomatic Medicine,* **52**, 558–70.

Suls, J. and Fletcher, B. (1985). The relative efficacy of avoidant and non-avoidant coping strategies: A meta-analysis, *Health Psychology,* **4**, 247–88.

Suls, J. and Rittenhouse, J. D. (1990). Models of linkage between personality and disease. In H. S. Friedman (ed.) *Personality and Disease,* Wiley-Interscience, New York, pp. 38–64.

Taylor, S. E. (1983). Adjustment to threatening events: A theory of cognitive adaptation, *American Psychologist,* **38**, 1161–73.

Thomas, P. D., Goodwin, J. M. and Goodwin, J. S. (1985). Effects of social support on stress-related changes in cholesterol level, uric acid level and immune function in an elderly sample, *American Journal of Psychiatry*, **142**, 735–7.

Tobin, D. L., Holroyd, K. A., Reynolds, R. B. and Wigal, J. K. (1989). The hierarchical factor structure of the Coping Strategies Inventory, *Cognitive Therapy and Research*, **13**, 343–51.

Turk, D. C., Meichenbaum, D. and Genest, M. (1983). *Pain and Behavioral Medicine. A Cognitive-Behavioral Perspective*, Guilford, New York.

Ursin, H., Baade, E. and Levine, S. (eds) (1978). *Psychobiology and Stress: A Study of Coping Men*, Academic Press, New York.

Ursin, H., Olff, M. and Godaert, G. (eds) (in press). *Quantification of Human Defence*, Springer-Verlag, Berlin.

Verrier, R. L. (1987). Mechanisms of behaviorally induced arrhythmias, *Circulation*, **76**, (Suppl.), 148–56.

Vitaliano, D. P., Russo, J., Carr, J. E., Maiuro, R. D. and Becker, J. (1985). The Ways of Coping checklist: Revision and psychometric properties, *Multivariate Behavioural Research*, **20**, 3–26.

Vögele, C. and Steptoe, A. (in press). Emotional coping and tonic blood pressure as determinants of cardiovascular reactions to mental stress.

Ward, S. E., Leventhal, H. and Love, R. (1988). Repression revisited: Tactics used in coping with a severe health threat, *Personality and Social Psychology Bulletin*, **14**, 735–46.

Watkins, J. and Salo, M. (eds) (1982). *Trauma, Stress and Immunity in Anaesthesia and Surgery*, Butterworth, London.

Watson, D. and Pennebaker, J. W. (1989). Health complaints, stress, and distress: Exploring the central role of negative affectivity, *Psychological Review*, **96**, 234–54.

Weidenfeld, S. A., O'Leary, A., Bandura, A., Brown, S., Levine, S. and Raska, K. (1990). Impact of perceived self-efficacy in coping with stressors on components of the immune system, *Journal of Personality and Social Psychology*, **59**, 1082–94.

Weinberger, D. A., Schwartz, G. E. and Davidson, R. J. (1979). Low anxious, high anxious, and repressive coping styles: Psychometric patterns and behavioral and physiological responses to stress, *Journal of Abnormal Psychology*, **88**, 369–80.

Williams, R. B. and Barefoot, J. C. (1988). Coronary-prone behavior: The emerging role of the hostility complex. In B. K. Houston and C. R. Snyder (eds) *Type A Behavior Pattern: Research, Theory and Intervention*, Wiley-Interscience, New York, pp. 189–211.

Chapter 10

Individual Differences in Health Behaviour

Ethel Roskies, University of Montreal, Canada

Individuals today living in industrialized countries have more control over their health than at any previous time in history. Lifestyle decisions—what we eat, whether we smoke, drink or exercise—play an important role in at least seven of the ten principal causes of mortality in the United States and Canada, and half of the deaths resulting from these causes could presumably be prevented by appropriate changes in individual health behaviour (Lalonde, 1974; US Dept of Health, Education and Welfare, 1979a). As the US Surgeon General succinctly stated the issue, "You, the individual, can do more for your own health and well-being than any doctor, any drug, any exotic medical device" (US Department of Health, Education and Welfare, 1979a, p. viii).

But while lifestyle may be a matter of individual choice, the repercussions of lifestyle decisions extend far beyond the individual: what an individual decides to do or not do in protecting his or her own health affects society as a whole via the costs of medical care, costs of supporting the medically unemployable and lost productivity. Furthermore, these social costs of illness have been escalating rapidly, outpacing rises in gross national product even in wealthy countries. This, in turn, has spurred government funding for research in individual health behaviour and has spawned a major white-collar industry in the last 25 years devoted to promoting health and preventing illness via modification of individual lifestyles (Matarazzo, 1984).

In spite of the importance of preventive health action, and the amount of writing generated on the topic, the determinants that lead individuals to attach a seat belt or not, start or stop smoking, eat a prudent, low-fat diet compared to one excessive in calories and fats and so on, are not easy to decipher. Not only is there a wide gap between attitudes and beliefs compared to actual practices (Salovey, Rudy and Turk, 1987), but behaviour itself varies over time (Mechanic, 1979) and, most confusing of all, even at the same moment in time is inconsistent from one health action to another. Surveys of a

Personality and Stress: Individual Differences in the Stress Process. Edited by C.L. Cooper and R. Payne
© 1991 John Wiley & Sons Ltd

variety of a health behaviours in a number of samples have shown that different behaviours are either not correlated at all, or else the intercorrelations are low (Kirscht, 1983). Rather than being unidimensional, health behaviour is multidimensional, and far from being able to categorize individuals on the basis of global lifestyle, one must consider each health practice separately. The title of this chapter is a misnomer; a more accurate appellation would be "Individual differences in health *behaviours*".

At the time I accepted the invitation to write this chapter, I was well aware of the relative independence of different health behaviours, but I expected to be able to provide a reasonable review of at least five or six of the most important lifestyle variables within my allotted consignment of pages. However, it soon became evident that my reach had exceeded my grasp; the literature is overwhelming, with thousands of articles spread across disciplines as disparate as epidemiology, cardiology, public health, preventive medicine, medical sociology, medical anthropology and health psychology. To keep this review at a manageable length, I would have to limit the number of health behaviours considered. Smoking and exercise were selected as representative illustrations, the first of a negative health practice and the second of a positive health action.

This review is further restricted to smoking and exercise as they are experienced in the industrialized countries. Preventing illness and promoting health is a world-wide problem and for tobacco use, at least, the health problems engendered may be even greater in developing countries than in their richer cousins (Dalenz, 1988; Masironi and Rothwell, 1988). Nevertheless, differences in environmental constraints and opportunities make it unlikely that data derived from research in industrialized countries can be generalized to developing ones, and as yet we lack sufficient research and clinical data specific to the latter.

SMOKING

Soon after Columbus and the first European explorers encountered the North American Indian custom of "drinking" the smoke of dried leaves, tobacco use and the cultivation of tobacco spread around the world (Ashton and Stepney, 1982). Almost from its inception, the smoking habit aroused widespread condemnation (Elizabeth I and James I of England, the papal bulls of 1642 and 1650) and provoked severe legal sanctions (the Romanoff empire in Russia and seventeenth-century Japan). The Turkish Sultan Murad IV even went as far as to order the death penalty for smoking! Nevertheless, no country that has learned to use tobacco has ever given up the habit (Brecher, 1972)—at least, not up till now.

In the United States, the introduction of the first "blended" cigarette in 1913 and the growing acceptability of smoking for women in the 1920s led to a surge of popularity for cigarettes, peaking about 1960 with more than half of adult males and about a third of adult females smoking (Shopland and Brown, 1985). But in 1964 the landmark report of US Surgeon General on the health risks of tobacco use (US Public Health Service, 1964) initiated a concerted public health effort towards smoking prevention and cessation that, in turn, led to a dramatic decline in the percentage of the population smoking (see below).

The Case against Smoking

Although cigarette companies and at least one respected psychologist have questioned the causal link between tobacco and disease (Eysenck, 1980), the more generally accepted view is that "cigarette smoking is the chief, single, avoidable cause of death in our society and the most important health issue of our time" (US Department of Health and Human Services, 1984). Tobacco use is a major risk factor for heart disease, various forms of cancer (lung, larynx, oral cavity, oesophagus, kidney and urinary bladder) and lung diseases such as chronic obstructive lung disease, bronchitis and emphysema (American Cancer Society, 1986; US Department of Health and Human Services, 1982, 1984). The degree of risk depends on the amount smoked, age of onset of smoking, amount of nicotine in the cigarettes smoked and the amount of inhalation, but there is no level of cigarette smoking, or even use of smokeless tobacco (US Department of Health and Human Services, 1986), that can be considered safe. Smokers have an overall death rate 70% higher than non-smokers and it is estimated that their average life expectancy is reduced by five to eight years (Fielding, 1985).

Smoking also has important economic costs. Compared to non-smokers, absenteeism and hospitalizations are 50% higher for smokers, while job-related accidents are twice as high (American Heart Association, 1981). A recent report by the Surgeon General indicated that smoking-related diseases cost the US more than $52 billion per year, an average of $221 per person (Montreal Gazette, 1990).

It is not necessary to smoke oneself to be harmed by tobacco use. Smoking in pregnant women increases the risk of spontaneous abortion, fetal growth retardation and death, low birthweight and neonatal death (US Department of Health and Human Services, 1980). Wives of smokers have a higher risk of cancer (Pershagen, Hrubec and Svensson, 1987; Garland et al., 1985), while children whose parents smoke have a greater incidence of bronchitis and pneumonia (US Department of Health and Human Services, 1984). As well, many non-smokers are among the 1500 people killed in the United States each year in accidental fires caused by smoking (Fielding, 1985).

The Smoking Career

Smoking shows intraindividual as well as interindividual variations. Not only do smokers differ from non-smokers, and male smokers from female smokers, but the same male smoker may be motivated by very different considerations at the moment he takes his first exploratory puff of a cigarette, compared to the period when he is firmly entrenched in smoking two packs a day, compared to when he has just made his third attempt to quit smoking. Thus, we shall consider separately the four major phases of what has been termed the "smoking career' (Wetterer and Troschke, 1986): the initiation phase, the habituation phase and, for some smokers, the cessation and relapse phases.

The Initiation Phase

Experimenting with cigarettes can begin as early as ages 3–7 (Moyer and Ouimet, 1988), and by age 16 the majority of adolescents (69% of boys and 62% of girls) have tried smoking at least once (Ramström, 1988). However, only a minority of those who try cigarettes become regular smokers and the process of initiation is a slow one, developing over a year or more after the first attempts (Ary and Biglan, 1988). It may take several more years before the individual's rate of smoking reaches its eventual adult level (Pechacek et al., 1984). Adolescence is clearly the critical period for smoking initiation with very few individuals beginning regular smoking either before the age of 12 or after the age of 20 (Evans, 1984).

Prevalence of adolescent smoking

A World Health Organization survey of smoking by 16 year old boys in 14 industrialized countries in 1983–5 (Geizerova and Masironi, 1988) reports prevalence rates of 16% for the US compared to 27% for Canada, 29% for Australia and the United Kingdom, up to a high of 55% for the Democratic Republic of Germany. In all countries surveyed, this signalled a decline during the previous five to ten years with decreases ranging from 3% in the Democratic Republic of Germany to 41% in the United States and 48% in Sweden and Australia.

Teenaged girls are not decreasing their smoking at the same rate as their male counterparts; in five of the fourteen countries surveyed, there was an actual increase in percentage of female adolescents smoking. The result is that in all countries, except the Democratic Republic of Germany, the smoking prevalence of teenaged females is currently higher than that of males, with smoking rates ranging from 21% in the United States to 45% in New Zealand and 48% in Norway.

Smokers vs. non-smokers

The pleasure to be derived from smoking is not a major factor in its initiation, since the first attempts at smoking are more likely to be described as aversive rather than pleasurable. Nor is ignorance a rationale for the behaviour, since most teenagers are well aware of the health risks of smoking, including 90% of those who smoke (US Department of Health, Education and Welfare, 1979b).

A frequently invoked explanation for teenage smoking is that it constitutes an anticipation of adulthood. Via smoking, the adolescent emulates the behaviour of attractive, mature, strong adults and in so doing associates these attributes to himself or herself. However, restrictions on media advertising and the declining percentage of smoking adults in the general population mean that adolescents as a whole are less likely than in former times to view smoking as a "normal" part of growing up.

More recent research on the correlates of adolescent smoking have highlighted instead the interaction of two major factors: an immediate environment in which key persons favour smoking, coupled with characteristics of the individual favourable to smoking. The influence of the immediate environment is shown by numerous studies showing that smoking teenagers are more likely than abstainers to have smoking parents, siblings and friends (Ahlgren et al., 1982; Gordon, 1986; Lawrance and Rubinson, 1986; McAlister, Krosnick and Milburn, 1984; Castro et al., 1987). Friends are particularly important in initiating smoking since teenagers usually smoke their first cigarette in the presence and with the encouragement of peers (Leventhal, Prohaska and Hirschman, 1985). Thus, even in the face of generally declining tobacco use, teenagers exposed to specific environments in which smoking continues to be widely practised have an increased probability of becoming smokers themselves.

But environmental influences are only part of the story in that the same cues may be perceived quite differently by teenagers predisposed to smoking compared to those not so inclined. For instance, one study reported that adolescents who smoke or who intended to smoke greatly overestimated the prevalence of adult or peer smoking and greatly underestimated negative adult attitudes to smoking (Leventhal, Glynn and Fleming, 1987).

This predisposition to smoking has variously been attributed to genetic make-up, social pathology or psychological vulnerability. One of the best known proponents of the genetic viewpoint is Eysenck (1980) who argues that heredity influences personality characteristics such as extroversion which, in turn, influence smoking (see below). However, even Eysenck would allow that during the initiation phase genetic predisposition would be secondary to social pressures. Moreover, while there is some empirical support for the hypothesis that heredity plays a role in smoking, its contribution is generally considered relatively minor (for a review see Hughes, 1986).

Much more emphasis has been placed on the social situation and psychological makeup of the beginning smoker. Indices of poor social adjustment in teenage smokers include poor academic achievement (Marston et al., 1988; Sunseri, 1983), sexual precocity (Livson and Leino, 1985; Gritz, 1984) and rebelliousness (Gordon, 1986; Gritz, 1984; McAlister et al., 1984). Teenage smokers are also likely to feel psychologically inadequate, manifested via lower self-esteem and self-efficacy (Ahlgren et al., 1982; Dielman et al., 1987; Lawrance and Rubinson, 1986; Penny and Robinson, 1986; Tucker, 1984b), a greater sense of fatalism or helplessness as evinced in an external locus of control (Clarke, MacPherson and Holmes, 1982; Dielman et al., 1987; Penny and Robinson, 1986) and a higher level of trait anxiety (Penny and Robinson, 1986). Indeed some observers have suggested that smoking in teenagers is just one manifestation of a syndrome of high risk or problem behaviours (cigarettes, alcohol, marijuana, hard drugs), part of a general pattern of deviant or unconventional development (Donovan and Jessor, 1985; Newcomb, Maddahian and Bentler, 1986).

It is still unclear whether teenage smokers are actually exposed to more major life stressors and family pathology than non-smokers (Baer et al., 1987; Wills, 1986), or whether their poorer social adjustment and self-image simply lead them to exaggerate the ordinary stresses of teenage living (Baer et al., 1987; Mitic, McGuire and Neumann, 1985). In either case, however, the absence of alternative coping resources encourages the use of smoking as a means of reducing tension (Gordon, 1986; Castro et al., 1987). Indeed, Ahlgren et al. (1982) found that smoking in fifth and sixth graders who disliked school and were fearful of failure had a double purpose, serving both to reduce their failure anxiety and to help maintain self-esteem in the face of failure. Similarly, Tucker (1984a, b) found that teenagers who were either physically unfit or obese were more likely to express the intention to smoke than their more physically trim and presumably more socially acceptable counterparts.

In summary, smoking can be viewed as a way of coping with stress in adolescence that is particularly likely to be employed by teenagers who live in an environment favouring the behaviour, as well as lacking alternate means of reducing their stress and bolstering their self-esteem. Contrary to what the advertisements would have one believe, it is a coping strategy of the socially marginal and psychologically vulnerable.

Male vs. female adolescent smokers

As seen above, smoking is less of a deviant behaviour in adolescent females than in males, given the larger percentage of females who initiate the behaviour. Traditionally, too, smoking is less likely to be associated with poor school performance in girls compared to boys (Wetterer and von Troschke,

1986) and more likely to be linked to concepts of female emancipation such as masculinity, success, career orientation and upward social mobility (US Department of Health and Human Services, 1980). However, a recent marketing plan by a leading US cigarette maker targeted as potential consumers the "virile female", defined both as of low socio-economic status (secondary school leaver in entry level job) and of low independence (spends her time waiting for her boy-friend to initiate activities). Since cigarette companies are typically very knowledgeable about their potential markets, this may be an indication that the characteristics of the female teenage smoker are changing, becoming more similar to those of her male counterpart.

Habituation

Most teenage smokers believe that they will no longer be smoking in five years' time (US Department of Health, Education and Welfare, 1979b). Once regular smoking is initiated, however, it is often followed by habituation, where individuals become physiologically and/or psychologically dependent on the habit (see US Department of Health and Human Services, 1988).

Data from the 1986 US Adult Use of Tobacco Survey (Fiore et al., 1988) revealed a smoking rate of 29.5% among adult males and 23.8% among adult females. This is a dramatic drop for males, compared to their 52.1% smoking rate in 1965, but marks a much smaller decline in females compared to their 1965 percentage of 34.2%. It should also be noted that if fewer people are smoking at all, there is a rising percentage of heavy smokers among them; among current smokers in the United States, 31% smoke fewer than 15 cigarettes per day, 41% smoke 15–24 cigarettes a day and 27% smoke 25 or more a day (Foreyt, 1987).

The number of smokers differs according to family income and gender. For men, smoking is associated with lower income, blue-collar jobs and downward social mobility. More than 50% of truck drivers and construction workers still smoke compared with smoking rates of 20% in lawyers, 16% in engineers and below 10% in doctors (Foreyt, 1987). This is in sharp contrast to the situation in women where smoking increases as income rises. Thus, at the managerial and administrative levels the number of women smokers actually exceeds that of men (US Department of Health, Education and Welfare, 1979b).

Although habituation to smoking is generally ascribed to dependence, there is considerable controversy as to the specific nature of the dependency. Currently, the most generally accepted view is that smoking is a "psychological tool" (Ashton and Stepney, 1982) which can be used by different people at different times for purposes as varied as improving concentration, reducing anxiety, substituting for food or avoiding withdrawal symptoms.

Smoking as stimulation

Many smokers claim that smoking helps them think and concentrate, a claim supported by findings that nicotine improves the individual's ability to sustain attention, ignore distraction, acquire information, process information quickly and accurately, and divide attention between two tasks (Wesnes, 1987). According to the author, individuals' awareness of increased cognitive efficiency via smoking and their attribution of these positive effects to smoking is a major motivation for continued nicotine ingestion.

Whether or not an individual chooses to use nicotine as a stimulant depends both on internal needs and external pressures. Individuals with a strong need for outside stimulation (for example, those scoring high on extroversion) are likely to find the stimulant properties of nicotine particularly attractive, as would individuals placed in situations favouring fatigue and boredom. Thus, the interaction of an extroverted personality with a boring task requiring high vigilance would maximize the potential for the use of cigarettes as stimulants (Warburton, 1987).

Smoking to reduce negative affects (anxiety, anger and so on)

It may appear paradoxical that the same drug used to increase arousal can also be used as a depressant. However, smokers often claim that smoking has a calming effect on anxiety and anger (Pomerleau, Turk and Fertig, 1984; Russell, Peto and Patel, 1974) and they often cite anxiety and anger as motives for smoking. Observation of smokers in the laboratory confirms their self-reports in that they do use more cigarettes and inhale more deeply under stress. Furthermore, smokers as a group score higher than abstainers on measures of neuroticism and irritability (Cherry and Kiernan, 1978; Thomas, 1973) and it is the smokers who are most anxious and most susceptible to stress who show the most beneficial stress reduction effects of smoking (Warburton, 1987; Warburton and Wesnes, 1978). The use of smoking to control anxiety and anger is particularly striking in women, with female smokers being more likely to score high on neuroticism and more likely to smoke in stressful, high-arousal situations (Frith, 1971; Russell et al., 1974).

Smoking to produce euphoria and prevent withdrawal symptoms

If nicotine has the capacity to produce physiological dependence, individuals should be motivated, as they are for other addictive substances, to attempt to avoid withdrawal effects by actively striving to assure a steady nicotine level. In fact, nicotine ingestion strongly resembles the intake of other dependence-producing drugs, in that it is orderly, compulsive and occurs even in the face of individual and social damage (Henningfield, Goldberg and Jasinki, 1987).

Furthermore, after tobacco deprivation there is a withdrawal syndrome that occurs reliably and consistently in chronic smokers (Svikis et al., 1986). Based on their review of the evidence, Henningfield et al. (1987) have no hesitation in categorizing nicotine as a dependence-producing drug, similar to other psychoactive compounds. Physiological dependence in itself, however, is not a sufficient explanation for smoking since some individuals smoke even in the absence of withdrawal symptoms, and others retain the desire to smoke long after the withdrawal symptoms have ceased.

Smoking as a substitute for food or following food

Smoking may decrease appetite for food and particularly sweet foods by an action on the liver, on glucoreceptors in the brain, or by an effect on catecholamines similar to amphetamine. It also decreases weight by increasing oxygen utilization or metabolism (Jarvik, 1987). Therefore, smoking cessation is likely to be followed by weight gain (Wack and Rodin, 1982) and many smokers, particularly women, continue to smoke in order to prevent the real or imagined risk of weight gain (Klesges and Klesges, 1988).

A less well known association of tobacco and food is the desire for smoking immediately following a meal. According to Jarvik (1987), the postprandial cigarette is usually considered the favourite cigarette of the day and the one which is hardest to relinquish. Furthermore, based on some recent studies in his laboratory, he concludes that food produces a craving for tobacco stronger than that evoked by alcohol, caffeine or even stress. There are a number of explanations for this phenomenon, including the possibility that eating may cause a lowering of blood nicotine levels, or that food has a sedative effect which nicotine helps to encounter.

Smoking Cessation

Almost two-thirds of the US smokers have attempted to give up smoking one or more times (Fiore et al., 1988). The major reasons for giving up are concern for health, both future and current, the desire to set a good example for children and pressure from others. Heavy taxes on cigarettes do not appear to motivate smoking cessation, with only 8% of respondents invoking cost as a factor in their desire to give up.

In contrast to the general difficulty in changing lifestyle habits, smoking cessation efforts have been spectacularly successful; in the US today, 31% of the men and 18% of the women are former smokers (McGinnis, Shopland and Brown, 1987). The vast majority of smokers who successfully gave up smoking did so on their own and by far the most favoured method was to quit "cold turkey" (81%). Surprisingly, in view of the tremendous efforts devoted to the development of smoking cessation programmes and courses, less than

6% of those successful quitters mentioned following a programme or course (Fiore et al., 1988).

It is difficult to determine what percentage of smokers who attempt to give up smoking succeed in the attempt. Based on his survey of ex-smokers in two different communities, Schachter (1982) reports a success rate of 60%, while the figure for smoking cessation programmes and courses is generally assumed to be only 20–30%. Given, however, that the vast majority of smokers stop by their own efforts, Schachter believes that the clinic population may be atypical, self-selected on the basis of previous failure. Furthermore, figures reported for programmes and courses are for *single* attempts, and do not take account of the fact that the failures of one course may become the successes of a subsequent attempt. For both these reasons, the success rates of programmes and courses may be spuriously low.

About a quarter of smokers who give up their habit report no difficulty in doing so, an absence of withdrawal symptoms (Schachter, 1982; Shiffman, 1979). Among those who do, the most common symptom following cessation is anxiety (Shiffman and Jarvik, 1976). Smokers with a high degree of neuroticism (hence anxiety-prone) find it particularly difficult to give up smoking (Cherry and Kiernan, 1978), and women, among whom there is a greater proportion of neurotic smokers, are especially prone to anxiety following cessation (Shiffman, 1979). The fact that women tend to use smoking specifically for controlling unpleasant feelings and hence are more likely to experience anxiety upon withdrawal may be a factor in explaining their lower rate of smoking cessation.

Another group that experiences particular difficulty in stopping smoking is heavy smokers. Nearly half of heavy smokers who give up reported severe withdrawal symptoms, such as intense cravings, irritability, sleeplessness and cold sweats. Furthermore, while some studies report that heavy smokers are ultimately as successful as lighter smokers in obtaining long-term abstinence (Rzewnicki and Forgays, 1987; Schachter, 1982), others report that, on the contrary, heavy smoking is inversely related to abstinence success (Glasgow et al., 1988).

Smoking relapse

About 80% of smokers who initially succeed at stopping will relapse over a 12-month follow-up period (Hunt and Bespalec, 1974). The three major factors used to explain relapse are strikingly similar to those used to explain smoking onset: social environment, stress and low self-efficacy.

Social environment can either reinforce tobacco abstinence or undermine it. If people in the smoker's environment encourage the ex-smoker not to smoke, this can help him or her remain smoke free (Colletti and Brownell, 1982). Conversely, if the ex-smoker is in a restaurant and bar with other smokers (Shiffman, 1986), or if others offer him or her cigarettes and express doubts about the ability to remain abstinent, then the chances for relapse are greatly increased (Sorensen, Pechacek and Pollonen, 1986).

Stress also plays a role in that, compared to successful quitters, individuals who return to smoking are likely to actually experience—or at least perceive themselves as experiencing—more stressful events and to be less successful in coping with them (Abrams et al., 1987; Swan et al., 1988; Wewers, 1988). In tabulating the data of a telephone hot line for ex-smokers, Shiffman (1986) found that acute episodes of anxiety and frustration at work and at home frequently lead the ex-smoker to take the first cigarette.

However, even a lapse does not necessarily mean that the ex-smoker will return to regular smoking. The crucial element here is how the individual interprets his or her violation of abstinence (Marlatt and Gordon, 1985). Individuals who possess confidence in their ability to beat the smoking habit (high self-efficacy) are generally better able to quit and remain abstinent compared to those who don't (Baer, Holt and Lichtenstein, 1986). Conversely, individuals who interpret a single lapsed cigarette as a sign of personal failure and lack of motivation will be more likely to resume smoking (Curry, Marlatt and Gordon, 1987).

In discussing smoking relapse, one appears to have come full circle with smoking onset. In both cases social environment plays a role in discouraging or encouraging smoking. But the way smoking cues are perceived and reacted to depends on the general stress level in the individual's life and the resources he or she possesses to manage this stress.

EXERCISE

The need to protect health via physical activity during leisure-time is the paradoxical result of the decreasing need for physical exertion during work or other daily activities. Not only are white-collar service jobs rapdily replacing blue-collar manufacturing jobs in industrialized countries, but even within the traditional blue-collar sectors of manufacturing and construction, the worker is more likely to press a button or survey a computer monitor than to engage in heavy physical labour. Outside the work-place, the growing use of the automobile as a means of transportation, the proliferation of electric and electronic appliances in the home, and the rise in television watching as a favourite mode of recreation have all contributed to fostering a sedentary lifestyle. As a result, leisure-time exercise must now be used to replace the exertion that is no longer part of the normal daily routine.

The Case for Exercise

A major study—13 000 healthy men and women followed over eight years—of the health benefits of exercise recently reported its findings in the *Journal of the American Medical Association* (Blair et al., 1989) and the results were sufficiently newsworthy to be featured on the first page of the *New York Times* (Hilts, 1989). Individuals in the highest fitness category (the sample was divided into five fitness categories) had only one-third the death rate from heart disease, cancer or other causes compared to those in the lower fitness category. Even more remarkable were the significant health benefits to be derived from even a moderate level of fitness; individuals in the second lowest fitness category (a level that according to Dr Blair could be achieved by a half-hour to an hour of daily walking) had only half the death rate of individuals at the lowest level. As the *New York Times* headline summarized it, "Exercise and longevity: A little goes a long way."

Dramatic as this report may be, it is only the latest in a long line of research efforts linking exercise to reduced risk for a variety of health disorders including heart attacks (Paffenbarger et al., 1984; Paffenbarger and Hyde, 1988), cancer (Frisch et al., 1985; Gerhardsson et al., 1986; Paffenbarger et al., 1986) and osteoporosis (Dalsky et al., 1986; Krolner et al., 1983). Exercise has also proven of value in the treatment of health disorders once they occur, such as slowing joint deterioration in arthritics (Nordemar et al., 1981), facilitating weight loss in the obese (Hagan et al., 1986; Pacy, Webster and Garrow, 1986) and maintaining metabolic equilibrium in non insulin-dependent diabetics (Richter and Galbo, 1986; Zinman and Vranic, 1985).

The role of exercise in maintaining mental health, as opposed to physical health, is more controversial. Although a large number of studies confirm a consistently positive relationship between physical fitness and mental health (Raglin and Morgan, 1985), it is unclear whether mental health is the consequence or the antecedent of exercise. Most of the studies linking the two have been correlational or quasi-experimental, and it is just as likely that good mental health leads people to exercise more, rather than vice versa (Morgan and Goldston, 1987a). A state-of-the-art workshop on the relationship between exercise and mental health, sponsored by the Office of Prevention of the (US) National Institute of Mental Health in 1984, acknowledged the ambiguities in the data but concluded, nevertheless, that exercise does lead to short-term decreases in stress emotions (state anxiety) and stress indices (neuromuscular tension, resting heart rate, some stress hormones) and that long-term exercise is associated with a decline in neuroticism and trait anxiety. Consequently, exercise could be prescribed for its positive emotional effects for all ages and both sexes and even for people receiving psychotropic medication (Morgan and Goldston, 1987b).

One of the purported health benefits of exercise that has received a great deal of attention recently is its role as a stress buffer. There are a number of studies suggesting that fitness permits individuals to maintain general mental and physical well-being even in the face of job stress (Kobasa et al., 1985; Pavett et al., 1987) or negative life-events (Brown and Siegel, 1988; Long and

Haney, 1988). More controversial is the rapidly growing literature heatedly debating whether or not exercise diminishes cardiovascular reactivity to acute psychosocial stressors (Duda et al., 1988; Holmes and Roth, 1988; Light et al., 1987; Plante and Karpowitz, 1987), an issue of particular relevance to individuals who because of family history of hypertension or presence of the Type A behaviour pattern are considered to be predisposed to hyperreactivity in response to stress (Holmes and Cappo, 1987; Roskies et al., 1986). A recent overview of this research, employing a meta-analysis of 34 studies with a combined sample of 1,449 subjects, concluded that aerobically fit participants in the studies did indeed have a reduced stress response to psychosocial stress compared with either control group or baseline values (Crews and Landers, 1987).

Exercise Prescriptions

Exercise activity can vary in type, intensity, frequency and duration, and how much, how long and how intensely an individual should exercise depends on the specific goal envisioned (American College of Sports Medicine, 1978). Thus, to develop and maintain cardiorespiratory fitness in healthy adults there is a minimum requirement of at least two exercise sessions per week for at least 10 minutes duration each at no less than 50% of maximum oxygen uptake. To provide for body mass and fat weight loss, on the other hand, the exercise prescription is increased to at least three sessions weekly of at least 20 minutes duration each, and these sessions must be of sufficient intensity to expend a minimum of 300 kilocalories per session.

In order to maintain the training effect, exercise must be continued on a regular basis. After only two weeks of lack of exercise, there is significant reduction of working capacity. After anywhere from ten weeks to eight months of detraining, virtually all the benefits of an exercise programme are lost, with the individual returning to near pretraining level of fitness.

Prevalence of Exercise Behaviour

Of all the measures an individual can take to improve his or her health, exercise is the lifestyle change with the widest popular approval. In two recent surveys, 46% of Canadians rated exercise as "very important" to their well-being (Canada Fitness Survey, 1983) and 42% of the US population thought that people should exercise three or four times a week for at least 25 minutes each time (Thornberry, Wilson and Golden, 1986). Unfortunately for individual and public health, however, there is a large gap between what people believe about exercise and what they do.

At any given time about 40% of Americans do not exercise at all during leisure time, another 40% are active at levels probably too low and infrequent for fitness and health gains, while just 20% exercise regularly enough (Stephens, Jacobs and White, 1985) to meet the guidelines for fitness described above or to reduce their risk for several chronic diseases and premature death (Paffenbarger et al., 1986; Powell et al., 1986).

The 1990 objectives set by the United States Public Health Service were: 90% of the population to be active in the 10–17 age range, 60% to be active in the 18–64 age range and 50% to be active in the over 65 range (President's Council on Physical Fitness and Sports, 1985). However, a 1986 report (Powell et al.) revealed that only 68% of individuals in the 10–17 age range were active and this percentage dropped to below 20% for all succeeding age ranges. The authors of the report concluded that it was highly unlikely that the 1990 objectives would be met.

The exercise habit is not only difficult to initiate, but equally difficult to maintain. About one-half of those who begin or renew a personal exercise programme will fail to maintain it at the level initially intended, and a like proportion has failed in previous attempts. In the typical supervised exercise setting about 50% of the clients or patients will drop out of the programme within six months to a year. Only 20–40% of the employees eligible to use worksite exercise facilities will do so, and only one-third to one-half of the users will exercise on a regular basis at vigorous intensities (Dishman, 1988a).

Having reviewed the smoking data, one may not be surprised that individuals fall by the wayside in practising good health habits. Where exercise differs from smoking, however, is that this resistance remains high even among cardiopulmonary patients, a group who might be considered most receptive to the health message. In fact, adherence statistics are remarkably similar (Dishman, 1988a) across different exercise programmes (community, worksite and unsupervised, self-initiated) and for different population groups (apparently healthy persons, patients in supervised exercise programmes for primary and secondary prevention of cardiopulmonary diseases, and for persons being treated with exercise for obesity, diabetes and depression). Consequently, the following review will not treat separately different types of exercise programmes or participants of different health status.

Exercisers vs. Non-exercisers

Attitudes, beliefs and knowledge

Non-exercisers do not differ significantly from exercisers in their knowledge, beliefs and attitudes concerning the potential health benefits of physical activity (Andrew and Parker, 1979; Andrew et al., 1981; Dishman and Gettman, 1980). The majority of people (including exercise abstainers and drop-outs) share the conviction that exercise is good for one's health (Andrew and Parker, 1979).

Socio-demographic factors

The largest and most consistent difference between exercisers and non-exercisers is the higher socio-economic status of the former. Managers and professionals are more likely to exercise regularly than blue-collar workers (Dishman, Sallis and Orenstein, 1985; Oldridge et al., 1983), college graduates more than high-school graduates (Harris, 1970; Yates, Leehey and Shisslak, 1983), and this positive relationship between socio-economic status and physical activity has been replicated in widely disparate samples (Coleman, Washington and Price, 1985; Helmert et al., 1989). Age also makes a difference as the sharpest decrease in exercise participation occurs in late adolescence and leisure-time physical activity continues to decline with advancing age (Canada Fitness Survey, 1983; Stephens et al., 1985). Males are also more likely than females to be classified as active, especially if frequency or intensity of the activity is taken into account (Stephens et al., 1985). Finally, marital status also plays some role, with single people excercising more than married ones (Canada Fitness Survey, 1983).

Biomedical characteristics

The results here are inconsistent. In one sample of post-myocardial patients, those with the highest risk for CHD were also most likely to drop out (Oldridge et al., 1983), while in a different sample including both cardiac patients and healthy people, it was the disease-free individuals who had the highest rate of drop-out (Dishman, 1981). Similarly, in some studies individuals with high body weight and/or high fat composition were less likely to adhere to an exercise programme than their thinner, leaner counterparts (Brownell, Stunkard and Albaum, 1980; Massie and Shephard, 1971; Pollock et al., 1982), but in other studies the same factors had no value in predicting exercise persistence (Bruce et al., 1976; Oldridge et al., 1983; Ward and Morgan, 1984). Based on these conflicting findings, Dishman (1987) concludes that "biologic traits do not consistently show strong relations to exercise" (p. 61). However, Dishman (1981) has also suggested that the biologic traits of the individual may affect exercise motivation indirectly via interaction with the characteristics of the specific exercise programme. Thus, the severely overweight person who attempts advanced aerobics would probably experience unpleasant bodily sensations and soon desist. Conversely, a chronic back pain sufferer who enrols in a mild exercise programme would probably obtain pain relief and hence be encouraged to persist.

Personality factors

Once again, the results are inconsistent. The majority of studies have reported the same positive correlation between extroversion and adherence to exercise behaviour as that found between extroversion and smoking (Blumenthal et al., 1982; Howard, Cunningham and Rechnitzer, 1987; Lobstein, Mosbacher and Ismail, 1983; Young and Ismail, 1987), but at least one study reported diametrically opposed findings, in that extroversion predicted drop-out (Massie and Shephard, 1971). Similarly, ego strength has been found to be positively related to adherence among cardiac patients (Blumenthal et al., 1982), but unrelated to adherence in a sample of college women (Dishman, Ickes and Morgan, 1980).

More consistent results have been obtained with a trait measure of self-motivation, defined as "a generalized non-specific tendency to persist in the absence of extrinsic reinforcement" (Dishman and Gettman, 1980, p. 297). Self-motivation has successfully discriminated between adherers and drop-outs at different levels of initial fitness in a wide variety of programmes, including commercial spas, community-based programmes, corporate fitness and coronary rehabilitation (Dishman, 1987). However, a recent attempt to predict exercise behaviour, combining self-motivation with measures of body weight and composition, successfully predicted adherers, but not drop-outs (Ward and Morgan, 1984).

Dishman (1987) suggests that the failure to find a consistent effect of personality disposition on exercise behaviour is due to the same oversight that makes the predictive value of biomedical variables appear spuriously low: a failure to consider possible interaction between the characteristics of the person and the characteristics of the exercise programme. Thus, the predisposition of extroverts to exercise would show itself most clearly in programmes meeting their specific needs, such as a group programme with high social interaction (Shephard, 1988). On the other hand, one could reduce the impact of a personality trait detrimental to adherence, such as low self-motivation, by designing programmes that emphasized the compensating motivations of social support and external reinforcement (Wankel, Yardley and Graham, 1985).

Previous exercise experience and current lifestyle

There are no reliable data on whether childhood participation in physical activity predisposes the adult to continue exercising. Even among adults, no clear relationship has been determined between pre-enrolment exercise and programme adherence (Dishman and Dunn, 1988). Thus, Bayles et al. (1984) found that programme activity (number of city blocks walked per day, stairs climbed and so on) positively predicted adherence to a walking programme for post-menopausal women, while in another study of a more general sample of adults, Dishman (1981) found no correlation between the two.

The one lifestyle factor that is consistently related to exercise is smoking. A smoker is both less likely to enter into a supervised exercise programme

(Shephard et al., 1980) and more likely to drop out of it (Oldridge et al., 1978). In fact, smokers more frequently give up exercising rather than giving up smoking (Taylor, Buskirk and Remington, 1973).

Emotional state

One of the professional benefits of exercise is its purported positive effect on tension, anxiety and depression (Berger and Owen, 1983; Dyer and Crouch, 1988; Morgan, 1985; Thayer, 1987). Regrettably, the more an individual might need the tension-reducing qualities of exercise, the less likely he or she is to obtain them since anxiety and depression themselves serve as barriers to the initiation of exercise activity or persistence in it (Blumenthal et al., 1982; Lobstein, et al., 1983; Rape, 1987; Ward and Morgan, 1984). Even competitive athletes are affected by negative mood with depressed and stressed individuals manifesting inconsistent training and greater tendency to drop out (Dishman, Ickes and Morgan, 1980; Knapp et al., 1984).

Social environment

Exercise behaviour can clearly be influenced by the explicit or implicit messages about the activity conveyed by important others. Thus, the spouse's attitude has been found to be as potent a predictor of exercise behaviour as the individual's own attitude (Andrew et al., 1981; Heinzelmann and Bagley, 1970). Still more striking, the amount of vigorous physical activity during free play engaged in by 3–5 year old children at their pre-school is related to the exercise activity of their parents (Sallis et al., 1988).

Is there a prototype drop-out?

Based on these and similar findings, Martin and Dubbert (1982) have drawn a composite profile of men who tend to drop out of exercise programmes. The prototype of the drop-out is an

> overweight, blue collar smoker with an inactive job and few leisure pursuits, with low self-motivation and a spouse who is indifferent towards his exercise participation, who lives or works farther away from the exercise facility, and who exercises infrequently, alone and at high intensity.
>
> (p. 22)

It should be remembered, however, that there are far more sedentary people in the United States than there are blue-collar workers or smokers. One must question whether the "prototype" non-exerciser represents more than a small fraction of the sedentary.

Can Exercise Become Addictive?

In contrast to most people who do not exercise enough, a tiny percentage of the population (I have seen no estimates of the size of this group) develop a single-minded commitment to exercise that "preempts all other interests in life" (Yates et al., 1983, p. 252). In fact, just as I was writing this section a local newspaper profiled a community resident, a 59 year old businessman whose business and family obligations were sandwiched between six to eight hours of exercise daily. Still more extreme cases have been reported (Katz, 1986; Little, 1969, 1979; Morgan, 1979; Peele, 1981; Yates et al., 1983) of runners who refused to abandon their goal of running 160–220 km weekly even after being advised by a physician that continued running would lead to permanent physical damage. They even preferred losing their jobs and marriages to giving up running. When in some cases the individual was finally forced to stop running because of hospitalization for a chronic running injury, he (the compulsive exerciser is typically a male) became clinically depressed.

Yates (Yates et al., 1983; Yates, 1987) has suggested that compulsive running may be the male equivalent of anorexia nervosa in the female. While the obligatory runner is apt to be a depressed male and the obligatory dieter a depressed female, both groups assume extreme and restrictive patterns of food intake and exercise, and both groups tend to forfeit libido and sexual activity. But this categorization of extreme exercise behaviour as a form of psychopathology has not gone unchallenged; the 1987 article provoked a storm of opposing responses (see Callen, 1987; Powers, 1987; Sacks, 1987).

While there is general agreement that regular exercise occupies a pre-eminent place in some peoples' lives, disagreement concerning the value and connotation of this behaviour has led to its being described by a variety of labels: addicted, dependent, committed, obligated or fanatical (Morgan and O'Connor, 1987). One way out of this semantic jungle (Peele, 1981) is to place exercise behaviour on a continuum of addictiveness ranging from (a) daily routines to (b) dependencies, (c) compulsions and (d) addictions. A true addiction exists "when the person ceases to be able to make choices" (p. 27) and continues in the behaviour even when it is no longer pleasurable, hinders other involvements and lowers self-esteem.

Whatever the behavioural resemblances of exercise addiction to other forms of addiction, some writers strongly dispute that any biochemical dependence is involved (Dishman, 1985, 1987; Morgan, 1985; Risch and Pickar, 1983). Furthermore, even psychological dependence is seen not as the *result* of exercise, but as the result of a pre-existing vulnerability concerning personal identity for which exercise is used as the solution (Dishman, 1987). Viewed from this perspective, individuals who exercise—even to abusive levels—have found a relatively benign fashion of resolving personal problems that might otherwise be expressed in a manner more damaging to the individual's mental and physical health.

Psychological Models of Exercise Behaviour

Not surprisingly, most attempts to develop explanatory models for exercise behaviour have concentrated on the large majority of people who do not exercise enough rather than on the small minority who exercise to excess.

In contrast to smoking, asking people their reasons for remaining inactive has proven singularly unhelpful in understanding exercise behaviour. Lack of time, inconvenience and family scheduling conflicts are some of the typical reasons given for remaining sedentary (see Dishman, 1987), but these are more likely to constitute socially acceptable rationalizations rather than real reasons. In fact, in one study people who claimed that they dropped out because the exercise facility was inconveniently located actually lived closer to it than those who remained (Gettman, Pollock and Ward, 1983).

There are two psychological models that have been developed specifically to explain exercise behaviour: the first (Sonstroem, 1978, 1988) invokes interest in the activity and the self-perception of ability as determining factors, while the second (Dishman and Gettman, 1980) emphasizes the predictive role of percentage body fat, body weight and self-motivation. Regrettably, both models have yielded only modest results in empirical trials. Measures of interest and self-perceived ability have shown some value for predicting initial participation in athletics by adolescents (Sonstroem and Kampper, 1980), but have proven singularly unsuccessful in predicting adherence either in adolescents or adults (Dishman and Gettman, 1980; Morgan and Pollock, 1978). The Dishman and Gettman model, in contrast, predicts adherence, but not dropouts (Ward and Morgan, 1984).

The goal of predicting exercise behaviour, and thereby influencing it, remains elusive. What people say and believe about exercise behaviour is not related to what they do, and self-explanations of exercise behaviour provide rationalizations rather than reasons. Furthermore, there is no single factor (be it demographics, exercise history, general lifestyle practices, biological characteristics, personality traits or emotional states) that satisfactorily explains all the variance observed in exercise behaviour. Even the attempt to develop models using combinations of factors has had only limited success.

Changing Exercise Behaviour

While some polls and data from selected population groups do suggest that the amount of time spent by US adults in vigorous leisure time activity has increased in the past 10–20 years (Powell and Paffenbarger, 1985; Stephens et al., 1985), the fact remains that only a small minority of the population (20%)

currently exercises at desirable levels of frequency and intensity. Exercise behaviour has proven resistant to change partly because of the inability to identify the relevant motivators and partly because those determinants that have been identified are themselves very difficult to alter (for example, blue-collar status, age).

Approaches used to influence exercise behaviour include media campaigns directed to the population at large and behavioural interventions directed to individuals and small groups. Media campaigns designed to promote public involvement in recreational sport and exercise have proven very effective in enhancing knowledge and favourable attitudes (McIntosh, 1980), but very ineffective in changing actual behaviour (McIntosh, 1980; Meyer et al., 1980). The relative failure of media approaches in altering exercising behaviour, in comparison to other health behaviours, is seen as one example of how exercise is motivated differently from other health behaviours (Meyer et al., 1980).

The cognitive and behavioural strategies used in individual and small group programmes include: (1) a decision balance sheet procedure in which the person consciously balances the costs and benefits of exercise (Wankel, 1984); (2) contracting via a deposit or signed agreement (Epstein et al., 1980; Oldridge and Jones, 1983); (3) changing exercise-related cognitions (Martin et al., 1984); and (4) skill-training for anticipating and managing relapses (Bélisle, Roskies and Lévesque, 1987). Following interventions of this type, one can generally expect a 10–25% improvement in the usual rate of adherence, but this result has been shown mainly for short time periods (3–10 weeks) and the few follow-up studies suggest that this effect is largely lost within six months to a year after the intervention ceases (Dishman, 1988b).

SMOKING AND EXERCISE AS ALTERNATIVE STRESS BUFFERS

Smoking is a health vice and exercise a health virtue, and much of the enormous outpouring of research concerning them in the last 30 years has been motivated by the desire to suppress the former and promote the latter. This has led to smoking becoming more and more a deviant social act, a harmful health practice resorted to by the socially marginal and psychologically vulnerable. Exercise, in sharp contrast, is increasingly valued by society and most likely to be engaged in by those of good education, high social status and sound mental health. In short, smoking implies weakness, physical and moral, while exercise connotes the opposite qualities of a strong will and a fit body.

Underlying these apparent differences, however, is one fundamental similarity: both for smoking and exercise, health is only one among many other considerations entering into the decision to engage or not. In addition to the health consequences, the individual must also weigh a multitude of biological needs (avoiding withdrawal symptoms, controlling weight, minimizing effort expenditure), psychological needs (relieving stress, increasing vigour) and social needs (obtaining social approval, fulfilling role obligations) and then evaluate the degree to which smoking or exercise fulfils or conflict with these manifold needs at a given moment in time. Therefore, understanding smoking and exercise as individual behaviours involves going beyond their health implications and developing a bio-psycho-social model that does justice to their multidimensional nature.

Central to this model is the role of both smoking and exercise as multipurpose stress buffers, alternate ways of coping with the varied stresses and strains of everyday living. The early morning jogger and the early morning smoker look very different, but both may be engaged in the same task of working themselves up for the coming day. Similarly, the need to unwind at the end of the day can be met either by smoking or by exercise. The two strategies are also alternate means of controlling weight, mastering anxiety or countering boredom. Significantly, the inverse correlation between smoking and exercise is one of the strongest relationships found among different health behaviours (Mechanic, 1979), suggesting that individuals who choose one of these coping strategies have less need for the alternative.

This ability of either smoking or exercise to serve as a stress buffer raises some intriguing questions concerning their differences. Why do some people choose smoking and others exercise to regulate the same stress situation? Why has it been so much easier to convince people to avoid smoking than to exercise regularly? Why do women smoke more and exercise less than men in contrast to their general predisposition to conform with health recommendations?

One striking difference between smoking and exercise is the contrast in the amount of effort involved. Compared to smoking, exercise is a high-effort strategy; to achieve its benefits one must expend considerable time and energy. In sharp contrast, the habitual smoker can reach for a cigarette at a moment's notice without conscious effort or thought. This discrepancy in exertion may help explain why, paradoxically, exercise is the mental health strategy of choice for individuals who are not already overburdened by stress, anxiety or depression.

Despite the many attractions of smoking, interventions directed at modifying smoking behaviour have experienced more success than those focused on exercise. Here, too, there are a number of differences between the two health practices that can be used to explain their differential responsiveness to change. For one, the case *against* smoking is clearer than the case *for* exercise; on the basis of the existing data, anyway, the negative health consequences of smoking appear stronger than the positive health benefits of exercise. Second, the social sanctions against smoking are more powerful than the social support provided to encourage exercise. In the light of the growing prohibitions against smoking in the work-place and in public spaces, the smoker is often a

social outcast; in fact, the initiation into and continuation of smoking behaviour is increasingly restricted to specific environments in which these
pressures have not yet made themselves felt. Nowhere, however, is there an
equivalent hero status available for the individual who attends an exercise
class or walks to work. Finally, smoking withdrawal may be painful, but the
effects are time-limited; even the committed exerciser, in contrast, must con-
tinuously do battle against the barriers of inertia, fatigue, competing claims
for time expended, or bodily aches and pains.

These differences between smoking and exercise also help to explain why
women show greater attraction to the first and resistance to the second. Given
the much higher prevalence of depression among women and time pressure
many women experience in fulfilling the multiple roles of worker, spouse and
mother, the combined features of emotional and weight regulation with a low
cost in effort makes smoking particularly attractive to them. Socially, too, the
pressures against smoking may be counterbalanced by the message of emancipation and independence that smoking still connotes to many women.
"You've come a long way, baby" is a message that is particularly hard for
many women to resist, especially those who are still experiencing difficulty
with the road ahead.

FUTURE PROSPECTS

Public health efforts in the last few decades have convinced substantial proportions of the population to abstain from or cease smoking, but have proven
far less successful in enticing individuals to exercise at the frequency and level
of intensity considered desirable by the experts. Because of this dissimilarity,
the coming years are likely to witness a divergence in the type of individual
differences considered salient.

As countries like the United States move towards a smoke-free status, the
smokers remaining will probably become increasingly homogeneous in social
and psychological characteristics and, even more important, will be perceived
and labelled by others as a specific, deviant sub-population. Consequently, the
emphasis will shift from intragroup (within smokers) to intergroup differences
(smokers vs. non-smokers). How many cigarettes an individual smokes, and
whether they are smoked primarily for stress relief or stimulation, will fade in
importance compared to the fact that the person smokes at all. A similar
situation currently prevails in organizations such as Alcoholics Anonymous
and Narcotics Anonymous where the focus is entirely on the shared addiction
and any discussion of individual differences among addicts is actively
discouraged.

The outlook for exercise, in contrast, is towards increasing heterogeneity,
both in the characteristics of people exercising, and in the range of activities
classified as exercise. At present, only 20% of the US population exercises in a

manner considered optimal by experts and 20 years of information and exhortation has done little to raise this percentage. It is obvious that the universal, one-size-fits-all exercise prescription does not meet the needs of a large number of potential consumers and it makes little sense to continue to market it. The challenge, instead, is to assess the specific needs of different groups, and to develop tailor-made programmes to meet these needs. Parking the car a block away from the office and substituting stairs for elevators may not be considered as aerobically desirable as jogging three times a week. But if this is all a working mother can manage, it is better than nothing. In short, meeting government objectives for physical activity will largely depend on understanding individual differences in needs and responding to these differences appropriately.

REFERENCES

Abrams, D. B., Monti, P. M., Pinto, R. P., Elder, J. P. and others (1987). Psychosocial stress and coping in smokers who relapse or quit, *Health Psychology*, **6**, 289–303.

Ahlgren, A., Norem, A. A., Hochhauser, M. and Garvin, J. (1982). Antecedents of smoking among pre-adolescents, *Journal of Drug Education*, **12**, 325–40.

American Cancer Society (1986). *1986 Cancer Facts and Figures*, American Cancer Society, New York.

American College of Sports Medicine (1978). The recommended quantity and quality of exercise for developing and maintaining fitness in healthy adults, *Medicine and Science in Sports*, **10**, vii–ix.

American Heart Association (1981). *Why Risk Heart Attack: Seven Ways to Guard Your Health*, American Heart Association, Dallas, Texas.

Andrew, G. M. and Parker, J. O. (1979). Factors related to dropout of post myocardial infarction patients from exercise programs, *Medicine and Science in Sports and Exercise*, **11**, 376–8.

Andrew, G. M., Oldridge, N. B., Parker, J. O., Cunningham, J. A. and other (1981). Reasons for dropout from exercise programs in post-coronary patients, *Medicine and Science in Sports and Exercise*, **13**, 164–8.

Ary, D. V. and Biglan, A. (1988). Longitudinal changes in adolescent cigarette behaviour: Onset and cessation, *Journal of Behavioural Medicine*, **11**, 361–82.

Ashton, H. and Stepney, R. (1982). *Smoking: Psychology and Pharmacology*, Cambridge University Press, Cambridge.

Baer, J. S., Holt, C. S. and Lichtenstein, E. (1986). Self-efficacy and smoking re-examined: Construct validity and clinical utility, *Journal of Consulting and Clinical Psychology*, **54**, 846–52.

Baer, P. E., McLaughlin, R. J., Burnside, M. A., Pokorny, A. D. and others (1987). Stress, family environment, and multiple substance use among seventh graders, *Psychology of Addictive Behaviors*, **1**, 92–103.

Bayles, C., Laporte, R., Petrini, A., Cauley, J. and others, (1984). A comparison of compliers and non-compliers in a randomized exercise trial of 229 post-menopausal women, *Medicine and Science in Sports and Exercise*, **16**, 115 (abstract).

Bélisle, M., Roskies, E. and Lévesque, J. M. (1987). Improving adherence to physical activity, *Health Psychology*, **6**, 159–72.

Berger, B. G. and Owen, D. R. (1983). Mood alteration with swimming—swimmers really do 'feel better', *Psychosomatic Medicine*, **45**, 425–33.

Blair, S. N., Kohl, H. W. 3rd, Paffenbarger, R. S. Jr., Clark, D. G. and others (1989). Physical fitness and all-cause mortality: A prospective study of healthy men and women, *JAMA*, **262**, 2395–401.

Blumenthal, J. A., Williams, R. S., Wallace, A. G., Williams, R. B. and others (1982). Physiological and psychological variables predict compliance to prescribed exercise therapy in patients recovering from myocardial infarction, *Psychosomatic Medicine*, **44**, 519–27.

Brecher, E. M. (1972). *Licit and Illicit Drugs*, Little Brown, Boston.

Brown, J. D. and Siegel, J. M. (1988). Exercise as a buffer of life stress: A prospective study of adolescent health, *Health Psychology*, **7**, 341–53.

Brownell, K. D., Stunkard, A. J. and Albaum, J. M. (1980). Evaluation and modification of exercise programs in the natural environment, *American Journal of Psychiatry*, **137**, 1540–5.

Bruce, E. H., Frederick, R., Bruce, R. A. and Fisher, L. D. (1976). Comparison of active participants and dropouts in cardiopulmonary rehabilitation programs, *American Journal of Cardiology*, **37**, 53–60.

Callen, K. E. (1987). Eating disorders and long-distance running: The ascetic condition: Commentary, *Integrative Psychiatry*, **5**, 210–11.

Canada Fitness Survey(1983). *Fitness and Lifestyle in Canada*, Government of Canada Fitness and Amateur Sport, Ottawa.

Castro, F. G., Maddahian, E., Newcomb, M. D. and Bentler, P. M. (1987). A multivariate model of the determination of cigarette smoking adolescents, *Journal of Health and Social Beahviour*, **28**, 273–89.

Cherry, N. and Kiernan, K. (1978). A longitudinal study of smoking and personality. In R. E. Thornton (ed.) *Smoking Behaviour*, Churchill-Livingstone, Edinburgh, pp. 12–18.

Clarke, J. H., MacPherson, B. V. and Holmes, D. R. (1982). Cigarette smoking and external locus of control among young adolescents, *Journal of Health and Social Behaviour*, **23**, 253–9.

Coleman, M., Washington, M. A. and Price, S. (1985). Physical exercise, social background, and the well-being of older adult women, *Perceptual and Motor Skills*, **60**, 737–8.

Colletti, G. and Brownell, K. D. (1982). The physical and emotional benefits of social support: Application to obesity, smoking and alcoholism. In M. Hersen, R. M. Eisler and P. M. Miller (eds) *Progress in Behaviour Modification* vol. 13, Academic Press, New York, pp. 109–78.

Crews, D. J. and Landers, D. M. (1987). A meta-analytic review of aerobic fitness and reactivity to psychosocial stressors, *Medicine and Science in Sports and Exercise*, **19**(5, Suppl.), 114–20.

Curry, S., Marlatt, G. A. and Gordon, J. R. (1987). Abstinence violation effect: Validation of an attributional concept with smoking cessation, *Journal of Consulting and Clinical Psychology*, **55**, 145–9.

Dalenz, J. R. (1988). Smoking control in developing countries—Summary. In M. Aoki, S., Hisamachi and S. Tominaga (eds) *Smoking and Health 1987: Proceedings of the 6th World Conference on Smoking and Health*, Elsevier, New York, pp. 609–10.

Dalsky, G. P., Ehasani, A. A., Kleinheider, K. S. and Birge, S. J. (1986). Effect of exercise on lower bone density, *The Gerontologist*, **26**, 16A.

Dielman, T. E., Campanelli, P. C., Shope, J. T. and Butchart, A. T. (1987). Susceptibility to peer pressure, self-esteem and health locus of control as correlates of adolescent substance abuse, *Health Education Quarterly*, **14**, 207–21.

Dishman, R. K. (1981). Biologic influences on exercise adherence, *Research Quarterly for Exercise and Sports*, **52**, 143–59.

Dishman, R. K. (1985). Medical psychology in sports and exercise, *Medical Clinics of North America*, **69**, 123–43.

Dishman, R. K. (1987). Exercise adherence and habitual physical activity. In W. P. Morgan and S. E. Goldston (eds) *Exercise and Mental Health*, Hemisphere, Washington, pp. 57–83.

Dishman, R. K. (1988a). Overview. In R. K. Dishman (ed.) *Adherence: Its Impact on Public Health*, Human Kinetics Books, Champaigne, Ill., pp. 1–7.

Dishman, R. K. (1988b). Epilogue and future directions. In R. K. Dishman (ed.), *Exercise Adherence: Its Impact on Public Health*, Human Kinetics Books, Champaign, Ill., pp. 417–26.

Dishman, R. K. and Dunn, A. L. (1988). Exercise adherence in children and youth: Implications for adulthood. In R. K. Dishman (ed.) *Exercise Adherence: Its Impact on Public Health*, Human Kinetics Books, Champaign, Ill., pp. 155–202.

Dishman, R. K. and Gettman, L. R. (1980). Psychobiologic influences on exercise adherence, *Journal of Sport Psychology*, **2**, 295–310.

Dishman, R. K., Ickes, W. and Morgan, W. P. (1980). Self-motivation and adherence to habitual physical activity, *Journal of Applied Social Psychology*, **10**, 115–32.

Dishman, R. K., Sallis, J. F. and Orenstein, D. O. (1985). The determinants of physical activity and exercise, *Public Health Reports*, **100**, 158–71.

Donovan, J. E. and Jessor, R. (1985). Structure of problem behaviour in adolescence and young adulthood, *Journal of Consulting and Clinical Psychology*, **53**, 890–904.

Duda, J. L., Sedlock, D. A., Melby, C. L. and Thaman, C. (1988). The effects of physical activity level and acute exercise on heart rate and subjective reponse to a psychological stressor, *International Journal of Sport Psychology*, **19**, 119–33.,

Dyer, J. B. and Crouch, J. G. (1988). Effects of running and other activities on moods, *Perceptual and Motor Skills*, **67**, 43–50.

Epstein, L. H., Wing, R. R., Thompson, J. K. and Griffiths, M. (1980). Attendance and fitness in aerobics exercise: The effects of contract and lottery procedures, *Behaviour Modification*, **4**, 465–79.

Evans, R. I. (1984). A social inoculation strategy to deter smoking in adolescents. In J. D. Matarazzo, S. M. Weiss, J. A. Herd, N. E. Miller and S. M. Weiss (eds) *Behavioral Health: A Handbook of Health Enhancement and Disease Prevention*, Wiley, New York, pp. 765–74.

Eysenck, H. J. (1980). *The Causes and Effects of Smoking*, Sage, Beverly Hills, Calif.

Fielding, J. E. (1985). Smoking: Health effects and control, *New England Journal of Medicine*, **313**, 491–8, 555–61.

Fiore, M., Novotny, T., Lynn, W., Maklan, D. and others (1988). Smoking cessation: Data from the 1986 adult use of tobacco survey. In M. Aoki, S., Hisamichi, and S. Tominaga (eds) *Smoking and Health 1987: Proceedings of the 6th World Conference on Smoking and Health*, Elsevier, New York, pp. 189–94.

Foreyt, J. P. (1987). The addictive disorders. In G. T. Wilson, C. M. Franks, P. C. Kendall and J. P. Foreyt (eds) *Annual Review of Behaviour Theory and Practice*, Volume 11, Guilford, New York, p. 177–233.

Frisch, R. E., Wyshak, G., Albright, N. L., Schiff, I. and others (1985). Lower prevalence of breast cancer and cancers of the reproductive system among former college athletes compared to non-athletes, *British Journal of Cancer*, **52**, 885.

Frith, C. D. (1971). Smoking behaviour and its relationship to the smoker's immediate experience, *British Journal of Social and Clinical Psychology*, **10**, 73–8.

Garland, C., Barrett-Connor, E., Suarez, L., Criqui, M. H. and others, (1985). Effects of passive smoking on ischemic heart disease mortality of smokers: A prospective study, *American Journal of Epidemiology*, **121**, 645–50.

Geizerova, H. and Masironi, R. (1988). Cigarette smoking in children and adolescents. In M. Aoki, S. Hisamichi, and S. Tominaga (eds) *Smoking and Health 1987: Proceedings of the 6th World Conference on Smoking and Health*, Elsevier, New York, pp. 601–8.

Gerhardsson, M., Norrell, S. E., Kiviranta, H., Pedersen, N. L. and others (1986). Sedentary jobs and colon cancer, *American Journal of Epidemilogy*, **123**, 775–80.

Gettman, L. R., Pollock, M. L. and Ward, A. (1983). Adherence to unsupervised exercise, *The Physician and Sportsmedicine*, **11**, 56–66.

Glasgow, R. E., Klesges, R. C., Klesges, L. M. and Somes, G. R. (1988). Variables associated with participation and outcomes in a worksite smoking control program, *Journal of Consulting and Clinical Psychology*, **56**, 617–20.

Gordon, N. P. (1986). Never smokers, triers and current smokers: Three distinct target groups for school-based antismoking programs, *Health Education Quarterly*, **13**, 163–79.

Gritz, E. R. (1984). 'Cigarette smoking by adolescent females: Implications for health and behaviour', *Women and Health*, **9**, 103–15.

Hagan, R. D., Upton, S. J., Wong, L. and Whittam, J. (1986). The effects of aerobic conditioning and/or caloric restriction in overweight men and women, *Medicine and Science in Sports and Exercise*, **18**, 87–94.

Harris, D. V. (1970). Physical activity, history and attitudes of middle-aged men, *Medicine and Science in Sports*, **2**, 203–8.

Heinzelmann, F. and Bagley, R. W. (1970). Response to physical activity programs and their effect on health behaviour, *Public Health Reports*, **85**, 905–11.

Helmert, U., Herman, B., Joeckel, K. H., Greiser, E. and others (1989). Social class and risk factors for coronary heart disease in the Federal Republic of Germany: Results of the baseline survey of the German Cardiovascular Prevention Study (GCRP), *Journal of Epidemiology and Community Health*, **43**, 37–42.

Henningfield, J. E., Goldberg, S. R. and Jasinki, D. R. (1987). Nicotine: Abuse liability, dependence potential and pharmacologic treatment of dependence. In W. R. Martin, G. R. Van Loon, E. T. Iwamoto and L. Davis (eds) *Advances in Behavioral Biology*, vol. 31, Plenum, New York, pp. 81–100.

Hilts, P. J. (1989). Exercise and longevity: A little goes a long way, *New York Times*, 3 November, p. 1.

Holmes, D. S. and Cappo, B. M. (1987). Prophylactic effect of aerobic fitness on cardiovascular arousal among individuals with a family history of hypertension, *Journal of Psychosomatic Research*, **31**, 601–5.

Holmes, D. S. and Roth, D. L. (1988). Effects of aerobic exercise training and relaxation training on cardiovascular activity during psychological stress, *Journal of Psychosomatic Research*, **32**, 469–74.

Howard, J. H., Cunningham, D. A. and Rechnitzer, P. A. (1987). Personality and fitness decline in middle-aged men, *International Journal of Sport Psychology*, **18**, 100–11.

Hughes, J. R. (1986). Genetics of smoking: A review, *Behavior Therapy*, **17**, 335–45.

Hunt, W. A. and Bespalec, D. A. (1974). An evaluation of current methods of modifying smoking behaviour, *Journal of Clinical Psychology*, **30**, 431–8.

Jarvik, M. E. (1987). Does smoking decrease eating and eating increase smoking? In W. R. Martin, G. R. Van Loon, E. T. Iwamoto and L. Davis (eds) *Advances in Behavioral Biology*, vol. 31, Plenum, New York, pp. 389–400.

Katz, J. L. (1986). Long-distance running, anorexia nervosa, and bulimia: A report of two case studies, *Comprehensive Psychiatry*, **27**, 74–8.

Kirscht, J. P. (1983). Preventive health behaviour: A review of research and issues, *Health Psychology*, **2**, 277–302.

Klesge, R. C. and Klesges, L. M. (1988). Cigarette smoking as a dieting strategy in a university population, *International Journal of Eating Disorders*, **7**, 413–19.

Knapp, D., Gutmann, M., Foster, C. and Pollack, M. (1984). Self-motivation among 1984 Olympic speedskating hopefuls and emotional response and adherence to training, *Medicine and Science in Sports and Exercise*, **16**, 114 (abstract).

Kobasa, S., Maddi, S., Puccetti, M. and Zola, M. A. (1985). Effectiveness of hardiness, exercise and social support as resources against illness, *Journal of Psychosomatic Research*, **29**, 525–33.

Krolner, B., Toft, B., Pors, N. S., Tondevold, E. and others, (1983). Physical exercise as a prophylaxis against involuntary bone loss: A controlled trial, *Clinical Science*, **64**, 541–6.

Lalonde, M. (1974). *A New Perspective on the Health of Canadians*, Information Canada, Ottawa.

Lawrance, L. and Rubinson, L. (1986). Self efficacy as a predictor of smoking in young adolescents, *Addictive Behaviors*, **11**, 367–82.

Leventhal, H., Glynn, K. and Fleming, R. (1987). Is the smoking decision an 'informed choice'?: Effects of smoking risk factors on smoking beliefs, *JAMA*, **257**, 3373–6.

Leventhal, H., Prohaska, T. R. and Hirschman, R. S. (1985). Preventive health behaviour across the life span. In J. C. Rosen and L. J. Solomon (eds) *Prevention in Health Psychology*, University Press of New England, Hanover, NH.

Light, K. C., Obrist, P. A., James, S. A. and Strogatz, D. S. (1987). Cardiovascular responses to stress: II. Relationships to aerobic exercise patterns, *Psychophysiology*, **24**, 79–86.

Little, J. C. (1969). The athlete's neurosis: A deprivation crisis, *Acta Psychiatrica Scandinavica*, **45**, 187–97.

Little, J. C. (1979). Neurotic illness in fitness fanatics, *Psychiatric Annals*, **9**, 49–51, 55–6.

Livson, N. and Leino, E. V. (1985). Adolescent personality antecedents of adult cigarette smoking: A longitudinal study, *Journal of Genetic Psychology*, **146**, 343–55.

Lobstein, D. D., Mosbacher, B. J. and Ismail, A. H. (1983) Depression as a powerful discriminator between physically active and sedentary middle-aged men, *Journal of Psychosomatic Research*, **27**, 69–76.

Long, B. C. and Haney, C. J. (1988). Long-term follow-up of stressed working women: A comparison of aerobic exercise and progressive relaxation, *Journal of Sport and Exercise Psychology*, **10**, 461–70.

McAlister, A. L., Krosnik, J. A. and Milburn, M. A. (1984). Causes of adolescent cigarette smoking: Tests of a structural equation model, *Social Psychology Quarterly*, **47**, 24–36.

McGinnis, J. M., Shopland, D. and Brown, C. (1987). Trends in smoking and smokeless tobacco consumption in the United States, *Annual Review of Public Health*, **8**, 441–66.

McIntosh, P. (1980). *'Sports for All' Programs Throughout the World*, UNESCO, New York.

Marlatt, G. A. and Gordon, J. R. (1985). *Relapse Prevention: Maintenance Strategies in the Treatment of Addictive Behaviors*, Guilford, New York.

Marston, A. R., Jacobs, D. F., Singer, R. D., Widaman, K. F. and others (1988). Adolescents who apparently are invulnerable to drug, alcohol, and nicotine use, *Adolescence*, **23**, 593–8.

Martin, J. E. and Dubbert, P. M. (1982). Exercise and health: The adherence problem, *Behavioral Medicine Update*, **4**, 16–24.

Martin, J. D., Dubbert, P. M., Kattell, A. D., Thompson, J. K. and others (1984). Behavioral control of exercise in sedentary adults, *Journal of Consulting and Clinical Psychology*, **52**, 795–811.

Masironi, R. and Rothwell, K. (1988). Worldwide smoking trends. In M. Aoki, S. Hisamichi and S. Tominaga (eds) *Smoking and Health 1987: Proceedings of the 6th World Conference on Smoking and Health*, Elsevier, New York, pp. 47–52.

Massie, J. F. and Shephard, R. J. (1971). Physiological and psychological effects of training—comparison of individual and gymnasium programs with a characterization of the exercise 'drop-out', *Medicine and Science in Sports*, **3**, 110–17.

Matarazzo, J. D. (1984). Behavioral health: A 1990 challenge for the health services professions. In J. D. Matarazzo, S. M. Weiss, J. A. Herd, N. E. Miller and S. M. Weiss (eds), *Behavioral Health: A Handbook of Health Enhancement and Disease Prevention*, Wiley, New York, pp. 3–40.

Mechanic, D. (1979). The stability of health and illness behaviour: Results from a 16-year follow-up, *American Journal of Public Health*, **69**, 1142–5.

Meyer, A. J., Nash, J. D., McAlister, A. L., Maccoby, N. and others (1980). Skills training in a cardiovascular health education campaign, *Journal of Consulting and Clinical Psychology*, **48**, 129–42.

Mitic, W. R., McGuire, D. P. and Neumann, B. (1985). Perceived stress and adolescents' cigarette use, *Psychological Reports*, **57**, 1043–8.

Montreal Gazette (1990). Smoking: $52 billion a year, 21 February, p. C7.

Morgan, W. P. (1979). Negative addiction in runners, *The Physician and Sportsmedicine*, **7**, 57–70.

Morgan, W. P. (1985). Affective beneficence of vigorous physical activity, *Medicine and Science in Sports and Exercise*, **17**, 94–100.

Morgan, W. P. and Goldston, S. E. (1987a). Introduction. In W. P. Morgan and S. E. Goldston (eds) *Exercise and Mental Health*, Hemisphere, Washington, pp. 3–7.

Morgan, W. P. and Goldston, S. E. (1987b). Summary. In W. P. Morgan and S. E. Goldston (eds) *Exercise and Mental Health*, Hemisphere, Washington, pp. 155–9.

Morgan, W. P. and O'Connor, P. J. (1987). Exercise and mental health. In R. K. Dishman (ed.) *Exercise Adherence: Its Impact on Public Health*, Human Kinetics Books, Champaign, Ill., pp. 91–122.

Morgan, W. P. and Pollock, M. L. (1978). Physical activity and cardiovascular health: Psychological aspects. In F. Landry and D. Orban (eds) *Physical Activity and Human Well-Being*, Symposium Specialists, Miami, pp. 163–81.

Moyer, C. A. and Ouimet, L. (1988). Smoke-free: A pre-school non-smoking program. In M. Aoki, S. Hisamichi, and S. Tominaga (eds) *Smoking and Health 1987: Proceedings of the 6th World Conference on Smoking and Health*, Elsevier, New York, pp. 579–82.

Newcomb, M. D., Maddahian, E. and Bentler, P. M. (1986). Risk factors for drug use among adolescents: Concurrent and longitudinal analyses, *American Journal of Public Health*, **76**, 525–31.

Nordemar, R., Ekblom, B., Zachrisson, L. and Lundquist, K. (1981). Physical training in rheumatoid arthritis: A controlled long-term study, *Scandinavian Journal of Rheumatology*, **10**, 17–23, 25–30.

Oldridge, N. B. and Jones, N. L. (1983). Improving patient compliance in cardiac rehabilitation: Effects of written agreement and self-monitoring, *Journal of Cardiac Rehabilitation*, **3**, 257–62.

Oldridge, N. B., Donner, A., Buck, C. W., Jones, N. L. and others (1983). The Ontario exercise heart collaborative study experience, *American Journal of Cardiology*, **51**, 70–4.

Oldridge, N. B., Wicks, J. R., Hanley, R., Sutton, J. and others (1978). Non-compliance in an exercise rehabilitation program for men who have suffered a myocardial infarction, *Canadian Medical Association Journal*, **118**, 361–4.

Pacy, P. J., Webster, J. and Garrow, J. S. (1986). Exercise and obesity, *Sports Medicine*, **3**, 89–113.

Paffenbarger, R. S. Jr. and Hyde, R. T. (1988). Exercise adherence, coronary heart disease, and longevity. In R. K. Dishman (ed.) *Exercise Adherence: Its Impact on Public Health*, Human Kinetics Books, Champaign, Ill., pp. 41–73.

Paffenbarger, R. S. Jr., Hyde, R. T., Wing, A. L. and Hsieh, C. C. (1986). Physical activity, all-cause mortality, and longevity of college alumni, *New England Journal of Medicine*, **314**, 605–13.

Paffenbarger, R. S. Jr., Hyde, R. T., Wing, A. L. and Steinmetz, C. H. (1984). A natural history of athleticism and cardiovascular health, *JAMA*, **252**, 491–5.

Pavett, C. M., Butler, M., Marcinik, E. J. and Hodgdon, J. A. (1987). Exercise as a buffer against organizational stress, *Stress Medicine*, **3**, 87–92.

Pechacek, T. F., Murray, D. M., Luepker, R. V., Mittelmark, B. M. and others (1984). Measurement of adolescent smoking behaviour: Rationale and methods, *Journal of Behavioral Medicine*, **7**, 123–40.

Peele, S. (1981). *How Much Is Too Much?*, Prentice-Hall, Englewood Cliffs, NJ.

Penny, G. N. and Robinson, J. O. (1986). Psychological resources and cigarette smoking in adolescents, *British Journal of Psychology*, **77**, 351–7.

Pershagen, G., Hrubec, Z. and Svensson, C. (1987). Passive smoking and lung cancer in Swedish women, *American Journal of Epidemiology*, **125**, 17–24.

Plante, T.l G. and Karpowitz, D. (1987). The influence of aerobic exercise on physiological stress responsivity, *Psychophysiology*, **24**, 670–7.

Pollock, M. L., Foster, C., Salisbury, R. and Smith, R. (1982). Effects of a YMCA starter fitness program, *The Physician and Sportsmedicine*, **10**, 89–102.

Pomerleau, O. F. and Pomerleau, C. S. (1984). Neuroregulators and the reinforcement of smoking: Towards a biobehavioral explanation, *Neuroscience and Biobehavioral Reivews*, **8**, 503–14.

Pomerleau, O. F., Turk, D. C. and Fertig, J. B. (1984). The effects of cigarette smoking on pain and anxiety, *Addictive Behaviors*, **9**, 265–71.

Powell, K. E. and Paffenbarger, R. J. (1985). Workshop on epidemiologic and public health aspects of physical activity and exercise: A summary, *Public Health Reports*, **100**, 118–26.

Powell, K. E., Spain, K. G., Christenson, G. M. and Mollenkamp, M. P. (1986). The status of the 1990 objectives for physical fitness and exercise, *Public Health Reports*, **101**, 15–21.

Powers, P. S. (1987). Eating disorders and long-distance running: The ascetic condition: Commentary, *Integrative Psychiatry*, **5**, 207–10.

President's Council on Physical Fitness and Sports (1985). *Mid-Course Review: 1990 Physical Fitness and Exercise Objectives, October, 1985*, President's Council on Physical Fitness and Sports, Washington, D.C.

Raglin, J. S. and Morgan, W. P. (1985). Influence of vigorous exercise on mood state, *Behavior Therapist*, **8**, 179–83.

Ramström, L. M. (1988). Smoking and children. In M. Aoki, S. Hisamichi, and S. Tominaga (eds) *Smoking and Health 1987: Proceedings of the 6th World Conference on Smoking and Health*, Elsevier, New York, pp. 87–98.

Rape, R. N. (1987). Running and depression, *Perceptual and Motor Skills*, **64**, 1301–10.

Richter, E. A. and Galbo, H. (1986). Diabetes, insulin and exercise, *Sports Medicine*, **3**, 275–88.

Risch, S. C. and Pickar, D. (eds) (1983). Symposium on endorphins, *Psychological Clinics of North America*, **6**, 363–521.

Roskies, E., Seraganian, P., Oseasohn, R., Hanley, J. A. and others (1986). The Montreal Type A Intervention Project: Major findings, *Health Psychology*, **5**, 45–69.

Russell, M. A. H., Peto, J. and Patel, U. A. (1974). The classification of smoking by factorial structure of motives, *Journal of the Royal Statistical Society, A*, **137**, 313–33.

Rzewnicki, R. and Forgays, D. G. (1987). Recidivism and self-cure of smoking and obesity: An attempt to replicate, *American Psychologist*, **42**, 97–100.

Sacks, M. H. (1987). Eating disorders and long-distance running: The ascetic condition. Commentary, *Integrative Psychiatry*, **5**, 205–6.

Sallis, J. F., Patterson, T. L., McKenzie, T. L. and Nader, P. R. (1988). Family variables and physical activity in preschool children, *Journal of Deveopmental and Behavioral Pediatrics*, **9**, 57–61.

Salovey, P., Rudy, T. E. and Turk, D. C. (1987). Preaching and practising: The structure and consistency of health-protective attitudes and behaviors, *Health Education Research*, **2**, 195–205.

Schachter, S. (1982). Recidivism and self-cure of smoking and obesity, *American Psychologist*, **37**, 436–44.

Shephard, R. J. (1988). Exercise adherence in corporate settings: Personal traits and program barriers,. In R. K. Dishman (ed.) *Exercise Adherence: Its Impact on Public Health*, Human Kinetics Books, Champaign, Ill., pp. 305–20.

Shephard, R. J., Morgan, P., Finucane, R. and Schimmelfing, L. (1980). Factors influencing recruitment to an occupational fitness program, *Journal of Occupational Medicine*, **22**, 389–98.

Shiffman, S. M. (1979). The tobacco withdrawal syndrome. In N. A. Krasnegor (ed.) *Cigarette Smoking as a Dependence Process*, National Institute of Drug Abuse, Washington, D.C., pp. 158–84.

Shiffman, S. M. (1986). A cluster-analytic classification of smoking-relapse episodes, *Addictive Behaviors*, **11**, 295–307.

Shiffman, S. M. and Jarvik, M. E. (1976). Smoking withdrawal symptoms in two weeks of abstinence, *Psychopharmacology*, **50**, 35–9.

Shopland, D. R. and Brown, C. (1985). Changes in smoking prevalence in the US: 1955–1983, *Annals of Behavioral Medicine*, **7**, 5–8.

Sonstroem, R. J. (1978). Physical estimation and attraction scales: Rationale and research, *Medicine and Science in Sports*, **8**, 126–32.

Sonstroem, R. J. (1988). Psychological models. In R. K. Dishman (ed.) *Exercise Adherence: Its Impact on Public Health*, Human Kinetics Books, Champaign, Ill., pp. 125–54.

Sonstroem, R. J. and Kampper, K. P. (1980). Prediction of athletic participation in middle school males, *Research Quarterly for Exercise and Sport*, **51**, 685–94.

Sorensen, G., Pechacek, T., and Pollenen, U. (1986). Occupational and worksite norms and attitudes about smoking cessation, *American Journal of Public Health*, **76**, 544–9.

Stephens, T., Jacobs, D. R. Jr. and White, C. C. (1985). A descriptive epidemiology of leisure-time activity, *Public Health Reports*, **100**, 147–58.

Sunseri, A. J. (1983). Reading, demographic, social and psychological factors related to pre-adolescent smoking and non-smoking behaviors and attitudes, *Journal of School Health*, **53**, 257–63.

Svikis, D. S., Hatsukami, D. K., Hughes, J. R., Carroll, K. M. and others (1986). Sex differences in tobacco withdrawal syndrome, *Addictive Behaviors*, **11**, 459–62.

Swan, G. E., Denk, C. E., Parker, S. D., Carmelli, D. and others (1988). Risk factors for late relapse in male and female ex-smokers, *Addictive Behaviors*, **13**, 253–66.

Taylor, H. L., Buskirk, E. R. and Remington, R. D. (1973). Exercise in controlled trials in the prevention of coronary heart disease, *Federation Proceedings*, **32**, 1623–7.

Thayer, R. E. (1987). Energy, tiredness, and tension effects of a sugar snack versus moderate exercise, *Journal of Personality and Social Psychology*, **52**, 119–25.

Thomas, C. B. (1973). The relationship of smoking and habits of nervous tension. In W. L. Dunn (ed.) *Smoking Behaviour: Motives and Incentives*, Wiley, New York, pp. 157–70.

Thornberry, O. T., Wilson, R. W. and Golden, P. (1986). Health promotion and disease prevention, provisional data from the National Health Survey, United States, January–June, 1985, *Advance Data from Vital Statistics*, **126**, 19 September.

Tucker, L. A. (1984a). Cigarette smoking intentions and physical fitness: A multivariate study of high school males, *Adolescence*, **19**, 313–21.

Tucker, L. A. (1984b). Psychological differences between adolescent smoking intenders and nonintenders, *Journal of Psychology*, **118**, 37–43.

US Department of Health, Education and Welfare (1979a). *Healthy People: The Surgeon General's Report on Health Promotion and Disease Prevention*, US Government Printing Office, Washington, D. C. (DHEW (PHS) Publication No. 017-001-00416-2).

US Department of Health, Education and Welfare (1979b). *Smoking and Health: A Report of the Surgeon General*, US Government Printing Office, Washington, D.C. (DHEW (PHS) Publication No. 79-50066).

US Department of Health and Human Services (1980). *The Health Consequences of Smoking for Women, A Report of the Surgeon General, 1980*, Office of Smoking and Health, Rockville, Md.

US Department of Health and Human Services (1982). *The Health Consequences of Smoking: Cancer, A Report of the Surgeon General*, Office on Smoking and Health, Rockville, Md (DHHS (PHS) Publication No. 82-51079).

US Department of Health and Human Services (1984). *The Health Consequences of Smoking Chronic Obstructive Lung Disease, A Report of the Surgeon General, 1984*, Office on Smoking and Health, Rockville, MD (DHHS (PHS) Publication No. 84-50205).

US Department of Health and Human Services (1986). *The Health Consequences of Using Smokeless Tobacco*, US Government Printing Office, Washington, D.C. (NIH Publication No. 86-2874).

US Department of Health and Human Services (1988). *The Health Consequences of Smoking Nicotine Addiction. A Report of the Surgeon General*, US Government Printing Office, Washington, D.C. (DHHS Publication No. (CDC) 88-8406).

US Public Health Service (1964). *Smoking and Health: Public Service Report of the Advisory Committee to the Surgeon General of the Public Health Service*, US Government Printing Office, Washington, D.C. (PHS Publication No. 1103).

Wack, J. T. and Rodin, J. (1982). Smoking and its effects on body weight and the system of caloric regulation, *American Journal of Clinical Nutrition*, **35**, 366–80.

Wankel, L. M. (1984). Decision-making and social support strategies for increasing exercise adherence, *Journal of Cardiac Rehabilitation*, **4**, 124–35.

Wankel, L. M., Yardley, J. F. and Graham, J. (1985). The effects of motivational interventions upon the exercise adherence of high and low self-motivated adults, *Canadian Journal of Applied Sport Sciences*, **10**, 147–56.

Warburton, D. M. (1987). The functions of smoking. In W. R. Martin, G. R. Van Loon, E. T. Iwamoto and L. Davis (eds) *Advances in Behavioral Biology*, vol. 31, Plenum, New York, pp. 51–62.

Warburton, D. M. and Wesnes, K. (1978). Individual differences in smoking and attentional performance. In R. E. Thornton (ed.) *Smoking Behaviour*, Churchill-Livingstone, Edinburgh, pp. 19–43.

Ward, A. and Morgan, W. P. (1984). Adherence patterns of healthy men and women enrolled in an adult exercise program, *Journal of Cardiac Rehabilitation*, **4**, 143–52.

Wesnes, K. (1987). Nicotine increases mental efficiency: But how? In W. R. Martin, G. R. Van Loon, E. T. Iwamoto, L. Davis (eds) *Advances in Behavioral Biology*, vol. 31, Plenum, New York, pp. 63–80.

Wetterer, A. and von Troschke, J. (1986). *Smoker Motivation: A Review of Contemporary Literature*, Springer-Verlag, New York.

Wewers, M. E. (1988). The role of postcessation factors in tobacco abstinence: Stressful events and coping responses, *Addictive Behaviors*, **13**, 297–302.

Wills, T. A. (1986). Stress and coping in early adolescence: Relationships to substance use in urban school samples, *Health Psychology*, **5**, 503–29.

Yates, A. (1987). Eating disorders and long-distance running: The ascetic condition, *Integrative Psychiatry*, **5**, 201–4.

Yates, A., Leehey, K. and Shisslak, C. M. (1983). Running: An analogue of anorexia?, *New England Journal of Medicine*, **308**, 251–5.

Young, R. J. and Ismail, A. H.(1977). Comparison of selected physiological and personality variables in regular and nonregular adult male exercisers, *Research Quarterly*, **48**, 617–22.

Zinman, B. and Vranic, M. (1985). Diabetes and exercise, *Medical Clinics of North America*, **69**, 145–57.

PART V

Some Outstanding Issues

Chapter 11

Stress, Health, and Well-being: The Role of Individual Differences

Stanislav V. Kasl, Yale University School of Medicine, and
Stephen R. Rapp, Wake Forest University

INTRODUCTION

The purpose of this chapter is to provide an overview of some of the research practice issues (both conceptual and methodological) which arise when one considers the broad topic of the role of individual differences in the research domain which links stress to indicators of health and well-being. This chapter is *not* intended as an evaluative, integrating commentary on the various contributions to this volume. Rather, we wish to consider a number of issues from a perspective which is broader than any one individual chapter could undertake; in effect, we do not wish to be confined by the boundaries of this topic implicitly suggested by the collective coverage of the various chapters. Thus, to the extent that our approach to the topic is based on our own evaluations of this research area, and not on the coverage of the different chapters, we may in fact be offering a somewhat different view of this domain than was visualized by the editors when they defined the various contributions they intended to request. Clearly, this volume is not like a textbook (e.g. introduction to social science statictics) where there is wide consensus on what needs to be included and how the various topics ought to be handled. Rather, identifying what the issues are—recognizing them and giving them some degree of explication—is part of the intellectual struggle of presenting this topic in an edited volume such as this.

We are somewhat uneasy about the title of this volume, *Personality and Stress: Individual Differences in the Stress Process*, as providing us with the optimal springboard for our discussion. Since in the course of our explorations we will inevitably comment on the meaning of such terms as "personality trait" and "individual differences", and will attempt clarifications and distinctions, then we find it highly desirable to anchor solidly our discussion to other

Personality and Stress: Individual Differences in the Stress Process. Edited by C.L. Cooper and R. Payne
© 1991 John Wiley & Sons Ltd

concepts which are represented by clear, noncontroversial, and agreed-upon conceptual and operational definitions. But anchoring our discussion to the concept of "stress", the remaining term in the title, left us with the hopeless feeling of an insuperable handicap, for stress continues to be a most difficult and unmanageable term. The recent exchange between Lazarus (1990) and some of the commentators (e.g. Ben-Porath and Tellegen, 1990; Breznitz, 1990; Brown, 1990; Costa and McCrae, 1990; Krohne, 1990; Moos and Swindle, 1990) clearly demonstrates the many unresolved issues: is stress (to be conceptualized as) a stimulus condition, a response, or some complex transactional term or process? Is stress necessarily subjective, or objective, or what? Are there unique criteria for defining stress (either as a stimulus or as a response)?

Given these difficulties with stress, we propose to center the discussion of individual differences not on stress alone, but on the stress–disease association. This is, after all, one of the primary payoffs in studying stress. Such a shift enables us to adopt an etiological perspective in which both stress and individual differences are seen as potential risk factors for, or antecedents to, health outcomes. This moves the concept of stress into the category of a stimulus condition (i.e. a stressor) in relation to the health outcome, but does not rule out using stress also as an acute response (i.e. distress) which can be antecedent to a more distal health outcome. Of course, when rather similar measures (e.g. those based on self-reports of symptoms) are used to assess the stressor, the acute distress, the distal health outcome, as well as the trait or individual-difference variable, then no amount of redefinition of the task for discussion will enable us to clearly separate different concepts from each other.

HEALTH AS A FUNCTION OF PERSONAL AND ENVIRONMENTAL CHARACTERISTICS

Fundamentally, there are two classes of variables available to us to understand and explain health, well-being, and behavior: characteristics of the person and characteristics of the environment. Within the social sciences, major research programs such as the one at the Institute for Social Research, University of Michigan, have utilized this formulation (French and Kahn, 1962) and have elaborated on it in many landmark studies, particulalry those of the occupational setting (e.g. Caplan et al., 1975; Kahn et al., 1964). Within public health, it is more common to consider an ecological system which includes three classes of variables, rather than two: agent, host, and environment (e.g. Susser, 1973). However, since the vast majority of the stress and disease studies in psychosomatic medicine, psychosocial epidemiology, behavioral medicine, medical sociology, and health psychology are either concerned with chronic diseases or infectious diseases in which the separate characteristics of the agent are not viewed as relevant, then it still remains true that the etiological dynamics are seen as a function of two classes of variables, host and environment.

It is true, of course, that in some research programs and some theoretical formulations (e.g. The Person–Environment Fit approach; French, Caplan, and Van Harrison, 1982), the interaction between specific characteristics of the person and specific characteristics of the environment takes on such an important and unique role that this interactive term might be viewed as a third, separate class of determinants.

The fact that health is seen as a function of characteristics of the person and of the environment does not mean that over the years actual studies have implemented this orientation in an even-handed and comprehensive fashion. A number of authors (e.g. Costa and McCrae, 1987a; Holroyd and Coyne, 1987; Suls and Rittenhouse, 1987) have suggested that there has been a recent (1980s) resurgence of interest in personality variables as determinants of health status, and that this has followed a period in which environmental influences on health held center stage (1960s and 1970s). Furthermore, the early beginnings of psychosomatic medicine (1940s and 1950s) are seen as a period in which person characteristics also dominated the etiological picture, but the present resurgence of interest in personality is not interpreted as a return to early psychosomatic formulations.

This kind of historical reconstruction has very limited accuracy or value. For example, it is much more appropriate to trace the research popularity (if not the actual bandwagon effect) of specific instruments (e.g. the Holmes and Rahe [1967] list of stressful life events) and of specific concepts (e.g. social support, Type A behavior, hardiness). Then any secular changes in relative emphasis on personality vs. environmental characteristics are better seen as derivative of the aggregation of poupularity of these specific research areas, rather than as a function of changes in programmatic commitment of investigators to personal vs. environmental characteristics as a class of etiologically important variables. Furthermore, there is generally a big difference between the theoretical formulation which embeds a construct and the actual execution of studies which utilize the construct; the latter may represent a drastic impoverishment of the theory. For example, the classical formulations of etiology in Alexander (1950) focused on specific intrapsychic conflicts, but did not neglect the situations which would arouse those conflicts. Thus, the early study of the etiology of duodenal ulcer (Mirsky, 1958) remains a model of research design which utilizes psychomatic (psychoanalytic) formulations, uses a prospective approach, and achieves a good balance of biological risk factors and personal and environmental characteristics; however, such a study was more the exception than the rule for research on psychosomatic etiology of disease. Similarly, while Type A behavior is conceptualized as the result of a predisposition stimulated by appropriate environmental challenges— Friedman and Rosenman (1974) state that "an environmental challenge must always serve as the fuse for this" behavior pattern—the actual studies have tended to treat it as a stable personality characteristic which by itself is an adequate predictor of coronary heart disease.

It is also important to take into consideration the theoretical and operational origins of a particular personality variable which has been utilized as a possible risk factor for physical illness. Many variables come to us from personality theory and are assessed by standard, often used instruments; the Califiornia Personality Inventory, the MMPI, and the Cattell 16 Personality Factors are several such examples. Traits in these instruments generally do not have an explicit theoretical link to health outcomes and no relevant environmental conditions are specified in their theoretical explication which might apply to the study of health outcomes. Thus these trait measures are very likely to end up being used as risk factors in isolation from environmental conditions, though not necessarily in isolation from established biological risk factors for that particular disease (e.g. Ostfeld et al., 1964). However, there are other personality variables, notably Type A behavior and Hardiness, which were formulated as stable characteritics of people which are intended to have some explanatory power in accounting for health outcomes; that is, their origins are not in personality theory (or, God forbid, factor analysis) but in health psychology, behavioral medicine, and psychosocial epidemiology. Their theoretical formulations explicitly target health outcomes and generally include the hypothesized additive and/or interactive contribution of environmental variables or exposures. This tends to promote a broader look at psychosocial determinants of disease, including a better balance of person variables and environmental conditions.

One interesting consequence of the above distinction is that when the construct validity of a measure is heavily dependent on the prediction of health outcomes, then the measure of the construct—and the construct itself— are likely to be challenged when less than satisfactory empirical evidence about health status linkages accumulates. Thus, recent research on Type A shows many attempts to fine-tune the construct and the measurement, and to identify the truly pathogenic components (e.g. Dembroski and Costa, 1987; Houston and Snyder, 1989; Siegman and Dembroski, 1989). Similarly, criticisms of the Hardiness concept and measure (e.g. Funk and Houston, 1987; Hull, Van Treuren, and Virnelli, 1987) have been partly based on the state of the evidence linking it to health outcomes. However, when construct validity of the trait measure is based on psychological theory and on linkages to other traits and other behaviors, then the lack of an association between the trait and health status outcomes does not challenge the construct and its measurement. In fact, fine-tuning the construct and its measurement specifically to enhance the empirical linkage to health status should be seen as inappropriate, since health status is not part of the nomological net surrounding the construct.

It is also important that trait measures allow for the study of specific bio-behavioral associations and thus permit the eventual establishment of linkages to biological mechanisms of disease causation (Krantz and Hedges, 1987). Here again, trait measures which come to us from psychological theory make this task of determining the underlying biological mechanisms more difficult than trait measures based on concepts formulated for the exploration of the psychosocial etiology of disease. Incidentally, the need to pay more attention to biological mechanisms applies equally well to characteristics of the psychosocial environment; for example, the whole research domain on social support and health can profit greatly from just such an emphasis.

The viewpoint that health is a function of personal and environmental characteristics gives rise to a number of questions and issues which we want to address in the remainder of this chapter. Two sets of issues will be discussed. One set concerns the need to make distinctions among variables, our ability to do so, and the reasons why such distinctions may or may not be useful; the distinctions to be made involve both the separation of personal characteristics from environmental variables, as well as within types of personal characteristics. The second set of issues will deal with some methodological implications of research efforts trying to clarify the role of individual differences in the stress–disease association.

WHAT KINDS OF INDIVIDUAL DIFFERENCES ARE THERE AND HOW DO THEY DIFFER FROM ENVIRONMENTAL EXPOSURE VARIABLES?

Suppose we are dealing with a strong prospective epidemiological design: (1) a broadly representative cohort initially free of target disease, (2) baseline data collection which includes psychosocial and biomedical variables, (3) complete monitoring of incident (initial) events of disease during specified follow-up, and (4) assessment of "hard" disease endpoints (e.g. myocardial infarction and sudden death for coronary heart disease). If we are dealing with a purely biostatistical model of predictors, we would enter all potential predictors and the logistic regression, or survival analysis (time till events), would identify the significant contribution of a subset of variables, where the contribution of each is independent of the others in the model. Withing the limits of this approach (i.e. how well can we predict the outcome with some multiple risk formula), we do not need to agonize over the distinction between person characteristics (individual differences) and environmental exposures. However, with any attempts to sort out relationships among the baseline variables in order to build hierarchical models which might permit assumptions about causal priorities and which might reveal direct and indirect effects, we are confronted with the necessity of having a more precise understanding of our variables, their temporal location and their probable manner of influence. This applies, of course, to the biomedical variables as well as the psychosocial ones, but the task is usually more difficult within the set of psychosocial variables, or with the broader set that combines both biomedical and psychosocial predictors.

As soon as one attempts to come to grips with the distinction between person characteristics and environmental exposure variables, one realizes how easily the distinction becomes blurred and somewhat unworkable. However, the frequent difficulty of clearly separating the two types of variables is only part of the problem; we also need to be able to think through the consequences—for etiological interpretations and for prevention and/or intervention—of not being able to make such a distinction in particular instances, or of misclassifying the status of a variable.

The issue is that person characteristics can index primarily an environmental exposure and that, conversely, environmental exposures can indicate primarily the role of personal characteristics. Consider, for example, the apparently straightforward socio-demographic variable, race. It is, of course, viewed as an attribute of a person and in most studies the investigator goes no further than trying to disentangle it from socio-economic correlates, especially education and income. However, being Black in the USA is also a broad indication of specific exposures and experiences, particularly so when one partials out general effects of low social class, which would be shared with poor whites. Therefore, any particular association with race can be seen either as a function of race-linked differences in personal predispositions or as a result of the specific exposures. (In fact, public health and social science research on race differences in the USA has become somewhat politicized and the Black community has criticized investigators for their great readiness to accept the predisposition interpretation.) For example, the fact that Black adolescents have a lower sense of internal control (e.g. Gurin et al., 1969) may be seen as a stable personal predisposition or as a cumulative impact of chronic exposures. It might also be noted that to a great extent the above discussion regarding race could be repeated with respect to other "simple" (but in fact quite opaque) socio-demographic characteristics, such as gender and age.

There is something quite unsatisfactory about making the above observations and stopping the discussion there. Fundamentally, if a person characteristic, such as race, is strongly related to chronic exposures which have chronic consequences, such that the impact of exposure in effect becomes a trait-like predisposition, then why do we need to be concerned with distinguishing environmental variables from personal predispositions? (In effect, the discussion threatens to drift toward the issue of the social origins of traits.) There are several partial answers: (1) If the effect of the exposure is reversible when exposure ends—even though in the natural setting the exposure is typically chronic—then the interpretation that this is a trait-like consequence of exposure is inappropriate. (2) Investigators may become more sensitized to the need for additional statistical controls (above and beyond the usual ones, such as education and income), provided relevant exposures can be measured; this will necessarily alter the "residual" meaning of the characteristic of the person, such as race, and may alter the pattern of associations. (3) In conceptual model building, such as that involved in LISREL analysis, misspecification of a variable naturally alters the model which we may accept as compatible with the findings. Insensitivity to the issue of what environemntal exposure variables may underlie a person characteristic, such as race, will lead to a possibly incorrect assumption that race is temporally antecedent to most other variables in the model.

The issue of underlying stable person characteristics masquerading as apparent environmental exposure variables is the opposite issue to the one just discussed. The recent discussions of the role of such variables as neuroticism and negative affectivity (e.g. Costa and McCrae, 1987b, 1990; Krohne, 1990; McCrae, 1990; Schroeder and Costa, 1984; Watson, 1990; Watson and Clark, 1984; Watson and Pennebaker, 1989) has helped sensitize many investigators to the various possible ways a general stable trait can influence the underlying etiological dynamics in stress–disease studies. There are several ways in which a stable trait may be the underlying, etiologically significant variable behind an association between environmental exposure and health:

(1) *Self-selection:* certain types of individuals may select themselves into certain kinds of existing settings (e.g. Type A behavior and occupational setting);
(2) *Changing the environment:* certain types of individuals may alter the environment in which they live, particularly the social environment; thus, differences in level of social support may be a function of differences in social skills, affiliative tendencies, and neuroticism (Heller, 1979; Henderson, Byrne, and Duncan-Jones, 1981);
(3) *Appraising the environment:* subjective evaluations of environmental conditions can be primarily a function of stable predispositions, such as negative affectivity, positive affectivity (Watson and Pennebaker, 1989), and dispositional optimism (Scheier and Carver, 1987).

It should be noted that the strategy of including objective measurements of the environmental exposure does nothing to eliminate the role of stable predispositions in the first two of the above three examples.

Thus far we have discussed issues in distinguishing characteristics of the person from those of the environment. There is also considerable difficulty in developing satisfactory distinctions among types of characteristics of the person—that is, types of individual-difference variables. One important distinction is between: (a) the view of traits as "transsituational 'situation blind' action tendencies" and (b) specific "if S, then R dispositions"—that is, dispositions to make certain responses R under certain conditions S (Ben-Porath and Tellegen, 1990). When Lazarus and his colleagues (e.g. Folkman et al., 1986) in effect reject the trait approach to stress and coping, they have in mind the broad notion of traits as transsituational response tendencies. However, as Ben-Porath and Tellegen (1990) point out, the second conception of traits is fully sensitive to the situational context which is so important in the Lazarus approach. One would suppose that the primary difference between the two views is one of specificity–generality of the trait in question. It is interesting to note, however, that measures of rather broadly conceived traits, such as neuroticism and extroversion, show systematic relationships to coping (e.g. Costa and McCrae, 1989; McCrae and Costa, 1986); thus it is not just some narrowly defined trait which influences coping.

Individual differences in how people react are presumably part of the domain of individual differences which are of interest in our discussion of the stress–disease research area. However, such reactions are generally seen as being apart from traits, such as in the state–trait distinction (Spielberger, Gorsuch, and Lushene, 1970). Unfortunately, it is difficult to separate the concept of a trait from the notion of a reaction (whether acute or chronic) on the basis of measurement alone. The fact is that while traits may be conceptualized as predispositions, they are seldom assessed with content-unique items intended to get at predispositions; what is measured are reactions, such as symptoms, mood, and so on. The state–trait distinction is sometimes accomplished by the most simplistic procedures, such as asking for self-reports characterizing previous week vs. previous year (or "usual times"). The whole concept of negative affectivity is based on interpreting a body of findings involving a number of similar measures; it is an inference. There was no measurement breakthrough involved in which a predisposition is measured independently of the reactions of interest. Thus, measures of negative affectivity reflect acute reactions, chronic reactions, and trait-like predispositions, and the relative proportions of these components are difficult to determine across individuals and across life circumstances in which the individuals find themselves.

The above issues translate into major research difficulties when one is attempting to carry out observational longitudinal studies of mental health status changes. Depue and Monroe (1986) offer a fine analysis of the research difficulties one encounters when: (1) one is using a non-specific measurement approach to disorder; (2) one has the usual heterogeneous sample, including those with chronic disorder, prolonged life difficulties, acute stressors, and high scores on neuroticism or negative affectivity (if measured); (3) data on disorder and events (life circumstances) are measured over time but not sufficiently frequently (e.g. once a year or less often as is the usual case); and (4) one is trying to disentangle stress-initiation effects on disorder from stress-maintenance effects. The authors strongly endorse the inclusion of individual-difference variables in life stress research but unlike others who have made similar recommendations, they note that "a great deal more conceptual and measurement work is required in this area" (Depue and Monroe, 1986, p. 48).

If stress and disease research tends to underestimate the importance of stable traits and individual differences in general, this is particularly true of biological variables. For example, psychosocial formulations of health consequences of shiftwork (e.g. Rentos and Shepard, 1976; Tasto et al., 1978) do not seem adequate and the role of biomedical variables looms large (Winget, Hughes, and LaDou, 1978). Specific complaints, such as those regarding sleep, depend partly on individual differences in diurnal variations in levels of activity, such as preferring high levels of activity in the morning vs. in the evening (Torsvall and Akerstedt, 1980). Psychomatic complaints associated with night-work appear to be related to changes in serum gastrin levels as well as to a stable trait variable, neuroticism (Akerstedt and Theorell, 1976).

Among biologically based individual differences, the concept of psychophysiological reactivity looms particularly important (e.g. Krantz and Manuck, 1984; Manuck, Kasprowicz, and Muldoon, 1990), even though prospective longitudinal data linking reactivity to disease are still rare (e.g. Menkes et al., 1989). Reactivity, of course, is not purely a stable individual-difference variable but is usually a function of the experimental situation and person characteristics, such as hostility (Suarez and Williams, 1989). When one looks closely at reactivity, the picture becomes quite complicated. In the program of research by Schneiderman and his colleagues (e.g. Ironson et al., 1989; Saab et al., in press; Tischenkel et al., 1989), one finds that while reactivity is stable—in the sense of repeatability of amount of change when faced with the same experimental challenge—there is a good deal of specificity:

(1) reactivity is associated with gender and race;
(2) reactivity is rather task-specific;
(3) total reactivity (such as blood pressure change) may be the same but the underlying mechanisms (cardiac output vs. peripheral resistance) may differ by person characteristics such as race;
(4) ambulatory blood pressure (i.e. outside of the laboratory) may be predicted from reactivity to some experimental tasks but not others.

In short, the notion of individual differences in physiological reactivity representing an important marker for pathogenic processes in disease development remains promising, but the high specificity (fractionation) of this "trait" makes it difficult to know just what to measure in what settings so that there may be some payoff in a prospective study of disease.

The adequacy of our understanding of the role of individual differences is heavily dependent on the data collection schedules. Specifically, a mixture of idiographic (ipsative) and nomothetic data collection (people over many occasions) yields valuable information. For example, Lazarus (1990) has found that the frequency of hassles (on the Hassles Scale) is highly stable over time and this has led him to conclude that it "acted much like a trait" (p. 11). One would presume that the high association of hassles with neuroticism would make it difficult to continue to use it as a clearly separate and separable construct. Similarly, a repeated measurement design by Luborsky et al., (1976) in their study of recurrent herpes labialis (RHL) and moods in nursing students was able to show that (a) a general unhappiness factor on the Clyde Mood Scale predicted total frequency of RHL during one year follow-up, but (b) daily mood fluctuations were not related to onset of any particular episode of RHL. Thus, the etiological factor was a trait-like variable, rather than the acute state of the person. Somewhat different results were reported by Conway et al., (1981): daily ratings of stress and daily consumption of cigarettes showed an association, but monthly (aggregated) data on these two variables showed no association. In this study the authors computed, for each individual, an intraperson correlation between stress and substance use; these revealed important individual differences in tendency to increase or decrease habitual substance consumption in response to varying levels of stress. De-Longis, Folkman, and Lazarus (1988) reported a wide range of intraindividual correlations (high positive to high negative) between hassle score and next-day number of somatic symptoms. It needs to be noted that neither the Conway nor the Delongis study established that these individual differences represented a stable person characteristic; for that, they would need to have another time series in order to show that, for example, those individuals for whom the two variables were negatively correlated once were then negatively correlated again. If this were to be the case, however, this kind of a variation in intraperson associations between stressors and outcomes would be a powerful reminder of the need to study individual differences in our general approach to stress and health. Thus far the documentation of stability of individual differences is adequate only for fairly general personality traits (e.g. Conley, 1985; Costa and McCrae, 1988; West and Graziano, 1989).

SOME METHODOLOGICAL CONSIDERATIONS

It should be abundantly clear from the previous comments that the inclusion of traits and individual-difference variables in studies of stress and health has two broad benefits: firstly, it enables us to improve our prediction of health status changes because our base of psychosocial predictors becomes more comprehensive; and second, it enhances our chances of arriving at the correct interpretation of the underlying dynamics and mechanisms, particularly in sorting out the role of the various psychosocial predictors in relation to each other. The latter point is a methodological one and we wish to amplify it with some additional comments.

There are a number of methodological points which are quite standard and which need not be elaborately discussed in this context. For example, within psychometric theory and practice which deals with adequacy of tests and measurements, we have classical notions of reliability and validity (including convergent and discriminant validity) which provide reasonably straightforward guidelines. Thus there is no need to rehash one more time such issues as the multiplicity of measures for the Type A behavior construct, how well or poorly they correlate, which ones relate to health outcomes, and so on.

Similarly, within epidemiology we have widely available methodological guidelines which discuss such issues as: (a) the desirability of prospective designs in which an initially healthy cohort is followed; (b) the need for an unbiased detection of the endpoints; (c) the measurement of endpoints which is uncontaminated by biased self-reports, by differences in medical care, and by subjective clinical judgments which may be influenced by unknown variables; (d) the need to identify potential confounders and to control for their influence in the analysis. Thus, there would seem to be no need to rehash one more time, for example, the importance of longitudinal designs, particularly when one does not fully understand how little may actually be accomplished by adding a second data collection point to a cross-sectional sample (see Kasl, 1983, 1985).

Many of the relevant issues have been covered in a recent volume on stress methodology (Kasl and Cooper, 1987) and a recent chapter on indvidual differences (Payne, 1988).

There are three issues which appear to us to call for some additional commentary. The first concerns negative affectivity and neuroticism (e.g. Costa and McCrae, 1987b; McCrae, 1990; Watson and Clark, 1984; Watson and Pennebaker, 1989). There is no question that the fundamental points of this whole literature need to be made, to be heard, and to be accepted by stress investigators: (a) there is a likely source of influence on both measurements of diverse variables as well as on etiological processes themselves (no matter how measured), which (b) appears to be a stable personal characteristic (trait) and (c) which can seriously distort our understanding of what the dynamics are when it remains unmeasured and uncontrolled. At the same time, it appears to us that soon this message may become too loud and too broad, given the evidence on which it is based. The negative affectivity (NA) issue threatens to dominate the picture of individual differences, stress, and health, and we can look forward to a plethora of studies in which the only innovation is the inclusion of some measure of NA and in which the inevitable conclusion is: it's just neuroticism or NA (e.g. Smith et al., 1989). The stress field is too susceptible to the bandwagon effect and after 20 years of cross-sectional studies correlating stressful life events and symptoms, we may look forward to

20 more years of cross-sectional studies correlating stressful life events and symptoms, but now also partialing out the effects of NA.

A few modest suggestions can be made. First, we do not yet have an adequate direct measure of NA as a disposition, the content of which would be uniquely different from measures of distress, dysphoric mood, and symptoms. Second, because of possible problems with measurement, the full statistical partialing out of the role of NA may be an undesirably conservative worst case scenario. Third, the assumption that NA is a stable trait "locates" this variable in time as antecedent to most other variables one studies in a typical stress and disease project (e.g. when sorting out causal priorities in cross-sectional data). We need to move beyond making mere assumptions and study the origins of NA and of the influences on it. Fourth, we need studies which more explicitly, more directly, and under a variety of controlled and uncontrolled circumstances, address the presumed or postulated role of NA, e.g. its influence on self-reports, such as of stressful life events, or its influence on social processes, such as seeking and receiving social support. Finally, if NA is to be routinely included as a potential confounder, then it would seem quite desirable to include other trait-like measures, such as positive affectivity (Watson and Pennebaker, 1989). This should provide a useful comparison and may possibly reduce the concern (expressed in the second point, above) with over-adjustment.

The second issue about which we wish to comment very briefly concerns the possibility that this volume and our own chapter will be interpreted as giving the message that greater concern with individual differences, and their inclusion in studies of stress and health, is by itself an adequate, sufficient strategy for meaningfully improving stress research. This is not our intended message. We believe that greater commitment to individual differences as a class of variables in stress research should go hand in hand with greater attention to, first, aspects of research design and, second, to the possible underlying biological mechanisms of causation. Some possible design issues: (1) creating homogeneous subgroups of subjects, such as with respect to baseline health and mental health characteristics (including history) so that the subsequent course of health status changes may be more clearly interpretable; (2) selecting subjects not to represent the total community but to be representative of those who have been exposed to specific situations and experience; (3) scheduling data collection in relation to the onset of exposure so that one maximizes the chances of detecting the various phases of impact and adaptation. Elsewhere (Kasl, 1983) these issues were discussed under the general recommendation of searching for opportunities to carry out "natural experiments". The issue of greater sensitivity to underlying biological mechanisms means that instead of blindly including some selected personality trait measures, we should also attempt to formulate explicitly a plausible pathway of influence. This will suggest to us additional variables which need to be assessed (e.g.

health habits, medications, medical care received) and, possibly, when they need to be assessed and how.

The final point we wish to make is that the notion of individual differences, and what variables might be included in future stress–health studies, is almost completely open-ended. Certainly, the list could be, and should be, much bigger than is represented by the coverage of this volume. In general, what is reasonably well represented are socio-demographic variables, personality traits, and health-related behaviors. Clearly underrepresented are individual differences which reflect skills and abilities, and needs and motives. This is a limitation inherited from the general stress field but need not be continued as we increase our commitment to the study of individual differences. In fact, it might be argued that our notions about relevant potential individual differences are exclusively grounded in the psychology of the person. However, since stress research is concerned with environmental variables as well, these come to represent a new source of formulations for potential individual-difference variables which may turn out to be important. For example, the large and extremely active research area on social support and health has very little in it which would represent specifically relevant individual-difference variables such as need for emotional support, preferences for types of support, tolerance for social isolation, beliefs about reciprocity of social support, and so on. Similarly, the literature on crowding and health has pretty much failed to develop any individual-difference variables which would be specifically coordinated to the study of health effects of this environmental exposure. And as stress researchers begin to study new environments altogether, such as automation and electronic equipment in white collar jobs, we may look forward to conceptualizing and trying to measure individual-difference variables which did not "exist" a short time ago.

REFERENCES

Akerstedt, T. and Theorell, T. (1976). Exposure to night work: serum gastrin reactions, psychosomatic complaints and personality variables, *Journal of Psychosomatic Research*, **20**, 479–84.

Alexander, F. (1950). *Psychosomatic Medicine*, Norton, New York.

Ben-Porath, Y. S. and Tellegen, A. (1990). A place for traits in stress research, *Psychological Inquiry*, **1**, 14–17.

Breznitz, S. (1990). Theory-based stress measurement? Not yet, *Psychological Inquiry*, **1**, 17–19.

Brown, G. W. (1990). What about the real world? Hassles and Richard Lazarus, *Psychological Inquiry*, **1**, 19–22.

Caplan, R. D., Cobb, S., French, J. R. P., Jr., Van Harrison, R., and Pinneau, S. R., Jr. (1975). *Job Demands and Worker Health*, NIOSH, CDC, PHS, USDHEW, Washington, DC.

Conley, J. J. (1985). Longitudinal stability of personality traits: A multitrait-multimethod-multioccasion analysis, *Journal of Personality and Social Psychology,* **49**, 1266–82.

Conway, T. L., Vickers, R. R., Jr., Ward, H. W., and Rahe, R. H. (1981). Occupational stress and variation in cigarette, coffee, and alcohol consumption, *Journal of Health and Social Behavior,* **22** 155–65.

Costa, P. T., Jr. and McCrae, R. R. (1987a). Personality assessment in psychosomatic medicine. In T. N. Wise (ed.) *Advances in Psychosomatic Medicine,* Vol. 17, Karger, Basel, pp. 71–82.

Costa, P. T., Jr. and McCrae, R. R. (1987b). Neuroticism, somatic complaints and disease: Is the bark worse than the bite?, *Journal of Personality,* **55**, 299–316.

Costa, P. T., Jr. and McCrae, R. R. (1988). Personality in adulthood: A six-year longitudinal study of self-reports and spouse ratings on the NEO Personality Inventory, *Journal of Personality and Social Psychology,* **54**, 853–63.

Costa, P. T., Jr. and McCrae, R. R. (1989). Personality, stress and coping: Some lessons from a decade of research. In K. S. Markides and C. L. Cooper (eds) *Aging, Stress, and Health,* Wiley, Chichester, pp. 269–85.

Costa, P. T., Jr. and McCrae, R. R. (1990). Personality: Another hidden factor in stress research, *Psychological Inquiry,* **1**, 22–4.

De Longis, A., Folkman, S., and Lazarus, R. S. (1988). Hassles, health and mood: Psychological and social resources as mediators, *Journal of Personality and Social Psychology,* **54**, 486–95.

Dembroski, T. M. and Costa, P. T., Jr. (1987). Coronary prone behavior: Components of the Type A pattern and hostility, *Journal of Personality,* **55**, 211–35.

Depue, R. A. and Monroe, S. M. (1986). Conceptualization and measurement of human disorder in life stress research: The problem of chronic disturbance, *Psychological Bulletin,* **99**, 36–51.

Folkman, S., Lazarus, R. S., Dunkel-Schetter, C., DeLongis, A., and Gruen, R. J. (1986). Dynamics of stressful encounter: Cognitive appraisal, coping, and encounter outcomes, *Journal of Personality and Social Psychology,* **50**, 992–1003.

French, J. R. P., Jr. and Kahn, R. L. (1962). A programmatic approach to studying the industrial environment and mental health, *Journal of Social Issues,* **18**(3), 1–47.

French, J. R. P., Jr., Caplan, R. D. and Van Harrison, R. (1982). *The Mechanism of Job Stress and Strain,* Wiley, Chichester.

Friedman, M. D. and Rosenman, R. H. (1974). *Type A Behavior and Your Heart,* Knopf, New York.

Funk, S. C. and Houston, B. K. (1987). A critical analysis of the Hardiness Scale's validity and utility, *Journal of Personality and Social Psychology,* **53**, 572–6.

Gurin, P., Gurin, G., Lao, R. C., and Beattie, M. (1969). Internal–external control in the motivational dynamics of negro youth, *Journal of Social Issues,* **25**, 29–53.

Heller, K. (1979). The effects of social support: Prevention and treatment implications. In A. P. Goldstein and F. H. Kanfer (eds) *Maximizing Treatment Gains: Transfer Enhancement in Psychotherapy,* Academic Press, New York, pp. 353–82.

Henderson, S., Byrne, D. G., and Duncan-Jones, P. (1981). *Neurosis and the Social Environment,* Academic Press, New York.

Holmes, T. H. and Rahe, R. H. (1967). The Social Readjustment Rating Scale, *Journal of Psychosomatic Research,* **11**, 213–18.

Holroyd, K. A. and Coyne, J. (1987). Personality and health in the 1980s: Psychosomatic medicine revisited?, *Journal of Personality,* **55**, 359–75.

Houston, B. K. and Snyder, C. R. (eds) (1989). *Type A Behavior Pattern: Research Theory and Intervention,* Wiley, New York.

Hull, J. G., Van Treuren, R. R., and Virnelli, S. (1987). Hardiness and health: A critique and alternative approach, *Journal of Personality and Social Psycholgoy,* **53,** 518–30.

Ironson, G. H., Gellman, M. D., Spitzer, S. B., Llabre, M. M., Pasin, R. D., Weidler, D. J., and Schneiderman, N. (1989). Predicting home and work blood pressure measurements from resting baselines and laboratory, reactivity in Black and White Americans, *Psychophysiology,* **26,** 174–84.

Kahn, R. L., Wolfe, D. M., Quinn, R. P., Snoek, J. D. and Rosenthal, R. A. (1964). *Organizational Stress: Studies in Role Conflict and Ambiguity,* Wiley, New York.

Kasl, S. V. (1983). Pursuing the link between stressful life experiences and diseases: A time for re-appraisal. In C. L. Cooper (ed.) *Stress Research: Issues for the Eighties,* Wiley, Chichester, pp. 79–102.

Kasl, S. V. (1985). Environmental exposure and disease: An epidemiological perspective on some methodological issues in health psychology and behavioral medicine. In J. E. Singer and A. Baum (eds) *Advances in Environmental Psychology,* vol. 5, Erlbaum, Hillsdale, NJ, pp. 119–46.

Kasl, S. V. and Cooper, C. L. (eds) (1987). *Stress and Health: Issues in Research Methodology,* Wiley, Chichester.

Krantz, D. S. and Hedges, S. M. (1987). Some cautions for research on personality and health, *Journal of Personality,* **55,** 351–7.

Krantz, D. S. and Manuck, S. B (1984). Acute psychophysiological reactivity and risk of cardiovascular disease. A review and methodological critique, *Psychological Bulletin,* **96,** 435–64.

Krohne, H. W. (1990). Personality as a mediator between objective events and their subjective representation, *Psychological Inquiry,* **1,** 26–9.

Lazarus, R. S. (1990). Theory-based stress measurement, *Psychological Inquiry,* **1,** 3–13.

Luborsky, L., Mintz, J., Brightman, V. J., and Katcher, A. H. (1976). Herpes Simplex virus and moods: A longitudinal study, *Journal of Psychosomatic Research,* **20,** 543–48.

McCrae, R. R. (1990). Controlling neuroticism in the measurement of stress, *Stress Medicine,* **6,** 237–41.

McCrae, R. R. and Costa, P. T., Jr. (1986). Personality, coping and coping effectiveness in an adult sample, *Journal of Personality,* **54,** 385–405.

Manuck, S. B., Kasprowicz, A. L., and Muldoon, M. F. (1990). Beahviorally-evoked cardiovascular reactivity and hypertension: Conceptual issues and potential associations, *Annals of Behavioral Medicine,* **12,** 17–29.

Menkes, M. S., Matthews, K. A., Krantz, D. S., Lindberg, L. A., Qaquish, B., Liang, K., Thomas, C. B., and Pearson, T. A. (1989). Cardiovascular reactivity to the old pressor test as a predictor of hypertension, *Hypertension,* **14,** 524–30.

Mirsky, I. A. (1958). Physiologic, psychologic and social determinants in etiology of duodenal ulcer, *American Journal of Digestive Diseases,* **3,** 285–314.

Moos, R. H. and Swindle, R. W., Jr. (1990). Person–environment transactions and the stressor-appraisal-coping process, *Psychological Inquiry,* **1,** 30–2.

Ostfeld, A. M., Lebovitz, B. Z., Shekelle, R. B., and Paul, O. (1964). A prospective study of the relationship between personality and coronary heart disease, *Journal of Chronic Diseases,* **17,** 265–76.

Payne, R. (1988). Individual differences in the study of occupational stress. In C. L. Cooper and R. Payne (eds) *Causes, Coping, and Consequences of Stress at Work,* Wiley, Chichester, pp. 209–32.

Rentos, G. P. and Shepard, R. D. (eds) (1976). *Shift Work and Health, A Symposium*, DHEW (NIOSH) Publication No. 76–203, Washington, DC.

Saab, P. G., Llabre, M. M., Hurwitz, B. E., Frame, C. A., Reineke, L. J., Fins, A. I. McCalla, J., Cieply, L. K., and Schneiderman, N. (in press). Myocardial and peripheral vascular responses to behavioral challenges and their stability in Black and White Americans, *Psychophysiology*.

Scheier, M. F. and Carver, C. S. (1987). Dispositional optimism and physical well-being: The influence of generalized outcome exepctancies on health, *Journal of Personality*, **55**, 169–210.

Schroeder, D. H. and Costa, P. T., Jr. (1984). Influence of life event stress on physical illness: Substantive effects or methodological flaws?, *Journal of Personality and Social Psychology*, **46**, 853–63.

Siegman, A. W. and Dembroski, T. M. (eds) (1989). *In Search of Coronary-Prone Behavior: Beyond Type A*, Erlbaum, Hillsdale, NJ.

Smith, T. W., Pope, M. K., Rhodewalt, F., and Poulton, J. L. (1989). Optimism, neuroticism, coping, and symptom reports: An alternative interpretation of the Life Orientation Test, *Journal of Personality and Social Psychology*, **56**, 640–8.

Spielberger, C. D., Gorsuch, R. L., and Lushene, R. E. (1970). *Manual for the State–Trait Anxiety Inventory*, Consulting Psychologists Press, Palo Alto, Calif.

Suarez, E. C. and Williams, R. B., Jr. (1989). Situational determinants of cardiovascular and emotional reactivity in high and low hostile men, *Psychosomatic Medicine*, **51**, 404–18.

Suls, J. and Rittenhouse, J. D. (1987). Personality and physical health: An introduction, *Journal of Personality*, **55**, 155–67.

Susser, M. (1973). *Causal Thinking in the Health Sciences. Concepts and Strategies in Epidemiology*, Oxford University Press, New York.

Tasto, D., Colligan, M. J., Skjei, E. W., and Polly, S. J. (1978). *Health Consequences of Shiftwork*, DHEW (NIOSH) Publication No. 78–154, Washington, DC.

Tischenkel, N. J., Saab, P. G., Schneiderman, N., Nelesen, R. A., Pasin, R. D., Goldstein, D. A., Spitzer, S. B., Woo-Ming, R., and Weidler, D. J. (1989). Cardiovascular and neurohumoral responses to behavioral challenge as a function of race and sex, *Health Psychology*, **8**, 503–24.

Torsvall, L. and Akerstedt, T. (1980). A diurnal type scale. Construction, consistency and validation in shift work, *Scandinavian Journal of Work Environment and Health*, **6**, 283–90.

Watson, D. (1990). On the dispositional nature of stress measures: Stable and non-specific influences on self-reported hassles, *Psychological Inquiry*, **1**, 34–7.

Watson, D. and Clark, L. A. (1984). Negative affectivity: The disposition to experience aversive emotional states, *Psychological Bulletin*, **96**, 465–90.

Watson, D. and Pennebaker, J. W. (1989). Health complaints, stress, and distress: Exploring the central role of negative affectivity, *Psychological Review*, **96**, 234–54.

West, S. G. and Graziano, W. G. (1989). Long-term stability and change in personality: An introduction, *Journal of Personality*, **57**, 175–93.

Winget, C. M., Hughes, L. and LaDou, J. (1978). Physiological effects of rotational work shifting: A review, *Journal of Occupational Medicine*, **20**, 204–10.

Index